Rio Grande #17, California Zephyr, at East Portal, Col., about to enter the Moffat Tunnel with James Peak in the foreground. Pueblo Division. Courtesy, Rio Grande RR.

RAILROADING THE MODERN WAY

S. Kip Farrington, Jr.

RAILROADING THE MODERN WAY is a streamlined book about a streamlined industry, and the title gives the most accurate description of its contents. It boasts 143 photographs all taken since 1948, captioned with places, Divisions, locomotives, and direction of the train. There are also interior views of many of the new cars. New trains, operating practices, C.T.C., yards, and radio of fifteen modern Class-1 railroads are completely covered.

Nine new railroads, not in any of Mr. Farrington's previous railroad books, are treated fully. They are the Bessemer and Lake Erie, Chicago and Eastern Illinois, Frisco Lines, Kansas City Southern, Pittsburgh and West Virginia, Seaboard, Virginian, Wabash, and Western Pacific.

The author takes up the most important part of a railroad's business — freight. Descriptions are also given of new ultra-modern passenger trains such as the Wabash Bluebird, the Rio Grande and Western Pacific's California Zephyr, the Baltimore & Ohio's Columbian, Southern Pacific's Cascade, Shasta Daylights and Sunsets, Seaboard's Gulf Wind and Silver Comet, C. & E. I.'s Georgian, Frisco's Meteor, Milwaukee's Olympian Hiawatha, and others. New yards described are the Santa Fe's Argentine at Kansas City, Southern Pacific's Taylor at Los Angeles, the Frisco's Springfield, and Chicago and Eastern Illinois's Wansford at Evansville, Indiana.

Major movements of ore, wheat, phosphate, coal, meat, and other perishables and the Florida citrus move are discussed.

The Sperry rail detector car, emphasizing the railroads' great foresight and ingenuity in their never ending search for safety devices, is included, as well as a chapter on the electrified portion of the Virginian Railroad. Electro-Motive Diesel locomotives, for yard as well as road service, are taken care of in another chapter. CTC comes in for its share of recognition. The last two chapters take up the unfair truck competition the railroads are receiving as well as automobile and truck hazards at highway crossings.

The book is a "must" for those of other countries, as well as the United States, who are interested in this great industry, for railroad fans, model enthusiasts, and railroad men. The author's books on American railroads are practically the only ones on present-day railroad operations and are more widely read by every type of railroader throughout the world than any others. These men praise them for their factual correctness, attention to detail, and handsome illustrations.

General George C. Marshall has contributed the introduction.

---

on railroads is attested by the fact that his books are sold by the thousands to railroad men throughout the world who know what they want to read and who know the real thing.

Books by S. Kɪᴘ Fᴀʀʀɪɴɢᴛᴏɴ, Jʀ.

FISHING THE ATLANTIC OFFSHORE AND ON

PACIFIC GAME FISHING

SPORT FISHING BOATS

A BOOK OF FISHES

ATLANTIC GAME FISHING

THE DUCKS CAME BACK

SHIPS OF THE U. S. MERCHANT MARINE

INTERESTING BIRDS OF OUR COUNTRY

GIANTS OF THE RAILS

RAILROADING FROM THE HEAD END

RAILROADING FROM THE REAR END

RAILROADS AT WAR

RAILROADS OF TODAY

RAILROADING THE MODERN WAY

Juvenile

BILL THE BROADBILL SWORDFISH

RAILROADING
The Modern Way

S. KIP FARRINGTON, Jr.

Coward-McCann, Inc.   New York

To

Tony Hulman, Chairman of the Board of the Indianapolis Speedway, athlete, sportsman, and businessman, who as an active director of a leading railroad is of service to the whole railroad industry.

CONTENTS

ix

INTRODUCTION

Two world wars have demonstrated the critical importance of our transportation system to national defense, particularly the railroads. Our ability to get men and supplies to where needed has been a fundamental reason for our military successes.

The sudden development of events in Korea required the immediate transportation of men and vast quantities of supplies to ports of embarkation. The railroads swung into action and expanded their operations to meet the sudden requirements. Deliveries of general cargo at the ports jumped from 400,000 measurement tons in June to more than a million in August. A million tons translated into boxcars would constitute a freight train one hundred miles long. This gives some indication of the magnitude of the American railroads' operations in this emergency.

Our railroads sent some of their experts to Korea, and assisted the South Koreans to operate the railroads in handling the greatly increased traffic and in repairing damages. Further, our people introduced some up-to-date American equipment and the technique of controlling and expediting traffic, which facilitated the urgently necessary quick movement of troops and supplies from the ports to the front.

The railroads are adding another page to their history of effective performances consistent with their record in two previous wars and with a promise of readiness to face any test in the service of the country.

GEORGE C. MARSHALL
Secretary of Defense

Pentagon Building
Washington, D.C.
November 27, 1950

FOREWORD

During the last two years it has been my good fortune to travel over and inspect the railroads of sixteen foreign countries. Some years before I did the same thing in six other countries. After having the opportunity of viewing all of their very fine railroads and territories plus the tremendous job they accomplish with their tedious and tough operations, I am even more thoroughly convinced that United States rail transportation is the best and most luxurious in the world. Nowhere else on earth are there so many passengers and so much freight on the move with such speed, such regularity, such safety, and such punctuality as in the states.

Nearly all of us, at one time or another, have paused as we drive along the highways to watch a freight train go thundering by—and maybe to wonder what all the different cars from the different railroads are carrying, and where they come from, and where they are going.

And you might well give a thought to those freight trains—for they are an indispensable part of our daily lives. They provide the basic transportation which makes possible the nationwide distribution of the vast output of U.S. farms and factories, mills and mines.

To the harassed motorists on some of our more crowded highways, it might very well seem that pretty nearly all the freight in the United States is moving by motor truck. But, of course, that isn't the case—for most of the freight that moves, and even most of the freight which is moved by truck, is *not* moved on the intercity highways.

There are two sorts of truck traffic, and by far the more important part is *not* the intercity traffic carried by the big long-distance haulers you meet in such numbers out on the highways.

The most important and the most useful service performed by trucks—and the service in which the overwhelming majority of trucks are engaged—is *local* traffic. This local traffic includes the farm-to-market movements, made in farm trucks, and the traffic carried in local transfer and delivery trucks in and around towns and cities. It is this local and farm traffic in which most trucks— probably five out of every six—are engaged.

The big long-distance haulers which you meet on the main highways are engaged in a different kind of business. These are the trucks which are doing the same sort of freight business as railroads. Last year, the railroads hauled more than seven times as much intercity freight traffic as did the trucks. Did you ever stop to think how important it is to you, both as a taxpayer and as a user of the highways, that so much of the nation's intercity freight hauling is done on the special highways of steel provided, maintained, and paid for by the railroads? If this traffic which moves by rail, or any considerable part of it, were to be moved on the public highways instead of on the railroads' special highways of steel, just imagine what you, as a motorist, would be up against.

Highway engineers have learned by experience the same thing which the engineering staffs of the railroads learned—that roads and bridges must be protected from overweight, and from the added impact due to excessive speed of heavy vehicles. Failure to protect them means damage and even destruction. And that means added costs—costs to be borne by the taxpayers and the motorists who, in the long run, must pay the bills. So let's make this our motto: "Always travel and ship via the railroads of the United States."

My one regret in writing this book is that it is not possible to include all of the United States railroads in it. The great majority of them very definitely practice railroading the modern way. It is a privilege to acknowledge and thank the publishers of the *Railway Age Magazine* for the excellent help they gave me in preparing this book. I am indeed grateful to Olive B. Flannery, Edna Brooks, and Charles Tyler for their work on the manuscript. I extend my deep appreciation to Preston George and Richard H. Kindig for the outstanding photographs they made to be included in this volume. H. Reid and Les Logue each generously contributed a photograph. The work of these men is certainly a real addition to the book. My sincere thanks to all of them. My Dictaphone Timemaster has again proved itself as the machine to use to write a book the Modern Way.

S. KIP FARRINGTON, JR.

Montauk, New York
February 1, 1951

RAILROADING THE MODERN WAY

CHAPTER I

THE AMERICAN FREIGHT CAR

The one thing around a railroad that never gets its face washed is a freight car. From the day it leaves the shop and, in new paint, self-consciously takes its place with the older rank and file on the road, the freight car receives little primping and may get to look as seedy as the hobo who rides it.

And yet freight cars are seen by countless millions every day. Railroads show off their sleek and shiny speed queens, and their autumn-colored Diesels, and their modernistic railroad stations, but few people are ever invited down to the railroad tracks to inspect a new freight train. Try to imagine a freight train with all silver cars, each with a broad red band on the side, and decorative trade-marks with reflective sheeting that glow at night, a Diesel to match, plus a stainless steel caboose with matching treatment—no modern streamliner would begin to get as much attention.

The nearest approach to this dream freight has been the introduction of the Southern Pacific's overnight freights, some reefer trains, the Union Pacific's yellow stock trains, and a few roads that have brought out rather breathless freight cars like those of the B.&O.'s Sentinel Service. However, there is a trend toward making the freight car, the boxcar, in particular, both an ambassador and a better advertiser. Paints that hold their color and gloss over long periods are being used more and more. An increasing number of roads are adding to the fast freight fleets, with built-in individuality. In 1949 a total of 110 "overnighters" on thirty railroads were offering shippers late-afternoon closings with first-morning delivery of l.c.l. or first-day placement of carload freight between points 300 miles or more distant.

1

Fast freight name trains were in operation as early as about 1910, but it was not until after World War II that fast freight began to dress up. Obviously, only trains operating between home-road terminals can cherish that "new look." An ordinary freight car is a tramp of the first water and often spends the best years of its life away from home. If it becomes incapacitated in foreign fields it is patched up and hustled on its way again.

While a railroad wants a freight car when it wants it, once it has it, there is an immediate urge to get rid of it. For every day the stranger remains on foreign rails it costs the host $1.75. In plain talk, this is rent. Nothing can make a railroad scream louder than having a lot of freight cars on its hands that it can't get rid of, as, for instance, a terminal railroad that receives from other railroads a ratio of cars greater than it consistently can send out. One such terminal road paid out over $5,000,000 in per diem charges on foreign-owned cars, while taking in less than half that amount for use of its own on other lines. (Per diem means "by the day" and indicates the amount paid by one railroad to another railroad for the use of a freight car.)

These per diem rates have increased over the years. In 1902, they were 25 cents per day; in 1907, 50 cents; 75 cents in 1916; $1.00 in 1920; then $1.15, $1.25, $1.50, and $1.75, starting on November 1, 1949.

Regardless of the fact that the casual observer finds the present-day freight car pretty much as he remembered it a number of years ago, "just eight wheels and a box," there have been constant changes and improvements. In 1880, except for trucks, truss rods, couplings, fittings, and a few accessories, a freight car was built of wood. Cars then were short lived and forever needing repairs.

Next came steel underframes, the backbone of a freight car; then there were steel ends, steel body framing, and finally steel sides and roof. Continuous research has developed the freight car until it is a pretty rugged character, but anything that takes the beating that a freight car does is bound to need repairs. Freight car maintenance in 1949 took $430,000,000 out of the pockets of the railroads. One road, owning about 60,000 cars,

2

employed 4,500 men in the car department and paid them $15,000,000. The cost of heavy repairs to this railroad was just a bit under $400 per car.

In February, 1950, the Class I railroads of the United States had available for service 1,758,144 freight cars. Broken down, this figure represented 726,882 boxcars, 65,005 flat cars, 51,882 stock cars, 852,312 gondola and hopper cars, 8,196 tank cars, 20,816 refrigerator cars, and 9,146 other types, including special-service cars. Cars retired and new and rebuilt cars placed in service each year constantly change the number in operation.

The capacity of the freight car has increased about 25 per cent from 1918 to 1948, or from 41.6 tons in 1918 to 51.9 tons in 1948. Around the turn of the century it was 27 tons. The average length of freight cars is forty-three feet, outside overall, but cars vary from twenty-four feet to seventy-five feet.

We have used the initials "l.c.l." earlier in the chapter, and many nonrailroaders may wonder what these initials mean. L.c.l. means "less than carload," or any shipment of freight which is too small to move on a carload rate, like boxes, crates, barrels, and the like.

Another term some nonrailroaders probably regard with a puzzled look is "ton-miles." A ton-mile is a measurement of freight service which has to do with the transportation of one ton of freight one mile. In 1948, Class I railroads in the United States performed approximately 638,000,000,000 ton-miles of service. The average freight train that you wait for at a railroad crossing turns out 18,779 ton-miles of service for each hour it is on the road, measured by 1948 standard. This represents two and one-half times as much hourly transportation output per train as was accomplished in 1920.

This gain in efficiency has resulted from putting 53.1 per cent more cars in the 1948 train and 12.3 per cent more tons in the average car and moving the train 57.3 per cent faster, or an increase in transportation output averaging 157 per cent.

What does it cost to haul a ton of freight one mile?

Charges vary according to commodity, distance, and the amount of care and risk involved. Between 1933 and 1946,

3

Class I railroads received an average of less than one cent per mile. In 1948, the average was 1.251 cents per ton-mile, and in 1921, the high point following World War I, it was 1.275 cents. Over this same period wages, fuel, materials, and supplies virtually doubled, while in 1948 the average freight revenue level was a trifle under that of 1921.

We go into a big market and we see shelves stacked with canned goods. We see many fruits and vegetables. United States railroads haul in one year 13,240,460 tons of canned goods; they carried over 12,000,000 tons of fruits and vegetables. They haul perishables to the tune of 1,124,000 carloads for distances ranging from a few miles to more than 3,000 miles. This fruit and vegetable haul is made in refrigerator cars, or reefers, and is a specialized service that is a marvel of speed and efficiency.

No matter where you see a spur track, even a weed-grown and rusted spur track, a freight car has been there. Remote though it may be from the roaring mainline, it is part of a vast rail network. Perhaps you see one of these spur tracks in the San Fernando section of Southern California, and there is a Boston & Maine boxcar there. You wonder about it.

How did it get there? When will it get home? Does the Boston & Maine know about this boxcar in the San Fernando Valley in California? Let us say that it arrived on this spur track via the Southern Pacific Lines with a load of plane parts. No one has the slightest idea when it will get back to its home road, but the Boston & Maine knows where this boxcar is all right because every time it goes from one railroad to another its number is recorded and a report is sent to the Boston & Maine's Car Record Office, an office maintained by every railroad.

Someone may ask, "Even when the home road knows what railroad this particular freight car is on, how could the local road find it?" The answer is: through "wheel reports," which chart all cars in a freight train. Agents or yardmasters at initial points deliver a wheel report to the conductor before the departure of a freight train.

You often read or hear the term "Class I railroad." A Class I

4

railroad, if the designation is not exactly clear, is a railroad which has an operating revenue above $1,000,000 a year. A Class II railroad has an operating revenue above $100,000 and not exceeding $1,000,000.

The ordinary freight car is a wanderer and it may travel on all of the Class I railroads in the United States during its lifetime. As of January 1, 1949, there were 133 Class I roads. A freight car travels as much as 5,000 miles a month; it may visit all the major cities, and also travel in Canada and Mexico, as there are sixty-six interchange points on the Canadian border and fourteen points on or near the Mexican border.

Happily, the United States, Canada, and Mexico, our good neighbors to the north and to the south, operate a vast and closely knit transportation system of some 280,000 miles. About 99 per cent of these lines are the standard gauge of four feet eight and one-half inches, allowing the uninterrupted movement of trains from one country to the other.

We hear people say, "The railroads mustn't buy many new freight cars; I never see any." Between and including 1945 through 1949, the railroads purchased close to 337,000 new freight cars, or over 67,000 each year. Between the close of World War I and mid-1950, the Southern Pacific bought 31,639 freight cars of all types, including 8,100 refrigerator cars for the Pacific Fruit Express, which is half owned by the Southern Pacific. These new cars would have made a freight train 265 miles long.

America's economy is gauged by a freight car. Freight carloadings are watched as carefully as a weather observer watches atmospheric conditions. Business analysts regard carloadings as one of the best current indicators of business activity, and weekly carloading figures are released each Thursday by the Association of American Railroads, and these are published in newspapers throughout the United States. (The Association of American Railroads is the central co-ordinating and research agency of the American railway industry.)

We hear the term "common carrier" used in connection with railroads. A common carrier is required to carry all goods offered

5

when accommodations are available, and when the fixed price for such service is tendered. The result is that a freight car is called upon to haul just about everything under the sun—anything that doesn't hang over or stick up too far. The Santa Fe, in 1944, was called on to move a fractionating tower weighing 500,000 pounds, or 250 tons, from Tulsa, Oklahoma, to Borger, Texas. The total length of the tower was 150 feet and it required three flat cars. It was the heaviest load ever shipped in one piece by any railroad.

Operating with horses as motive power, the Baltimore & Ohio Railroad was the first common carrier, beginning operation in 1830. The first common carrier operating with steam power was the South Carolina Railroad, which inaugurated regular service on Christmas day, 1830. This road is now part of the Southern Railway System. In that year twenty-three miles of railroad were in operation. In 1948, there were 225,149 miles of railroad owned, with 397,203 miles of track operated.

Every railroad freight car tells a story. First, it proudly offers the name of the railroad, or, perhaps, the name by which it is more commonly known, as the "Nickel Plate," and the initials of the line, N.Y.C.&St.L.—New York, Chicago & St. Louis— and the car number. Then there may be an advertisement, like "The Route of Phoebe Snow" on a Lackawanna car, or an M.K.T. car will boast that "The Katy Serves the Southwest." The freight car of your modern railroad believes in utilizing some of that space for a commercial.

And why not? A freight car trundling by that simply says U.&I. Railroad won't get much attention. But put on the car "The Land You Love," and it will catch the eye and also leave an impression in your mind.

Included in the information painted on the side of a freight car is the date it was built and the place, date, and initials of the road on which it was repaired. There are figures which indicate the overall width and height; the inside length and inside width, and the cubic feet. The weight of the empty car, the capacity of the car, and the load limit are given in pounds.

6

Also, on an attached steel plate, or painted on the car will be the name of the owner, trustee, lessor. There will usually be the type of axles, the kind of wheels, and the spring travel. Chalk marks usually originate in the classification yard and were placed there by switchmen. Freight cars have carried the chalked signatures—in the past more than in the modern age—of famous hoboes or of nationally known boomers.

Many railroads become famous for their symbols; perhaps none more so than the Great Northern with its famous goat, "Old Bill." The symbol of the Northern Pacific is centuries old, having originated in China and was once emblazoned on the national flag of Korea, and it serves today with the Northern Pacific's slogan, "Main Street of the Northwest." There is always a story behind the symbol of a railroad. Many of these symbols have undergone changes and streamlining through the years, but they are always eye catching and immediately stir the imagination of the watcher beside the track, creating the urge to travel yonder around the curve to these worlds where the rails reach.

Modern railroading has developed many new freight-car types for handling unusual shipments. A big Eastern road offers shippers sixteen-wheel flatcars that will carry up to 198 tons. Railroads provide covered, weather-proof hopper cars; new types of gondolas that have been designed for girders, pipes, and over-size loads go far toward helping the shipper to solve his transportation problems, and in wartime these cars are particularly adaptable to the needs of the Army and the Navy. New refrigerator cars carry frozen foods safely and further implement the great reefer fleets.

Some freight cars employ six-wheel trucks to take care of their heavier loads, and trucks and draft gears of newly engineered standards have taken a lot of grief out of railroading and saved shippers anguish and the Claim Department dollars. Freight progress is marked by new kinds of steels and alloys, providing more economical and more dependable transportation. Advancement in the engineering of one-piece cast-steel underframes spell longer life, provide greater strength, and do away with a lot of repair bills.

7

For years Pullman was a name associated with de luxe passenger travel, but today Pullman-Standard is associated with the up-to-date freight car. Pullman-Standard and other freight-car builders turn out cars by assembly-line production methods. Nothing on wheels takes the beating, year in and year out, that a freight car does. It is treated as though everyone in the world were mad at it. Never a gentle hand is laid on it. Coupled in a train, a freight car, through its draft gears, may be subjected to blows as high as 300 tons. Actual dynamometer tests reveal that forces of 500 tons may batter the freight car under certain conditions.

A freight car may suffer the equivalent of a thousand collisions of varying violence every day it is in service; it receives constant trip-hammer blows at higher speed from forces built up by so little a thing as the wheels clicking over the rail joints. It is attacked by rust canker and slugged by shifting consist. It is blistered by the molten sun of the southwestern deserts and iced up by northern blizzards. It is the most abused thing that rolls or flies or floats, and yet without it the fires of industry would turn into cold ashes almost overnight.

A freight car has to be built to certain rigid specifications, which allow it to travel and work hand in hand with every other freight car, to be repaired as speedily in Maine and California as in Florida or North Dakota. In modern railroading, the freight car has more and more enjoyed the company and attention of professors and scientists, who, on behalf of the Association of American Railroads, are every day discovering new ways to improve the inherently robust railroad dromedary called the freight car.

Those with a socialistic lean feel that if the government owned the railroads, things would be different. Everything would come out of the same mold, from jacknives to boxcars. The trouble would be that the freight car today probably would be about on a par with the ancient vintage mail trucks that we see on the streets. Many railroads and many car builders have combined their brains and experience to produce the best tough-haul transport unit on the face of the earth.

8

There was a time when a tank car only hauled oil. The modern tank car hauls just about everything liquid, including such commodities as fish oil, molasses, propane, caustic soda, sulphuric acid, asphalt, linseed oil, gasoline, lube oil, muriatic acid, wine, chlorine, and milk, to name a few. Many of these tank cars are built by freight-car manufacturers and leased to the railroads to meet the needs of shippers.

More and more, the freight car is becoming a specialist. Dump cars are built to handle pulp logs, with a built-in mechanism that tilts the car body for quick unloading. On the other hand, there is the rotary machine dumper that grabs a seventy-ton hopper car loaded with coal and empties it in *sixty seconds.*

Dock and freight-house loading and unloading is largely mechanized and a freight car spends less idle hours and more main-line hours than it used to. It has to. Competition is a roaring monster with a heavy foot on the gas. Today's boxcar is as busy as a bee—busy hauling things for our way of life, busy hauling military supplies. Each week 850,000 freight cars are loaded and sent bustling down the track, helping to maintain both the civilian economy and America's national defense.

Pacing the fast-stepping freight car of the modern era is a communications system that covers land, sea, and air. Radio is becoming a very important factor in modern railroad practice. It does not replace signals or the various types of communication that have always been a part of train movement; it supplements them. For a long time the railroads have been conducting experiments in the use of radio and inductive carrier systems. The former uses the air in transmission, while the latter employs rails and adjoining line wires as a medium of transmission.

Radio makes possible instant communication between conductor and engineer and between dispatcher and crew members. In a subsequent chapter we will find it at work on the Kansas City Southern. The Santa Fe, at the beginning of 1950, had installed radios on twenty-eight locomotives and thirty-six cabooses used on through freights in three operating districts, centering at Barstow, California.

Radio in yard and terminal work has become invaluable. We

9

will see it at work in the following pages in such important yards as the Denver yard of the Denver & Rio Grande Western, in the Springfield, Missouri, yard of the Frisco Lines, and in Taylor Yard on the Southern Pacific in Los Angeles, California.

Everything points to speeding up the freight car, in streamlining its service, both in hauling full loads and l.c.l. shipments. The shipper likes this; he likes the attention he is getting and the fine help in delivering the goods. This service is playing a major part in the door-to-door schedules that are speeding shipments by such great modern roads as the Baltimore & Ohio.

Enormous gains have been made in freight handling—another method of speeding up the freight car. There are the so-called "fork trucks," powered conveyors, electric-powered tractors, mobile cranes. The trend of mechanization has moved on from the larger stations to the smaller stations. "Get that freight car loaded and rolling!" is the credo.

Paper work has been reduced through the scientific application of streamlining by means of timesaving devices. A waybill used to go through a lengthy routine that involved bent clerks at ink-spattered desks; now they photograph it quicker than you can dip a pen.

Through the pages of this book the reader will find constant reference to the manifest, the Red Ball train, the time freight, and you will travel up and down the country with these great modern trains. You will go to market with the orange and ride with the wheat. You will tour the River Line and look at the ore haul out of Conneaut, and see the black diamond come down from the coal fields, from tipple to tidewater. You will see fast freights scheduled as second sections of crack limiteds. You will meet the American freight car in busy terminals and on the booming main line, and you will find the freight car a vital part of the nation's life.

The crack streamliners, reared in luxury and to the manor born, have set a pattern for styles unequaled by queens anywhere, but the horny-handed freight car is ambassador of the railroad.

CHAPTER II

THE SOUTHERN PACIFIC

Diesels Tame Tehachapi

The Tehachapi is the toughest piece of mountain railroading on all of the vast Southern Pacific Lines. That takes in a lot of territory and is a large statement. The Southern Pacific lines include many famous stretches of mountain railroading, including Paisano Summit, in Texas; Steins Pass, New Mexico; and such California grades as Beaumont Hill, San Fernando, Santa Susanna Pass, Santa Margarita, Donner Summit, the Big Hill over the high Sierras, Dunsmuir to Grass Lake, Cascade Summit, and the Siskiyous—all tough mountain railroads. And there are a lot of lesser grades. But this Tehachapi wall, curve for curve, tunnel for tunnel and mile for mile is the granddaddy of spectacular mountain-climbing track in my book. I have looked at them all, and I have given the palm to this roughneck of the rails.

You do not toss off these Tehachapis as just another grade, for the simple reason that nowhere is there a formation like the Tehachapi. It is neither a mountain nor a hill, in the strict meaning of the words, but rather a thousand hills stacked together to make a barrier between California's great central valley and the vast Mojave Desert.

Crowning it all is the mile-long, world-famous Tehachapi Loop that completely circles a high, bald hill, a crowning achievement in a railroad construction job performed by William Hood away back in 1876. In the twenty-five miles between Caliente, the start of the major climb, and Tehachapi station, just west of the summit, there are fifteen tunnels and fifty-eight ten-degree curves, an indication of what this Tehachapi is like.

11

I have ridden every name railroad train in the United States—the head end and the rear end of both freight and passenger trains—as well as railroads in many parts of the world, including grades as high as 14 per cent, but I have never seen tonnage go up much harder than it does over this Tehachapi. There are steeper grades in the United States, but none so completely dominated by curves.

Fortunately, with these straight-up and straight-down mountainsides, the Southern Pacific does not have to fight snow. It does fall in the Tehachapi but in no quantity. However, there is rain in season, and in a bad year it can play havoc. The East experiences floods, vast and terrible at times, but nowhere else can flood water generate in amount and ferocity so quickly as in the Western mountains, and in particular in the Tehachapis.

I am going to digress just a moment here. In years past, the Southern Pacific has fought storm and flood havoc that has wiped out, completely erased, miles and miles of right of way, and the railroad replaced the track at its own expense. When highways are washed out, the truckers hunt a detour until the state has made repairs; yet they are in competition in freight haul with this railroad that has to maintain and supply not only its rolling equipment but the roadway over which it travels.

The Tehachapi subdivision is single track for thirty-two miles, between Bena and Tehachapi station, and the track is used jointly with the Santa Fe, and during the early years of World War II, or until centralized traffic control was installed, it was a bottleneck and a railroad man's nightmare, with as many as one hundred train and helper movements handled over it on an average twenty-four hours.

From about 1928 the famous Mallets, the Southern Pacific's AC locomotives—articulated consolidation—hauled the freight trains over these Tehachapis. Not long after World War II, or as soon as deliveries could be made, Diesels made their appearance on this portion of the San Joaquin Division. The Diesels eliminated the water stop at Woodford, about halfway up the grade, and, with the dynamic brake, eliminated stops to cool wheels, which heated under the drag of brakes when retainers

12

were employed. The Diesels handled the trains to advantage when stops and slowdowns were necessary, and in the modern today the entire operation over the Tehachapi grade has been smoothed and speeded to a point of extreme efficiency.

Riding a Diesel on Tehachapi

Sometimes a railroad will attempt to put its best foot forward when the word is passed that a railroad writer is riding one of its trains, but not so on the Southern Pacific or any other place for me in the Tehachapis—everything was strictly routine when I went out for another look at this mountain operation. It was probably about the one hundred twenty-fifth (as well as I can remember) eastbound trip I have made.

I rode to Bakersfield, California, from Los Angeles in the cab of the locomotive pulling No. 51, the San Joaquin Daylight. This is one of the Southern Pacific's famous fleet of Daylights, and a very popular train. After having lunch with Superintendent B. W. Mitchell, we drove to the yard. Extra 6128 East had been called for 1:15 P.M.

All Southern Pacific trains out of San Francisco are eastbound. Into San Francisco, all over the system, trains are westbound.

The motive power is one of the new Electro-Motive Diesels. Coupled behind it are seventy-one loads and fourteen empties, for eighty-five cars and a tonnage totaling 7031 Ms. An M. is a unit of weight on the S.P., which counts two Ms. to the ton. This road is the only one that continues employing this system. At one time, the Lackawanna and some of the other Eastern railroads used it.

So translating our 7031 Ms. into tons we have 3515½. We leave Bakersfield at 1:55 P.M. with an AC helper, the 4255, cut into the train ten cars ahead of the caboose. The double track reaches in a long tangent toward Bena, fifteen miles away. The grade is practically level for a short distance, but it soon stiffens to 1.50 per cent as we roar down on milepost 323.

At Bena we leave the double track and also come under cen-

13

tralized traffic control. We are past Ilmon and fighting a 1.70 per cent grade before reaching milepost 333 at Tunnel ½. The freight now attacks a mile of 2.50 per cent compensated as we approach Caliente, where we have a meet with Extra 6125 West. We watch it coming down the hill and start the long sweep around the great horseshoe curve. The Caliente curve has never been given the attention it deserves, for it is one of the finest in the United States.

A mile and a half east of Caliente we enter Tunnel No. 1, 231 feet in length, moving on a full 2 per cent grade. All of the way from milepost 336½ to milepost 359½ we will be fighting a ruling grade of 2.5 per cent, except for a brief drop to 1.44 per cent near Tehachapi. There is a little 1.80 per cent, 1.83 per cent, and 2.20 per cent.

The big Diesel works beautifully. The crew maintains a constant watch of the train, snaking slowly around these curves behind us. Back there somewhere is the helper, but we never see it, only its smoke, spouting upward from among the bald-domed hills.

We are by Bena at 2:27 P.M., and out of Caliente at 2:49 P.M. No sooner are we off one ten-degree curve than we are moving into another one. We move through Tunnel No. 3, 700 feet long. And No. 4, 337 feet long. At milepost 341 we go into Tunnel No. 5 for 1,180 feet of blackness. Milepost 342—Tunnel No. 6, 355 feet in length. And, remember, this line was built in the year 1876 when a Chinese and a wheelbarrow were considered labor-saving machinery.

The train moves across the face of a high cliff, slowly but steadily, and the world is spread out below—a world of great slopes with corsages of live oaks set on rounded bosoms.

Another ten-degree curve. Then a 9.30, and another ten-degree. Right and left. We squirm between steep embankments and now look squarely at the black and yawning mouth of Tunnel No. 7, 519 feet, portal to portal. The headlight is on all of the way, as though half expecting to come on some unchartered bore in these vast hills.

The AC locomotives, the Mallets, were a mighty smooth piece

of machinery, from the old "mudhens," right on to the AC-6-AC-12's, the 4100-4274 Class, built up to 1943, but the Diesel is better—with smoother riding qualities, and, of course, easier on the track.

East of milepost 344 there is Tunnel No. 8, 690 feet long. In a little while the engineer whistles for Rowen. Tehachapi Creek is on our left. Now only a creek bed—there is not much water in it—but it can be a roaring demon, as witness the great flood in September, 1932, that swept down on Woodford completely burying two engines and part of a train. We cross the trestle that went out that year and stop at Woodford at 3:45 P.M.

The dispatcher puts us into the passing track to let No. 24, the Santa Fe's Grand Canyon Limited pass. (The joint traffic rights of the Southern Pacific and the Santa Fe extend from Mojave, California, to Bakersfield.) Following No. 24, two light engines coupled together came up the hill as Extra 1265 East for the Santa Fe. Ten minutes behind them is No. 52, the eastbound San Joaquin Daylight, with road engine 4429 and helper 4351.

We get out of Woodford at 4:14 P.M., having been in the hole there twenty-nine minutes. A mile east of the station we cross Tehachapi Creek for the fourth time, moving over a gradient that varies between 2.17, 2.2, and 2.20 per cent in the next mile.

The thrill of the Tehachapi comes with never knowing just where a train is going to appear against the mountainside. We look ahead and see a splash of color. It is the vivid-colored Daylight streamliner, moving on toward the famed Tehachapi Loop. Later we see the bright-hued train still higher up above Walong. It is a beautiful picture in this fading day.

Just east of milepost 350, we cross Tehachapi Creek again. The fifth time. Now we are approaching the Loop. Here between mileposts 351 and 352 there are curves of the following degrees: 9.30, 10.03, 9.20, 7.38, 9.36, 9.40, 8.05, 10, then 9.18, 10.05, and 10 degrees. What a masterful achievement! Seventy-five years ago! And then, as a final stroke, these railroad builders

15

ringed this hill with steel, a marvel of construction—the great Loop of the Tehachapi!

We start around the Loop, making our entrance by passing through Tunnel No. 9. Right here is the big moment. Our Diesel crosses over our AC helper as it emerges from the tunnel which we passed through in starting our swing. In other words, at this point, the head end of the train crosses over the rear end.

We then come to Tunnel No. 10, 307.1 feet long. Tunnel 11, which has been daylighted, is only 120 feet long. This is at milepost 353. We crawl around curve after curve, many of them of eight, nine, and ten degrees. The Diesel motors are roaring, building power for the traction motors that keep us moving. We are by Marcel and its long sidings.

We move into Tunnel No. 14, which is 513 feet long. We are still fighting the great Tehachapi grade. Tunnel No. 15 yawns before our Diesel, with 330 feet of darkness, and Tunnel 16, 258 feet long. At milepost 356 is Tunnel No. 17, 259 feet in length, and between milepost 356 and 357 we make the sixth crossing of Tehachapi Creek.

At Cable, the dispatcher sticks us three minutes with a yellow signal as we meet Extra 6123 coming down the hill. They put them through the passing track, as we have the reverse grade. East of milepost 358 we make the seventh crossing of Tehachapi Creek, and continue to climb steadily upward but the Diesel is not even smoking. A great piece of power.

Now we come onto a long tangent for the first time and move up toward Tehachapi depot, coming onto double-track territory again at milepost 360. This is the end of C.T.C. We are by the station at 5:08 P.M. At 5:13 P.M. we stop at Summit Switch, where we cut off the helper, AC-4255. The helper backs around the Y in preparation for its return down the hill to Bakersfield. We are out of Summit at 5:20 P.M.

With steam power, retainers would be set up but they are not necessary with a Diesel and the dynamic brake. The descending grade is ½ to 1 per cent to about milepost 371. Here we start a 2.20 descent, with Cache Creek bed along the right of the right of way. We pass Warren at milepost 374 and roll into Mojave

16

at milepost 381 at 6:06 P.M., having made the run down from Summit, sixteen miles, in forty-six minutes. The speed limit for this train is 30 miles an hour. The dynamic brake was used entirely; the air brake was not touched until we reached the Mojave yard limits.

We have finished our run on the Tehachapi subdivision, and now we are on the Mojave subdivision and running as First No. 806. We are given an order to run four hours late from Mojave to Burbank Junction. The grade is slightly descending and tangent across the vast flatlands of Lancaster. Once I rode an AC class engine, which was pulling a passenger train, over this stretch at sixty miles an hour. I never go through Lancaster that I do not think of it. These Mallets, of course, are the cab-ahead locomotives that have been used on the Southern Pacific for a great many years; in fact, I believe Baldwin built the first ones as the old 4,000 Class, 2-8-8-2, in 1909, as the AC-1. The one I rode was a later type, a 4-8-8-2, which began with the 4,100 Class.

The grade starts to lift at Lancaster and we move on through Palmdale, climbing, and get a flag at 7:22 P.M. west of Vincent. The "flag" is a red fusee, carried by a state trooper, who, when we stop, informs us that No. 52 hit an automobile at the Vincent highway crossing. We are delayed about an hour before we crawl slowly past the scene of the accident, where two motorists were killed.

The automobile driver who approaches and drives over a railroad track without first being sure that no train is approaching is foolhardy beyond words. Reckless with his own life and absolutely indifferent to the danger he invites for those riding with him, he further endangers the lives of railroad men. This kind of a motorist is the greatest menace the American railroader has to face.

Our long freight rolls on down the grade, having tipped over the summit at Vincent. We get train orders at Paris for meets down the canyon, the first of which is with No. 57, the Owl, at Ravenna. We meet No. 59, the West Coast, at Lang. Westbound trains face a grade on this stretch of track as high as 2.24 per cent. Between Vincent and Saugus there were numerous tun-

17

nels at one time, but many of these have been opened up, forming cuts now in these steep-walled hills. This is nothing like the Tehachapi but it is heavy going and in the past has been the scene of enormous flood damage.

We are by Saugus at 9:46 P.M. Saugus is a small but interesting railroading spot. Grimy helper engines used to wait here to do their bit in getting freights up the hill, but Diesels have changed the picture. First No. 806 moves on to Newhall and we wait here for No. 55, the San Joaquin passenger. Newhall is an old town, with the home of the late William Hart looking down from a hill close by. In the tumbled hills to the south, oil was first discovered in California.

Between Newhall and San Fernando we pass through the longest tunnel on the line, 6,925 feet in length. Leaving the tunnel, we enter San Fernando Valley and roll on to Burbank Junction, reaching there at 11:00 P.M., just in time to get the red signal, holding us for No. 72, coming in on the Los Angeles Division of the Coast Line from San Francisco. We follow him into Glendale, and the author dropped off the Diesel at the station.

It was another good run, coming down from the San Joaquin Valley over the unforgettable Tehachapi with another 3,500 tons for the new retarder hump in Taylor Yard, Los Angeles, a short distance from the Glendale station.

It was a remarkable performance and one of the toughest tests that can be given Diesel power.

Except for howling blizzards, the Tehachapi experiences all kinds of weather. Some idea of the summer heat in the San Joaquin Valley and the Mojave area may be gathered from the fact that temperatures of around one hundred degrees have been recorded in the Valley at midnight.

CHAPTER III

DENVER & RIO GRANDE WESTERN

California Zephyrs

The Denver & Rio Grande made history in the West a long time ago. That was in 1871. The pages recording that great era are beginning to turn dim and yellow. Little engines then, hurling their weight at the Rockies in magnificent conquest. And they built a monument in the city of Colorado Springs and set upon it little old No. 168, a narrow-gauge Baldwin in 1883, in everlasting memory—a shrine of iron and steel on the footstool of the range, celebrating the sixty-second anniversary of Colorado statehood in August, 1938.

And then on September 14, 1950, another monument was unveiled—a monument to progress, to a man named Cy Osborn, to a streamlined train with glass rooftops, the California Zephyr.

At exactly the spot where the Vista-Dome was first conceived, at exactly the spot where the east- and westbound California Zephyrs meet in the grandeur and the solitude of Glenwood Canyon, dedication ceremonies were held by the Denver & Rio Grande Western Railroad and General Motors in tribute to the conception of the glass-domed car by C. R. Osborn, now a vice-president of General Motors.

The ceremony took place under the eyes of the passing trains, with the deep-throated Diesels shouting their salutes before this big, new monument cairn surmounted by a nine-foot scale model dome coach, an exact replica of the passing dome coaches that are part of the silver trains gliding past.

God gave Colorado the Rockies and the Denver & Rio Grande Western and Cy Osborn made it possible for the traveler to enjoy these mountain monarchs by daylight and from a vantage point previously enjoyed by a select few.

To review briefly: In 1944, Cy Osborn, studying wartime freight movements through the Colorado Rockies, was riding the fireman's seat of a Diesel freight locomotive. He was struck by the fabulous mountain scenery and sensed the impact it would make on the train traveler, once he was afforded the opportunity to view it as he had. Cy Osborn took the idea back to the engineering department of the Electro-Motive Company at La Grange, Illinois, and the answer was the Vista-Dome car.

The California Zephyrs made their debut on March 20, 1949, and became the first transcontinental trains carrying Vista-Dome cars. Those who ride them never forget the breath-taking beauty of these Colorado Rockies.

Six sets of eleven-car California Zephyrs cross the Rockies and the Sierra Nevadas, in California, in daylight, which means that six of these trains are constantly roaming the rails between Oakland–San Francisco, California, and Chicago, Illinois.

The California Zephyr makes the run over this Colorado-mid-continent route in fifty hours and thirty-one minutes eastbound, and fifty-one hours and twenty minutes westbound. The California Zephyr replaced the Exposition Flyer, which required sixty-three hours eastbound and over sixty-nine hours westbound. The California Zephyr was scheduled to put the passenger at the points of most spectacular scenery in daylight, where the earlier Flyer passed through this startlingly beautiful high country, both in the Rockies and in the California Sierra Nevadas, during hours of darkness.

Make-up of the Train

Each California Zephyr consists of a baggage car, three Vista-Dome coaches, a Vista-Dome buffet-lounge car, two six-bedroom-and-ten-roomette cars, a dining car, one sixteen-section sleeper, one six-bedroom-and-ten-roomette car, and a Vista-Dome lounge-observation, with one drawing room and three bedrooms.

Each car of the California Zephyrs was given a prefix word "Silver" because of the stainless steel surface of these beautiful and unique trains. The baggage cars have been named for wild animals of the Western plains and mountains, and we find these cars with such names as the Silver Buffalo, the Silver Antelope, the Silver Stag. And then the coaches with such characteristic names of Western life and environment as the Silver Lariat, the Silver Mustang, the Silver Sage.

The names of the buffet-lounge cars, the diners, and the buffet-observation suggest the kind of service rendered, like the Silver Hostel, the Silver Banquet, the Silver Penthouse. The room cars carry names representative of Western scenery—Silver Butte, Silver Pass, Silver Surf. The open-section sleepers have been given the names of trees, like the Silver Maple, the Silver Pine, the Silver Palm.

Everything possible has been done to surround these California Zephyrs with the atmosphere of the great open spaces of the West, the breadth and freedom of life there. Each breath-taking morning raises the curtain on new worlds for the traveler who for the first time is looking at the West.

No. 17, the westbound California Zephyr, leaves Chicago at 3:30 P.M. and the passenger is given a preview of great prairies before darkness closes in. The next morning there are still vast prairie lands spread out but the wide plains of Nebraska are behind, and this is Colorado now, and off there ahead you, from your seat in the Vista-Dome, find something startling and fascinating reaching across the horizon—blue it is, with a white-lace edging. You are getting your first look at the Rockies, and that first look will leave its impression strongly in your memory.

From that moment every waking hour will be filled with such sheer, titanic grandeur as dreams are made of. You can ride these trains again and again and find something new every time —new cloud effects, new snow formations, new green meadows, leaves set aflame in the high country, new waterfalls, storms driving down, sudden sunny vistas opening up.

You haven't seen America until you have seen it from "upstairs" on a train, from a seat in one of these modern railroad penthouses, the Vista-Dome cars.

The Budd people, of Philadelphia, built the California Zephyrs, and they turned out cars capable of meeting the wide variation of requirements that have made them truly "blue ribbon" trains, with many innovations and improvements incorporated in their structure and design.

Few trains, as this is set down, have as many varied "downstairs" as the Vista-Domes of the California Zephyrs, for here we find not only domes on the coach cars but on the mid-train buffet-lounge, the rear room-buffet-observation car. In other words, there are no two Vista-Dome cars alike in the train's consist, which has five Vista-Domes altogether.

The eleven-car trains provide 138 seats for coach passengers, plus seventy-two in the Vista-Domes and 107 in the sleepers. To provide care for certain of the passengers, ten young women have been specially trained to serve as hostesses on the six sets of equipment. They are known as the Zephyrettes and they devote themselves to looking out for women, children, and aged people who are traveling alone. Each train also provides valet service.

In the dormitory car, the steward has a bedroom; also the hostess. Back of these two bedrooms are the dormitory quarters with three sets of three-tier bunks. There are also toilet and shower facilities in addition to the separate washroom.

Lighting features on the California Zephyrs include a cylindrical magnifying ceiling unit in the coaches which is formed to control the light to the aisle only. This design produces a low level of soft light in the seat area without glare.

As you go up the stairs to the dome for night observation, lighting gradually changes from a high to an extremely low level so that the reflections on the glass dome do not restrict the passengers' ability to see out. Two small lights are concealed on the sides of the stairway on each tread. Smaller lights of a similar design illuminate the leading edge of the elevated platform on which the seats are located.

A continuous row of lensed glassware, built into the ceiling on each side of the air duct, makes the Vista-Dome an outstanding feature of the car when the train is in a terminal.

Night lighting has come to occupy a most important niche in our lives, and the lighting of a modern train is, indeed, a far cry from the days of the Pintsch-Burner lamps or even the later electric lighting systems. Lights on the train of today make easy reading and also provide the same atmosphere of luxury you find in the finest of hotels.

We have in the dining car on the California Zephyr a soft glareless light and cheerful ceiling illumination from a continuous row of Luminator lensed glassware mounted in the coves on the side of the ceiling. The steward's desk in the foyer is accented by a special ceiling light.

A row of Luminator lensed glassware is used in the buffet-lounge, similar to the arrangement in the diner. In the double-seat sections at the end of the car a small cornice light is employed transversely over the seats in a way that directs the light over the passenger's shoulder. Individual fluorescent ceiling units are located over the tables and seats.

In the open-section sleeper individual fluorescent ceiling lights are located opposite each section. This unit has large prisms pressed into the side walls of the controlled lens to give additional illumination to the ceiling. The down lighting floods the car from side to side, with ample light for reading but still no glare to disturb your relaxation. The upper and lower berths have incandescent lights.

In the roomettes two fluorescent tubes are placed one on each side of the mirror, with the lensed glassware controlling the light so it does not disturb the occupant while using the mirror, or while sitting beside it. The main light source is in the ceiling over the reading area. An incandescent berth light at the side can be used either in the daytime or at night.

In the observation-lounge the lighting is from a continuous row of lensed glassware in the soffit over the top of the windows, directing the light to the reading area. The ceiling is illuminated by lights over the seats. The buffet ceiling units are arranged to illuminate the various seating arrangements in the proper manner.

We have referred here to "Luminator lensed glassware," as some stress has been placed on the lighting of the California Zephyr. Streamlining of the lighting system of the train was accomplished in a very pleasing manner by the Luminator manufacturers. Their engineers and designers created a lighting that accented tremendously the modern trend of the interiors. The combination of lensed glassware and fluorescent light produced both softness and a fascinating highlighting of detail.

The entire lighting system was developed especially for this streamliner. Travelers are immediately impressed by these modern developments in lighting technique. You have only to stand on a station platform to know that there have been far-reaching achievements in putting glamour aboard this new kind of train.

We find pleasure in the underdome sections of the California Zephyr. There is particular charm and coziness here—it is a kind of snug-harbor feeling, enhanced by murals and kindly surroundings.

Needless to say, the artists, when they start to work on these interiors, do something that has never been done before—they take the background colors of the country beside the track and weave them into something as warm as a blanket. Here we have gold and Indian red; there it is nut pine and light dust. Eight major color schemes are employed. The coaches and the various types of car have their own distinctive combinations.

An outstanding feature in the buffet-lounge is a series of large stylized maps of cities along the route, carved and painted on linoleum.

The California Zephyrs, of course, are equipped with radio and public-address systems. Two two-spool wire reproducers can give twelve hours' continuous entertainment. A train telephone system allows members of the crew to communicate with each other. The radio system consists of two sets, each having seventeen pretuned crystal receivers, thus making available as many as thirty-four broadcasting stations.

Modern air conditioning and heating provide for the sudden temperature changes that may be encountered.

How much modernity enters into the make-up of these California Zephyrs is exemplified in a slender control panel we find conveniently located to the berths in the rooms. These are for: (1) air conditioning, (2) push button for porter service, (3) switch for ceiling light, (4) four-position fan switch, (5) potentiometer for heat control, (6) volume control for radio, and (7) selector switch for radio and public-address system.

There is one car in the train that has just about everything in the way of accommodations, and that is the last car. At the rear end of this car there is the luxurious lounge and observation section, with accommodations for thirteen passengers. From this section stairs lead to the Vista-Dome. The underdome section provides a luxurious buffet and service bar. There are seats here for twelve. Forward is a drawing room and three bedrooms, and, next to the vestibule the porter's seat and berth. The drawing room offers outstanding de luxe appointments.

Big Diesels pull the California Zephyr over the entire distance. Usually a three-unit Electro-Motive locomotive of 4,500 horsepower goes through from Chicago to Denver. In the Rockies the motive power is normally the only two 6,000-horsepower Alco Diesels the Rio Grande are running between Denver and Salt Lake City. Across the western deserts and over the Sierra Nevadas, Salt Lake to Oakland Pier, California, the power is Electro-Motive units combined to produce 4,500 horsepower.

These California Zephyrs provide coach and Pullman accommodations at no extra fare. All accommodations, of course, must be reserved in advance.

Generous-sized and conveniently located men's and women's dressing rooms are provided down the length of the train, and they have every facility for the passengers' comfort, even down to the electric receptacle for bottle warmers in the women's rooms.

Absolutely nothing has been omitted on these trains to make the transcontinental traveler feel like royalty away from home.

The undercar equipment is as new and modern as the general

furnishings, with Timken roller bearings, coil bolster springs, and vertical shock absorbers. The air brakes are the Westinghouse High-Speed-Control type, with antislide devices to prevent wheels locking. A lever-type hand brake operates through the Budd-type disc brakes with which the trucks are equipped.

Copper tubing is used for all brakes, steam and water pipes on the car bodies.

All buffet and dining-car kitchen facilities include Frigidaire electromechanical refrigeration, which also takes care of the ice-cube production.

The thirty-six-inch rolled-steel wheels of the cars are machine balanced, and we find rubber pads placed under the center plates, under the equalizers over the journal boxes, and at the ends of the bolsters. These are the things that help cushion your train and silence it when the miles are streaking behind.

Safety has been built into the California Zephyrs beneath their beauty and the passengers are surrounded by structural-tested walls and roof sections. Safety has been built into the roadbed, and the last word in signaling is used, including the centralized traffic control system of train dispatching over all of the districts of the silver miles which these silver cars of the California Zephyrs speed that are not double track.

CHAPTER IV

WABASH MANIFEST TRAINS

Fast Freight Is King

The manifest train is king of the railroad. Manifest freight means a long, fast haul. It is the shippers' delight and the railroad's pride. The best in power heads the manifest train on its run for it is the railroad's bid for traffic lost to truckers. In a time of national emergency, the fast freight is a vital factor in war transport.

On the Wabash we find crack fast freights thundering through, linking up important cities, having a part in the coast-to-coast haul of perishables, in the movement of livestock and merchandise. Such trains are important to our economy.

Eastbound, from Kansas City, the Wabash operates No. 90, departing at 5:30 A.M. This train handles fruit and vegetables from California, Arizona, the Pacific Northwest, Oregon, and Idaho; livestock, which required feed, water, and rest, at Kansas City; and manifest freight from California, Texas, and Colorado.

Primarily, No. 90 is a Chicago fruit and vegetable train, providing seventh-morning arrival in Chicago from California Zone 1 (this is the unit perishable schedule); sixth-morning from Imperial Valley, California; and fifth-morning arrival from Arizona's Salt River Valley. Connection is made with the Pennsylvania at Logansport, Indiana, with the Erie at Huntington, Indiana, and with various lines at Buffalo, New York, providing third-morning arrival for such Eastern seaboard points as New York City, Jersey City, Philadelphia, Baltimore, Washington, and other points; and also third-night arrival at New England points. Moving by way of Detroit, this service provides second-morning arrival at Toronto, and second-night arrival at Montreal, Canada.

Train No. 90 operates on an exceedingly fast schedule. Because of its acceptance of perishables up to train time, it stops only at division points and consequently does no intermediate work.

A second section of No. 90 is operated out of Kansas City about 8:00 A.M., arriving in St. Louis at 5:30 P.M. the same evening. Here connection is made with early morning trains of Eastern and Southeastern lines from East St. Louis.

Train No. 82 on the Wabash departs from Kansas City at 3:40 P.M., accepting traffic connections up to 1:00 P.M. This train handles fresh meat and packing-house products from Kansas City, and also from connecting lines, originating principally in Oklahoma and Texas.

Train No. 82 arrives in St. Louis early the following morning, making connection with Eastern and Southeastern lines' trains leaving St. Louis around noon. This manifest arrives in Chicago the following day and connection is made with early evening trains for Eastern lines. No. 82 also protects perishables received too late for No. 90. It connects with the Pennsylvania at Logansport and with the Erie at Huntington, Indiana, providing third-morning arrival on the Eastern seaboard, and a third-night arrival at New England points. This train also does some intermediate work between Kansas City and Detroit.

Train No. 98, scheduled to leave Kansas City at 8:20 P.M., accepts traffic up to 6:30 P.M. This train handles livestock, merchandise, and Kansas City proper traffic, petroleum products, and fruit and vegetables from Colorado. The livestock is loaded at the Kansas City stockyards up to 7:00 P.M.

No. 98 arrives in Buffalo the second evening, making possible third-night arrivals at New England cities. Through its connections with the Pennsylvania and Erie at Logansport and Huntington, it provides third-afternoon arrivals at Eastern seaboard points.

A connection from No. 98 reaches St. Louis the morning following its night departure from Kansas City, and deliveries are made to Eastern and Southeastern lines for trains leaving East St. Louis around noon. This train also performs intermediate work between Kansas City and Detroit.

Fast freight No. 92 is scheduled to depart from Omaha, Nebraska, at 6:45 P.M., arriving in St. Louis at 10:30 A.M. the next day. This train carries, principally, livestock and meat from the South Omaha stockyards. It also picks up livestock and perishables at Shenandoah, Iowa, and Stansberry, Missouri. Because of its fast schedule No. 92 makes no other intermediate stops. It connects at Moberly, Missouri, the following morning with Kansas City No. 90 for the East.

Also operating out of Omaha is Manifest No. 96, departing at 12:15 A.M. This is practically a local train to Moberly, Missouri, doing cleanup work, also handling some merchandise. The train performs intermediate work between Moberly and St. Louis, principally at Centralia and Mexico, Missouri. No. 96 connects at Moberly with Kansas City No. 82 for the East.

From Des Moines, Iowa, we have Manifest No. 98, with a scheduled departure at 1:00 P.M. No. 98 handles merchandise, connecting-line livestock, and packing-house products, principally from Sioux City, Iowa; Minneapolis & St. Louis Railway connection at Albia, Iowa, from the Twin Cities to St. Louis and Kansas City; meat from Ottuma, Iowa.

No. 98 arrives in St. Louis the morning following its departure from Des Moines for connection with Eastern and Southeastern lines' trains leaving East St. Louis around noon. The train picks up livestock and perishables between Des Moines and Moberly and connects at Moberly with Kansas City No. 98 to the East.

These brief outlines of manifest movement on the Wabash indicate something of the fine co-ordination that keeps the wheels of the fast freights moving down the rails. America can be proud of roads like the Wabash, built and grown up in the American tradition of free enterprise, and producing, day in and day out, the finest kind of modern transportation.

We have mentioned Kansas City No. 82, out of Kansas City, and now we have Train No. 82 from East St. Louis, departing at 2:00 A.M., with cutoff for accepting freight at 1:30 A.M. This train handles California, Arizona, and Texas fruit and vegetables for Chicago, and, via Logansport and Huntington, Indiana, Eastern points; merchandise, locally loaded dairy freight, meat, etc.; meat and livestock from Texas and Oklahoma; reconsigned perishables and miscellaneous freight for Eastern destinations and to and via Chicago.

Two sections of 82 are usually operated—one to Chicago and one to the East. The Chicago section arrives in Chicago at 12:30 P.M. the same day. The Eastern section consolidates at Decatur, Illinois, with Kansas City No. 82. No. 82 from East St. Louis provides the same kind of service to the East as Kansas City 82, except it is one day earlier.

East St. Louis No. 98 leaves this city at 10:30 A.M., with cutoff time at 9:00 A.M. This No. 98 handles Texas fruit and vegetables, manifest and other freight arriving by way of various connections, also meat and packing-house products from Oklahoma and Texas.

East St. Louis 98 arrives in Chicago early the following morning. It consolidates at Decatur with Kansas City No. 98, providing the same Eastern arrivals one day earlier.

Train No. 96 is scheduled out of East St. Louis at 4:30 P.M. No. 96 handles livestock and meat from the National Stockyards, Illinois; early-loaded local traffic; merchandise for Detroit; seasonal movements of fruit and vegetables, such as some Texas onions and tomatoes and vegetables from Louisiana; perishables and other freight from New Orleans and Memphis. No. 96 provides following morning arrival in Chicago, third-morning arrival on the Eastern seaboard, third-night arrival at New England points, via the Pennsylvania and the Erie at Logansport and Huntington, respectively, and various lines at Buffalo. This train does considerable intermediate work between East St. Louis and Detroit.

The Wabash operates Train No. 82 out of Chicago at 9:00 A.M. The Indiana Harbor Belt Railroad and the Belt Railway of Chicago deliver Western lines' traffic for this train. No. 82 handles fruit and vegetables from California, Arizona, and the Pacific Northwest; dairy freight, meat, and packing-house products, principally from Iowa, Nebraska, Minnesota, and Wisconsin; miscellaneous freight loaded at Chicago industries the previous day. No. 82 is consolidated at Detroit with Kansas City and St. Louis No. 82's, and it provides the same service to the East beyond Detroit as St. Louis No. 82.

Train No. 98 is scheduled out of Chicago at 8:30 P.M. The Indiana Harbor Belt Railroad and the Belt Railway of Chicago, as in the case of No. 82, deliver Western lines' traffic for the train and cutoffs have been arranged to co-ordinate with these deliveries.

No. 98 handles merchandise, local traffic, and the early stockyards' pull. The train consolidates with Kansas City and St. Louis No. 98's at Detroit, providing the same service to the East beyond Detroit as St. Louis No. 98.

Train No. 96 is scheduled out of Chicago at 11:30 P.M. It handles late stockyards pull, late-loaded merchandise, and early-released industry loads. Chicago No. 96 does the intermediate work between Chicago and Detroit, consolidating at Detroit with St. Louis No. 96.

From Toledo to the East, the Wabash offers No. 182, with a 7:30 A.M. departure and a 6:00 A.M. cutoff. No. 182 handles all business from Toledo and the Toledo connections for Detroit and the East. This business is mostly coal and grain. No. 182 is scheduled into Detroit at 11:45 A.M. the same day, and it connects with No. 96, leaving Detroit (Windsor) in the afternoon.

Westbound Movement

Westbound from Buffalo, Wabash Train No. 97 leaves Niagara Falls (Buffalo) at 10:30 P.M., and Train No. 91 leaves Fort Erie (Buffalo) at 6:00 P.M. Various sections of these trains are operated as required and consolidated out of Detroit at 1:00 P.M. the following day as No. 91.

This manifest movement provides following-morning arrival in Detroit; first-midnight arrival at Chicago; second-morning arrival at East St. Louis; and second-night arrival at Kansas City.

31

These trains from Niagara Falls and Fort Erie are co-ordinated to protect traffic from Eastern connections in New England and on the Eastern seaboard, providing arrival from those origins on second morning to Detroit, second midnight to Chicago, third morning to East St. Louis, and third night to Kansas City.

A special merchandise service is also operated out of Niagara Falls and Fort Erie about noon, protecting Eastern lines' seaboard departures the previous night and providing a through schedule from the seaboard for second-morning arrival to Chicago, and second-noon arrival to East St. Louis.

From Detroit, Train No. 91 is scheduled to depart at 1:00 P.M. This is a connection for Canadian lines' inbound trains. No. 91 also handles Detroit industry traffic as well as freight traffic off the Buffalo Division. Sections are operated to Chicago, East St. Louis, and Kansas City, providing the same arrivals (one day earlier) as No. 91 and No. 97 from Buffalo.

The Wabash also operates Train No. 89 from Detroit at 8:00 P.M. This train handles merchandise and early industry traffic, providing arrival at Chicago the following morning, at East St. Louis the following afternoon, and at Kansas City the second morning. This train also performs considerable intermediate work.

Two trains are operated out of Toledo—No. 77 at 10:00 A.M. and No. 79 at 9:30 P.M. These trains handle miscellaneous connecting-line traffic, and also a heavy movement of Eastern coal for Chicago. A connection is made at Montpelier, Ohio, with Trains Nos. 91 and 89 from Detroit to the West. Turn-around runs are operated on the Toledo Division from Delta, Ohio, to Montpelier to handle a heavy movement of automobiles and automobile parts received from the Detroit, Toledo & Ironton Railroad. Various sections of Nos. 91 and 89 operate as required to accommodate these turn-around runs.

From Chicago, No. 93 is scheduled to leave at 7:00 P.M. This train handles Chicago proper traffic, merchandise, and freight from connecting lines; also early stockyards pull. No. 93 connects with No. 91 at Decatur, Illinois, for Kansas City. It ar-

Sentinel freight really moves on the B.&O. First Chicago #97, with Diesel 108, passing C.S.D. #97 with engine 6120, Class S-1, 2-10-2 type, meeting eastbound Potomac Yard #94 at Sir John's Run on the east end of Cumberland Division. Courtesy, B.&O. RR.

S.P. Extra 6124 above Woodford climbing 2.36 grade headed for tunnel #9 at Tehachapi Loop. San Joaquin Division. Courtesy, S.P. RR.

S.P. Extra 6124 east is now leaving Tehachapi Loop at Walong, Calif., still on C.T.C. grade 2.2. San Joaquin Division. Courtesy, S.P. RR.

S.P. Extra 6124 east, solid train of iron pipe entering C.T.C. leaving Bena, Calif., on 1.5 grade. San Joaquin Division. Courtesy, S.P. RR.

S.P. Extra 6124 east coming out of tunnel #9 at Walong, Calif., rounding famous Tehachapi Loop, curve #81, on 2.36 grade. San Joaquin Division. Courtesy, S.P. RR.

View from the Vista Dome of Rio Grande #1, the Royal Gorge, approaching the Sangre de Cristo Range, Col., on the Pueblo Division. Courtesy, Rio Grande RR.

Monument to an idea. Replica of Vista Dome coach at Grisley, Col., where Cy Osborn, Vice-President of General Motors, first thought of the idea of having domes on the roofs of cars. The eastbound California Zephyr, #18, is shown on the opposite side of the Colorado River, Glenwood Canyon. Grand Junction Division. Courtesy, Rio Grande RR.

Western Pacific Extra 907 west, with E.M.D. 5,400 h.p. F-3 Diesel, east of Keddie, Calif., on the Western Division. Courtesy, W.P. RR.

Western Pacific #18, California Zephyr, passing through the Honeymoon Tunnels at Rock Creek Dam, Calif., on the Western Division. Courtesy, W.P. RR.

Interior of the Vista Dome on the Wabash's new Bluebirds #21 and #24 in operation between Chicago and St. Louis looking toward the rear with exit showing. Courtesy, Wabash RR.

Wabash #98 crack Redball Fast Freight with three E.M.D. F-7 2,000 h.p. units heading into Decatur Yard, Ill. Decatur Division. Courtesy, Wabash RR.

Virginian Time Freight #71 with 3,000 tons crossing the New River Bridge at Glenlyn, Va., on the New River Division, hauled by one of the fine new electric engines Class EL-2B. Courtesy, Virginian RR.

The Virginian's magnificent power plant at Narrows, Va., which puts the 11,000 volts into the lines that operate their electrification. Courtesy, Virginian RR.

The Santa Fe Chief #19 hauled by Diesel 19 at Chapelle, N.M., on the Third District of the New Mexico Division with Starvation Peak in background. Photo by Preston George.

Santa Fe Extra 5017 west, the great 2-10-4 type, arriving at Vaughn, N.M., on the First District of the Pecos Division. Photo by Preston George.

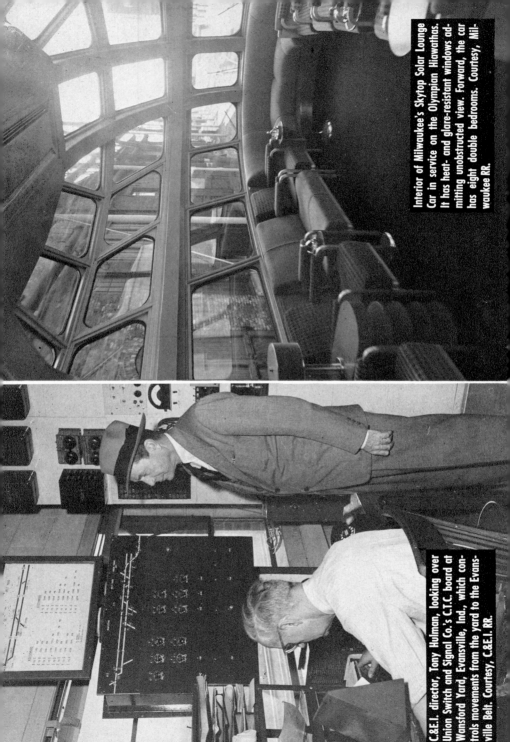

Interior of Milwaukee's Skytop Solar Lounge Car in service on the Olympian Hiawathas. It has heat- and glare-resistant windows admitting unobstructed view. Forward, the car has eight double bedrooms. Courtesy, Milwaukee RR.

C&E.I. director, Tony Hulman, looking over Union Switch and Signal Co.'s C.T.C. board at Wansford Yard, Evansville, Ind., which controls movements from the yard to the Evansville Belt. Courtesy, C.&E.I. RR.

rives at East St. Louis the following morning and at Kansas City the following night.

Train No. 83 is also operated out of Chicago at 8:30 P.M. No. 83 handles late-loaded merchandise and the late pull from the stockyards. It connects with sections of No. 89 at Decatur, arriving in East St. Louis the following afternoon and in Kansas City the second morning. It also does considerable intermediate work between Chicago and Decatur.

Train No. 97 leaves St. Louis at 7:10 P.M., with a cutoff time at 5:30 P.M., arriving in Kansas City the following morning. This manifest handles Florida fruit and vegetables and miscellaneous freight from connecting lines for Kansas City and beyond, also early-loaded local traffic.

Scheduled out of St. Louis at 8:20 P.M. is Train No. 95. This train operates in sections to Des Moines and Omaha, arriving in Omaha the following afternoon and in Des Moines the following noon. No. 95 handles Florida fruit and vegetables, miscellaneous freight from connections, all business for the Minneapolis & St. Louis, via Albia, Iowa, merchandise for Omaha, Des Moines, Twin Cities, and beyond. It provides following-night arrival at the Twin Cities by way of Albia and the Minneapolis & St. Louis road.

The Wabash, with its finely synchronized manifest service, offers a general cross section of the kind of fast freight service in operation all over the nation. Through this kind of service, the average speed of the freight car has increased amazingly. It is speed the shipper wants, and it is speed he is getting, with the so-called "overnighters" alone operating almost 45,000 miles nightly at the time this is set down.

This means better power, better rolling stock, better roadbed, and better train dispatching and signaling. It means railroading the modern way.

The Wabash offers fine service from New England and Eastern seaboard points, via Buffalo, Detroit, and Chicago, to all points West through its connecting gateways. It provides excellent service from St. Louis to Denver, Salt Lake City, San

Francisco, Seattle, Portland, and other destinations over connecting lines.

The Wabash has earned a fine fast freight reputation through its ability to highball its manifest traffic, day in and day out, in storm and fair weather. Its operating men, its two-fisted railroaders, rank high on the roster of American railroads.

CHAPTER V

WESTERN PACIFIC

Youngest Transcontinental Line

The Feather River Canyon, in the California Sierra Nevadas, ranks high among scenic rail lines. It was one of the roughest, toughest stretches of track that was ever spiked down on a mountainside. That was in the old days. Today the rail of the Western Pacific still searches out the wild, breath-taking canyon passage for its pathway, but it is a safe, modern line that for one hundred and twenty miles provides the traveler with a thrill a minute.

The men who pioneered the Western Pacific and the men who have run trains over it since were, and are, a hardy lot. Spanish explorers poked into the Feather River Canyon country in 1820, and, like so many places in California, it carries the name they gave it, though now it is the English version. The Spaniards called it El Rio de las Plumas, because of the great number of wild fowl feathers they found floating down the river. Even today the Feather River country is a favorite haunt of wild ducks and geese, just as it is becoming increasingly popular with the human species of migratory birds.

The Feather River Canyon is largely confined between the towns of Oroville and Portola, California. Oroville stems from the Spanish word for gold, and Portola is a Spanish surname, one Gaspar de Portola, leader of what was called the "holy expedition" to Upper California in 1769. Gaspar de Portola was later the Golden State's first governor. So back and beyond the scenery of the canyon there are legends and traditions that have been in the making for nearly two hundred years.

The Western Pacific, the youngest of the transcontinental

lines, was completed in 1909 and transcontinental service was begun the following year. Compared with the older transcontinental roads, the Western Pacific was able to employ many modern engineering techniques, thus meeting the challenge of the mountains with the ability to manufacture easier grades.

It was not until 1934 that the Western Pacific was linked up with the Denver & Rio Grande Western at Salt Lake City, Utah, to make a Colorado–mid-continent route. This hookup was made when the thirty-eight-mile Dotsero Cutoff was opened between Orestod and Dotsero, Colorado. (The name Orestod is simply Dotsero spelled backward.) The Cutoff linked the D.& R.G.W.'s main line, up there on the top of the Rockies, with the great Moffat Tunnel. This effected a route shortening of 175 miles.

God gave the choicest of the Rockies to Colorado, and to California the Sierra Nevadas and Feather River Canyon, and the Western Pacific and the Denver & Rio Grande Western made it possible for the train traveler to enjoy a part of this rich mountain scenery by daylight through the medium of the California Zephyrs.

In days gone by Western Pacific telegraphers and train dispatchers experienced stern adventures in moving trains down the canyon. It was wild and rugged and lonesome, and many an operator walked away from it before he started talking to the crickets.

In 1944, the Western Pacific installed centralized traffic control over some 250 miles of line. A further expansion increased C.T.C. to 360 miles, and when 1950 drew to a close the single track between San Francisco, California, and Gerlach, Nevada, had 438 miles of this modern type of train operation by direct signal indication handling traffic. Indications are that C.T.C. will be in Salt Lake City in late 1951.

Prior to 1944, the Western Pacific was running trains with practically no block signaling. Trains moved by timetable and train order, just as railroad men, for a great many years, figured they were meant to. But there came a day when the time card and so-called "flimsies" were not enough—flimsies being train orders, inscribed on very thin paper because of the necessity of making several copies.

The Western Pacific, confronted with an increased tempo in train movement, had its choice of installing the conventional automatic block type of signal or centralized traffic control. These were men of vision on this rugged Western Pacific, with its Feather River country and inland valleys and deserts, and they chose a modified system of C.T.C., finding that it could be adapted economically to meet traffic requirements, and at the same time dovetail nicely into the general physical characteristics of different subdivisions.

We will first review train movements, traffic volume, and right-of-way contour that the operating problems may be more clearly defined, and then delve into the more intricate details of C.T.C. and its application to this Western Pacific line.

The road runs two passenger trains each way. In connection with other railroads, we have the crack California Zephyr, running between San Francisco and Chicago, and the Zephyrette, triweekly, in operation between San Francisco and Salt Lake City. Freight traffic and the number of freight trains vary on the different subdivisions.

Freight traffic centers at Stockton, California, located ninety-two miles from San Francisco and in the great valley of one of the most productive areas in the world. Stockton has a large freight yard, and here are assembled through trains for the East. Here, too, the arriving westbound trains are broken up for distribution over the rails of the Western Pacific to the San Francisco Bay area and throughout certain portions of the Sacramento and San Joaquin valleys.

At Stockton, the W.P. exchanges considerable traffic with the Santa Fe, and in less volume with the Tidewater Southern and the Southern Pacific lines. Ordinarily, the east-west freight traffic between Stockton and Salt Lake City requires about four to six through trains each way daily. This does not include the local freight trains, or the turn-around runs, which pick up fruit, vegetables, and sugar beets.

Beside the east-west San Francisco-Salt Lake traffic, the

Western Pacific forms part of a north-south link which ties in Oregon and Washington points at a place called Keddie, California. Keddie is in the Feather River Canyon, 189 miles east and north of Stockton, making a junction for trains going to Bieber, California, 112 miles to the north. At Bieber connection is made with an outflung line of the Great Northern which dips south from its east-west line along the Columbia River. This provides the Western Pacific with a north-south route, in conjunction with the G.N., between Seattle-Portland-Spokane, on the north, and San Francisco on the south. Through its interchange with the Santa Fe at Stockton, this north-south route is extended to Los Angeles and other points in southern California.

Two through trains, on an average, are handled over the Western Pacific's north-south route between Stockton and Bieber via Keddie. Around 15 per cent of this traffic is to and from the San Francisco Bay area and the rest is interchanged with the Santa Fe at Stockton.

Including the daily passenger trains and the freight drags on the Salt Lake and Seattle-bound runs, a total of fourteen to sixteen through trains are operated daily on the Stockton-Keddie section.

The distance between Oroville and Portola is 116 miles. This Feather River Canyon section is winding, with a lifting grade eastbound. It is not a heavy grade, being the lightest in the Sierra Nevadas. For fourteen miles out of Oroville the rail ascends at 0.4 per cent; then it becomes 1 per cent all of the way to Portola. Consistently uniform eastward, locomotives can handle trains of uniform tonnage. The Class M-80 power is rated at 2,200 tons, and the M-137 at 4,000 tons. Westward the tonnage is limited only by the capacities of the sidings, which range from eighty-five to ninety-five cars. Curves are almost continuous, with most of them up to six degrees, but a considerable number are between eight and ten degrees, except in a few locations where the spirals have been extended and the curvature slightly exceeds ten degrees.

Train speeds, accordingly, are limited more by curvature than by grades. Between Bloomer, east of Oroville, and Gray's Flat the maximum for the California Zephyr for the fifty-five miles is forty miles per hour, and thirty-five miles per hour for other passenger trains using conventional cars. Limit for freight trains is twenty-five miles, making the average about twenty miles per hour and thirty-five miles per hour for passenger.

Because Feather River Canyon was the tight spot, the Western Pacific decided in 1944 that this would be the first section to be signaled. Power switch machines were placed at sidings, and these switches and the signals at these locations authorizing train movement are controlled by the dispatcher.

From Oroville, the Western Pacific track extends westward through the broad, level Sacramento River Valley and the San Joaquin Valley to Stockton, a distance of 113 miles. The line here is practically level and is tangent for long distances. The few curves are light. For these reasons there was no urgent need to install signaling on this subdivision in 1945. But physical conditions between Stockton and Clinton (Oakland), 84.3 miles, made consideration of signaling on this first subdivision necessary.

In this territory the railroad passes over a range of hills which have a maximum elevation of 750 feet at Altamont. From Stockton the grade is generally ascending up to 0.6 per cent westward for 23.3 miles; then 1 per cent for the 12 miles to Altamont, from which point the grade descends at 0.8 per cent for 26.5 miles down through Niles Canyon. From Niles to Oakland the 22.5 miles lays level. The decision with reference to types of signaling to be installed on this subdivision was based on the reduced volume of traffic as compared with other subdivisions.

About 150 to 175 cars or more are handled over this first subdivision between the Bay area and Stockton westward, and around 175 cars move eastward to the Stockton yard. This is roughly about one third of the traffic handled on the territory extending from Stockton to Keddie. Thus, the scheduled trains on the first subdivision of 93.8 miles include four passenger trains and about four through freight trains. A local freight train is operated each way daily except Sunday, and, in certain seasons, a switch run is operated between Stockton and Carbona and down a branch to Kerlinger and return to Stockton.

Because fewer trains were operated on the first subdivision, the first consideration at that time was to provide complete track-circuit-controlled signaling as a safety measure. Based on the benefits attained through authorizing train movements by signal indication on the Oroville-Portola C.T.C. territory, the Western Pacific inaugurated a study which would create like benefits for the Stockton-Oakland subdivision. However, G. W. Curtis, division superintendent of the Western Division, pointed out that the cost of C.T.C.—over and above that for conventional automatic block—did not seem justified at that time by the number of trains.

The Wabash Railroad had a single-track signaling installation in which the siding switches were operated by hand-throw stands, and the signals at these switches, which were under the control of the dispatcher, displayed aspects to authorize train movements. A committee was sent to look over this installation, and on the strength of the report submitted the Western Pacific decided to adopt this system for the first subdivision.

It might be pointed out, for those not familiar with the usual centralized traffic-control installation, that C.T.C. hookups usually employ siding switches that are thrown by means of electrical forces set in motion by the train dispatcher at the centralized traffic-control cabinet. But in the situation on the first subdivision of the Western Pacific only the signal authorizing train movement came under the hand of the train dispatcher.

The initial costs of this type of installation were not much more than they would have been for straight automatic block. Be it understood, the automatic block offers protection but cannot dispatch trains, not being controlled by the dispatcher. Now let us see how this Wabash system worked out on the Western Pacific's first subdivision.

Train Operation by C.T.C.

The installation on 84.3 miles of line between Oakland and Stockton provided the dispatcher with controlled signals, authorizing train movements as follows: (1) proceed from one siding layout to the next, (2) to enter a siding, (3) to depart from a siding and proceed to the next siding, and (4) stop.

The signals used are the searchlight type. On each station-entering signal and on each leave-siding signal there is a second "unit" which consists of a normally dark lamp, and when lighted this displays a black letter S on a circular white background a little over eight inches in diameter.

At the end of each siding, the main-track station-leaving signal and the leave-siding signal are in line, opposite the clearance point on the siding, as is customary practice. Also, at each siding the station-entering signal is located opposite the fouling point and in line with the other two signals. This practice allows a train, for example, to stop short of the switch and pull into the siding without the confusing procedure of being required to pass a signal indicating "stop."

Further, the location of the station-entering signal permits the elimination of a short track circuit through each switch; hence, one track circuit extends from the leave-siding signal to the approach signal, located a mile and one half distant.

We will take two stations, Midway and Altamont, on the Western Pacific line between Oakland and Stockton for an example of how this particular C.T.C. layout operates. Normally, the main-track westward station-leaving signal at Midway displays a red aspect, indicating, of course, stop. If there is no train between this signal at Midway and the station-entering signal at Altamont, to the west, and if the dispatcher sends out a proper control the signal at Midway will show green, authorizing the train on the main track to proceed to the station-entering signal at Altamont.

If there is a westbound train on the siding at Midway, and the dispatcher is ready for it to depart, he will send out a control which causes the leave-siding signal at Midway to display red

41

over the illuminated S. Then the head brakeman throws the switch, after which the aspect of the signal changes to green, authorizing the train to pull onto the main track. The rear brakeman closes the switch, or returns it to normal, which is the manner of referring to it in centralized traffic procedure.

We now have the train proceeding westward. A mile and one half east of Altamont the train will come to Altamont's "approach" signal. If the signal at Altamont is displaying red the approach signal, naturally, will show yellow. But if the signals at Altamont have been cleared for the train, allowing it to proceed on the main track at normal speed through Altamont, the approach signal will display green.

On the other hand, if this westbound train is to be directed to stop and enter the siding at Altamont, the dispatcher will send out a control which will put the station-entering signal at red, with the lower unit displaying the illuminated S. It follows out that the engine crew of the approaching train will have a "yellow approach" providing advance information. In all railroading, absolute obedience of signal indication is necessary to safety. With C.T.C., there can be no loose interpretation of the meaning of a signal, for that signal is a train order, as imperative as though the engineer and conductor carried written train orders over the signatures of the division superintendent and the train dispatcher. The engineer cannot take liberties with a yellow signal.

Neither the centralized traffic-control machine nor the man operating it can set up a dangerous condition. Any possible threat to safety has to come from the runner at the controls, and that is extremely remote, thanks to the high caliber of our railroad men.

This Western Pacific train approaching Altamont under control will stop clear of the east switch, which the head brakeman will "reverse," or line for the siding. With the train in the siding, the rear-end man will close the switch, or return it to "normal."

If the dispatcher wants our W.P. train to wait here in the siding he simply does not clear the station-leaving signal until such time as he is ready for the train to proceed. If there is reason for direct communication with the crew of the train the dispatcher sends out a control that lights a "call" lamp, located on the side of a relay house, situated in close proximity to each switch. A telephone is located in the relay house at each switch, providing a speedy and effective means of straightening out any problems that arise.

Continued Modernization

To better expedite train movement and promote safety over an increased mileage the Western Pacific decided in 1948 to install signaling on the second subdivision of 113 miles between Stockton and Oroville. It has been pointed out that the area around Stockton is highly productive, and also that there is a very considerable amount of traffic in and out of Stockton, as there is also in and out of Sacramento, the state capital city.

Sacramento has an approximate population of 120,000. About forty to fifty cars are handled daily. For about sixty days during the sugar-beet season the Western Pacific operates a turn-around run out of Stockton to Sacramento and return to Stockton. This picks up about fifty to sixty cars of beets daily. At several points the Western Pacific connects with its subsidiary, the Sacramento Northern Railway, which has trackage through much of the Sacramento Valley and on through the industrial areas on the northern end of San Francisco Bay. The Western Pacific exchanges about sixty to seventy cars daily to Sacramento with the Southern Pacific and the Sacramento Northern. The Western Pacific also interchanges about twenty to twenty-five cars daily at Marysville, California, with the Sacramento Northern.

This 113-mile subdivision is in the broad, flat valleys where the track is level and tangent for long distances. However, because this subdivision is part of not only the east-west but the north-south route we find a larger number of trains in operation. The daily traffic on this second subdivision includes four passenger trains and twelve to eighteen through freight trains, which

43

are, of course, in addition to the local freights and the turn-around pickup trains, which operate as required.

On account of the heavier traffic, the signaling adopted for this subdivision included power switch machines with its C.T.C. setup. The signals at sidings are located in accordance with conventional practice. With certain exceptions, the station-leaving signals have two aspects. There are no intermediate signals in this arrangement, other than the approach signals, such as were mentioned earlier. In general, the signaling is similar to that employed on the first district between Oakland and Stockton.

The station to station as a single block was considered to be the most practical for nearly all blocks in the Stockton-Oroville territory because of the straight, level track, permitting comparatively quick acceleration and sustained high speeds. On a few of the station-to-station blocks, which were more than ten miles long, intermediate automatic signals were installed. This made possible a following train movement, something not provided for in the first subdivision installation.

Control Panel Normally Dark

In drawing the preliminary specifications for the control machine to be used on the Oakland-Stockton installation, the Western Pacific called for the following: (1) all indication lamps to be normally dark, and (2) the "signal-clear" indication to be carried on the track model adjacent to the involved switch.

The opinion held was that the important advantage gained by the normally dark panel was that of the ability to notice a changed condition, as indicated on the control panel, more readily. The reaction of the operators was most gratifying.

This system of indication was arranged by Western Pacific engineers, and it was patterned in part after the system of indication for the Oakland-Stockton machine, which was designed by the Union Switch & Signal Company. It is particularly interesting in view of its introduction of something different.

Above the track diagram, and between each location of controlled signals, there is a blue lamp which is lighted when westbound traffic is established in the corresponding block by the clearing of the westbound signal. This lamp continues to show until the train movement has cleared the block. If the signal is placed to "stop" by lever control, the blue lamp continues to show until the time locking at the field station has expired, and a corresponding indication has been transmitted to the control machine. A second blue lamp, located on the panel below each block, operates in a similar manner for eastward traffic.

On the track diagram the three signals at each power switch layout are represented by a symbol including a green lamp. When a signal on the ground is cleared for a main-track movement in either direction, or for a movement from the siding, the lamp on the panel which corresponds in location with the signal that has been cleared, will be lighted and show steadily. If the lineup is for a train to take siding, this lamp indication starts flashing.

Above each *switch* lever there are three lamps—a green one to the left above the "normal" position, an amber one to the right above the "reverse" position, and a white one in the center. The white lamp above the center of the lever is lighted only when the switch in the field is out of correspondence with the lever. The green, normal, lamp or the amber, reverse, lamp is lighted only after a signal is cleared over the switch or the "OS" track section is occupied.

Above each *signal* lever there is only one white lamp, which is normally dark. When a signal, which has been cleared, is taken away, the lamp above the signal lever is lighted until the time locking interval has expired. This exact notice of the expiration of the time period permits the dispatcher to make other lineups at once.

The track-occupancy lamps on the track diagram are red, and these are normally dark. One lamp represents each OS section at a power switch, and such a lamp is lighted steady when the

45

corresponding switch detector track circuit is occupied, or when the dual-control switch machine lever is in the hand-throw position. One track occupancy lamp is used for each section of the diagram which represents the main track between controlled switches of a siding. In addition, one lamp is used for each section of the diagram which represents the main track between two sidings.

A white lamp, with black letter C, above each code-sending push button is lighted when code is going out, or when code is being received from corresponding field station. A circuit network in the machine prevents code from going out to a clear signal that is not consistent with the position of a switch or in conflict with a signal already cleared. The objective of this feature is to prevent setting up time locking unnecessarily.

Coded Track Circuits

Coded track circuits have done more to advance modern railroad signaling than any other single factor. The coded track circuit was pioneered by the Union Switch & Signal Company, with the first installations being placed in service in 1933 in both electrified and steam-service territory. The original steady-energy track circuits, invented in 1872, have been employed in railway signaling by the Union Switch & Signal Company since its organization in 1881.

A coded track circuit, briefly, is a circuit in which the current fed to the rail is broken into recurring pulses to form a so-called code. A code is made up of "on" period energy pulses, separated by "off" period intervals. The development and modern-day employment of coded track circuits and their use in connection with centralized traffic control were fully described in the Union Switch & Signal Company chapter of my book, *Railroads of Today*.

Now we will examine coded track circuits as applied to the Oroville-Portola, or the Feather River, section of the Western Pacific.

46

Except for switch-detector sections, short releasing sections for outlying electric locks and the yard area at Oroville and Portola, coded track was used exclusively on the Oroville-Portola installation, completed in 1945.

The successful operation of long track circuits (some over 11,000 feet), the improved broken-rail protection, and the facility of block signal operation without the use of line wires have been the factors which influenced the W.P. to use coded track on all subsequent installations. Where highway crossing protection or interlockings are present in a coded-track controlled block, the Western Pacific uses the conventional coded line-jumper method of getting around the conventional track-circuited section.

As the signal program progressed, the Western Pacific worked with the Union Switch & Signal people in applying new ideas as they concerned coded track circuits and their application to later operational systems. Some affected the overall operation, others were more in the nature of innovations. One of the most important of these changes was providing a means of returning the direction of feed for steady current normally energizing the track circuit to a given direction (westward on the Western Pacific).

In the station-to-station blocks on the Oroville-Portola installation, steady energy is fed into the block behind the train, regardless of direction; therefore, circuits in a block were left feeding eastward or westward, depending on the previous movement. With this arrangement, the discharge on the track cells shifting from "no load," when the circuit was feeding from the opposing end, to over 1.2 amp. when actually feeding the track. As a consequence, the regulation of the charge on the track cells was a real problem. No trouble was experienced in maintaining the proper battery condition in the siding areas where steady energy fed normally in one direction only; and a conclusion was that on future installations the station-to-station block should be arranged in a similar manner. The result was that the Union Switch & Signal Company developed a scheme which has been used successfully on the Western Pacific.

Because of its highly technical nature and the limits of space, we will not attempt to cover it here.

In connection with remote instances where the mechanism or the lamp itself may fail, the signal must be regarded as displaying its most restrictive indication, which is also an operating rule on the Western Pacific, as well as other roads, when any signal lamp remains dark upon the approach of a train that it would normally affect.

Three Control Machines in One Office

The use of carrier equipment on the centralized traffic control code line circuits made it possible to locate the three C.T.C. control machines for all three subdivisions in the division offices at Sacramento.

The carrier equipment is in duplicate at each machine location. Thus, if a set fails, the stand-by set can be brought into service. In case the line relay at the involved field station is released due to an open line or other causes, the stand-by equipment is automatically placed in service. Since the stand-by units are adjusted so as to receive at lower power level and transmit at a higher power level ordinary losses to the carrier circuits are automatically compensated.

In addition to the carrier for control and indication codes, other carrier equipment, known as individual carrier, is used for special purposes, i.e., (1) to transmit indications at twenty-three kilocycles from a rock-slide fence at M.P. 260.94 to Rich Bar; (2) to transmit controls at forty-one kilocycles from Sacramento to release an electric lock on a hand-throw switch at the Campbell Soup spur; (3) to transmit at twenty-seven kilocycles drawbridge indications from San Joaquin River bridge to Lathrop field station; and (4) to transmit "OS" indications at forty-one kilocycles from Radum interlocking to the field station at East End of Livermore.

To reach the subdivisions where they are to operate the C.T.C. conventional D.C. codes and the carrier frequencies are on one two-wire line circuit. West from Sacramento, this circuit is on No. 8 copper wire with plastic weatherproof covering. East from Sacramento to Oroville, this circuit is on No. 6 copper wire; and from Oroville to Portola the circuit is No. 8 bare Copperweld wire.

At some locations, important highways cross the single-track main line of the Western Pacific within one hundred feet of power-operated C.T.C. controlled siding switches. The control circuits for the flashing-light signals at such a crossing are arranged so that the crossing signals do not start to operate until a signal has been cleared for a train movement over the crossing. If a locomotive with cars makes a move to pull over the crossing and then back again, the flashing-light signal will operate because the so-called "stick" relay which controls this function is "knocked down" when the signal for the back-up move is cleared.

To look down a stretch of railroad track, seeing the unchanged ties and rails that have become so commonplace, it is difficult for the layman to understand the advances in rail transportation that have been made. The flashing streamliner, appearing on the scene, indicates the progress made in motive power and in cars. And the signal lights, somehow, are different. The station, perhaps, has come under the airy hand of the modernistic architect. And there is the public-address system, telling you where your car will stop along the platform. Too, someone has told you that when you are aboard the train and speeding along you can telephone your home or your office. But it is not until you have looked inside of a C.T.C. instrument house out along the line or inside of a modern C.T.C. dispatching cabinet that you are fairly confronted with the astonishingly intricate maze of wires and instruments that go to make up the signaling and communication systems of your modern railroad.

We have searched out a little of the mysteries of the centralized traffic control system as applied to train operation on the Western Pacific, and we now turn our attention to general communications.

Communication Facilities

The general offices of the Western Pacific are located in San Francisco. From here communications reach out to Salt Lake City, 928 miles to the east, and to all important points affecting rail service on the line. A tie-in is made with the Denver & Rio Grande Western at Salt Lake where the first link is made with the present transcontinental route.

The modern railroad could not operate without its communication network, no more than railroads could have operated at the turn of the century without the Morse circuit. These communications involve not only train movements but all business associated with rail transportation.

The telegraph key is still clicking in places, but feebly. The telephone long ago began crowding it out for train dispatching and general long-distance communication. Then, back around 1907, the printing telegraph machine entered the picture and has more and more been employed by the modern railroad.

Turning the half-century mark, the Western Pacific had completed extensive communication improvements—improvements that meant the saving of thousands of dollars annually in long-distance telephone calls alone. These modern installations, in addition to long-distance telephone facilities, included printing telegraph circuits between operating headquarters, yards and traffic offices, and the last word in such things as electronic devices on carrier equipment by means of which existing line wires could be used to carry impulses of several high frequencies, such as, for instance, the employment of centralized traffic control line wires for telephone conversations.

Modern railroading would be a far cry from the ultraefficient facility that it is today without these magic electronic devices.

Let's examine for a moment the printing telegraph facilities that reach out from the headquarters' offices of the Western Pacific in San Francisco to the offices of the Santa Fe, the Southern Pacific, the Pacific Fruit Express, the Reservation Bureau, and Oakland. Also this service links the San Francisco offices with Stockton and Sacramento, California, and Elko, Nevada.

Before undertaking the communications improvement program, the Western Pacific made little use of the printing telegraph, and, in consequence, depended on the Morse system for most of its "message traffic." There will never be another age like that of the old telegraph key and sounder for romance and adventure down the path of the "singing wires," but that is gone; the page is dimming, the words are blurred. Never again will we know men and women who gave our nation so much as the telegraphers. Without them there would be no modern railroad story; they were the communication pioneers, and today the last of them are forever signing that wistful "30," which over the years has signaled the finished copy—the end.

Headquarters of the Western Pacific's Eastern Division are located at Elko, Nevada; those of the Western Division at Sacramento, California. In the San Francisco Bay area the Western Pacific serves numerous docks, industries, and warehouses. A branch extends from Niles along the east side of the bay to San Jose and on to a fruit-growing area. At Sacramento and Marysville, California, the Western Pacific connects with its subsidiary, the Sacramento Northern, which serves many towns in the Sacramento Valley, as well as industrial areas in the northern part of the San Francisco Bay area. There is a connection at Stockton with another subsidiary, the Tidewater Southern, which reaches through part of the great San Joaquin Valley.

The principal through route of the Western Pacific is east and west between Salt Lake City and points in California. On this east-west route, from Keddie, California, 281 miles from San Francisco, the Western Pacific has a secondary line extending north 112 miles to Bieber, California, where it connects with the Great Northern for points in Oregon and Washington. Thus the section of the Western Pacific between Stockton and Keddie is part of a north-south route linking Seattle and Portland on the north with San Francisco and through its Santa Fe connections, with Southern California.

The old Morse telegraph system of communications could only handle the most urgent railroad business, with the result that some communications had to be handled by outside commercial companies. No attempt was made to transmit passing reports and train consists in advance of or concurrently with train movements so that the information would be available ahead of train arrivals. Telephone train dispatching was employed on the main line between San Francisco and Salt Lake City, but no through telephone circuits were available between important offices, and many long-distance calls had to be made over commercial lines.

The new communications facilities, on the other hand, were planned with the objective of providing complete and adequate communications, employing printing telegraph for the transmission of all messages, including passing reports and train consists, and making the telephone generally available for conversation locally on the railroad, as well as for long-distance connections between important offices. A "train consist" is a list of cars in a train which shows car initials, numbers, weights, and destination. The "passing report" includes that information plus all further notations on waybills that are necessary for the work of the car-service bureau, as well as of the traffic department in contacting shippers and consignees.

The additional Teletype and long-distance telephone circuits were obtained in various ways, including direct wire, the simplex leg of phone pairs, and by carrier circuits superimposed over existing train dispatching telephone pairs. Except on the direct-wire circuits in San Francisco, all message traffic on the Western Pacific is handled by tape transmitters at the rate of sixty-one words a minute.

It has been the practice since the days of the old Morse circuits to indicate communication offices by letter combinations. So we find the main communications offices of the Western Pacific with the letters "GO." Here we find printers, transmitters with tape reperforators, and transmitters associated with the perforators.

In the GO office all of the Teletype equipment, such as printers, transmitters, reperforators, and incoming printer circuits, is connected to a specially constructed switchboard known as a "switching center." This is handled by an operator with a monitor and send-receive printer.

When a distant office "rings in" the signal lamp on the affected circuit is lighted and there is also a buzzer signal, which provides both a visible and an audible signal to indicate what office is calling. The operator then inserts the monitor in the answer jack and ascertains whether the calling office wishes a printer or wants to be connected through to an office or offices beyond. If the latter is desired the "cut-through" circuits are used and the calling office is cut through to the office desired.

The advantage of this method is that all offices addressed will receive the message as it is being transmitted from the originating office, thus expediting the service as well as eliminating the necessity of reperforating and handling the tape for a second transmission through the facilities of the GO office.

If a line to one or more of the offices addressed is busy at the time of transmission the operator can insert a reperforator into the circuit. This will produce a tape which can be run as soon as the busy circuits are cleared.

A modern railroad has an amazing network of communication facilities. This network is a veritable nerve center of the rail system and it is one of the major factors in helping to speed the traffic of the rails.

There could, perhaps, be no better example of the number of lines required by a railroad than is offered by the Western Pacific, which is comparatively a small railroad. This road has in operation manually operated private branch telephone exchanges in nine cities.

We find San Francisco with 300 lines; Stockton with 60 lines; Sacramento, 100 lines; Oroville, 20 lines; Keddie, 20 lines; Portola, 20 lines; Winnemucca, Nevada, 10 lines; Elko, Nevada, 20 lines; and Salt Lake City, Utah, with 240 lines. These exchanges are at the present time (the fall of 1950) connected by 13 long-distance circuits, which for the most part were created through the installation of single-channel carriers.

Local telephone service between division headquarters and all local stations at which agents are on duty, as well as to the homes of section foremen and signal maintainers, is available through a circuit with selector calling, as is employed in telephone train dispatching. The general telephone facilities, other than train dispatching, includes the P.B.X. at ten cities, the local selector calling lines to all wayside stations, and the long lines to connect the P.B.X. boards. Calls can be handled between any two persons anywhere on the railroad. A great many times train time is saved and important decisions made which affect savings in labor and material—all a result of these modern-day communications which have been applied to a rail line that has fought to the top the hard way, the Western Pacific.

The Zephyr Gets a Bath

Grimed and dusty from the sand and sagebrush miles across Utah and Nevada, the California Zephyr is given a brisk shower upon its arrival at Portola each morning. It departs down the canyon, fresh and clean. The operation requires seven minutes, and it is one of the things passengers remember in connection with their trip.

This special brushless train washer was designed and constructed by the Western Pacific under the direction of T. L. Phillips, a retired chief engineer. The apparatus is very simple, consisting of three sets of curved pipes beside the track. When in position these pipes form half arches, each of which has eight spray nozzles, which are about twenty inches from the car.

When the train starts through the shower curtain the first set of spray nozzles apply a special cleaning solution to the car tops and sides. This is then followed up by two rinsing operations from clear water. Spraying is done through fan-type nozzles which give sufficient pressure to remove, first, the film of grime accumulated during the run, and, second, to completely remove the last vestige of rinsing solution and leave the surface sharp and sparkling.

Travelers on board the train usually try to obtain seats in the dome sections for the show. This "Portola shower" is an innovation and a train-freshening process that would have given old-time railroaders a big laugh, if they survived the shock of those Vista-Domes. The old mountain railroaders had troubles enough getting the trains over the road without fussing over their appearance.

We can imagine chattering telegraph sounders up and down the division carrying the word that No. 17, the westbound California Zephyr, was "getting a bath at Portola." It probably would have been charged off to "cabin fever," which meant crazy in the head.

A concrete basin was constructed under the track in the washing area to protect the roadbed. This was provided with suitable drains. A train taking a shower is protected by train signals and floodlights. With all arches in nonoperating position the floodlights go out and the signals display a "lunar white" indication. But with one or more of the shower arches leaving the nonoperating position for the wash operation the six floodlights immediately light up and the signal indication changes to purple.

Only westbound trains are provided with shower facilities for the reason that trains out of Oakland, California, do not require a bath at this point. At the Chicago and Oakland terminals of the run the California Zephyrs get a thorough cleaning with Whiting washers.

Many weird and wonderful tales have come out of the high Sierras since the trek of the forty-niners, but it was left to the Western Pacific Railroad to add a new page for writers to record in connection with the Feather River Route, and President F. B. Whitman and Operating Vice-President Harry Munson, both crack all-around railroad men, are the gentlemen who have put the road to work in the modern way.

CHAPTER VI

THE PITTSBURGH & WEST VIRGINIA RAILWAY

Freight Road—Modern Operations

The Pittsburgh & West Virginia is one of the really great little railroads in the United States, and it has the distinction of being one of the very few main-line roads anywhere that hauls only freight. Though small in mileage the road is big in efficiency, and it certainly is richly deserving of a place in any work that deals with modern railroading.

In times of peace or war, these little railroads are vital links not only in our national economy but in the transportation system that keeps our very life blood flowing. They are a part of the greatest rail network in the world. When we think of small rail lines we are more or less prone to think of them as second- or third-raters in roadbed and rolling stock, and that is a mistake, for some of these little roads are the most compact and completely adequate rail plants imaginable.

The Pittsburgh & West Virginia Railway extends from Connellsville, Pennsylvania, where it connects with the Western Maryland Fast Freight Line, to Pittsburgh Junction, Ohio, crossing the upper corner of West Virginia, for a total 111-mile main line. The remaining twenty-one miles go to make up branches to Donora, Clairton, Mifflin Junction, Pittsburgh West End, and Bellfield, Pennsylvania.

The line has twenty-three spring switches, six rail oilers, and a slide fence hooked up with the C.T.C. machine at Rook.

The Pittsburgh & West Virginia Railway as it now exists was formed with the building in 1904 by Jay Gould of the link from

Pittsburgh Junction, Ohio, to Pittsburgh, Pennsylvania, to connect with the West Side Belt, which was then already in existence and which had important industrial connections in the Pittsburgh district. In 1930 the road was extended to Connellsville, Pennsylvania. This was known as the Connellsville Extension and it made the through route to and from the Atlantic seaboard possible.

The Pittsburgh & West Virginia links up the shortest route between the Great Lakes and the Eastern seaboard, and a fast, dependable freight service is maintained.

Since 1938, an extensive roadway rehabilitation program and equipment rebuilding program has been in progress. The new equipment program initiated in 1947 resulted in the delivery in the first quarter of 1949 of 600 new all-steel, self-clearing sixty-ton hopper cars. The road has some 3,500 cars at this writing, and approximately 35 per cent of these were built following the program begun in 1947.

The rail on the P.&.W.V. is all 112 and 115 pound. All ties are completely creosoted. The AB type of modern freight brake equipment has been installed on all cars. A high type of maintenance and progressive improvements provides a plant that is kept thoroughly modern.

The road has seven excellent 2-6-6-4-type Mallet locomotives in service. These were built in 1934, 1936, and 1937.

Rook, fifty-six miles from Connellsville and close to Pittsburgh's great steel mills, is the road's division point, its operating headquarters and the seat of its centralized traffic-control system. Centralized traffic control completely eliminates the operation of trains by "timetable and train order" on the entire main line, as well as the Mifflin and Clairton branches.

This means that the dispatcher at the C.T.C. cabinet in the modern, fireproof centralized traffic-control building at Rook has at his fingertips the control of every train on the road every minute of the day and night. This is railroading the modern way.

The Pittsburgh & West Virginia right of way does not wind in-and-out and up-and-down these rolling Allegheny foothills, as perhaps you might expect; instead it seems to more or less skim over the top of them, which is why it is called the "High Line." This is accomplished through the use of magnificent high bridges, spanning gorges and ravines, and tunnels which bore through the hills. The result is a maximum 1.35 per cent grade, and very little of this. The main line to Connellsville is 1 per cent maximum. West of Rook the grades are 0.7 compensated.

The bridges and tunnels, unlike what you might expect on a "little" railroad, were built to sustain the heaviest loads and to allow plenty of clearance for outsize shipments. Heavy power of other roads can be detoured over the P.&W.V. without trouble. In particular, in wartime the advantage of having bridges and tunnels of a size and strength to handle any kind of freight is of vital importance. The road has twenty-two of these full-size tunnels, all with excellent drainage.

A number of older type of motive power, such as the Consolidation and Mikado-type locomotives, have been retired. They were replaced with 2,000-horsepower Fairbanks-Morse Diesels. These are used back to back in through service and will handle 2,400 tons easily. The road also has a 1,000-horsepower Baldwin Diesel switch engine.

Along the line of the Pittsburgh & West Virginia lies a black diamond treasure chest in the form of coal. Five hundred fifty million tons of it unmined in the Pittsburgh No. 8 Seam alone. Think of it! And then there is the Freeport Seam below, vast in its earth-bound hoard. The road receives and moves about 150 loads of coal per day, mostly for western connections.

Located at Avella, Pennsylvania, the railroad, through its Acme Coal Cleaning Company, maintains a coal cleaning plant which is available to anyone loading coal on its lines. This has been a great boon to the small coal operator and is proof of the wide-awake traffic solicitation on the part of the Pittsburgh & West Virginia.

The chief freight movements are (1) steel, (2) coal, (3) ore from various lake ports and the port of Baltimore, (4) manufactured products, and (5) meat. Fortunately the road does not have to worry about passenger service.

Fast Freight

When the Reading, Western Maryland, P.&W.V., and Nickel Plate put the PCS-1 into service it was just about the hottest thing on wheels, and this in a day when fast freight is king of the railroad. We defer, of course, to the queen and her streamlined train.

There may be more spectacular fast freights than PCS-1, but this is a truly crack train and one that these roads can be proud of. Of course, an aid to rapid movement on the Pittsburgh & West Virginia is the fact that there are no large terminals on this route, which permits movement of freight without the delays common to big freight terminals.

PCS-1 leaves Philadelphia at 9:00 P.M. every night except Sunday. It is scheduled for five hours on the Reading and leaves Lurgan on the Western Maryland at 2:00 A.M., arriving at Connellsville, eastern terminus of the Pittsburgh & West Virginia, at 8:30 A.M.

The Western Maryland, the Fast Freight Line, having wheeled PCS-1 into Connellsville, the P.&W.V. couples on its motive power and highballs at 9:00 A.M. The train reaches Rook at 11:25 A.M. There is a thirty-minute inspection and the crews change and the highball is given at 11:55 A.M. PCS-1 passes Pittsburgh Junction, in Ohio, at 2:45 P.M.

The Nickel Plate gets it to Bellevue, Ohio, at 7:30 P.M. The train is due in Chicago at 4:45 A.M. the second morning and it is usually there two or three hours ahead of time. The connection from Bellevue to St. Louis arrives in St. Louis at 1:30 P.M.

Other crack trains received from the Western Maryland are Western Maryland No. 3, and, eastward, Nos. 94 and 90 from the Nickel Plate. No. 90 carries most of the Eastern meat.

One of the most fabulous trains in the United States originates on the Pittsburgh & West Virginia and the name of it is the Michigan Steeler. This train carries a great deal of the steel which goes into the fabrication of your automobile.

The Steeler pulls out of Rook at 3:00 A.M. every morning and is delivered to the Nickel Plate lines at Pittsburgh Junction,

Ohio, at 6:00 A.M., roaring through the dawn in these tumbled hills with clocklike precision. It reaches Brewster, Ohio, over the Nickel Plate at 7:45 A.M., leaving there at 9:15 A.M. The final delivery by the Nickel Plate's Wheeling & Lake Erie Division is at Toledo at 2:00 P.M. where the train makes connections with all lines into Michigan, namely: the Chesapeake & Ohio, the Grand Trunk, and the Detroit, Toledo & Ironton.

In spite of its workhorse existence, compared with the roads of the sparkling luxury trains, the Pittsburgh & West Virginia has a certain freshness about it that bespeaks the generous employment of fresh paint. This may not come under capital improvement in the annual report but it does leave an impression of general well-being.

Nothing is so ruinous as a rundown look, and nowhere does it become more readily apparent than on a railroad, and often on big railroads. The Pittsburgh & West Virginia maintains its roadway and train equipment and terminals in a manner that reflects pride of accomplishment, pride of ownership.

Railroad accomplishment stems from the office of its president and in Charles J. Graham the Pittsburgh & West Virginia has a completely competent leader, one of the best-liked men in the business. Because of time spent in various cities of the country he remains close to his own and other traffic representatives, which is an excellent practice for any railroad head for it brings him closer to the shipper, his views, and his needs.

"High Line"

The Pittsburgh & West Virginia has direct connections with the Nickel Plate Road, Western Maryland, Baltimore & Ohio, Pennsylvania, Montour, Union (Bessemer & Lake Erie), Pittsburgh & Lake Erie (New York Central), Donora Southern, and the Monessen Southwestern (Pittsburgh Steel Co.).

These roads have their roots deep in the teeming centers of steel and coal, the very foundation of our economical existence, and the pulse of them is hot. They have provided vital supply lines in past wars, and in a world of suspicion and chaos they are continuing to rank among the leaders in support of the nation.

During World War II, the Pittsburgh & West Virginia handled enormous quantities of vital oil and the essentials of the constant flow of war traffic, living up to its name "High Line."

The Pittsburgh & West Virginia is fortunate in having an exceptionally competent and vigorous board of directors, led by Charlie Graham. At the end of 1949, the road's average of investment for every employee was $66,000. This not only included the cost of locomotives and other rolling stock used by employees but also represented the cost of rights of way for tunnels, bridges, ties, rails, ballast, the shops, enginehouses, fuel stations, shop and power plant machinery.

Safety is an important factor on the Pittsburgh & West Virginia and safety campaigns are carried on vigorously. There are frequent safety meetings with motion pictures being shown. Awards are made to departments standing highest in nonreportable injuries.

A feature of each year's work is the safety slogan contest which results in the submission of hundreds of slogans. Cash awards are made to the employee submitting slogans which, in the opinions of the judges, are of winning caliber.

The P.&W.V., in line with many other roads, has a suggestion program, with cash awards being made to employees whose suggestions for improvements in connection with service and operation efficiency were adopted.

The road also puts out a monthly bulletin, well named the *Hi-Line*. This bulletin is of importance in the improving of relationship between the employee and the employer, and it serves to weld closer the entire Pittsburgh & West Virginia railroad family. Such a bulletin as *Hi-Line* also has great educational value and it serves to keep all employees informed.

The Pittsburgh & West Virginia road maintains traffic representatives in Portland, Oregon, and San Francisco, California, on the Pacific Coast, and in New York City and Baltimore, Maryland, on the East Coast. It has representatives in six other

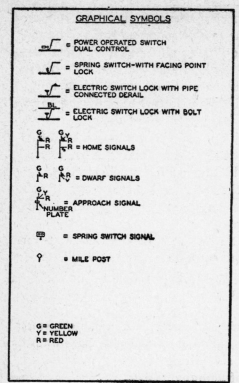

GRAPHICAL SYMBOLS

= POWER OPERATED SWITCH DUAL CONTROL

= SPRING SWITCH—WITH FACING POINT LOCK

= ELECTRIC SWITCH LOCK WITH PIPE CONNECTED DERAIL

= ELECTRIC SWITCH LOCK WITH BOLT LOCK

= HOME SIGNALS

= DWARF SIGNALS

= APPROACH SIGNAL

= SPRING SWITCH SIGNAL

= MILE POST

G = GREEN
Y = YELLOW
R = RED

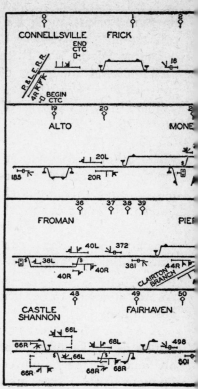

CONNELLSVILLE   FRICK

ALTO   MONE

FROMAN   PIER

CASTLE SHANNON   FAIRHAVEN

large Eastern and Midwestern cities. This indicates the progressiveness of this little freight railroad in the Allegheny foothills.

In the office of general traffic manager, freight agents, superintendents of transportation, chief engineer, and right on down the line we have found men who know their business and are

62

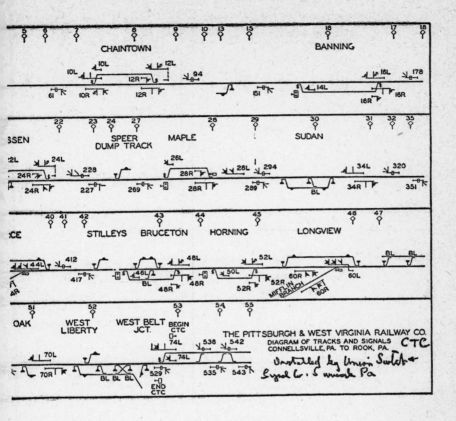

proud to be a part of the Pittsburgh & West Virginia organization.

It is truly a great little road, forming a strong steel link between two other great roads, which tie together a vitally important route between the Atlantic seaboard and the Great Lakes and Middle West. A real "high line."

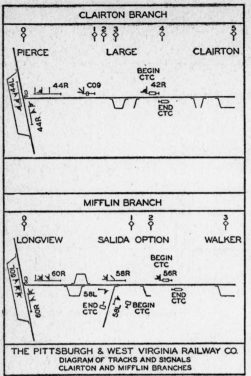

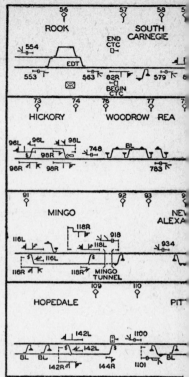

THE PITTSBURGH & WEST VIRGINIA RAILWAY CO.
DIAGRAM OF TRACKS AND SIGNALS
CLAIRTON AND MIFFLIN BRANCHES

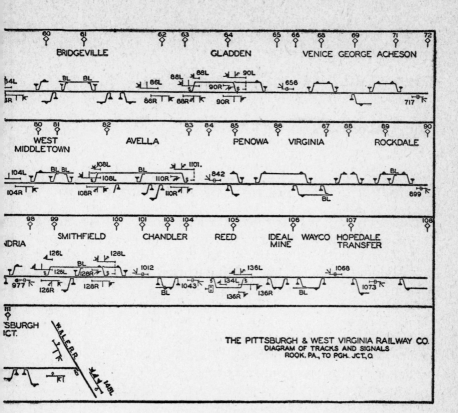

THE PITTSBURGH & WEST VIRGINIA RAILWAY CO.
DIAGRAM OF TRACKS AND SIGNALS
ROOK, PA., TO PGH. JCT, O.

65

CHAPTER VII

ARGENTINE YARD

The Santa Fe Modernizes Its Great Terminal

During World War II the Santa Fe realized that something was going to have to be done to reduce train delays at Argentine, Kansas. The big yard was just choking up, with as many as a hundred switching tracks being worked in the yard during a twenty-four-hour period. In 1943 engineers began a study of conditions, with the one idea of developing and converting it into a modern plant. The first dirt was turned in June, 1947, and in April, 1949, portions of the new hump yard went into operation. May 9 saw around-the-clock operations, and by October all of the facilities were in full operation.

Previously, Argentine had been a "flat" yard, meaning that the shuffling of cars in the classification yards was done by switch engines and crews working from leads. Multiply the operation of a locomotive setting one or more cars off on a side track by the same locomotive and crew-switching cars on a dozen or fifteen tracks and you have switching in a flat yard.

About 4,000 freight cars, during peak movements, are handled through Argentine every day. About 25 per cent are interchanged locally with twelve connecting lines. The load movement is predominatingly eastward.

Before the modernizing of Argentine was begun the yard consisted of a westbound and an eastbound yard and a yard for handling and storing cars of wheat. The latter was adjacent to what was claimed to be the largest elevator in the world. Included in the general layout was a big engine terminal and car-repair layout, also a high-level icing dock, 2,700 feet long. The area occupied as a whole was some four miles long and about a quarter of a mile wide, being flanked by the road's double-track transcontinental main line.

Of vast importance since the modernization of the yard has been the reduction in the average time required to move loaded cars through the terminal, amounting to about an hour and forty minutes. There has been also a reduction of about ten hours in the detention time for empties.

It is easy to see what this means over a period of a year—around 192,000 car days. There is, in consequence, an important reduction in per diem. Not to be overlooked is the good will of shippers because of the faster service.

A clogged flat yard during peak movements, or in time of national emergency, can play havoc with important train schedules. And when perishables are involved there are the possible damage claims to worry the road. Switching time and costs have been reduced under the new classification system and a completely new type of efficiency introduced.

The new Argentine Yard is built around the fifty-six-track hump-retarder yard, located north of the old yard. Cars are humped in a westerly direction. At its west end the classification yard is connected with the new westbound and eastbound departure yards by means of six working leads. Each of these yards has seven tracks, and between them there is an additional track that may be used for either direction. Tracks in the eastbound yard handle 79 to 129 cars; those in the westbound yard can accommodate from 85 to 125 cars.

Trains departing westbound move almost directly from the departure yard onto the main line, but eastbound trains pass along the north side of the classification yard and cross to the south side by means of an underpass beneath the crest of the hump. The underpass also carries a westbound drill track which extends around the north side of the classification yard. A modern car-repair layout, including four tracks and a service building, was built at the west end of the classification yard and south of the working leads.

Consisting partly of existing trackage, a westbound receiving yard, made up of fifteen tracks of 41- to 141-car capacity, was constructed east of the classification yard. Cars can be humped directly from this yard. The head-in switches of eight tracks are part of a modern electric switch system, controlled from an interlocking tower. Existing trackage south of the classification yard was converted into an eastbound receiving yard, with nine tracks of 65- to 150-car capacity. Four of these tracks have head-in switches, powered by switch machines, which, with similar units in adjacent routing crossovers, are incorporated in a centralized traffic-control system. Other existing trackage on the south side of the eastbound receiving yard can be used for receiving eastbound trains during a rush. Otherwise, the trackage is available for the storing of cars, for flat switching, or for holding grain cars to be inspected.

When cuts of cars from the eastbound receiving yard are to be classified they are pulled over the hump in the reverse direction. Two separate tracks are provided for these movements so they can be carried out without interfering with humping operations.

Town Moved

Some idea of the enormity of the yard modernization project undertaken by the Santa Fe at Argentine may be gained by the revelation that swelling trackage expanded to an extent which required moving the entire town of Turner, Kansas, lock, stock, and barrel.

Stores, business blocks, homes—everything had to go to a new location to make room for the new Argentine facilities. A viaduct was built across the tracks at this location to carry a highway called Key Road.

On the alignment of an existing viaduct carrying Carlisle Road over the old yard, a new 1,216-foot viaduct was constructed across the body of the new classification yard. This structure had to be designed to carry two sixteen-inch gas mains and a ten-inch water main.

Further construction involved was the relocation of a power line, a Bell Telephone line and a six-inch crude-oil line. Another aspect of this enormous task was the relocation of two miles of state highway on the north side of the new departure yard.

Dominating everything else in this great Argentine freight terminal is the new hump-retarder yard. These tracks, holding thirty-one to fifty-four cars each, have a capacity of 2,310 cars. The tracks are divided into eight groups. At the hump.end these converge on three leads; thence uniting with the single lead coming down the hump incline.

In designing the grades and track arrangement at the hump a particular point was made of reducing to the minimum the distance required for cars to pass the clearance points after leaving the crest. This was accomplished by employing lap switches, and by extending the protective circuits of the switches back into the retarders. This was done with a desire to obtain classification tracks of the greatest possible length so that the frequency of "trimming" operations, and their interference with humping operations, would be reduced so far as possible.

(Trimming involves the use of a switch engine and crew whose job it is to make proper adjustments of cars in the classification yard, such as removing a car accidentally placed on the wrong track or moving cars not properly spotted to the correct location.)

Beyond the clearance points, the classification tracks descend on a grade of about 0.2 per cent until the west end of the yard is reached; then there is a slight lift to the grade in conjunction with which "skates" are used to bring cars to a stop.

Car retarders are installed in Argentine Yard at twelve locations. These, along with the power-operated switch machines, are of the electro-pneumatic type manufactured by the Union Switch & Signal Company. The retarders and switch machines are controlled from three towers.

Two northerly groups of tracks in the classification yard are reserved for cars to be transferred to connecting lines. In addition to passing into the departure yards these cars may be pulled back over the hump. When such movements are in progress the switch leading to these groups is locked.

The construction and revamping of Argentine Yard involved the creation of a stable subgrade protected so far as possible from water. Among the unusual and extraordinary measures employed was that of applying a surface mat to prevent rain from penetrating into the subgrade. This protective mat was applied over an area of about 190,000 square feet, which reached out from the crest of the hump down through the retarder area in a general fan shape. It consisted of a mixture of limestone, sand, and emulsified asphalt, ranging in depth from four inches under the ties to two inches in the open spaces between and alongside the tracks. The area thus paved is graded to manholes, providing an escape for rainfall into an extensive system of subsurface drains.

The Argentine Yard drainage system consists of some 5,400 feet of Armco corrugated metal pipe, paved and fully coated with asphalt. Pipe diameters range from eight inches to eighteen inches. Except the mains, these pipes are all perforated.

Car retarders are supported on reinforced concrete foundations because of the unstable nature of the fill. A twelve-inch drain of perforated pipe was installed under all fifty-six tracks to dispose of water collecting at the sag in the grade. This empties into open ditches on both sides of the track area.

Considerably over a million cubic yards of grading was involved in modernizing Argentine Yard, which indicates something of the size of this vast project.

Buildings

The work at Argentine involved the construction of new buildings, towers, and other facilities. Original buildings which continue to play a vital role in the operation of the yard include a yard office building, which was remodeled as part of the project, and the main yard office building on the south side of the yard beside the main-line tracks and a little west of the Argentine passenger depot.

Structures in the hump area are the hump conductor's building at the crest of the hump, a tower office for the humpmaster opposite the first retarder location, and three control towers. The first two buildings are more or less conventional, but the control towers offer something different in design. A form of construction was employed consisting of a skeleton steel supporting superstructure topped by a cabin for the operator. These cabins have flat roofs and wide overhangs. There are large window areas on three sides. The remaining wall areas are of Transite, both inside and out.

The appointments in the operator's cabin include a sealed-beam bulb with a blue lens. When illuminated over the operator's desk at night the soft blue light presents no interference with vision through the windows.

A concrete-brick service building in the hump area houses two oil-burning boilers which supply steam for heating all the buildings on the hump, two motor-driven compressors, repair shops for electricians and signal repairmen, and toilets.

An office building for the "bowl" yardmaster was built at the west end of the classification yard; also a "west-end" yard office, located near the new Key Road viaduct at Turner. The bowl yard office is a four-story tower, with the yardmaster's office on the top floor. Located on the first floor are an operator's office for telegraph and Teletype, a relay in the pneumatic tube system, welfare facilities for employees, and a room containing an oil-burning hot-water heater.

The west-end yard office is an attractive one-story building, which, besides the office of the yardmaster, contains an office for the agent and the Teletype and centralized traffic-control operators, a locker room for carmen, and toilets and showers.

Looking over a great yard like Argentine, the eye finds the high towers with their banks of light for night illumination, the control towers, the vast maze of tracks, spun out like tight-woven threads building a pattern in a loom, the countless cars, but hidden from the onlooker's curious gaze is one of the vital sustain-

71

ing elements of a great modern freight terminal—the *pneumatic tube.*

In Argentine Yard there is a total of 18,400 feet of five and one-half-inch aluminum-alloy pneumatic tubing. In addition, car cards are delivered from the main yard office to the hump conductor through a three-inch tube.

Incoming trains drop off waybills at the east-end yard office and they speed 4,700 feet through the pneumatic tube to the main office. Waybills from incoming eastbound trains are delivered by conductors to the west-end yard office and they rush 7,200 feet through the tube to the "bowl" yard office, and from here are relayed over a distance of 6,500 feet through the pneumatic tube to the main office building. The reverse movement takes place in connection with outward-bound trains.

Of immense importance in the efficient operation of a modern freight yard is the chattering Teletype machine. By means of the Teletype circuits the consist of the approaching train is received considerably in advance of the freight's arrival. For instance, the consist of westbound trains is teletyped from Shopton, Iowa, 221 miles east of Argentine. The consist of eastbound trains is sent ahead from Emporia, Kansas, 118 miles west.

Switch lists then are prepared in the main yard office and sent by Teletype to the humpmaster's office and the three control towers. A duplicating printer in the office of the humpmaster turns out an extra copy which is sent by pneumatic tube to the hump conductor. These methods are a long step from the day of the telegraph operator and the hump rider.

Modern Yard Communications

The Diesel-electric switching locomotives working the Argentine Yard are all radio equipped. Two frequencies are used. One is for communication between the humpmaster and the hump conductor, on the one hand, and for humping locomotives on the other. The second frequency is for communication with locomotives engaged in the yard and transfer service.

72

Nine engines used in the humping area have radios equipped to operate on both frequencies; the radios in all other yard locomotives have only the "all-yard" frequency.

Walkie-talkie sets are used by car checkers in both receiving and departure yards to transmit car numbers to the bill clerks.

Almost anywhere you go in a modern railroad yard there are speakers similar to those employed in all public-address systems. In fact, you are never out of hearing of them. These are the paging speakers, and then there are talk-back speakers, keeping the personnel in the yard in close contact with the various offices. At Argentine there are 112 Jensen talk-back speakers and more than 30 Jensen paging speakers. The speakers in this system are arranged in four groups, one centering in the east-end office, one in the hump tower, one in the tower of the bowl yard office, and one in the west-end yardmaster's office.

The mechanical department is provided with a separate communication system, making it possible to exchange information between the rip-track foreman or a car foreman in the bowl office, or between foremen and carmen working in the yard. In this system paging speakers are used to summon the men in the yard, after which there can be the necessary exchange of information over the telephone. For this purpose a telephone is mounted either directly on the paging speaking standard, or at some nearby location.

Some of the paging speakers have dual controls, allowing use by both the operating and mechanical departments. The mechanical department system has ten paging speakers and five telephones in the departure yards, seven paging speakers and the same number of telephones in the eastbound receiving yard, a corresponding number of paging speakers and telephones in the westbound receiving yard, and four paging speakers and two telephones at the rip track.

The Argentine Yard is equipped with two separate intercommunication systems. One connects the humpmaster, the hump conductor, the three control towers, and an undertrack inspection pit. The other furnishes a hookup between the east-end yard office, the interlocking tower at the east end of the yard,

73

the humpmaster, the bowl yardmaster, the west-end yardmaster, the office of the superintendent, the trainmaster, and the general yardmaster in the main yard office.

Inspection Pits

Built in under the lead track to the hump at Argentine is a concrete pit with a shatter-proof glass through which the inspector can give the undersides of the cars passing over him a close examination. An oil-operated windshield wiper keeps the glass clean. Normally the inspector sits in a swivel chair, looking downgrade at the underbodies, wheels, and trucks as they approach. If he desires he can swing his chair for a second look at the running gear after it has passed the pit.

Conveniently located in the pit is a lever by means of which he can spray whitewash on a wheel of the car on which defects have been located. Other equipment in the pit includes a telephone and an intercommunication unit which is a part of a hookup between the hump conductor, the humpmaster, and the three control towers. As the cars go over the hump, those marked with whitewash are routed to the rip track, situated adjacent to the classification yard immediately to the south. The car numbers are transmitted by means of the intercommunication system to the inspector in the pit. He then gives the rip track a complete report by telephone.

The reader may feel that this glass-covered inspection pit is not a healthy place to be if something is loose and dragging. However, every safety precaution is taken through advance warning mechanisms and lights and bells if equipment is down, for instance, dragging detectors of a so-called "high-type" signal with an intermittent bell and light when dragging equipment is approaching.

"Low" detectors cause a bell and lights to function continuously in the case of very low hanging parts. This is a signal for the inspector to leave the pit.

Lubrication of car journals is made from an oil injection sta-

74

tion on the upgrade side of the inspection pit. Here is located a shallow concrete pit on each side of the track. Over these pits are shelters which are open on the track side. Oilers stationed at this point operate squeeze-type nozzles to control the flow of oil. In the floors of these pits are radiant heating coils employed as a foot-warming measure during cold weather.

The car-repair facilities adjacent to the classification yard include a service building and four repair tracks. The latter are built with seven-foot ties and are separated by concrete platforms, or runways, which are so designed that the edges can be used as jacking blocks. Here light repairs are made to loaded cars, but if major repairs are required the car is sent to the larger car-repair facilities in the engine-terminal area.

The servicing of switchers in the Argentine Yard before its modernization was taken care of at two points—one at the engine terminal and the other near the main yard office. The latter facility has been replaced with a new and enlarged servicing plant on the south side of the westbound receiving yard and somewhat toward its western end. An additional servicing installation is located near the west end of the classification yard. This is provided especially for the use of trimmer engines.

Reefer Icing the Modern Way

Husky young football players have found wrestling cakes of ice at railroad icing docks during vacations a good way to both keep in condition and to earn money. These young men did a good job, but hand icing of refrigerator cars is being supplanted at various points on the Santa Fe by machine power in the form of giant icing machines.

As part of the modernizing project at Argentine Yard, the icing dock, located in what is now the eastbound receiving yard, was subjected to important changes. These included the addition of new types of equipment designed to increase the speed and efficiency with which reefers could be iced. Icing, prior to the revamping of the yards, was taken care of at an ice dock that

75

consisted of a high-level structure of sufficient length to take care of sixty-five cars on each side. Here bunker ice was delivered to the cars.

Reefers that required "top" icing had to be moved to another location before the revamping of Argentine took place. A word here regarding top icing. A fruit train is the baby of the road over which it is moving. Its load is perishables, of one kind or another. It is inspected frequently. Temperatures in the cars have to be maintained at predetermined levels to prevent deterioration of the consist. If the fruit in some cars of the train shows a tendency toward premature ripening, top icing becomes necessary, and the cars will be cut out and moved to a top-icing platform where machines blow shaved ice over the fruit, covering it with a snow blanket six or seven inches in depth.

The modernized Argentine Yard increased the capacity and speed of its old dock through the addition of two icing machines. One of these, a Rico platform icer, operates on a track on the high-level dock that extends 1,530 feet west of the Carlisle Road viaduct, which spans the fifty-six-car classification yard. This is a self-propelled machine that picks up blocks of ice from the conveyor on the platform, breaks them into pieces of the desired size and delivers the chunks directly into the bunkers of cars on both sides of the platform through chutes.

The second machine, also self-propelled, operates on a standard-gauge railroad track on the ground. This is designed for both bunker and body icing. The track over which this machine operates extends westerly from the end of the dock a sufficient distance to allow for the icing of ninety-seven cars on each of two tracks. Block ice for this machine is delivered by a conveyor that extends the full length of the icing docks.

The 540-foot portion of the Argentine icing dock east of the viaduct, since the advent of the icing machines, is used for storage and for handling "strays."

The icing machines were developed jointly by the Railways Ice Company and the Link-Belt Company, both of Chicago. They are being manufactured and sold by the Link-Belt people.

The dock-type, or platform, car icer is mounted on four

76

double-flanged wheels and moved along standard rails secured to I-beam girders on the deck of the icing platform. Normally, track gauges are nine to twelve feet. The machine straddles a dock chain conveyor which brings the ice cakes from the storage house. An inclined pickup conveyor receives the cakes of ice from the dock conveyor and moves them to a feeder conveyor, which passes them to the crushers. For bunker icing the processed ice is then delivered to the bunker chutes.

Salt is carried in a bin supported on a trailer which travels on the same rails as the machine. When salted ice is desired, salt is taken from the bin to the boom chute in operation by a conveyor. This conveyor can be set by the machine operator at the controls on top to deliver the quantity required.

When this type of machine is used for top icing the blocks of ice are diverted by a feeder conveyor directly to the crusher-slinger, where they are shaved and delivered into the refrigerator cars on either side of the dock by an impeller and a flexible hose.

The second type of icing machine used in the Argentine Yard, the Master car icer, is designed to service two lines of refrigerator cars, one on each side. The machine is approximately fifty-four feet long and is mounted on three axles. Electric motors, receiving current from trolley wires beneath the ice conveyor, power it.

Carried on one end of the machine is a thirty-one-foot tower, propelling motors and machinery, an ice crusher, bunker-ice elevator, a salt bin, salt feeder and elevator, an operator's control panel and platform, and the two boom chutes, one on each side.

At the machine's other end there is a conventional crusher-slinger, with a swiveling discharge elbow for top icing. Between the crusher-slinger and the tower there is a reversible feeder conveyor which removes the ice cakes from the storage-house conveyor by a power-operated retractable plow, delivering them either to the bunker-ice crusher at the tower end or to the crusher-slinger.

A single operator on the control platform, about twenty-six feet above the rails, controls all mechanical operations. In addition, the icing operation requires a few men for opening and closing bunker hatches and for directing the flow of slinger ice.

After the ice blocks are removed from the conveyor, if they are to be used for bunker icing, they are carried to the bunker-ice crusher by the feeder conveyor. The crusher can be adjusted to reduce the ice block to any size desired. An enclosed elevator then lifts the crushed ice to the boom chutes, which in turn deliver it to the car bunkers. The operator controls the raising and lowering of the chutes; also the opening and closing of a gate in each chute for the distribution of the ice into the near or far hatch.

Bunker ice can be handled at the rate of eighteen 300-pound blocks per minute, or thirteen 400-pound blocks per minute. The latter adds up to about 160 tons an hour when the machine is in steady operation.

Salt is carried on the machine in a 15,000-pound capacity bin. A salt-feeder conveyor at the base of the bin delivers the salt horizontally to a separate bucket-type elevator, which raises and discharges the salt into the boom chute simultaneously with the crushed ice. A salt counter, set by the machine operator for increments of twenty-five pounds of salt per second, automatically measures the amount required for each bunker. A feature of the equipment is that the salt-feeder conveyor and elevator are also used to refill the salt bin.

For top icing, the blocks are carried by the feeder conveyor into the crusher-slinger where they are reduced to snow ice, which is delivered through the side doors of the cars with the usual impeller and flexible tube. The machine can produce this snow ice at the rate of nine 300-pound blocks or seven 400-pound blocks a minute, or at the rate of about eighty tons an hour.

The normal procedure with this robot iceman is to fill the bunkers of the reefers standing on one track, and then those on the second track on the return movement. In this manner, one string of cars can be pulled when iced and a new string switched in while the machine is working the other string.

Since the operator can quickly divert ice either to the bunker icing unit or to top icing, both operations can readily be accomplished as the machine moves along, thus eliminating lost motion in backtracking. Usually only about five to ten cars in a string of one hundred cars normally require top icing.

C. E. Merriman, construction superintendent, was handed the assignment for the modernization of the Atchison, Topeka & Santa Fe yard at Argentine in 1943, and he did a masterful job. The general supervision was by T. A. Blair, chief engineer of the system, and F. D. Kinnie, chief engineer of the Eastern lines.

And so Argentine Yard at Argentine, Kansas, completely modernized at the close of 1949, has taken its place among the great yards of the United States having facilities adequate to meet the demands of a country at peace or a country at war.

Where Is That Freight Car?

"Where's that car of freight?" says the shipper. "When do I get it?"

The Santa Fe Red Ball Information Service never fails to come up with the answer. It knows, practically every minute of every day, where that Red Ball car is. The Santa Fe maintains 300,000 wire miles of private telephone, telegraph, and Teletype circuits in order to give the shipper his answer—and fast.

This wire service employs the latest in multichannel message-carrying equipment—copper wires which carry five telephone conversations at once, or three telephone conversations and twenty-eight printing-telegraph messages (fourteen each way on duplex circuits) all at once.

Let us take a Santa Fe car—say, A.T.&S.F. 141617—and see what happens. This is one of 80,000 freight cars in motion on the Santa Fe every day.

We'll say A.T.&S.F. 141617 was loaded at a big fish cannery in San Diego, California. It is consigned to a distributor near Boston, way across the continent, routed Santa Fe to Chicago. It is loaded and ready to roll. First, it must have identity other than its number and so it is given a Red Ball symbol—SD-100. "SD" is for San Diego, "100" is an identifying number which no other can have while this particular SD-100 is on the system.

When the train with SD-100 in its consist pulls out of San Diego, the first report goes by wire to the Red Ball Information Service in Topeka, Kansas, giving the exact hour and minute that SD-100 pulled out of the yards.

Topeka immediately teletypes this report on SD-100 to the Santa Fe freight representative in Boston. This representative calls the consignee, saying, in effect, "Your car of canned fish from San Diego just left." So the consignee gets the word, and quickly—no more than two hours after it left San Diego.

The consignee gets another report from Belen, New Mexico, when SD-100 goes through as one of the cars of a fast Santa Fe freight train, pulled by a big blue-and-yellow, 6,000-horsepower Diesel. He gets another report from Wellington, Kansas; another from Kansas City; and, finally, from Chicago, where the Santa Fe delivers SD-100 to another railroad.

Now what happens if SD-100 develops a hotbox around Clovis, New Mexico—something that may happen on any railroad? The Red Ball service is immediately informed and this information clearing house in Topeka notifies the Boston office, and the consignee gets the word.

The wire from Clovis reads, SET OUT CLOVIS, 11:15 P.M., ACCOUNT BAD ORDER SD-100.

However, at Clovis men are already working to get SD-100 rolling again. As soon as the hotbox has been repaired and the car is moving, another report is flashed through, telling the consignee his shipment has left.

Another service rendered deals with "diversion." The consignee may want to change the destination of his car, for the reason of a possibly better market in some other city. He notifies the railroad and the wires flash the necessary orders. The agent in the new delivery city begins receiving reports of the progress of the car.

This service works for the shipper—at no extra cost—whenever

Western Pacific #17, California Zephyr, descending 1-per-cent grade in C.T.C. territory east of Belden, Col., third subdivision, Western Division. Courtesy, W.P. RR.

Pittsburgh and West Virginia P.C.S.-1 fast freight hauled by two 1,500 h.p. road-switching Diesels coupled back to back west of Frick, Pa. Courtesy, P.&W.V. RR.

B.&L.E. 1,500 h.p. switching Diesel with cut of ore cars being loaded by Hulett machine from Lake ore carrier at Conneaut Dock at Conneaut, Ohio. Courtesy, B.&L.E. RR.

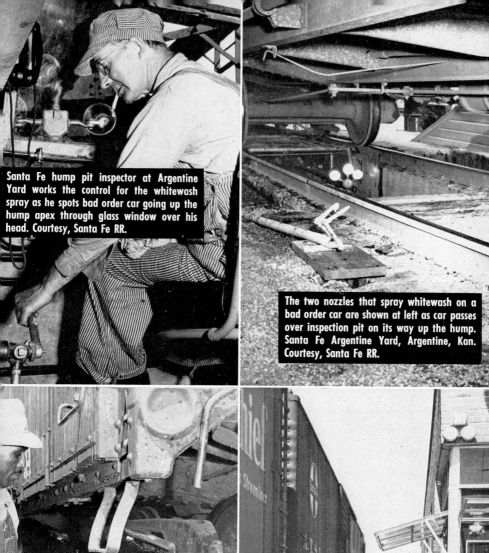

Santa Fe hump pit inspector at Argentine Yard works the control for the whitewash spray as he spots bad order car going up the hump apex through glass window over his head. Courtesy, Santa Fe RR.

The two nozzles that spray whitewash on a bad order car are shown at left as car passes over inspection pit on its way up the hump. Santa Fe Argentine Yard, Argentine, Kan. Courtesy, Santa Fe RR.

Oiler squirts just the right amount of oil from pneumatic oil can in journal box of freight car as it nears top of hump at Santa Fe's Argentine Yard. Courtesy, Santa Fe RR.

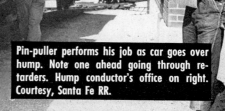

Pin-puller performs his job as car goes over hump. Note one ahead going through retarders. Hump conductor's office on right. Courtesy, Santa Fe RR.

Santa Fe's bowlmaster at Argentine gives order to engine crew of switcher that can be seen behind microphone on his talk-back. Yard engine pulling string of cars to westbound departure yard. Courtesy, Santa Fe RR.

Hump yardmaster checks cars over the hump in tower office. Classification yard with fifty-seven tracks in background. A. tower on right, C. tower at left, cars going through Union Switch & Signal Co.'s retarders, Courtesy, Santa Fe RR.

Frisco #2, the crack Texas Special, approaching Lindenwood Yard, Mo., on the Rolla Subdivision of the Eastern Division with 1,000 h.p. Diesel switcher on the right. Courtesy, Frisco Lines.

Excellent Frisco wharf and some of their facilities in the fine and rapidly growing port of Pensacola, Fla. Courtesy, Frisco Lines.

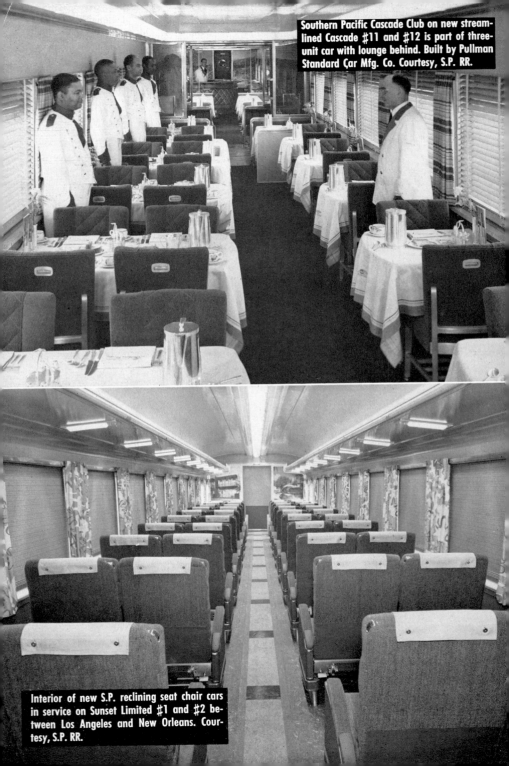

Southern Pacific Cascade Club on new stream-lined Cascade #11 and #12 is part of three-unit car with lounge behind. Built by Pullman Standard Car Mfg. Co. Courtesy, S.P. RR.

Interior of new S.P. reclining seat chair cars in service on Sunset Limited #1 and #2 between Los Angeles and New Orleans. Courtesy, S.P. RR.

Milwaukee #101, the Afternoon Hiawatha, running over the First Subdivision of the Milwaukee Division showing Skytop observation car. Courtesy, Milwaukee RR.

Interior of Milwaukee's coaches used between Chicago and Twin Cities on the Hiawatha trains. They seat fifty-two in the body of the car in foam-rubber reclining chairs. Courtesy, Milwaukee RR.

Southern Pacific #2, the new Sunset Limited, on the Rio Grande Division. Courtesy, S.P. RR.

he starts a car rolling. It works for all consignees automatically and for all shippers just for the asking.

In the new and modern railroad era, the Santa Fe's Red Ball Information Service is tailor-made to fit the needs of their customers—these consignees and shippers—who supply the railroad with the business so necessary to its life blood.

The Santa Fe football team doesn't miss any signals or muss up many plays, and what team would with a fine line of traffic department heads, general managers, engineers, and mechanical officers, plus a backfield composed of F. G. Gurley, R. G. Rydin, G. H. Minchin, and C. R. Tucker.

CHAPTER VIII

NEW TRAIN STYLES ON THE S.P.

The Cascade and Sunset Limiteds

The Southern Pacific put into operation on two successive Sundays in August, 1950, two completely new streamliners, the Cascade, operating between San Francisco, California, and Portland, Oregon, and the Sunset Limited, running between Los Angeles, California and New Orleans, Louisiana. Both trains flashed the famous "Daylight red," the predominant color of the road's coastal trains, the Daylights.

The new and faster Cascade night trains went into service on August 13, clipping two hours from the schedule of the fastest previous sleeping-car train schedules on this world-famous Shasta Route. The new Cascades made their initial 718-mile runs just a bit over a year after the inauguration of the new Daylights, the day streamliners described in another chapter.

The new Cascades operate under the numbers 11 and 12— No. 11 is the southbound train; No. 12, the northbound. At the time the sleek new trains began their runs, trains operating between San Francisco and Portland on the Southern Pacific carrying these numbers had been in operation fifty-one years, except for about seventeen months when they were assigned to local trains. Then Nos. 11 and 12 were known as the Shasta Express, although the better part of two days were required to make the trip. Names changed but old Nos. 11 and 12 rolled on. For about ten years prior to 1927 the train was the Shasta Limited.

The pioneer trains of the route rode the rails of the original Siskiyou Line, laid across the famous Siskiyou Mountains and with the final spike driven home in 1887. In 1927 a line with easier grades, less curvature, and twenty-five miles shorter was completed by way of Klamath Lake over the Cascade Mountains of southern Oregon. This appropriately was named the Cascade Line, and its premier train was the Cascade, and it carried on its locomotives the numbers 11 and 12.

During World War II the original Siskiyou Line provided the Southern Pacific with a route over which a lot of the war traffic flowed, and in spite of its heavy grades and winding rail.

Compared to the almost two days of travel on the first Nos. 11 and 12, the new Cascades go through in sixteen and one-half hours. They carry cars to accommodate travelers bound for Seattle, Washington, and each train is made up of eleven passenger-carrying cars, which include eight sleeping cars with a total of 130 private rooms, and the triple-unit Cascade Club, which has a room more than 130 feet long for dining and lounging.

Two cars ahead next to the Diesel locomotive are for baggage, express, and mail. The exterior color scheme of the train was patterned after that of the road's famous Coast Line Larks, running between Los Angeles and San Francisco. This is a subdued two-tone gray with lighter striping, sedate and prim as the attire of a lady to the manor born, but the Diesel retains the red and orange that has been brightening the right of way of some of the S.P.'s California lines since the inauguration of the first Daylight.

The Cascade, No. 12, leaves San Francisco at five o'clock in the afternoon, reaching Oakland Pier, across San Francisco Bay, at 5:20 P.M. and departing at 5:30 P.M. It makes stops at Sixteenth Street, Oakland; Berkeley; Richmond; and Crockett. Then it swings on north to cross the Martinez-Benecia Bridge and continues its swift flight up the great valley to Redding, California, to Dunsmuir and the closing high country, on into historic southern Oregon, Klamath Falls, Chemult, Eugene, Albany. It pulls into Portland at 9:30 A.M. Pullmans going through to Seattle reach the Washington state city at 2 P.M.

The Cascade Club—Triple-unit Car

Sometimes we try to visualize things behind the Iron Curtain, and somehow find it hard to imagine Ivan taking junior down to the railroad station to look at the trains. But in America it is more or less a ritual in a great many cities and towns. And these days father has to keep his guard up, for sonny has a sharp and inquiring eye.

Watching the new Cascade, he is apt to impale father with a query concerning the "long car that doesn't have any outside doors for folks to get in through." However, if father has been keeping posted in regards to modern railroading on the Coast, he should be able to advance the information that this is the three-car articulated arrangement that had made its appearance on the new trains of the Southern Pacific.

In this case it is the Cascade Club, and its dining-lounge space is spread over one room more than 130 feet long, and is served by the kitchen unit. Looking into the Cascade Club for the first time you are not only astonished by its expanse but by the luxury of its appointments. Travelers become more enthusiastic about it than, perhaps, anything else on this fine train.

The color interest in the dining-lounge section is heightened by enough accent on red and cedar tones to provide plenty of sparkle. And here is where the decorators called on the scenic attractions of the fabulous Shasta Route for their inspirations, as they artistically blended in canyon tan, Odell blue, and the deeper Cascade blue for the basic colors.

The lobby ends of the club have the Cascade blue in the ceilings, with walls of redwood-burl finish. The semicircular seats in the lobbies have a deep Columbia blue for the leather upholstery; the floors are cedar red and canyon tan; and, at the articulation, there is an inlay star in cedar red in the marbleized rubber tile, surrounded by canyon tan. Blue-leather curtains hide the diaphragms at the articulation, completely concealing the point of joining of the cars. Walking through you have a feeling of freedom of movement and you are aware of a pleasant broadening of horizons in car design where in standard practice there formerly were vestibule doors and tight passageways.

The Pullman-Standard Manufacturing Company and the Southern Pacific have done a remarkable job in this three-car combination, and California-Oregon travelers appreciate the added zest it has given to train travel; it is one of the things they remark on in reviewing their trip.

In the dining section of the Cascade Club, we find the light canyon-tan ceiling descending through deepening blues to the carpet, a striking tone arrangement. Table tops are pearlescent and inlaid. The bar section in the center of the car is done in gold, silver and blue, with gold-tone mirrors. And there are murals, which always add so much to these modern interiors. The venetian blinds, the attractive drapes, the color-bordered linens, the gleaming silver—all add to an atmosphere that reflects the finest de luxe service possible.

The Cascade Club veritably smiles a welcome. "This is your home!"

The triple-articulated unit is over 200 feet, total length, and it includes, of course, a modern stainless-steel kitchen with every scientifically designed convenience to aid in the quick and easy preparation of the best in food.

The service in the Cascade Club exemplifies the slogan of the road—"The Friendly Southern Pacific." A smile costs nothing, but it is the greatest ambassador in the world.

Pullman Sleepers

The Cascade provides five types of sleeping-car accommodations. These include roomettes, bedrooms, bedrooms *en suite*, compartments, and drawing rooms. No open-section space is provided on the train.

A bane of the old-type sleeping car was the swaying journey down the curtained aisle to reach the bathroom facilities. If you wanted to sleep a little late, there was some embarrassment attached to parading through a car in which some of the berths were made up and occupied by washed and attentive observers. It took a hardened traveler to make the trip with complete indifference to the car's audience.

There is nothing that appeals so much to today's train traveler as the sleeping facilities behind closed doors, with the compact but convenient arrangements that offer the traveler the opportunity to become presentable before appearing in public. From the roomette on up to the drawing rooms you have these general features for restful sleep: locomotive power transmitted through the train by tight-lock couplers, velvet-operating electro-pneumatic brakes with anti-wheel-slip devices, soundproofing, deep carpets, fluorescent lighting, and the last word in air conditioning.

Now let's look at the most modest of the sleeping accommodations, the roomette. The premade bed can be used for immedate occupancy. It is easily lowered from the wall behind the wide foam-rubber-upholstered sofa-type seat. There is a private washstand, with hot and cold running water, which folds into the wall in the corner opposite the seat. Below the washstand is a private toilet with a hassock-type cover.

And that is not all. Each roomette has a full-length wardrobe closet and mirror, circulating ice water, plenty of space for hand luggage, and other comfort-travel features that are a part of the new Cascade.

Cascade blue and other blue tones enter into the color scheme of part of the roomettes, with carpeting in garnet with a fern pattern, door curtains in rust color, and window shades in coral. Other of the roomettes employ apricot shades in varying tones. In these the seats are upholstered in red instead of Cascade blue.

Where bedrooms are used in the car make-up we find ample space for two persons. The seating and bed arrangements are alternated crosswise or lengthwise of the car. These are paired so that two bedrooms—one lengthwise and one crosswise—can be used *en suite* by opening the folding partition between them.

Because of this arrangement we discover a new designation employed in the railroad formula, and that is "BC" and "BL." The first refers to "beds crosswise"; the second to "beds length-

wise." The BL seat arrangement is similar to that of the roomette, but with the addition of a comfortable, foam-rubber
movable lounge chair. In the BL type the bed raises into the
ceiling instead of into the wall.

Certainly matchless ingenuity was used in designing the modern Pullman, and it makes possible a thoroughly restful journey
for the traveler, who at the end of the trip can step down with
a complete sense of well-being.

The bedroom *en suite* make an ideal arrangement for family
travel, or for businessmen who wish to have a conference room
en route.

Colorings of the rooms are matched in pairs. We find one set
employing beige color schemes, with cream-yellow ceilings, walls
of medium beige and dark beige for the doors. Carpeting is rust
with leaf patterns, curtains of coral shade, and sofas and chairs
done in a turquoise-colored fabric. Another set of bedrooms goes
into the tans. For variety, some bedroom sets have Cascade-blue
carpets, some turquoise shades.

All bedrooms have an enclosed washroom and toilet annex.
There is ample space in each bedroom for a service table for
writing or for games.

Compartment accommodations are more spacious than the
bedrooms, and they may be combined *en suite* with another
compartment or with a drawing room. The compartments have
a washroom-toilet annex, a movable foam-rubber upholstered
lounge chair and a foam-rubber lounge-type sofa. When the
beds are down the lounge chair is still available for use.

Each of the Cascade's drawing rooms have three beds. One
is a disappearing wall bed, one is an upper bed that raises into
the ceiling, and the third is a bed that becomes a wide foam-
rubber lounge-type sofa. There is plenty of space for the daytime
use of two movable foam-rubber upholstered chairs, which
gives the space a living room effect. The drawing room has two
large windows.

The compartments and drawing rooms employ the same tasteful color-tone combinations as those we have previously de-

87

scribed, and these do much to lend variety and enchantment to the atmosphere of the train.

All sleeping rooms have individually controlled heat and air conditioning.

The total number of roomettes on the Cascade are eighty-four, and the various types of larger rooms are forty-six.

Mr. C. E. Peterson, vice-president in charge of system passenger traffic, has every reason to be proud of the twin Cascades, the trains that make night travel a pleasure.

The Sunset Limited

The new streamlined Sunset Limited, which made its bow to railroad America on Sunday, August 20, 1950, was the culmination of sixty-seven years of rail travel over the Sunset Route, which reached from San Francisco, California, to New Orleans, Louisiana, originally, but which since 1942 has had Los Angeles, California, as its western terminal.

The new Sunset Limited cut five hours off the former eastbound running time and three and one-half hours off the westbound time for the 2,070-mile trip through the states of Louisiana, Texas, New Mexico, Arizona, and California. This made the schedule forty-two hours, a long step from the time prior to the turn of the century when the Sunset Limited of that era made the journey once a week; then twice a week; then three times weekly until 1902 when it became the premier daily train of the Sunset Route.

It was on November 1, 1894, that the first "palatial" Sunset Limited made the run, San Francisco to New Orleans, in seventy-five hours. The train consisted of four wooden cars, pulled by little eight-wheel locomotives. But even then the train was an aristocrat and the passengers were enthused about the Composite Car, with its large parlor and wicker chairs, separate smoking room, and buffet for light lunches.

And there was the Ladies Compartment Car, which had a parlor, library, and seven elaborately furnished sleeping rooms with a maid in attendance. The dining car, also, was extremely fashionable with its wicker chairs and potted plants. This blue-blood strain has become traditional on the Sunset Route and was important in the sharply modern trend of the years following World War II. More, this train was the first solid vestibule train to operate from the Pacific Coast.

The five sets of equipment that went to make up the new Sunset Limited cost a total of about $15,000,000, including the Diesel locomotives.

The consist of one of these Sunset Limited trains includes four chair cars, six sleeping cars, two baggage cars, a coffee shop–lounge car, a full-length dining car, and a full-length mid-train lounge car. Fifteen cars. East of Del Rio, Texas, two-unit Alco Diesels of 4,000 horsepower are used; west of Del Rio the train is pulled by three-unit 6,000-horsepower General Motors Diesels.

Train designers found plenty to work with when they made their preliminary surveys and they employed this background material to good advantage. The route is historical and beautiful and these artists made the most of the material assembled. They, of course, had to make a painstaking study of the whole, discarding all but the most pleasing possibilities.

Hundreds of Kodachromes were taken, and they included scenes all the way from the blue Pacific, through Southern California, into old Mexico, across the mountains and desert country of southern Arizona, on across the vast breadth of Texas, into the picturesque bayou country of Louisiana, and to the old French Quarter of New Orleans.

As a result, the new Sunset Limited was beautiful beyond words, and it was as luxurious as it was beautiful. It has been difficult to learn which of the three feature cars of the train received the most popular acclaim—the French Quarter Lounge, the Audubon Dining Room, or the Pride of Texas Coffee Shop–Lounge. They all have proved very popular, and more than that, they have something that the traveler carries away. Other travelers may boast of the feature cars on their favorite trains, but the man or woman who has ridden the Sunset Limited will be quick to rush to the defense of these sparkling cars pleasantly closing the gap between the Pacific Coast and the Gulf.

All windows of the train are the wide picture windows, shatterproof and nonfogging. Chair-car seats are reclining and of the modern Sleepy Hollow type, each with its own comfortable leg rest, which creates a chaise-longue effect. They are foam-rubber upholstered and they cradle perfectly every human size, shape, and weight. When you drop into them, they fit—and you simply sigh and relax. All doors of the Sunset are the fingertip type that open automatically. The days of struggling with car doors has gone to return no more.

The Sunset Limited crosses vast expanses of desert country, and to create a barrier against seeping dust a thing called "pressurized air conditioning" has been employed. This is a new method of so handling air that a slight positive pressure is maintained at all times inside of the car, something that not only aids in the elimination of dust and dirt by preventing its ingress, but predetermines a fixed amount of ever fresh circulated air.

An unusual high level of lighting intensity has been achieved in the chair cars by use of 110-volt, 30-watt fluorescent tubes running the length of the ceiling above the aisle. These are positioned in fixtures so as to shed a maximum amount of completely glareless light over all seating areas.

Supplementing these ceiling lights are individually controlled reading lights of eight-watt fluorescent tubes located in the overhead parcel rack above each set of reclining chairs. These fixtures also hold small blue night lights. All ceiling fixtures are provided with incandescent emergency lights.

An improved type of radio equipment makes possible an even, low-level distribution of broadcasts to all parts of the cars.

Sleeping accommodations on board the Sunset Limited are pretty much the same as on all modern-day luxury trains. The complete roomettes provide space for one passenger, with all of the standard facilities, which include everything a passenger needs to thoroughly enjoy daytime traveling.

At night, the doorway curtain may be zipped and from the wall behind the sofa seat a premade bed is easily lowered by the occupant. The bed, which is also always handy for a daytime nap, has a deep, foam-rubber mattress thirty-two inches wide and seventy-four inches long. A mirrored corridor door may, for added privacy, be closed and locked.

The bedroom facilities on up to the Master Drawing Room employ the lengthwise and crosswise bed arrangements described earlier in this chapter, with all of the comfort features, including electric-shaver outlets, individual heat and air-conditioning controls, circulating ice water, and the bed reading lights.

Restful color schemes include tones of Mosul tan and light taupe beige, with doors a gun-metal gray and the carpeting a rich *tête-de-Negre* hue. Upholstery is done in two-toned striped mohair in ashes of roses and woodstone colors. Window shade interior surfaces are a colorful clay pink.

Some sleeping cars use light-bright navy and parchment tones, with flame-hued doors and light-turtle-egg-toned window-shade interiors. Another decorative scheme uses sand white, fountain green, and Waterloo green. Certainly, originality has flowed generously from the sketch pads and drawing boards of the decorators.

Hardware surfaces throughout are of stain-finish aluminum or stainless steel. The effect is a triumph in clean-lined beauty.

Accommodations in the car called the baggage-dormitory car provide for twenty-seven members of the train's dining-car crew in five rooms that have bunks similar to those found on Navy ships. There is an individual room for the steward. Each of the crew's rooms has an individual washbasin. Located elsewhere in the car are wardrobes where the crewmen can hang uniforms and personal clothing. There is also a shower, water cooler, and toilets.

The baggage-postal car has a thirty-foot railway post office and a fifty-two-foot baggage room.

Each Sunset Limited has a newsstand space and an office for the conductor. The sleepers have a porter's roomette.

The kitchens of these Sunset Limiteds are completely equipped with stoves, refrigerators, sinks, and cabinets of gleaming stainless steel. Refrigerators are cooled with the dry-ice system, developed by Southern Pacific engineers in conjunction with the Carbofrezer Company. This is a new refrigeration development.

Among the mechanical features of the train we find that the brakes are a new type built by the Budd people—a disc brake, which is velvet smooth and quick acting. These do away with the usual brake shoe and in consequence reduce maintenance and replacement costs.

Intriguing, indeed, are the hundreds of innovations on the train in this day of modern railroading. We will mention again here the Rolokron Unit—the device that automatically releases the braking pressure on any wheel having a tendency to slide (generally caused by wet surfaces) and then when the wheel begins to roll properly again the braking pressure is automatically reapplied. Through the use of modern car couplings the cars of the Sunset Limited start and stop practically as a unit, and without jolts or jerks.

You ride on roller bearings and shock-absorbed-controlled springs. Trucks have derailment safety guides. The journals have hot-bearing alarm systems. The air brakes are electro-pneumatic. Everything is as new as tomorrow's sunrise.

Colorful Feature Cars

Train travel today offers a new adventure every time you open the door on the next car. Let's say you have boarded the Sunset Limited in Los Angeles, California, for the 8:00 P.M. departure. You have had your dinner. Before you retire you feel that you would like a snack, and you go into the Pride of Texas Coffee Shop–Lounge car.

You find here the atmosphere and hospitality of that fabulous state, and you find color and ornamentation that is at once amazing and alluring. Cattle brands catch your eye—real cattle brands of Texas' famous brands. There are reproductions of actual Mexican spurs and long-horn steer heads done in antique silver finish.

The curved bar sustains the Western flavor with its knotty pine. The flowering Yucca Cactus inlays of the table tops reflect the desert country that will greet you in the morning. Here the designers have been vastly original in these color tones, with adobe brown and gay sunflower yellow. Wall panels are of palomino-tan leather. The entire atmosphere invites relaxation with pleasant fellow travelers, a prelude to deep, soft-cradled slumber in the privacy of your sleeping-car quarters.

In the morning, somewhere over around Tucson, Arizona, you make your way to the Audubon Dining Room. Every effort was made to capture here the romantic and beautiful background used by the great artist-naturalist, John James Audubon, for his bird illustrations, many of which reflect the Louisiana bayou country.

Here the color hues are original and striking—bayou green, gulf blue, egg shell, and others. The woodwork, in keeping with the styles of the Audubon era, has been done in maple, with walnut and ebonized-birch inlays.

Framed by the great windows are vistas of giant cacti, saguaros, against mountain backgrounds. It is almost as though you were in a resort hotel, with the great, colorful panorama of the Southwest turning its pages before the broad panes of the dining room.

The French Quarter Lounge car offers a preview of this famous section of New Orleans, with its traditional ornamental iron vine arbors, cast from actual patterns used in the grillwork found in this old Louisiana city. These treillages are applied at ends and on pier panels between the wide windows of the car. They appear in bone white against the striking watermelon red of the walls and ceiling. Small white stars are painted in varying sizes on the side panels of the ceiling.

Lounge seats have been done in comfortable deep foam rubber, upholstered with Pebbletweed-patterned watermelon-red mohair. While this gay Mardi Gras color predominates, it is complemented by the cypress gray of the lower walls and a carpeting in fern-feather design. The bar section is in cypress gray, with a smartly padded bar front of moss-gray leather, which is highlighted by satin-finish stainless-steel moldings and a watermelon-red ceiling. The mirrors are etched with frosty birds and bayou foliage.

A valet service is available, with an attendant to press your clothes and attend to minor repairs. In the car, also, there is a shower which is available for the use of sleeping-car passengers.

The cars of the Sunset Limiteds were styled by John Harbeson. Mr. Harbeson and the Southern Pacific collaborated in the selection of the three color combinations with which the sleepers are decorated.

The highest point of this great Sunset Route is at Paisano, Texas, 5,074 feet; the lowest point is at Salton, California, 202 feet below sea level.

They will tell you the Sunset Limited is "the streamlined train with the Southern accent," and you can appreciate this when you are introduced to these amazing feature cars which help speed the miles between the Pacific Coast and the Gulf.

CHAPTER IX

THE SEABOARD AIR LINE

Modern Road of the South

"Through the Heart of the South." This slogan of the Seaboard Air Line traces back to around 1907, and it indicates something of the potentiality of this really great southern railroad, which operates some 4,136 miles of road, 2,500 miles of which are laid with 132-pound rail. The Seaboard is a progressive road —a modern road.

The road is marked by its fast trains and its courteous service. Nowhere do you find finer railroad manners. Nor do you find finer food than in their dining cars. It might be called the road of hospitality.

The Seaboard reaches southward from Richmond, Virginia, crossing the lines of the Norfolk & Western at Petersburg, Virginia, and interchanging with them at this point. The Seaboard crosses the line of the Virginian Railway at Alberta, Virginia, and crosses the state line just above Norlina, North Carolina. Here the Seaboard's connecting branch line reaches out to the great ports of Portsmouth and Norfolk, Virginia, and the peanut center at Suffolk, Virginia.

At Henderson, North Carolina, a few miles south of Norlina, there is a branch line to Durham. Continuing south, we come to the fine city of Raleigh, the capital of North Carolina. From here the Seaboard's shining rails thread in down through the pine belt, with its great resorts and famous golf courses—all served by the Seaboard—at Southern Pines, Aberdeen, and Pinehurst.

Hamlet, on down in the southern part of the state, is one of the most important junction points on the Seaboard. Hamlet is 253 miles from Richmond, and here Seaboard's Atlanta & Birmingham line turns to the southwest, with Birmingham, the western terminus, 493 miles away. To the east is the Wilmington, North Carolina, branch, and to the southeast the magnificent "great shortcut" line, where passenger trains travel by way of Columbia, South Carolina, and the freights take the slightly longer low-grade route by way of Charleston, touching at Dillon, Potsan, and Andrews. From the latter point a branch leads to Georgetown. This freight line rejoins again with the main line at the port of Savannah.

The passenger line serves the winter and shooting resort of Camden, and Columbia, the capital of South Carolina, passing on down through Denmark and Fairfax over these fine high-speed tracks to Savannah.

The division of right of way makes for fast operation of both passenger and freight traffic. Centralized traffic control assures rapid-fire movement with all security over the entire main line and freight lines from Richmond to Jacksonville. One piece of double track is all that is not under C.T.C. The same modern signaling is employed from Jacksonville to Wildwood, Florida.

The Seaboard line from Hamlet to Atlanta also has C.T.C. This is the route of the sparkling Silver Comet, the flashing flight of which is guarded by centralized traffic control, with the newest section that between Atlanta and Birmingham. The growth and development of the South industrially has made it imperative that its rail service keep pace with the modern trend.

An important segment of the Seaboard runs westward from Savannah, Georgia, to Montgomery, Alabama, via Americus, Georgia. The road also has an important line extending west from Jacksonville to Tallahassee, Florida. At Gross, Georgia, and Jacksonville other lines connect from the Florida shrimp and paper port of Fernandina to Yulee and the cutoff that allows some of the trains to run around Jacksonville, which extends from Gross to Baldwin, the junction south of Jacksonville.

From Jacksonville west to Tallahassee an excellent piece of rail right of way carries the Seaboard's Gulf Wind.

Moving on down the great subtropical Florida peninsula, the Seaboard's steel reaches from Waldo over to Tampa, on the west coast, where the line splits. Passenger trains and most of such crack perishables as the Marketer operate through Wildwood from Plant City and Tampa. The St. Petersburg line, which takes in Clearwater, extends from Tampa in an arc along the peninsula that bounds Tampa Bay on the north and west. A branch extends down the east side of the bay into Sarasota and Venice.

Another line comes down to the west coast points of Fort Meyers and San Carlos, and a line turns off just south of Arcadia for Boca Grande, thrust out into the Gulf. At Port Boca Grande phosphate rock is loaded into the holds of ships, and Port Boca Grande also supplies the tops in tarpon fishing to the many sports fishermen who are drawn there.

From Wildwood south the Seaboard takes care of the busy winter traffic at Mountain Lakes, Winter Haven, West Lake Wales, Sebring, and across the Everglades through Okeechobee, Indiantown, and on to West Palm Beach and the Atlantic and the blue Gulf Stream. Continuing south the rails of the road reach Fort Lauderdale and Miami, a great tourist mecca, and to Homestead, close down to Royal Palm State Park, and the beginning of the fabulous Florida Keys.

Florida, from north to south, is a vacation land beyond compare, a port of escape from northern cold, and the Seaboard sets the visitor down at any one of a large number of famous resort cities.

Modern Speedliners

The Silver Meteor, a crack year-round train, operates from New York, Philadelphia, and Washington to Miami, St. Petersburg, and Tampa. With a late noon departure from New York City, the Silver Meteor has an afternoon arrival the next day in Florida's lower peninsula. Returning, this train leaves Miami in the morning and has a next morning arrival in the northern cities.

The Silver Star leaves the north in the morning and is in Florida the next morning. Returning, the Silver Star provides a convenient noon departure for those who want an extra day in the sun.

These trains have fine lightweight equipment, including modern sleeping cars, baggage-dormitory cars, excellent dining cars, lounge cars, modern coaches, and an observation rear end. The seats are reserved in the coaches.

The Silver Comet is the Seaboard's de luxe train from New York, Philadelphia, Baltimore, and Washington to Atlanta and Birmingham. It is modern, with sleepers and reserved seats in the coaches, plus tavern-observation and the touches that make for comfort.

Other trains on the Seaboard between New York and Florida are the Palmland and the Sunland, as well as the Cotton Blossom from Norfolk and Portsmouth, Virginia, to Atlanta and Birmingham, with New York, Washington, and Richmond connections.

The Seaboard mail trains are Nos. 3 and 4; also 17 and 18 out of Portsmouth. Baggage, mail, and express are also handled on Nos. 15 and 16 between Atlanta and Birmingham.

There is plenty of glamour to the names of these speedliners of the Seaboard Air Line, but it remained for the latest addition, the Gulf Wind, to really provide a tangy freshness to the Gulf run. The Gulf Wind! Wonderful!

The Gulf Wind began operation on July 31, 1949. It saves approximately five hours between Jacksonville and New Orleans. It is operated by the Seaboard to Chattahoochee, Florida, then it is handled by the Louisville & Nashville into New Orleans.

The Gulf Wind provides Pullman streamlined coach service, with direct connections at New Orleans for the Pacific Coast. It would be hard to beat a trip on the Gulf Wind, and going on through to the Pacific Coast on the Southern Pacific's fabulous Sunset Limited.

The public's response to the Gulf Wind can best be judged

by the fact that the patronage on this train has more than doubled that of its predecessor. The Seaboard also provides a good cross-Florida night service with sleeping cars between Tampa and Miami, with connections from St. Petersburg.

The Seaboard's streamliners are noted for their very capable, attractively groomed, and good-looking registered nurses, who have given fine service since the trains were inaugurated to both coach and Pullman passengers.

Outstanding Development

The development and modernization of the properties of the Seaboard Air Line following World War II have been progressive. Its centralized traffic-control development has been the most marvelous of any railroad in the United States.

The road's record during World War II was splendid, as it was when the Korean emergency arose. Serving, as it does, so many Army and Navy camps, as well as bases on the Atlantic Coast, the Seaboard was provided with an enviable opportunity to serve the American public as well as the Army and Navy.

The road owns a total of 655 locomotives, of which number only about 400 are steam. It is rapidly buying more Diesels for both road and switching service. Its car fleet includes some 20,607 freight cars, 458 passenger cars of later design, and 1,126 work-equipment cars. It owns nine barges and ferry boats for its tidewater assignments.

In 1949, the Seaboard carried 1,582,234 passengers, and in 1950 it exceeded that figure. The operating ratio is particularly good. Products of mines accounted for 45.39 per cent of the road's business; manufacturing and miscellaneous 27.99 per cent; products of forests 15.65 per cent; products of agriculture 6.37, and products of animals 0.60 per cent.

Development of any modern railroad includes Dieselization, and the Seaboard early recognized the handwriting on the wall. The road was the first railroad in the South to adopt the Diesel power for main-line service. The first General Motors Diesel went into service in 1938 on the New York–Florida run. The Diesel fleet grew, until the early part of 1950 saw 147 General Motors' units in service, and these units at this writing have accumulated well over 100,000,000 miles in all classes of service. More deliveries were scheduled for 1950, a year that saw 81 per cent of its freight service, 87 per cent of its passenger service, and 59 per cent of yard switching being done with Diesel power.

The Seaboard credits its great fleet of Diesels with being an important factor in improving earnings. For the first six months of 1950, earnings before fixed charges were $8,251,944, an increase of $2,134,237 over the preceding year.

The Seaboard Air Line, beside being the first with Diesel locomotives on its New York to Florida line, was the first to air-condition cars and the first to streamline the speedliners on this run.

The Seaboard was the first to better its schedule by by-passing Jacksonville with both freight and passenger, and the first not to go into Savannah.

This writer has always had an affection for the Seaboard, because it was on this road, back in 1913, that we rode its first locomotive, on the old Florida-Cuba Special, Nos. 1 and 2. Since then we have covered thousands of miles over this property. We saw the first of their Mountain-type engines arrive early in 1914, and we have watched the Seaboard grow ever since, with a keen appreciation of the wonderful development.

The Seaboard renders a great service to the South—the kind of service that any modern railroad offers the public and the area that carries its rails. Industry and agriculture and the promotion of prosperity are closely linked to the railroad.

We have an example in the perishable movement between Florida and the North, which will be covered in another chapter. The Seaboard has been among the leaders in developing this move to the highest state of perfection. Hauling many products of the soil, the railroad is constantly put to the test to deliver these perishables in A-1 shape. Watermelons, for instance, demand great attention and care, and the railroad reaps very little profit from handling them. However, it is part of the service the carrier provides.

The Seaboard's lumber haulage to the many paper mills along its line is another service handsomely rendered, and the paper tonnage that moves to the North and West is tremendous.

This is truly a great road with its silver rails spinning out the miles "Through the Heart of the South"—the Seaboard Air Line.

CHAPTER X

THE MODERN FRISCO

Five Thousand Miles of Service

Freights go booming through on the Frisco—freights between St. Louis and the Southwest; freights between Kansas City and the Southwest; freights between Kansas City, St. Louis, and the Southeast. Great fleets are on the move around the clock connecting the cities that have grown up in the tradition of the West, the Southwest, the South—Ellsworth, Wichita, Kansas City, Quanah, Fort Worth, Dallas, Fort Scott, St. Louis, Memphis, Birmingham, Mobile, Pensacola, Enid, Tulsa, Springfield. Springfield, Missouri, the crossroads of the Frisco, teems with freight cars from all points of the compass. Famous freights move in and out of this steel web. Nos. 30, 31, 32, 35, 37, 131, 134, 135, 136—rolling in, broken down, made up; highballing into the dawn of another roaring day on the railroad.

But before these, and more, great trains could attack the miles, there had to be a fine roadbed, good power, the best in signaling. The track is completely ballasted with chats, which is fine and firm, and 115-pound rail is used all over the system. Like the one at Springfield, yards have been enlarged, modernized. Only a modern yard can shuttle modern traffic in and out. Signal systems and train dispatching have been correlated during these modern years through the centralization traffic control. On heavy traffic lines over single track, in particular, the written train order has been outmoded and now the dispatcher has thumb-size switches to manipulate. And switch points move and signal lights spring to life as far as the last remote mile of this thing called C.T.C.

As an indication of how the Frisco has taken C.T.C. to its hearth and home we find on the busy main line, St. Louis to Tulsa, 386 miles of centralized traffic control out of the 424 miles between these points. The remaining thirty-eight miles is double track. The road also has eighty-seven C.T.C. miles between Fort Scott and Afton on the extremely busy Northern Division. On the main line, the heavy traffic Eastern Division carrying through freight from Kansas City to Springfield, Birmingham, and Memphis is C.T.C. from Springfield to Thayer, Missouri, a distance of 137 miles. On the Southern Division there is forty miles of it between Jasper and Birmingham—at a point where the Illinois Central uses the Frisco's tracks.

The last seventeen miles of the road's C.T.C. is between Madill and Lakeside on the Southwestern Division. This gives the Frisco 667 miles of Union Switch & Signal Company's centralized traffic control.

The Frisco has only about 363 steam locomotives left, and the majority of these are in storage. Complete Dieselization is scheduled as quickly as this modern power can be secured. At this writing, the road owns 72 A unit freight Diesels and 42 B units—a total of 114 units. The Frisco owns 23 passenger Diesel units, 17 of which are Electro-Motive E8's of 2,250 horsepower, described in the chapter on General Motors Diesels. Six are 2,000-horsepower E7's. We will stress, in a later chapter, the great "General Purpose" locomotive, the GP7, and the many power assignments it can master. Seventy-three of these locomotives are rendering fine service on the Frisco Lines. The total Diesel switching fleet numbers 101 locomotives of various horsepowers.

The Frisco's modernizing program after World War II included a spectacular line change on the difficult Dixon Hill and another at Hancock Hill between Springfield and Newburg, Missouri, where the grade was reduced from 2.3 per cent to a little over 1 per cent. There are no helper districts on the entire railroad. There has been a great deal of passenger-station modernization at many points, with very attractive structures replacing the outmoded depot of yesterday. Nothing so enhances a locality as the modern railroad station. The arriving passenger gets his first impression of the city from the station. The depot has been the ugly duckling over a long period, often through no fault of the railroad, for wars and depressions do not allow for architectural dressing up along that line.

Let us look briefly at some of the cities served by the Frisco Lines—Tulsa, Memphis, Kansas City, St. Louis, Birmingham, Oklahoma City, Springfield, Pensacola, Mobile, Fort Worth, Dallas—representing the states of Oklahoma, Tennessee, Missouri, Kansas, Florida, Alabama, and Texas.

Tulsa is famous for its fabulous oil properties, its steel fabrication business, its tank manufacturing, its oil well supply, and its wide reputation as a general distribution point. A vast amount of business originates in and moves in and out of this thriving Oklahoma metropolis. The Frisco road has secured important properties, and built spur tracks from their main line east of the city to the industries already beginning to locate there.

Birmingham, the "Pittsburgh of the South," with its great steel mills, its cast-iron pipe, its coal, its heavy machinery, plus the heavy movement of inbound grain, gives it top rating among the industrial cities of the United States. The Frisco plays a vital part in serving this city's heavy industry, and it interchanges here with the Seaboard and other Southern railroads. The Frisco's facilities for handling passenger traffic, as well as freight, is excellent.

Another great metropolis, thrusting up its remarkable skyline above the prairie, is famous Oklahoma City. Turning to the southeast and the Gulf, we find Pensacola and Mobile, cities providing heavy northbound tonnage.

Mobile, a recent addition to the list of cities served by the Frisco, bids fair to give the line considerable business in the future, as more and more South American ore is shipped to this port. By 1952, no doubt, this ore movement will be in full swing. The Frisco Lines took over the Alabama, Tennessee & Northern Railroad and now operate the road, which gave the Frisco access to this busy Gulf port.

Springfield, Missouri, the crossroads, beside being a busy railroad city, is the center of a greater dairy-producing area than any similar region in the United States. Within a radius of forty miles, the dairyman and the cow reign. The Frisco's shops, yards, and facilities provide employment for a large number of the road's 16,000 employees. Springfield is a fine city, a busy city.

The Frisco provides excellent passenger service. The Meteor, Nos. 9 and 10, is an overnight train between St. Louis and Tulsa and Oklahoma City. It is a lightweight type of speedliner on a good schedule. It provides buffet-lounge cars on the head end and the rear end of the train. Like all trains in the modern trend, it gives you a smooth start, a floating ride, and glide-in stops. The Meteor has evening departures out of St. Louis, Tulsa, and Oklahoma City and morning arrivals at the other end of the runs respectively.

The Will Rogers, Nos. 3 and 4, leaves St. Louis and Oklahoma City later in the evening and carries sleeping cars for Joplin, Missouri.

The famous Texas Special, Nos. 1 and 2, runs out of St. Louis as far as Vinita, Oklahoma, on the Frisco Lines; then the "Katy," Missouri-Kansas-Texas Railroad, handles the trains to Fort Worth, Dallas, and San Antonio. This train is streamlined, Diesel-powered all the way, with everything in the way of accommodations the traveler can desire—sleepers, lounge-observation, chair-lounge-buffet, reclining-chair cars, dining car. A crack train!

The Kansas City–Florida Special, Nos. 105 and 106, is another of the fleet of modern trains. This train has connections from the Santa Fe and the Union Pacific. It runs from Kansas City to Birmingham. The Frisco offers all sorts of connections for the Florida trade. Excellent service is provided and also overnight sleeping cars from Memphis to Pensacola. The Frisco's River Division offers excellent service from St. Louis to Memphis —the shortest and fastest route.

Some fine but lesser known trains do not carry dining cars but are equipped with coach diners, such as we find on Nos. 807 and 808, the Sunnyland. Another train that does not carry a diner but provides buffet-lounge meal service is the Black Gold, Nos. 507 and 508.

The Frisco Lines have left no stone unturned in their efforts to see that all of its passenger traffic is given an opportunity to obtain excellent food when traveling, and that is a real service rendered, though it produces no profit for the railroad and is usually provided at a loss.

"Home on the rails!" is one of the slogans of the Frisco Lines, and they have done everything to make available comfortable and dependable rail travel. Such trains as the Meteor and the Texas Special quickly made a reputation for modern luxury aboard a train, and though comparatively newcomers to American railroading they have set high standards.

CHAPTER XI

WABASH BLUE BIRD

Dome-car Streamliner

It has been called one of the most beautiful trains in America—the Blue Bird of the Wabash. It is one of those trains that when you see it you want to ride it. And this is the thing that is selling the railroads back to the public. The beauty and charm of the modern train is something that fascinates and intrigues every member of the family.

There was a time when it was only dad who wanted to drive down to the station with sonny to look at the trains. Now it is mother and sister and grandma. Dad looks at the Diesel, mother looks at the luxurious interiors behind the big picture windows and the children look at the dome cars.

People are riding the trains in this streamlined age "just for the ride," as a train conductor on the Wabash remarked shortly after the inauguration of the Blue Bird. There was a day when train passengers eagerly sought a seat on the open observation car, disdaining the discomforts of dust and cinders just for the view. Today they enjoy the comfort of the air-conditioned Vista-Dome and are presented with a bird's-eye view, which is included when you buy your ticket.

On the Blue Bird you are offered the utmost in luxury at no extra fare. It is, of course, a coach train, offering de luxe accommodations for daylight service between Chicago and St. Louis. Its three dome chair cars, dome parlor-observation, diner-lounge, and baggage-buffet-lounge provide opportunity for time disposal to a degree that makes this five-hour trip a pleasant interlude.

It doesn't make any difference how many trips you have made between Chicago and St. Louis, you will find the view from a Blue Bird dome different every time. The strange part of it is that the traveler is seeing a new America from these dome cars, and he is getting acquainted with his country all over again.

It was on a Sunday morning, February 26, 1950, that the Blue Bird was formally christened at the St. Louis Union Station. The conductor's highball signal waved No. 24, the crack new train, on its way at 8:55 A.M. It pulled into the Dearborn Station, Chicago, at 2:05 P.M. for a run of 285.7 miles, with stops at Delmar Station, Decatur, Illinois, and Englewood Station, Chicago. Northbound, the train makes flag stops at Granite City and Taylorville to pick up revenue passengers. The train makes a round trip daily.

The Blue Bird was the first dome-car streamliner between Chicago and St. Louis, and its entrance into high railroad society was spectacular for its color combination is striking, with bright stainless steel separating the skirt and the window panel of dark blue. The letter and number boards are blue and the lettering is gold. The roof is stainless steel.

From the Wabash flag at the front to the Blue Bird rear-end sign, the train is a streamlined symphony without and a complete luxury liner within. The emphasis is on comfort, as exemplified by the Heywood-Wakefield Sleepy Hollow coach seats, a design also used in the observation-parlor car. Tantamount to bodily ease is the excellence and taste of every decorative appointment.

This six-car Blue Bird is out of the shops of the Budd Company. The marvel is that the car builder can perform such perfection in a piece of railroad rolling stock, which daily must stand up to high speed, the weather, and hard use within.

One of the things which dresses up your modern train is the murals. Somehow your eye seems to catch them first. Then comes the drapery, the upholstery, the carpets, and other floor covering. At night, the lighting, of course, emphasizes certain features of the decoration motif.

On the Blue Bird, the murals painted in oils on canvas, are

by Auriel Bessemer. The ones that this writer likes in particular are those which depict aspects of the life of the territory through which the train operates—some are historical, some contemporary. These murals lend so much to the pleasing interiors.

You drop into a seat in the twelve-place cocktail lounge and let your glance run on through the adjoining forty-place dining section. The separating partition here establishes the decor for the entire car. Your eye catches the blue, patterned drapery and the Venetian blinds, the Canton blue wainscoting and partitions, the tan leather upholstery, the shining black Formica table tops, and the decorative partition screens between the dining section and the cocktail lounge.

Your gaze rests on these screens, as it does whenever it discovers something striking and unusual. Here are vertical Lucite rods —five on each side of the passageway—which are interwoven with bands of Chinese-red leather. Located at the base of the rods are reflector bulbs which cause the rods to light up for their entire length, while a red glow is given out through half-inch bands grouped along the length of the rods.

In the dining room there are ten four-seat tables with movable chairs upholstered in antique tan leather. The frames are of satin-finish metal. The appointments throughout are comparable to those of a fashionable hotel.

There are two four-place sofas in the cocktail lounge and four lounge chairs with combination smoking and beverage trays. Two table tops are built into each sofa arrangement. The upholstery is a brilliant Chinese-red leather. The carpet is blue and the table tops are of cobalt blue-gray Formica. The windows have light-ivory Venetian blinds with blue tapes for contrast.

The dome-observation-parlor car, located back of the diner, is divided into four sections—the observation lounge, the dome, and two parlors. At the rear the curved observation section has six upholstered lounge chairs and two tables recessed on the sides of the rear door. Next forward is a fourteen-passenger parlor section with large Sleepy Hollow lounge chairs, fully adjustable and rotating. The general lighting is fluorescent, but there are individual-controlled reading lamps above each chair in the base of the baggage rack.

The central area of the car beneath the dome section has lounges for ladies and gentlemen. Forward of these is an unusually designed drawing room with accommodations for five persons. It features a private, fully enclosed lavatory. Drawing-room fittings include a three-place sofa with adjustable armrests, two movable chairs of the lounge type, and a full-length illuminated wardrobe with double doors.

Beyond the drawing room toward the front is a second parlor section for nine passengers. It has movable barrel-backed chairs conveniently arranged before the seventy-inch-wide panorama windows.

The coffee shop–club car is located forward behind the Diesel locomotive. In the baggage section ahead provisions have been made for the crew. These include lockers, water cooler, and toilet. The center of the car contains a lunch counter with nine leather-upholstered stools. Beyond the partition toward the rear there is a twenty-three-passenger lounge section, with washrooms for ladies and gentlemen at the end of the car.

The lounge has two four-place, built-in banquette sections and twelve large lounge chairs. Forward of this section is a three-place curved sofa shaped around a cocktail table. Glass panels separate the lounge and lunch counter. Murals are included in the decorative scheme of the lounge. There are gold-tinted mirrors and Venetian blinds. The latter in grouse tan. The drapery is turquoise.

Gold-tinted Plexiglass mirrors are located forward of the bulkhead in the lunch-counter section. The walls are Arab tan and the ceiling light beige.

Various glass panels in the train carry out the Blue Bird theme with an etched blue bird on a vine. There are many details that reflect the touch of master craftsmen in this modern luxury train, craftsmen who have combined their skills and their arts to produce one of the outstanding trains in America.

Decorations

The interior decorations of the Blue Bird were created by the Wabash Passenger and Mechanical Departments, in collaboration with John Harbeson, of Philadelphia, one of the nation's leading industrial architects. The name, The Blue Bird of the Wabash, is a poetic combination if there ever was one, and the builders have utilized every possible practice and treatment in emphasizing it.

The dome coaches carry a variety of color schemes which prevent unpleasant monotony. Wainscoting and doors are Canton blue. The walls above are light stone gray and the ceilings are of ivory. A band of Canton blue runs along the edge of the baggage racks in a solid line. In one car we find a rose carpet, with seats upholstered in blue needlepoint; the second car has a light-gray needlepoint upholstering and blue carpet; and the third car offers ashes of roses upholstering and blue carpet.

Again, the outstanding decorative note of the coaches is the large oil paintings which form murals on the forward bulkhead of the dome sections. The scenes are historical.

Each dome coach is divided into two passenger sections below. The forward section seats twenty and the rear thirty-four passengers. The dome section provides seats for twenty-four. The color scheme of the car is carried out here. Seats on the main floor are individually reclining and rotating reversible, of the Sleepy Hollow type. The rubber-covered footrests are adjustable. The dome seats are reversible but do not recline. These have folding footrests and ash trays are built into the arms. Cushions and armrests of all seats are foam rubber.

The lounges of the dome coach are located beneath the dome section, or in the center of the car instead of at the two ends as in conventional equipment. The ladies' lounge has two attractive dressing tables, one for two persons and the other for one person. The adjacent washroom is separated from the lounge by a curtain. The latter has marbleized floor tile and the lounge has carpeting. The washroom has two washbasins and a toilet enclosure. The lounge has a comfortable upholstered sofa and the washroom a folding seat. Full-length mirrors are suitably located.

There is an equally generous-sized men's lounge, with three washbasins and two toilet enclosures. A curtain separates the lounge and washroom. The lounge has full-length mirrors, a leather-upholstered seat, and marbleized tile floor.

The stairway to the dome section leads from the rear passenger section. Glass in the dome windows is the tinted heat-resisting type which prevents glare. It is double glazed for safety and more efficient air conditioning. The inner layer is shatter-proof, with a hermetically sealed air space between the two layers of glass to increase resistance to heat and cold. Specially engineered air conditioning has been perfected to maintain an even temperature under all kinds of adverse weather conditions. All windows are curved to conform to the car lines.

Two rows of fluorescent lights along the roof of the dome provide general illumination, and small slits are installed along the step-up to the seats as a safety measure. To insure maximum vision the hermetically sealed double-paned forward and rear center windows also serve as air-conditioning ducts.

The corridor below the dome which joins the front and rear portions of the dome coach is entirely carpeted and is reached by two steps at each end. A Sunroc electromechanical water cooler is located in a recess formed by the dome's curved stairway. The doors of this modern train operate automatically, a feature that older people in particular appreciate.

The train is completely air conditioned and an even temperature is always maintained. Soundproofing largely eliminates train noises, making for greater journey comfort. All general illumination is the fluorescent type and all cars have individual reading lights set about each chair in the base of the baggage rack.

The Blue Bird's communication system is used normally for the playing of recorded music, but special announcements of interest to passengers also are made over the system. An unusual feature of the system is the pretuned radio which brings in one broadcasting station as soon as the other fades out due to the distance covered. Radio broadcasts throughout the train are made

Conductor on the Seaboard's northward Marketeer #80 prepares to inspect the Merchandiser #85 as these fast freights meet on double track just north of Hamlet, N.C. Virginia Division. Courtesy, S.A.L. RR.

K.C.S. #9, crack morning train to the Gulf, meets #88 with engine 905, the great 2-10-4 type of the K.C.S. at Grandview, Mo. Northern Division. Photo by Preston George.

B.&O. Capital Limited, #5, passing over the Monocacy River Bridge on the west end of Baltimore Division enroute from Washington to Chicago. Courtesy, B.&O. RR.

Frisco's new yard office complete with tele-type, telephone, and loud-speaker facilities as well as lockers and washrooms for the yard crews and general offices for the yard masters and operating officials. Courtesy, Frisco Lines.

Fine new Diesel shop built by the Frisco Lines at Springfield, Mo., has already been en-larged. Courtesy, Frisco Lines.

Interior of the Wabash's new Bluebird's dining car showing the cocktail lounge. Courtesy, Wabash RR.

Wabash #12, the streamlined City of Kansas City east of Delmar, Mo., on the St. Louis Terminal Division. Courtesy, Wabash RR.

New S.P. Cascade first #12 carrying flags at Oakland (16th St.), Calif., on first run, August 13, 1950. Western Division, Courtesy, S.P. RR.

S.P. first #671 with new E.M.D. Diesel 6262 F-7 at Odell Lake on the Portland Division. Courtesy, S.P. RR.

Rear end of one of the new coaches of the Wabash Bluebird showing mural and reclining seats. Courtesy, Wabash RR.

Interior of the new Wabash's coffee shop club for coach passengers from the kitchen end—the first car of the new Bluebird. Courtesy, Wabash RR.

Returning the empty ore cars to Conneaut, B.&L.E. engine 634, 2-10-4 type, Class H E, with 115 cars approaching K.O. Yard at Adamsville, Pa. Courtesy, B.&L.E. RR.

B.&L.E. Diesel #704 with 11,160 tons, 112 cars of ore at Kremis, Pa. Notice the excellent track, heavy rail, ballast, and turnout. Courtesy, B.&L.E. RR.

Milwaukee #16, new Olympia Hiawatha, in Montana Canyon near summit of Belt Mts. running along Sixteen Mile Creek between Sixteen and Canyon, Mont., Rocky Mt. Division. Courtesy, Milwaukee RR.

only when a program is of more than usual importance. The system has two channels for wired music, sixteen for pretuned radio reception, and one for public-address purposes.

The Wabash in creating the Blue Bird has done everything possible to bring to its riding guests the comforts they would find in any fine hotel, only, of course, in a more compact field. Train travel provides the opportunity to adapt the tastes of the individual to the whims of the moment. Father can adjust his Sleepy Hollow seat for a comfortable nap, while mother beside him sits up to read or embroider.

The traveler can move around, stretch his legs aboard this ultramodern streamliner, get a snack in the club car, step up to the dome to enjoy the view, go into the diner and enjoy the best in food—a great feature of Wabash travel. On the way to the diner he will perhaps want to stop for his favorite drink and a chat with fellow travelers. This is rail travel in the modern mode, something that it is very easy to become enthusiastic about, even for a veteran globe-trotter.

Comfort with Speed and Safety

Many people remark on the smooth starts of today's luxury train, as contrasted to the lumpy jolts of yesterday. One answer is the National Malleable tight-lock coupler which eliminates a lot of lost motion. On the Blue Bird there are the Waughmat draft gears. And there are the modern trucks with their combination coil and bolster springs, the roller bearings, the sound-deadening pads of rubberized fabric, applied on the center plates, equalizer spring seats, side bearings, and swing hangers.

More than seventy specialists in railroad equipment building had a hand in the construction of the Blue Bird, which required two years to build. Today's train, like the modern automobile, is a far cry from the 1920 model, even the 1940 model. There are a lot of things "under the hood" tuned to the traveler's comfort and convenience. All train vestibules have folding stainless steel handrails which are lowered into place when the train is in motion. These are for making passage from car to car easier.

The Blue Bird car-body structures are of Budd Shotweld construction in which stainless steel is used throughout, except for the welded alloy-steel combination ends, draft sills, and bolsters, which are joined to the stainless-steel center sills by rivets. Sound deadening is applied in the form of Insulmat, which is sprayed on the inside of the roof, sides, ends, and floor pans. The body insulation is three inches thick throughout.

Safety features built into the Blue Bird include a Mars rear-end light built as a part of the curved roof section of the dome-observation-parlor car at the extreme back. This red light flashes automatically when the train slows to twenty miles an hour or stops. Its flashes form a figure-eight pattern which makes it sharply apparent to any following train.

Two headlights are built into the front of the Blue Bird's Diesel. One sends a strong beam down the center of the track, providing excellent visibility. The other rotates, like the rear-end light, in a figure-eight pattern, which provides a visible warning to motorists approaching grade crossings.

A 2,000-horsepower General Motors Diesel pulls the Blue Bird. This locomotive is capable of a speed of 117 miles per hour, which is less important by far than its ability to maintain a high average speed. The weight of the Diesel is 315,000 pounds. It is seventy-one feet long and carries 1,200 gallons of fuel oil and 1,200 gallons of heating water. Its range between fuel and water stops is 600 miles, or approximately the distance, round trip, of the Chicago–St. Louis run of the train.

The Diesel cab has an insulated partition between motor compartment and the cab itself, and the roof of the cab includes sound-absorbing material. It is possible for the engineer and fireman to converse in ordinary conversational tones, more easily facilitating the exchange of signal observations. Automatic windshield wipers and defrosters assure the engineer a clear view in bad weather.

Sun visors cut off the glare for the crew when the streamliner is running into the sun. The controls have been designed for the most natural position and movement of arms and hands. The two whistles, one for town and one for the country, assure a clear signal always.

The Blue Bird's brakes are Westinghouse HSC type, which means high speed control. They are, of course, electropneumatic, which is a brake system that operates instantaneously down the entire train length and produces a soft, strong braking of all wheels whether they are on the first car or the last car.

The total seating capacity, including the seats in the domes, is 375. However, normal accommodations provide for 162 in the coach seats, 23 in parlor seats, and 5 seats in the drawing room. In addition, there are the 96 dome seats. The remaining seats are the 6 in the observation lounge and 24 in the lounge section of the coffee shop–club car.

Nothing has been omitted in the endeavor to make the Blue Bird completely new and completely modern. It is impossible to list here the more technical details and items that are a part of the train. The ventilating system alone is a finely engineered feature that makes for passenger comfort, as is the low-pressure zone heating with thermostatic control and fan radiation unit set in stainless steel ducts along the floor at the side walls, which operates in conjunction with an overhead heat coil. This is a Vapor Heating Company installation, and Vapor is but one of some seventy concerns, as we have mentioned, having a hand in the job of building the Blue Bird.

St. Louis–Chicago travelers are finding the Wabash's addition to the new streamliners a happy medium of transportation between the two cities. It leaves St. Louis every morning and Chicago every afternoon.

CHAPTER XII

KANSAS CITY SOUTHERN

Kansas City to Gulf Ports

The Kansas City Southern Lines reach straight south from the Kansas City Union Station over the shortest rail route to the tidewater at Beaumont and Port Arthur, Texas, to Lake Charles, Louisiana, also a Gulf port, and, of course, to New Orleans, gateway of the Mississippi Valley. From the "Front Door" of the "Heart of America" to the Gulf seaboard the rails stretch over the prairies, across the western Ozarks, over the Ouachitas, the highest mountains between the Appalachians and the Rockies, and there make the long glide down the coastal plains to the sea.

This is the way of the Southern Belle, the crack streamliner of the Kansas City Southern to New Orleans, and the more leisurely Nos. 9 and 10. Also it is the line of a famous king of fast freights, No. 77, a merchandise special operating between Kansas City, Port Arthur, and New Orleans.

The Kansas City Southern has vigorously carved a niche for itself in the railroad hall of fame through sheer grit and determination. It is a glorious example of what can be accomplished in a land of free enterprise by freeborn men, and such achievements should be chronicled on the walls of the world in a day when Communists and fellow travelers are crying down the American way of life.

The Kansas City Southern was born during the panic of the 1890's and it has survived subsequent hard times and recessions with amazing hardihood, thanks to the leadership of men like William N. Deramus, president. There have been times when it was sink or swim, with a millstone of debt around its neck. In fact, in the 1940's there were financial experts who were predicting that the road would be in receivership by 1950. But Bill Deramus, a man named Grant Stauffer, and Kansas City businessmen went to work on behalf of Kansas City's home railroad and pulled the Kansas City Southern out of deep water.

In 1890 a road called the Kansas City Suburban Belt began operation under the leadership of Arthur E. Stilwell, previously engaged in selling insurance. This man, Stilwell, was a born railroader and in his field he ranked with Hill and Harriman and the other railroad builders. He visioned a line to the Gulf and went to work on it with a fine disregard for the panic that was on. The Belt Line extended from Independence, Missouri, through the industrial and wholesale districts of Kansas City, Missouri, into the Argentine district of Kansas City, Kansas. Here it tied in with other lines in the area, serving packing houses, elevators, stockyards, and various industries.

Stilwell then organized the Kansas City, Nevada, Missouri & Fort Smith Railroad as a means of tapping the coal fields to the south. And so began his Gulf line. The road was completed to Hume, Missouri, late in 1891. In 1893 it was reorganized as the Kansas City, Pittsburg & Gulf Railroad. Hard times created difficulties but in 1893 the steel reached Joplin, Missouri, and two short lines were added to the project: one between Joplin, Missouri, and Sulphur Springs, Arkansas; the other between Texarkana, Arkansas-Texas, and Little River to the north.

In 1895 the line was completed to Shreveport, Louisiana. On September 11, 1897, about twelve miles north of Beaumont, Texas, the last spike was driven home, connecting the line between Kansas City and the Gulf, with the exception of eleven miles near Kansas City, where leased trackage was used. In 1929, the road built its Leeds-Grandview line for complete ownership between Kansas City and Port Arthur.

In 1900, the Kansas City, Pittsburg & Gulf Railroad became the Kansas City Southern Railway Company.

The Kansas City Southern operates in the states of Missouri, Kansas, Arkansas, Oklahoma, Louisiana, and Texas. The road has a mileage of 962 miles. It comes down from Kansas City to Shreveport, Louisiana, 560 miles, joining with the Louisiana & Arkansas system, which it owns, to tie in Dallas, Texas; Hope, Arkansas; Winnfield, Baton Rouge, and New Orleans, Louisiana. The Louisiana & Arkansas has a total mileage of 877 miles.

The Kansas City Southern and the Louisiana & Arkansas connect the Midwest with five great Gulf Coast ports. The country served enjoys a general temperate to subtropic climate, with varying soils that produce a great variety of agricultural products, including grains, vegetables, fruits, berries, grapes, cotton, and nuts. The land sustains extensive dairy herds, beef cattle, and other livestock.

It is easy for people to fall into the error of thinking that this is a country of rather meager natural resources, and all too little has been written of the country served by the Kansas City Southern and the other rail lines. In the first place, we have Pittsburg, Kansas, there in Crawford County. Everyone, of course, knows about the other Pittsburgh in Pennsylvania, for which Pittsburg, Kansas, was named, but many are not too familiar with the latter city.

It has been called the "Coal Capital" of Kansas, with an annual production running into millions of dollars. Its iron foundries, oil equipment manufacturers, and other industries are important. Here are located main shops and division offices of the Kansas City Southern. Other lines serving Pittsburg, Kansas, are the Santa Fe, the Frisco Lines, the Missouri Pacific, and the Joplin-Pittsburg Railroad.

The natural resources spread lavishly along the Kansas City Southern Lines include, coal, oil, natural gas, timber, iron ore, limestone, tripoli, dolomite, marble, salt, sulphur, lead, zinc, antimony, mercury, bauxite, slates, clays, shales, chalk, lignite, silica, and vanadium.

At Hume, Missouri, the Hume-Sinclair Coal Company operates strip-mining operations producing some 800,000 tons per year. Mulberry, Kansas-Missouri, was named for its mulberry grove. Industries include strip and deep coal mining and agriculture. Amsterdam, Missouri, some sixty miles south of Kansas City, was named for the old country Amsterdam because of early Dutch interest in the railroad.

From the great industrial, agricultural, and rail clearing house of Kansas City right on down the line to the Gulf we find lusty sinews of commerce employed in many and varied enterprises in country, town, and city. And there are the famous resorts, catering to vacationists, becoming more and more a big business in the Ozarks, which boast some of the finest scenery. There is certainly plenty of diversity on the K.C.S. lines.

Let us take, for instance, Siloam Springs, Arkansas, named for the Biblical pool of the miracle. Here we find diversified agriculture, a large milk plant, a fruit cannery, beef and dairy cattle, John Brown University, and the Ozarks. McCurtain, Oklahoma, is a coal mining and agricultural center. Mena, Arkansas, named for Queen Wilhemina, of Holland, in recognition of capital invested by the Dutch in the building of the Kansas City Southern. It is in the heart of the Ouachita Mountains, with a national forest handy, providing scenery, vacations, forest products, woodworking, and berries.

Texarkana is on the Arkansas-Texas border with the state line running down the center of one of the main streets. It is noted for its clay products, wood preserving, baskets, machine shops, tank cars, and it is a junction point for the Kansas City Southern, the Missouri Pacific, the St. Louis Southwestern, and the Texas & Pacific.

Shreveport, Louisiana, is the second largest city in Louisiana and Caddo Parish seat. The Kansas City Southern owns valuable Union Station properties there. Oil, natural gas, lumber, glass, furniture, chemicals, oil-well machinery, steel fabricating, fertilizer are the major industries. De Quincy, Louisiana, is a division point where the line branches to Lake Charles. Here is located a $2,000,000 naval stores plant. And up the line a few miles at De Ridder is the Crosby Naval Stores plant for the extraction of turpentine, resin, and pine oil from the stumps of cutover timber lands. De Ridder and Leesville are located in the heart of the old lumber country.

The tracks of the Kansas City Southern make the Sabine

119

River Crossing and thread on into Beaumont, Texas, which has one of the world's largest refineries. The famous Spindletop and other oil-producing fields are nearby. Shipbuilding, rice production, and milling are carried on in this area. Beaumont is also a famous deep-sea fishing port. Port Neches, on the Neches Belt Line of the K.C.S., has private deepwater facilities through the Neches River and the Port Arthur ship channel. Some twenty miles inland from Port Arthur, Beaumont receives at its docks ocean freighters.

Port Arthur, Texas, port and rail terminal, was named for Arthur Stilwell, founder of the Kansas City Southern. Port Arthur, on Sabine Lake, has excellent protection from the open sea, nine miles away. Extensive facilities include a 500,000-bushel elevator and a conveyor for loading coal from cars to ships. There is a million-dollar rice industry in the county, the great Sabine-Neches industrial areas, and extensive livestock and fur ranches. Port Arthur is the end of the run for the famous No. 77, Kansas City Southern fast freight.

We gauge our thinking along defined channels and are quite amazed sometimes when presented with facts that had escaped us. For instance, it is a little difficult to realize that this Kansas City Southern brings coal down to the sea. This coal comes from the fields around Heavener, Oklahoma, and on north.

Probably nowhere in the United States is there a more diversified area. Certainly the resources along the lines of the Kansas City Southern are rich and many. It is a land of progress and opportunity for the farmer, the industrialist, the mechanic. It is a tourist's heaven and a vacation world hard to beat.

Railroad Pioneers—The River Line

The New Orleans connection of the Kansas City Southern is made at Shreveport over the lines of the Louisiana & Arkansas. (The K.C.S. obtained control of the Louisiana & Arkansas through the acquisition of capital stock in 1939.)

William Edenborn, the first president of the American Steel

& Wire Company, began construction on the Shreveport & Red River Valley Railroad in 1896 and the line began operation between Shreveport and Coushatta, Louisiana, in 1898. The road reached Alexandria, Louisiana, in the spring of 1902, and Mansura, Louisiana, in the fall of that year.

The Louisiana Railway & Navigation Company was organized in May of 1903 to purchase the property of the Shreveport & Red River Valley Railroad and to complete construction of the line into New Orleans. Through service was inaugurated between Shreveport and New Orleans on April 14, 1907. On April 1, 1923, a branch of the Missouri-Kansas-Texas lines between the Louisiana-Texas line and McKinney, Texas, was purchased. Trackage rights were secured from the Texas & Pacific Railway into Shreveport, and the Louisiana Railway & Navigation Company of Texas began operation.

This road and the Louisiana & Arkansas Railway were acquired by Harvey Couch and associates in 1928 and the two lines were reorganized into the Louisiana & Arkansas Railway Company on May 8, 1929. In this year the L.&A. purchased the Louisiana Railway & Navigation Company of Texas and in April, 1930, the corporate name of the Louisiana Railway & Navigation Company of Texas was changed to Louisiana, Arkansas & Texas Railway Company.

The line was extended to Dallas on July 1, 1932, by Trackage rights with the Missouri-Kansas-Texas road, but the route was changed via the Gulf, Colorado & Santa Fe, at Farmersville, Texas, in September, 1937. The Louisiana, Arkansas & Texas Railway was purchased by and became a part of the Louisiana & Arkansas Railway Company in June, 1939.

The Louisiana & Arkansas Railway started out as a logging road, built by William Buchanan around 1896. It was chartered as a common carrier in 1898 and extended from Stamps, Arkansas, to Spring Hill, Louisiana. Later, Buchanan bought large timber holdings in the vicinity and the road reached out to cities of importance. With further rail construction and the acquisition of other small lines, Buchanan's railroad reached Winnfield, Louisiana, in May, 1902, when the Louisiana & Arkansas Railway Company was organized. The extension to Hope, Arkansas, connecting with the Missouri Pacific and the Frisco was completed in June, 1903.

The rail of the road continued to thrust on into the timber country, reaching Jena, Louisiana, in December, 1903. By July, 1906, the tracks had reached from Packton to Alexandria, Louisiana. The purchase of the Minden East & West Railroad in July, 1910, was a big step in the development of the property. Service to Vidalia, Louisiana, on the Mississippi River opposite Natchez, was effected in July, 1917, but the Louisiana & Arkansas holdings in this branch were disposed of in 1945.

William Buchanan, pioneer logger and railroad builder, was the first man to put logs down on the skids of a sawmill by rail. And in many ways he was a remarkable man, and from his meager logging road start in the early nineties there was completed by 1910 a railroad more than 300 miles in length. It is too bad that more has not been written of men like Buchanan; they are an inspiration and they further point out by their deeds the vast possibilities of free enterprise.

The railroads have been among the stoutest-hearted pioneers of the country in the face of adversity, from the conquest of raw frontiers to the present-day struggle to survive economically. Without the railroads, World War II would have been lost. Without the Kansas City Southern and the other railroads serving this richly productive area of which this chapter deals there would have been no great tidewater ports, no inland empire.

One of the things that every railroad must subscribe to is the modern trend. Steam is singing its swan song, the click of the telegraph key is a weak voice in the wilderness, switching methods have undergone radical changes. Through employment of radio the Kansas City Southern has demonstrated its readiness to railroad the modern way when and where it is possible, and radio communication is one of the factors that help expedite the movement of No. 77, which we have mentioned and which you will hear more about.

The River Line—Shreveport to New Orleans—on the Louisiana & Arkansas, upon leaving Shreveport, crosses the Red River and passes Barksdale Field, four miles south, one of the largest airports in the United States. It was named for a hero of World War I. Between Shreveport and Alexandria is Coushatta, the seat of Red River Parish, named for an Indian tribe, known for its forest products, agriculture, and cotton. It is historically significant because of the "Coushatta riots," which occurred in 1874, during the reconstruction period.

Alexandria, Louisiana, was named for Alexander Fulton, owner of the Spanish grant site of the first settlement. It was an outpost where wagon trains for Texas got supplies from steamboats. The parish is rich in agriculture, a diversified farming and livestock area. It ships lumber, flooring, cottonseed, and soybean products. Manufacturing includes such items as road machinery, shingles, staves, insecticides, pine-tar products, turpentine, and talcum powder. It was a military training center in World War I. It is a modern, bustling city of the South.

Mansura, about thirty miles south of Alexandria, is populated by descendants of the Acadians, of "Evangeline" fame. Here we find cedar water buckets and gourd drinking cups. The Angelus tolls at 6 P.M. each Saturday evening for the setting of clocks to avoid being late at Sunday Mass. Products of the soil are sugar cane, cotton, and shallots.

The original white settlers at Hamburg, a few miles south, were from Hamburg, Germany. The principal crop is Dutch clover. A little farther on is Simmesport, located on the Atchafalaya River near the confluence of the Red and Old rivers. Commercial fishing is the major industry. This is, too, a fine hunting country, with deer in the forests and plenty of small game.

Baton Rouge, about eighty miles north of New Orleans, is itself virtually a Gulf port, since ocean freighters come up the Mississippi to its docks, where they load for ports of the world. Nine flags have flown over Baton Rouge, the third largest Louisiana city. Baton Rouge is beautiful and intriguing. It is the capital city. A thirty-four story capitol building has replaced the old capitol structure, and it is the highest building in the South. Baton Rouge is the home of Louisiana State University and its more than 2,000-acre campus and 45,000-seat stadium. Here we find the only bridge across the Mississippi until New Orleans is reached.

This is the land of the French Acadians. It is rich in legend and folklore. It is a great industrial city, with plant investments exceeding $400,000,000 and a weekly payroll of more than $1,000,000. Synthetic rubber is produced here, Ethyl fluid, chemicals, acids, soda products, and aluminum. The railroads serving it are the Louisiana & Arkansas—for the parent Kansas City Southern—the Missouri Pacific, and the Illinois Central.

Between Reserve and Norco, south of Baton Rouge, is the Bonnet Carré Spillway, an emergency floodway protecting New Orleans and the lower Mississippi River area. Completed in 1935 at a cost in excess of $13,000,000, it has a 250,000 cubic-foot water capacity per second.

New Orleans, queen city of the South, has been called "America's most interesting city." Founded by Bienville as a French colony in 1718, and named for the Duc d'Orléans, the city was under Spanish rule from 1767 until 1803, then transferred back to France, and then sold to the United States as part of the Louisiana Territory for $15,000,000. The port facilities are state owned and among the finest in the country, with thirteen and one-half miles of public docks. Millions of tons of a vast diversified cargo move across these docks—cargo that has reached tidewater over the tracks of the Louisiana & Arkansas and the eight other railroads that serve the city.

A vast delta country reaches away south of New Orleans to the mouth of the Mississippi, 110 miles away. An important manufacturing city, New Orleans' industries include shipbuilding, sugar refining, bags, alcohol, celotex, roofing, petroleum, cottonseed products, coffee, syrup and molasses, textiles, clothing, twine, furniture, and fertilizers. It is a great summer and winter vacation land. It is famous for its French cuisine and Creole dishes, its French Quarter, its Mardi Gras, the Spring Fiesta, and the Sugar Bowl football classic.

New Orleans—Rampart Street Station—is the end of the run for train No. 1, the new Southern Belle. We will describe the streamliner in another chapter, a train that is modern in a land that is old.

Radio and Train Movement

The Kansas City Southern is not a fancy railroad. There are many things it does not have in the way of frills, but anything it may lack in the way of styling it more than makes up for in soundness and horse sense. If the Kansas City Southern had not been hardheaded and frugal it would have had a different financial story to tell as we set these words down.

There has been a lot of fine railroading on the Kansas City Southern, and the road was quick to seize on radio as a means to an end.

The Kansas City Southern was among the first to experiment with and to adopt the use of the radiotelephone on engines and cabooses and in yards and wayside stations. All of the new Diesels have the latest equipment of this type of communications.

It was a long step from the time Bill Deramus worked as a night telegrapher at a station in the pine woods on the Louisville & Nashville. Then the operator only talked with the train crew upon its arrival at the station; now he picks up his radiotelephone and his voice reaches out into the blackness to a Kansas City Southern train, toiling on the grade.

"Where are you, No. 15?"

And No. 15 answers. The report is then made to the dispatcher, which allows time to change a possible meet with an opposing train. This, of course, is done by means of the regular land circuits.

Back in the mid-forties, Bill Deramus said, "We'll modernize not only our equipment but in all other respects just as quick as it can be done economically and we have the funds for the purpose." The Kansas City Southern began to buy Diesels for both freight and passenger, speeding up train movement and reducing costs. It planned a new streamliner; purchased 1,200 new freight cars; scheduled ambitious track improvements, including curve reduction; began the reconstruction of the Arkansas River bridge at Redland, Oklahoma; and initiated other projects, to be begun as soon as funds became available.

It is this kind of faith in the future of the railroads that will maintain these lifelines of the nation in a manner that will keep them ready for any emergency. And it is men like William N. Deramus, who have learned the railroad game the hard way, the country will look to for the courage and the brains to lead the railroads through wars and panics.

In 1908, Bill Deramus was a telegraph operator in Pittsburg, Kansas. A little later he went to Heavener, Oklahoma, to take over the dispatcher's chair. He became manager of the entire system in 1928. He was named president of the Kansas City Southern and its allied Louisiana & Arkansas in 1941—another American success story.

No. 77, Merchandise Special

Out of the "Heart of America" at 8:40 nightly rolls No. 77, southbound fast freight. It highballs in the yards at Kansas City and slides away to the music of its big Diesel motors, bound for the Gulf with a consist of rush merchandise and reefers loaded with meat. This is a modern train in a day of modern railroading.

It rolls the 786.7 miles to Port Arthur over a sound roadbed and a heavy rail. It leaves Air Line Junction, Kansas City, and soon its trucks are clattering swiftly over the Missouri Pacific Crossing, the Alton and the Kansas City Terminal Crossings, the Santa Fe and the Sheffield Steel Crossings and then Fifteenth Street.

The Merchandise Special pulls into Pittsburg, Kansas, North Yard at 12:01 A.M. It has covered 127 miles in three hours and twenty-one minutes. No. 77 leaves the North Yard at 12:25 A.M. on the Second District, reaching Watts, Oklahoma, at 4:10 A.M., a distance of 235 miles from Kansas City's North Yard.

126

No. 77 reaches Heavener, Oklahoma, at 7:05 A.M.—102 miles. It is heavier going, stiffer grades, on the Fourth District between Heavener and De Queen, Arkansas, but No. 77 has covered the ninety-five miles by 10:30 A.M. Rich Mountain is behind, the highest point on the run. It is out of the De Queen yard, on the Fifth District, at 10:40 A.M. and pulls into Shreveport, Louisiana, yard at 2:15 P.M., a distance of 125 miles.

No. 77 is in the yards at Shreveport until 5:10 P.M., when it departs for Leesville, Louisiana, 110 miles away. The big Diesel noses into Leesville at 10:00 P.M. This is the Sixth District and the fast freight is getting close to tidewater. The final run over the Seventh District begins at 10:30 P.M. and the train crosses the Sabine River into Texas. Leaving Beaumont at 3:20 A.M., No. 77 arrives at Port Arthur, 117 miles, at 5:00 A.M.

This Merchandise Special of the Kansas City Southern is geared for top performance. The road knows what the shippers want and it has what it takes to deliver the goods. Such a train as No. 77 makes its weight felt and it is the best possible advertising medium a railroad can have. Every time it rolls past a country depot or pulls into a city, people are watching. "That's 77," they will say. "Comes down from Kansas City. Passes through six states."

When the old-timers watch No. 77 wheeling through, they say, "The Kansas City Southern has come a long way. I remember when it was the Kansas City, Pittsburg & Gulf Railroad and Arthur Stilwell was president."

In an annual report of the Kansas City, Pittsburg & Gulf road for the fiscal year ending June 30, 1898, Arthur E. Stilwell, president, wrote of the difficulties encountered, including rains and floods, affecting one third of its mileage; two yellow fever epidemics, which for weeks at a time prevented the movement of trains; the general depression and interest on bonds beginning to pile up with the road building program incomplete; and of a roadbed not yet shaken into a permanent right of way. At the same time, he wrote of unprecedented industrial and agricultural developments during the preceding two years. Experts in rice culture had found large areas suitable for rice growing;

experienced lumbermen were examining into the quality and quantity of the pine forests; settlers were being located along the line.

Towns were springing up, saw and stave mills were being erected, orchards were being set out, blue trap rock properties were being developed, stone quarries were supplying fine building material. In one year lumber tonnage jumped from 23,324 tons to 58,640 tons.

The equipment problem then, as in the later years, was one that presented the management with headaches and gray hairs. "Fifteen (15) ten-wheel engines," wrote President Stilwell, "will arrive in a few days from the Baldwin Locomotive Works, and 400 coal cars, 150 flat cars, and 489 boxcars have been ordered. . . . This will increase earnings, but at least 1,500 more box cars are needed. . . ."

The steamship business at Port Arthur was developing rapidly. Several vessels a month were being loaded for foreign ports. The coal business was growing with "smokeless" coal finding great favor. Wheat was rolling to the tidewater and trains were carrying back lumber, rice, and fruit. The country was new and raw, but it was developing and new records were being established.

Railroaders were hewing to the line—building, developing, working toward a greater tomorrow; paving the way for the day when the Southern Belle and No. 77 would be riding the rails. Great trains linking the "Heart of America" and the deep-water ports of the Gulf Coast.

CHAPTER XIII

A DOME ON THE CAPITOL LIMITED

The Baltimore & Ohio's Dome Sleeper

When Cy Osborn, a vice-president of General Motors, riding the head end of a Diesel-drawn freight in the Colorado Rockies in 1944, was struck by the notion of putting a dome on a passenger train he probably never dreamed that he was starting something that one day would cause a stir in the halls of Congress. But that, in effect, was what happened when the Baltimore & Ohio put a Strata-Dome car in the blue-blooded aristocrat of trains, the Capitol Limited.

"A dome on the Capitol?" An eyebrow arched. "Their Columbian has domes—a coach train."

The coach trains and their domes, trains one step lower in the social railroad order than the extra-fare and all-Pullman trains, in the early days of "upstairs under glass," had been the object of many an envious eye. The kind of people who ride extra-fare, or patronize the slightly exclusive train-secretary type of train, felt that they were being discriminated against.

The Baltimore & Ohio was the first steam railroad incorporated in the United States; it was one of the first railroads to put Diesel motive power on passenger trains, including the Capitol Limited; the first commercial radiotelephone call ever made was from the B.&O.'s Royal Blue on August 15, 1947; the first "bay window" caboose was put in service on the Baltimore & Ohio in 1930. We are not sure, as this is set down, whether or not the Baltimore & Ohio is the first "purple and fine linen" train to provide an observatory for its guests, but it is safe to say that they will have, at least, come close to leading the parade by putting in service on December 20, 1950, a Strata-Dome for the pleasure of those who ride the Capitol Limited between Washington and Chicago.

However, the Baltimore & Ohio does rate another "first," in that it is the first road in the East to put on a Strata-Dome *sleeping car*.

Of the three units built by Budd, two went into service the last part of 1950, on the Capitol Limited; the third operates, as this is written, on the Shenandoah, between Washington and Chicago, making the westbound trip one day and the eastbound trip the succeeding day.

These dome sleepers have the usual twenty-four seats on the upper level. On the lower level, each car has five roomettes, one single bedroom, and three large double drawing rooms. Each double drawing room is fitted with three arm chairs for daytime use and twin beds for sleeping.

Privileged travelers! In a day of modern railroading.

Dinner in the Baltimore & Ohio's excellent diner, then a visit to the Strata-Dome. Later, somewhere in the mountains, you come down the thick-carpeted stairs from the dome and in a few steps are at the door of your roomette or drawing room.

This Strata-Dome sleeping-car feature is probably one of the finest, most advanced innovations that has come out of the railroad world since the introduction of the observation car, when it was considered an advancement in the higher social order to be able to sit or stand on the brass-railed rear platform and breathe dust and get pelted with cinders for the sake of the view.

The departure of the Capitol Limited from Washington is an event. This train draws its clientele from the high-brass aristocracy of the nation's white-domed metropolis, and includes the heads of government, Army and Navy heads, foreign ambassadors, industrialists and representatives of the entire social register, also railroad officials with business in the capital.

The Capitol Limited is the "Who's-Who" train, and it carries a lot of pomp and splendor. There are stern senators and frowning dowagers, and bosses and bureaucrats, along with some lame-duck congressmen and some shiny-new and eager-faced congressmen-elect. And tonight there is the man from California and his wife, in the Santa Fe sleeper, en route to Los Angeles. The Capitol Limited connects in Chicago with the Chief, bound for the West Coast.

The passengers board the train at Union Station, Washington. There is a growing murmur in the motor compartments of the Diesel, wearing the emblem of the Capitol, and No. 5, Chicago-bound, heads out into the Potomac Valley and the land beyond, a land made sacred by the blood of patriots who died there.

The silver steel reaches out for its rendezvous with Harper's Ferry, Shenandoah, The Cherry Run, Sir John's Run, Great Cacapon, Green Ridge, Paw Paw, Okonoko, Cumberland.

Riding through the Potomac River area is always a pleasure, particularly during the cherry-blossom time when pink and white bank the green slopes and kindly valleys. The sun drops beyond the Alleghenies, scarlets and blues flash across the sky, twilight approaches and a patch of shadow moves stealthily from a bowered run. In the coolness in this twilight a homely scene appears—a farmhouse and pale faces watching the train glide around the curve, representing for these simple folk the glamour worlds somewhere beyond. Every eventide they watch for it.

"Kinda miss the old steam engine," the man says, "talkin' to the hills."

"It's so pretty," the woman says. "Might be some of you children will get to ride on it when you're grown up."

"It's a fairyland with dolls," the little girl says.

"Could war ever touch these people?" asks a city man in the Vista-Dome.

"Yes," replies the wife of the California man, "when those boys are old enough to fight."

There is nothing quite like it anywhere—this country of the Potomac and the Alleghenys—in cherry-blossom time, in the spring when those high peach orchards are corsages on the full breasts of the hills.

Deep in the great gorges, the sound of the shouting Diesel

131

horn is thrown back and forth from the ramparts, and the blade of the headlight slices the mountain face. Cumberland's lights glitter and the Capitol Limited whispers to a stop to pick up passengers for Gary, Indiana, and the West.

"All aboard!"

Past Ellerslie, Maryland; Cook's Mills, Pennsylvania; Hyndman, Pennsylvania—the train now works the Sand Patch grade, a 2.2 per cent grade. The Capitol Limited is fighting out of the mountains, struggling into the worrying hills. Down off Sand Patch, the Capitol speeds through Confluence and Ohiopyle, Pennsylvania, across Castleman's and the Youghiogheny rivers, past Indian Creek and Connellsville.

No. 5, the Capitol Limited, is performing beautifully. No. 5 is on time—10:49 P.M. The night is still young for these people in the Strata-Dome. A man comes up the stairs, a mite rumpled in trousers, slippers, and a shirt.

"Down there counting sheep," he mutters. "Say, where are we? What river is that?"

"The Youghiogheny."

"Look, there's a train!"

"Across the river. The Western Maryland."

Night in a Strata-Dome? Night is fascinating, mysterious, anywhere. In the dome there is adventure around every curve. The traveler looks for the unexpected, and finds it—perhaps in a few sleepy lights, in a sudden change of skyline, in the dull velvet sheen of the Youghiogheny, caught by the train lights, or in a freight on a siding with the glimmer of its marker lamps.

Someone starts talking about No. 97 of the B.&O. The Quick Dispatch and its night flight. The old Central States Dispatch, reaching from New England, the Jersey shore, and the Chesapeake to Cleveland, Columbus, Springfield, Chicago, and St. Louis—each city the destination of a fast-traveling No. 97.

"They're world famous," says a stocky man. "They deliver the goods. I know. I'm a commission man. Take those Banana Specials out of Locust Point, Maryland—they wheel them toward the Mississippi, toward Chicago and Akron, right over this line. You don't know the railroads until you know the fast freights."

Jacob's Creek, Fitz Henry, West Newton, Shanner, McKeesport. High, steep hills—it is getting on toward midnight.

Someone yawns. "I paid for sleeping accommodations on this train, I'm going to bed."

"Not yet," says the commission man. "You've got to see the Pittsburgh steel mills from the Strata-Dome."

The Capitol Limited glides through Braddock, Pennsylvania, ten miles from Pittsburgh, and moves on into this great industrial and river metropolis, where the Monongahela, the Ohio, the Allegheny converge. There is only one Pittsburgh, mighty beneath its shroud of smoke, the steel capital.

There is no show anywhere like this. The probing steel rails lead to the place of their birth, carrying this luxury train of the Baltimore & Ohio straight down the hot throat of the fiery hell where steel is made.

Rank on rank they stand, these batteries of fire-belching chimneys—torches against the night sky casting a yellow glow. Molten metal, crucibles, steam plumes, smoke, noise—the orchestration of the steel mills. Here the iron ore, come down from Conneaut and all the miles across the Lakes from the Mesabi Range, bound for South America through the Baltimore ports, is tortured into materials of peace and war—the plowshare and the sword.

Names are here, great names in steel—and here are the names you will see between McKeesport and New Castle:

National Tube Company (Seamless)—Left-hand side going West, Cristy Park Works, McKeesport, Pa.; National Tube Company, McKeesport, Pa. (same plant); U.S. Steel Company —Right-hand side going West, Braddock, Pa. (known as Edgar Thompson Works); Bethlehem Steel Company—Left-hand side, Rankin, Pa. (known as Rankin Plant); U.S. Steel Company— Left-hand side, Rankin, Pa. (known as Carrie Furnace); U.S. Steel Company—Both right- and left-hand side, Homestead, Pa.; Mesta Machine Co.—Left-hand side, West Homestead, Pa.; Jones and Laughlin—Both right- and left-hand side, Pittsburgh,

Pa.; Oliver Iron and Steel Company—Left-hand side, Pittsburgh, Pa.; Standard Steel Spring Co.—Left-hand side, Coraopolis, Pa.; Pittsburgh Forge Company—Left-hand side, Coraopolis, Pa.; Continental Rod Co.—Right-hand side, Coraopolis, Pa.; Russell Burdsell and Ward—Right-hand side, Coraopolis, Pa.; Jones and Laughlin (known as Aliquippa Works)—Right-hand side, Extends from West Economy to West Aliquippa; Falcon Steel Company—Right-hand side, West Aliquippa; Kidd Steel Company—Right-hand side, West Aliquippa; Colonial Steel Company—Right-hand side, Colona; Pittsburgh Tube Company—Right-hand side, Monessen; Superior Steel Company—Right-hand side, Monessen; Pittsburgh Screw & Bolt—Left-hand side, Monessen; Townsend Steel Company—Right-hand side, Fallston; Union Drawn Steel Company—Left-hand side, Beaver Falls; Moltrup Steel Products Co.—Left-hand side, Beaver Falls.

As seen while riding through the middle of this Dantesque extravaganza at midnight, in the observation dome of one of America's great name trains, the Capitol Limited, Pittsburgh steel and these gushing furnaces and stacks will be remembered for a long time. The passengers leave the dome with a new page, sharply etched, in their memory book.

Gary, Indiana, is reached at 6:54 A.M.—steel again. Travelers have come upstairs from the sleeping rooms. There is freshness in this spring morning; the land has been washed, it seems. Off to the side is Lake Michigan. It is South Chicago now, Sixty-third Street Station at 7:33 A.M. Chicago at 8:00 A.M.

The "On Time" performance of the Capitol Limited is nearly 100 per cent. It is remarkable.

The man and his wife in the Santa Fe sleeper, and other passengers for the Coast, enjoy the luxury of sleeping late. They do not have to get up and make the change across to the Dearborn Station. Later the Santa Fe sleeper will be switched into the make-up of the Santa Fe's No. 19, the Chief.

Travelers are enjoying, and will continue to enjoy, this contribution to modern railroading—the Strata-Dome sleeper—first

134

introduced in the East by the Baltimore & Ohio on its great Capitol Limited.

Finer L.C.L. Service

On the Baltimore & Ohio they have a slogan: "Constantly Doing Things—Better!"

In my book *Railroads of Today*, I told how the B.&O.'s Sentinel Service Speeds the freight car. This service was inaugurated in March, 1947, and all across the road's vast network the movement of carload shipments began moving with the same precision and under the same continuous control as does passenger traffic. I told about their traffic Blue Book, one of the most comprehensive features ever offered the railroad shipper.

And keeping pace with their slogan, the Baltimore & Ohio, in 1950, conceived and launched a new kind of service, quite in keeping with the modern railroad trend—a Time-Saver Service for Less Than Carload Freight. This is a streamline l.c.l. operation that provides door-to-door schedules with Sentinel Service dependability.

One third, or more, is saved in shipping time.

As we have pointed out in our opening chapter, the basis of American economic life is the freight car—common carrier transportation by rail. This is the *only* form of transportation which *can*—and *does*—handle *anything, anywhere, anytime,* in *any quantity*.

Though railroads do not agree on all points of the problems presented in the modern day concerning l.c.l.—and there are many—it still is a vital part of our way of life and the Baltimore & Ohio has contributed much, both from the point of view of the carrier and the shipper.

To provide a finer freight service, the B.&O. has set the pattern through combining three factors—management, methods, and men. *Management:* Constant planning to give shippers new and faster trains. *Methods:* Assuring speedy service and dependa-

135

bility. *Men:* Training and organization in yards, terminals, and offices.

Such a program provides for a better way of life in peacetime, and, through its effective co-ordination, becomes an important factor in days of stress and crisis.

The B.&O. has a great president in R. B. White, honored by the U.S. Army when he was made a colonel heading the Allegheny region when the government took them over during a strike. He knows his property and that of others. In Howard E. Simpson the road has one of this country's ablest traffic vice-presidents, and the same may be said of Operating Vice-President W. C. Baker.

CHAPTER XIV

THE VIRGINIAN

Building and Development—Coal Fields

The Virginian was built through the vision, resources, and courage of one man—H. H. Rogers.

Steel rails reached out from tidewater, searching into the Virginia hills. Eventually they reached from Sewalls Point, on Hampton Roads, Norfolk, Virginia, to Deepwater, West Virginia, a distance of 443 miles, and, thence, through the medium of the New York Central and a bridge connection over the Kanawha River, to other horizons in the Great Lakes region and along the Atlantic seaboard. And so an empire was born, an empire with its heart in the fabulous coal fields of the New River and the Pocahontas.

This man, the late H. H. Rogers, said, "It can be done!" And so ordered it—a railroad to be built out of his private funds. Such a thing had never been heard of. But H. H. Rogers said, "I will do it, for I am looking at this future railroad from the standpoint of tonnage, big tonnage." Accordingly plans were laid for a railroad that would handle traffic in the most economical and yet in the speediest manner possible. It was a pretty big order, but H. H. Rogers and those who came after were men of a caliber who do not include the word "failure" in their lexicon.

The initial moves executed by the engineers and attorneys in making reconnaissance and establishing locations for the new railroad were watched alertly by competitors, and eventually it became a game employing strategies and sharp wits.

The Virginian Railway was started in West Virginia in the name of the Deepwater Railway Company in 1896 when a four-mile construction project went up Loup Creek from Deepwater to Robson. In a chapter under the title "Virginian Coal Move," we will find a giant coal car, VGN 19146, loading at a tipple at Robson for a journey over a highly modern railroad out to Sewalls Point and a great modern coal pier.

The building of a railroad to the highly developed specifications which H. H. Rogers placed in the hands of his authorized agent was a radical departure from accepted practices, with the result that there was a lot of eyebrow lifting and a lot of skepticism; nevertheless the experts never took their eyes off the venture. And later these experts agreed that this was, indeed, modern railroad building with a vengeance.

The departure from the former methods employed in the construction and equipping of a railroad, in the light of economic results achieved, resulted in an intensive study of this sort of progressive engineering on the part of technical experts throughout the world. And the Virginian has been the model for railroad improvements, which later were applied to some of the largest and oldest systems in the United States.

Heavy was the work of blasting a right of way out of those West Virginia and Virginia hills. There was solid rock to be moved—a lot of it. But rock has never stopped the railroad builder, even when there were only strong backs and picks to do the job. Here in the Virginia hills, 10,000 laborers went to work. Fifty steam-shovels were brought in, 1,200 dump cars, and 124 locomotives.

The first grading out of Sewalls Point was started in May, 1905, and the first track put down in October near Algren, Virginia. Train service between Roanoke, Virginia, and Big Stoney began in September, 1908, and went on through to Princeton, West Virginia, in February, 1909.

Passenger service between Deepwater, West Virginia, and Roanoke was inaugurated on May 23, 1909, and through passenger service began on July 1, 1909.

The Virginian's incorporation was effected on March 8, 1907.

At the time the Virginian's originators began spiking down rails in the West Virginia hills there was not a single mine development on what is now the main line. Since that time, ninety-one mines have been directly developed by the road. It has also shared in the development of forty-seven mines on connecting branch lines which it has acquired or built. The total mines developed in this great coal field as a result of the pioneering of H. H. Rogers stand, therefore, at 138, and out of these come endless trainloads of the world's greatest economic mineral —the black diamond called coal.

The tie-up of the Virginian with the New York Central, which was effective on March 15, 1931, circumscribed at last the territorial path which H. H. Rogers originally intended to encompass. These two great railroad systems, with their lateral connections, unify the relationship of producers and shippers to the great consuming and distributing centers of the Midwest, the North Central area, and the Southeastern states by a service of the highest order.

This directness of route was the primary thought involved in the work of the engineers who planned and executed the course of the Virginian's line. To achieve this objective natural barriers had to be conquered through the construction of a chain of tunnels, bridges, and cuts. A great deal of attention had to be given to matters of grades and alignment, more attention, in fact, than had ever been characterized in the building of a railroad before.

At times the track seems almost to skip from one bridge to another. These bridges had to be high and strong, and cost had no consideration in the culmination of the builder's plan. The broad, comprehensive, far-seeing design of this undertaking also contemplated in structural phases a railroad which was to be installed with such ponderous equipment as had never before been seen.

Contrary to the practice of the older systems in routing their lines expressly to reach populous centers of passenger traffic, the Virginian, as has been pointed out, was built to render revenue from the timeless hills through brute strength. And today this road stands as an eternal monument, not only to the man who visioned it, H. H. Rogers, but to those great railroad men who came after him.

We deeply regret that space does not allow of a greater coverage of the Virginian Railway, or more of the story of these coal fields. We would like to list the coal operations and the coal operating companies along the Virginian, and the operating companies on the New York Central, the Campbell's Creek Railroad, the Kelley's Creek Railroad, and others in the Kanawha district—but it is impossible, there are too many of them.

What greater example of free enterprise in a land of free men than this Virginian.

The Virginian has been very fortunate in always having a fine board of directors. Today we find the work undertaken by the late H. H. Rogers being ably carried on by his son-in-law W. R. Coe, chairman of the executive committee, and a grandson, William Rogers Coe, Jr., vice-president and treasurer.

Always a great road, even in hard depression years, the Virginian has kept pace in the railroad world to the threshold of this modern era, and it has continued this trend through the able efforts of George D. Brooke, who arrived in 1943 from the presidency of the Chesapeake & Ohio to become chairman of the board. He was followed a year later by Frank D. Beale, who occupies the president's chair.

George Brooke brought a lot of hard-won railroad experience to the Virginian. He had been close to the roaring main line, having served as superintendent of three crack divisions on the Baltimore & Ohio. From the B.&O. he went to the Chesapeake & Ohio as assistant to the operating vice-president; then working up to general manager, operating vice-president and president. He was also president of the Nickel Plate and the Pere Marquette.

Frank Beale graduated from the University of Virginia, having majored in engineering. He spent his entire railroad life, before coming to the Virginian, with the Chesapeake & Ohio and the Nickel Plate railroads in many operating and engineering capacities before stepping into the Virginian presidency.

With the guns of World War II at last silent, the way was open for a modernization program. The Virginian, and every railroad, was war weary. Depression years had taken their toll, and war traffic had allowed time only for the most necessary of repairs. Bolts needed tightening all over the railroad, new ties went in and a general renovation put the roadway in readiness for a full load of traffic. Shops and storehouses had their faces lifted; cars and locomotives came out of the Princeton shops with that new look, ready to take their place in the coal move.

The Virginian purchased four giant 510-ton electric locomotives of 6,800 horsepower, which were delivered in 1948. They bought eight 900-class 2-6-6-6 Mallets and five 2-8-4 Berkshires for fast freight work. Heavy 2-8-8-2 Mallets were purchased from the Santa Fe, and fifteen exceptionally fine coal-burning 0-8-0 switchers were acquired for yard service.

The road has some 115 pieces of freight motive power. Six fine Pacific type engines handle the passenger traffic. Twenty-five new steel caboose cars brought this type of rolling stock to 104 and 2,500 new fifty-five-ton steel hopper cars, rebuilt in 1948 and 1949, raised the great fleet of hoppers and gondolas to around 15,360, which indicates the kind of traffic that pounds the rail from the tree-clad coal-country hills to the tidewater.

The Virginian employs centralized traffic control between Mullens and West Deepwater. Every siding on the road is equipped with a telephone at each end, making it easy for the conductor or engineer of a train to get into communication with the dispatcher. This is, indeed, a modern asset.

The longer sidings, east of Roanoke, average 7,600 feet in length with a capacity of 190 forty-foot cars; from Roanoke to Elmore, the longer sidings average 6,600 feet and will take about 150 cars. It has not been found feasible to operate trains of more than 170 cars.

The road is completely laid with 131- and 132-pound rail. The branches and passing tracks have been re-laid with 100- and 131-pound rail. New water and coaling stations have been erected. Water treating plants are located at the five major water stations. All water pumping is automatic.

When the engineers laid out the Virginian they put down the foundation for a real coal-haul road, and it has proved itself through the years. Between Victoria, 120 miles west of Norfolk, and tidewater there is no curve over 2 degrees, and, I believe, only one up to 8 degrees between Victoria and Roanoke, with very few up to 5 degrees. Near Elmore, at the edge of the West Virginia coal fields, there are a few up to 12 degrees, and from Elmore all the way to D.B. Tower, at the west end, only a few of 16 degrees. There is no restriction against any railroad equipment in service today being handled over the Virginian. Heavy grades were avoided so far as possible through the use of tunnels, of which there are thirty-four on the main line, fourteen on the various branches, an indication of the ruggedness of this coal-field country.

Practically all of the bridges on the Virginian have an E-75 Cooper's rating, which means, as explained in the Bessemer and Lake Erie chapter, that it is a very rugged structure, with a locomotive-axle loading capacity of 75,000 pounds.

The great electric power plant at Narrows, Virginia, about midway in the electrified zone of 134 miles between Mullens and Roanoke, is probably as fine a plant as you will find in the world. The electrical head is a man outstanding in his line in the United States.

In the handling of trains, particular attention is given to a rigid rule concerning tonnage. No locomotive is loaded above its rated capacity under any consideration. Never are these freight engines given extra tonnage, which means that the power is not abused. And in cold and severe weather strict measures are taken to see that the tonnage is reduced.

The Virginian has high-speed train-order stands at every open office. It has twenty-one spring switches and one hundred rail oilers. The latter are very important on a railroad that is handling heavy tonnage.

The 3,500 Virginian employees have been thoroughly indoctrinated in the railroad principles introduced by the new supervisory officials brought to the road. It is hoped that never again will it be necessary to bring in new officials from outside the

Virginian Railway family, and toward this end department heads have been directed to train capable replacements to take over at such time as it might become necessary.

The Virginian owners and the coal shippers and others are deeply appreciative of the excellent job done by these men who guide its destiny. The road performed a remarkable war service, rendering the Army and the Navy base at Norfolk every possible support in those critical days, just as in the perilous times that confront the country in the beginning of 1951 the Virginian, grown stronger through modernization, will provide the fiber and the genius for even greater transportation demands.

The entire personnel of the Virginian has proved itself loyal and efficient. The chief engineer and the maintenance-of-way engineer rank among the finest to be found anywhere. The division superintendents, the general manager, all of the officials are men of unusual railroad ability. Virginian stockholders are fortunate in having men of such caliber directing the operation of the railroad. All due credit must be given to F. D. Beale, president; G. D. Brooke, chairman of the board, and the board of directors for their accomplishments in making the Virginian a strictly modern railroad—a white diamond carrying black diamonds from the coal vaults of the hills to the great rail and water highroads of America and the world.

CHAPTER XV

THE MILWAUKEE ROAD

One Hundred Years of Progress

On November 20, 1850, old No. 1, a little eight-wheel, funnel-stack, wood-burning locomotive, out of the Norris Works in Philadelphia, hauled a little train on a little rail over five miles of the Milwaukee's parent segment, Milwaukee to Wauwatosa. And the first locomotive whistle in Wisconsin screamed its triumph.

On November 20, 1950, the Milwaukee Road—the Chicago, Milwaukee, St. Paul & Pacific—was operating over 10,670 miles of track in twelve states. Its locomotive fleet included 1,118 pieces of motive power, of which 61 were electric and 216 were Diesels; and its freight car fleet was over 57,000.

An empire of steel rails, spiked down by free enterprise.

From two open freight cars in 1850 to great fleets of modern streamliners, the most famous of which is the flashing Olympian Hiawatha, operating on a forty-five-hour schedule between Puget Sound, on the Pacific Coast, and Chicago, on the Great Lakes, one of the great name trains of America.

On September 1, 1950, the road's new head, J. P. Kiley, a great all around railroader, walked through the door marked "President" to take his place at the desk just as the Milwaukee Road was ending its first one hundred years and starting its *second century*—with "a bow to the past and a pledge to the future."

The Olympian Hiawathas

Thirteen years after the first Hiawatha took the rails for its dashing flight across the miles from Chicago to Minneapolis the Chicago, Milwaukee, St. Paul & Pacific inaugurated the present Olympian Hiawathas, operating between Chicago and Seattle-Tacoma, Washington. With the introduction of these sparkling new trains the Hiawatha service was extended 1,800 miles, as of June 29, 1947.

The Olympian Hiawathas, passing through eight states and crossing five mountain ranges, makes the 2,200-mile run to Seattle and Tacoma, in the Northwest, in forty-five hours, or nearly fourteen hours faster than former schedules. Half a day is saved to Montana and Yellowstone; a full night and part of a day to Puget Sound.

The Olympian Hiawathas are brilliant, they are different, and they are writing a new page in railroad history in the land of the Northwest. These thrilling and delightful trains have been presented pridefully by the Milwaukee as another contribution to modern railroading.

The road's former transcontinental train, the pioneer Olympian, continues in service and is now known as the Columbian. The Milwaukee Hiawathas, the four daytime streamliners operating between Chicago and the Twin Cities, celebrated their thirteenth anniversary on May 29, 1948, by appearing in completely new garb and with many major improvements and innovations.

Each of the six units of the Olympian Hiawathas represent an expenditure of $1,500,000, and they combine service, beauty, and luxury in their flashing conquest of time and space across the mountains and the plains where the first famous Olympian pathfinders wrote their story on burnished steel.

The exterior color scheme of the new Olympian Hiawathas is the traditional Milwaukee harvest orange and royal maroon. The car roofs are painted a dark sandy gray to offer the least change in appearance from dirt and weather. The trucks and entire underbody are painted out in a dull shadow black to minimize its irregularity, which contrasts with the sleekness of the upper car body.

Four-thousand-horsepower Diesel-electric locomotives haul the Olympian Hiawathas between Chicago and St. Paul–Minneapolis. Fairbanks-Morse three-unit 6,000-horsepower Diesels handle the trains between Minneapolis; Harlowton, Montana; Avery, Montana to Othello, Washington.

Giant electric locomotives are used on all Milwaukee Road trains through the Rocky, Bitter Root, and Cascade mountains, representing the longest electrified road operation in America.

The consist of the Olympian Hiawathas includes a mail-express car, baggage-dormitory car with accommodations for the dining-car employees, three day coaches, two Touralux sleeping cars, one combination coach-Touralux, a dining car, a grill-buffet-lounge car, and two Pullman cars.

Designed and built by Milwaukee engineers, the Touralux sleeping cars have fourteen lower and fourteen upper berths, offering a complete departure from the conventional type sleeping-car berths. They afford privacy and the utmost comfort by night or day. All berths are individually lighted and air conditioned. The lower berths are higher, wider, and longer. The rail fare is but little more than seat space in coaches, and considerably less than in standard Pullmans.

Combination cars offer day-coach seats and Touralux berths. Space in the combination cars is reserved for women traveling with small children.

Hiawatha Luxurest coaches have forty-eight individually controlled reclining chairs of the Sleepy Hollow type, padded with resilient foam rubber. Comfortable footrest and more room per passenger permit full relaxation.

The Tip Top Grill car provides additional dining and lounging space. This full car is radio-equipped and has a snack section serving coffee, sandwiches, and fountain specialties, and a smart cocktail lounge. This gay and original car, with its informal seating arrangement, radio, music, and entertainment, is open to all passengers aboard the Olympian Hiawatha.

Entering the dining car you have the impression of stepping

into the dining room of a fashionable hotel. There are crisp white tablecloths and a full silver and china service, set off with a real rose on each table. The usual long, narrow monotony of the conventional dining car is broken both by the table arrangement and by the use of a central break in the wall treatment, which features a three-dimensional effect in the paneling, terminating in an indirect lighting trough in the ceiling. The central areas are laminated plastic with gray-green background, relieved by a diagonal diamond leaf pattern of hawthorne leaves and flowers. The angle seating of the car strikes a new note, and the shape of the tables makes it possible to enter or leave without disturbing others.

The Olympian Hiawathas are equipped with a public-address system and radio. Carrying a portable microphone, your conductor can plug it in at the electrical switchboard in any car of the train to make station announcements, meal service announcements, or for other purposes.

In the central areas of the coaches, rectangular windows are arranged for the most satisfactory vision and without exposing the passenger to cold glass against his arm. Instead of rectangular windows, portholes are installed in lounge and vestibule sections of the coaches.

An improved type of vestibule has been built into the cars for convenience and safety. This includes a rubber tunnel between adjoining cars to keep out dirt and snow. All cars have the tight-lock type of couplers that prevent accidental uncoupling and also embrace other safety features.

The interior color schemes and motif throughout are both restful and pleasing. All lounge and dressing rooms for men and women are conveniently located and of fine appointment. The complete range of accommodations and facilities on these luxurious trains fulfill every ideal concerning modern rail travel.

The new bedroom and roomette sleeping cars with the glass-roofed Skytop Lounge represent the last word in near-hotel comfort as well as roof-top panoramas of the mountain beauty of the Cascades and the Rockies.

Let us turn now to a few of the factors engineered into these arrow-swift, shadow-smooth, and silent Olympian Hiawathas that whirl you across this scenic northern transcontinental route of the Milwaukee Road.

The car trucks are of Milwaukee design and have bolster springs located outside the truck frames to afford easier riding at the seat locations within the cars. Vertical and lateral shock absorbers, similar to those in your automobile, lessen jolts and shocks. The wheels are roller-bearing equipped. High-speed air brakes, activated by electricity, permit all cars in the train to brake simultaneously, as a unit, which makes for better and safer braking.

The new equipment embodies principles of design based on millions of miles of service. With their rigid frames and all-welded bodies of tough Cor-ten steel, the cars combine exceptional strength and moderate weight. Sidesway and annoying vibration have been eliminated to a large degree. Acceleration behind the powerful Diesel locomotives is smooth and fast; likewise, deceleration under the sure grip of the modern braking system, is accomplished with a velvet ease that is as gentle as it is effective.

Since the first Milwaukee Hiawathas were placed in operation the riding qualities of these fliers of the North have earned for the road a reputation second to none. And this in view of the fact that these Olympian Hiawathas are capable of cruising at 100 miles per hour, and of maintaining high speeds over mountain grades behind the 6,000 surging horses in the big Diesel or electric locomotives.

The deep and superfluous sheet metal skirts, used on some streamlined trains, have been omitted in the Olympian Hiawathas in order to facilitate maintenance work and also eliminate the accumulation of tons of ice and snow that collects on this skirting during the winter months.

The Milwaukee Road is the newest of the northern transcontinental lines. Its first through passenger operation was established in 1911 with the introduction of the Olympian and the Columbian, the first all-steel trains running between Chicago and Seattle-Tacoma.

Westbound, the Olympian Hiawatha leaves Chicago at 3:30 P.M., Central Standard Time, and arrives in Seattle at 10:30 A.M. and Tacoma at 11:45 A.M. the second day. Departure from Tacoma is at 1:30 P.M. and Seattle at 2:45 P.M., with arrival in Chicago at 1:45 P.M., Central Standard Time, the second day.

Your trip to or from the great Pacific Northwest is accomplished without an awareness of the passing of time and is comparable to a gay week end at your favorite resort. The tedium of train travel is completely eliminated through the luxury and comfort at your command. The constantly changing scene, your complete freedom to move through the train, the relaxation you enjoy in the Tip Top Grill and buffet car, the thrill that comes with your visit to the glass-roofed Skytop Lounge, with its bird's-eye view of majestic peaks, your enjoyment of the fine meals in the fashionable atmosphere of the dining car—all serve to create an enthusiasm for this new experience in rail travel and create regret when, all too soon, your destination is announced.

Never before have the designer's staff, you tell yourself, built so much into a train. And they have accomplished more than meets the eye, for they have built permanent beauty into these Olympian Hiawathas, not a surface shine and gloss that will quickly fade.

Too often the sparkling train of today becomes dull and shabby and travel-worn in the tomorrow that is forever charging down on us. Every train is intriguing on its maiden trip, but after the initial effort there is a speedy dimming of the luster of this proud beauty.

Fully aware of this, the designers of the Milwaukee Hiawathas have selected materials and color schemes with an eye to maintenance and long life in the original pleasing freshness of appearance. The general theme of these Hiawathas is bright, cheerful colors, a discreet use of woods and plastics in an effort to produce a homelike interior in contrast to the regimented look of transportation equipment in general.

The Olympian Hiawathas will always be new and brilliantly

different as these speed queens of the Milwaukee flash down the rails.

The New Milwaukee Hiawathas

The Chicago–Twin Cities Hiawathas have taken a prominent place in the gay parade of the trains of today. New in dress and new in motive power, these speed queens include every modern touch and feature emblematic of railroad progress.

With the speed of the wind and the color of autumn foliage they are among America's pacemakers in an era of rail transportation that transcends even the fondest dreams of yesterday's forward-looking builders.

The United States has always been travel conscious. Nothing so intrigues old John Q. Public as a time-saving piece of machinery, and any new piece of travel equipment that will get him somewhere else faster than previously instantly receives his full attention. Just let it be voiced around that the old Moonbeam Limited has a new kind of locomotive on the head end and you're going to have a struggle to get within a block of the depot at train time.

Things are a lot different on the head and rear ends than they were at the close of World War II—and in between also. The 1948 Milwaukee Hiawathas are different. With the easing of the postwar struggle to get materials, new passenger equipment began to roll out of the car shops and started breezing down the main line.

The super de luxe cars in operation in the Milwaukee Hiawatha service today are part of a total order for 127 placed with the Milwaukee shops in 1947. On May 29, 1948, some of these cars were included in the make-up of Twin-Cities Hiawathas that were making the 410-mile run out of Chicago in 375 minutes, making seven station stops.

The 4,000-horsepower Diesel on the head end of these Milwaukee Hiawathas is pretty much the same as any other Diesel, except for its distinctive color band and the winged identification lettering, but the rear-end Sky Top observation is something else again and strikes a distinctly original note. Its rounded rear is studded with a built-in Mars light, which flashes oscillating red beams as a warning to other trains when the Hiawatha slows or makes an unscheduled stop.

The consist of the four Milwaukee Hiawathas varies from ten to sixteen cars. A typical make-up includes a baggage car with office quarters for the conductor; day coaches with reclining seats and adjustable footrests; spacious lounge, smoking rooms, and buffet-lounge cars called Tip Top Taps for the serving of light refreshments; forty-eight-seat dining cars with stainless steel kitchens and deep-freeze units and all modern devices for the storage and preparation of food; reserved seat parlor cars that include drawing rooms; and the observation parlor car with the Sky Top lounge. All cars are air conditioned and equipped with public-address system and radio.

Improved roller-bearing trucks, of Milwaukee design, contribute to smoother riding at all speeds. Air brakes are of the Westinghouse high-speed-control type, incorporating the electric feature.

As in the Olympian Hiawatha, the exterior color scheme utilizes the traditional Milwaukee colors of harvest orange and maroon accented by a restrained touch of stainless steel and modern script lettering of the name Hiawatha.

The new cars constitute the fifth re-equipment of Hiawatha trains since 1935, making possible improved service over the entire road, since replaced cars will be thoroughly reconditioned and used in less important trains in other parts of the system.

The structural design of the new Hiawatha cars combines several important factors, namely: structural strength with minimum weight to create a car meeting all present-day requirements as to tests and design specifications; simplicity in design for ease of fabrication, assembly, and maintenance in coach yards; and balance, to give maximum stability and riding comfort at all speeds.

Heating is an important item on the Milwaukee and the designers have given it intensive study. Vapor Zone heat with copper-fin radiation is used along the side wall, and an overhead coil heats all fresh and recirculated air.

Air conditioning consists of Waukesha mechanical and safety steam jet. The steam-jet air-conditioning unit used on all cars built in 1946 and 1947 is completely new in its assembly and application to these cars. Further, Milwaukee engineers, drawing on their extensive experience in the operation, servicing, and maintenance of this type of equipment and working in collaboration with the Safety Car Heating and Lighting Company, have created an entirely new arrangement for this particular unit which is mounted inside of the car body. It comprises a steam-jet unit said to surpass any of the older conventional units, both in economy of operation and convenience for "on the train" servicing.

Primary lighting in all passenger-carrying cars is fluorescent, with incandescent emergency lights. Power for the fluorescent light is furnished from a motor alternator installed on the car and power for the emergency lighting is supplied directly from the batteries. An unusual feature in the body of the coaches and parlor cars is the development of the continuous fluorescent lighting along the front edge of the luggage rack.

Seats in the body of the coaches are the Sleepy Hollow type. Chairs and sofas in lounge rooms were designed and built at Milwaukee shops. Coach seat upholstery is done in chocolate brown and chartreuse yellow in one car, and cool green and gray in the other.

All lounge rooms are equipped with two porcelain washstands and a dental bowl arranged in a compact unit, with towels, paper cups, and convenient electric razor outlets.

The new Hiawatha coaches carry out cheerful interior color schemes in two alternating designs, using laminated plastic paneling for maintenance and beauty, coupled with the warmth of bleached walnut wood. The designer has produced practical interior wall treatments designed to look well for many years. Harmonizing walnut bulkheads are diagonally accented with the emblem of the Hiawatha Indian trade-mark, finished in gold lacquer, to pick up the continuity of the exterior vestibule emblem.

The lunch-lounge car is designed with its forward half arranged for serving sandwiches, soft drinks, and light meals, the galley and bar amidships, and the regulation lounge area in the rear half of the car. Diagonal seating and restaurant-type booths are featured in the snack room area, whereas cocktail lounge seating is employed in the lounge area. Bright and colorful fabrics are used to produce a clublike atmosphere. The car is completely carpeted in the mottled rust pattern found throughout the entire train.

The attractive dining car has places for forty-eight. Except for the seating arrangement, the general design follows the pattern of the same car on the Olympian Hiawatha. The new parlor car offers more seats than formerly, and the seats are of an entirely new and special design, created for this train. Soft gray-green laminated plastic is used on the walls, augmented by a blonde walnut trim. The drawing room at the end of the car is paneled in English oak realwood laminated plastic, with comfortable seating for four opposite each other in the window area, which is equally convertible into a complete lower berth for purposes of naps or illness. In addition there is a comfortable armchair. Toilet facilities are provided in an annex.

The Sky Top solar lounge has been carefully designed to retain impact strength and yet offer maximum visibility for the scenic views of the beautiful trip to and from the Twin Cities. On clear nights, the lighting can be arranged on the interior for full view of the moon and stars. The glass used in this area is special heat-and-glare resistant exterior and interior panes, and is of a triple-pane type. The dome area is 90 per cent transparent, with an aero-dynamic terminating shape. The solar lounge area features a curved davenport at the extreme rear and comfortable lounge chairs along each side, with magazine and end tables. Varying colors in shades of rust, green, gray, and lime are used in the identifying Hiawatha block pattern fabrics throughout the car.

The ladies' lounge in the coach cars is entirely feminine, utilizing soft gray-green and ivory laminated plastic paneling. The lounge divan is upholstered in a pleasing gray-green fabric. The walls are accented with carefully selected French costume prints on one wall and floral prints on the opposite wall. Adequate mirror facilities, with stainless steel trim, supply the keynote of the washbasin and vanity area.

The four-wheel cast steel high-speed trucks of the Milwaukee Hiawathas were designed by Milwaukee Road engineers and assembled at the Milwaukee shops. The design of these trucks is based on the results obtained from many tests conducted over a period of several years and they embody the most forward ideas developed in these tests.

In contrast to the Olympian Hiawatha trains, the treatment of the exterior paint scheme of the Milwaukee Hiawatha cars retains the continuous horizontal bands of maroon color through the letter-board area and the window area, terminating in an angular panel at the new Sky Top lounge car, the single note of family resemblance to the Olympian Hiawatha scheme. These individualized treatments, thoroughly harmonious, and in similar trend, give complete individuality and identity to the two well-known trains.

CHAPTER XVI

BESSEMER & LAKE ERIE RAILROAD

A Great Ore Carrier

The Bessemer opened its first line the year that the golden spike was hammered home at Promontory, Utah, in 1869. Today the Bessemer has a total mileage of 212 miles, with rails reaching from the Erie shore down to the great steel districts around Pittsburgh.

The fires of the steel mills light the night sky. Ore—iron ore —moves ceaselessly to feed the hungry furnaces that are breathing steel for American industry, steel for the sinews of war. And the Bessemer plays a vital part in the flow of ore that the railroads have brought from the Mesabi Range through the port of Duluth and across the Lakes by ore boat to Conneaut.

"Only 212 miles?" we hear someone say. "Small railroad, this Bessemer. Don't hear much about it out my way." No, perhaps not. But remember this. *More tonnage passes over each mile of the Bessemer in one day than any other Class 1 railroad in the United States.*

Let us say that we are driving between two metropolitan centers in our car. We will pass quite a lot of those behemoth trucks that are freighting on the highways. Maybe a couple hundred of them. Two hundred is quite a lot of trucks, when you take time to count them. Two hundred men at the wheels. A lot of truck drivers.

Yet it would take 950 ten-ton trucks to haul a Bessemer train of ore. Almost one thousand ten-ton trucks to haul a like amount of ore from Conneaut, say, down to XB Tower, North Bessemer Yard.

Let us consider these two cities between which we are driving

155

as being a hundred miles apart. If all of the Bessemer freight cars owned by them were placed in one train it would reach from city to city. One hundred miles of just freight cars.

We hear a lot about freight rates, and old John Q. Public groans. Someone has told him the railroads are robbers—capitalistic giants, tramping the little guy into the dust. Wait a minute.

The Bessemer must haul one ton of freight three miles to pay for a three-cent postage stamp, for the rate on ore is just one cent per ton per mile.

Old John Q. couldn't haul a suitcase in his automobile a mile for three cents. But we are not concerned here with economic comparisons, but a few small figures. A few simple figures such as these are easy to digest, easy to remember when all the shouting is going on.

The beginning of the Bessemer came when, in 1865, the Bear Creek Railroad was incorporated. However, it might be recorded that the *real* beginning was a contract for construction of twenty-one miles of track over the Otter Creek route from a connection with the Erie & Pittsburgh Railroad. In 1867 the original name was changed to Shenango & Allegheny Railroad Company. Construction authorized by an act of the legislature was completed to the coal mines of Pardoe, Pennsylvania, in 1869, and for many years Pardoe was the southern terminus of the road.

The Bessemer & Lake Erie Railroad Company was incorporated in 1900, and a railroad was constructed from Kremis, Pennsylvania, to KO Junction, 8.81 miles, which was opened for operation in 1902.

Previous to the incorporation of the Bessemer & Lake Erie Railroad Company, we find such progressive incorporations as the Connoquenessing Valley Railroad in 1881, changed in 1882 to the West Penn & Shenango Railroad by court order. This company was reorganized as the Pittsburgh, Butler & Shenango Railroad Company in 1889, and was operated by the Shenango & Allegheny Railroad until its consolidation with the Pittsburgh, Shenango & Lake Erie Railroad in 1890.

There were further reorganizations and consolidations, with

156

new construction from time to time probing the countryside. A lot of this railroad building followed old tow paths, which offered sound and stable roadbeds.

In 1888, the Northeastern-Ohio Railroad Company was organized and secured right of way and valuable rights at the harbor of Conneaut, Ohio. This road consolidated with the Pittsburgh, Shenango & Lake Erie Railroad Company, and, following another name change, pushed the steel through from Albion, to Conneaut Harbor, beginning operation in 1892.

The Bessemer & Lake Erie Railroad Company by lease and agreement effective April 1, 1901, made with the Pittsburgh, Bessemer & Lake Erie Railroad Company, assumed control and operation of the Pittsburgh, Bessemer and Lake Erie Railroad Company and the Meadville, Conneaut Lake & Linesville Railroad Company.

In 1906, the Bessemer leased that portion of its lines extending from North Bessemer to East Pittsburgh—8.04 miles of main line, with lands and tracks. The Pittsburgh, Bessemer & Lake Erie Railroad Company and the Meadville, Conneaut Lake & Linesville Railroad Company were merged with the Bessemer & Lake Erie Railroad Company under a joint agreement of merger dated June 28, 1948, and filed in the office of the Secretary of the Commonwealth of Pennsylvania on October 31, 1949.

The Bessemer & Lake Erie Railroad Company, at the close of 1949, owned and operated 211.54 miles of main line, 202 miles of sidings and yards, 139 miles of second track, and 23 miles of traffic spurs.

Line Modernization

The Bessemer has consistently followed the policy of revising its line in order that better transportation service could be rendered. The rail size has been increased at intervals since the original track carried those first trains of the Shenango & Allegheny road. Those rails were very light. Then came the sixty-pound rail of the Pittsburgh, Shenango & Lake Erie Railroad.

This was raised to a hundred pounds per yard in 1896-97, and this weight was standard for many years.

It was in 1917 that the 130-pound standard of rail was adopted. In 1934, this rail was replaced by 131-pound rail. The 152-pound rail was adopted in 1939, and in 1948 a standard of 155 pounds was adopted.

At the beginning of 1950 the Bessemer had spiked down about ninety miles of the 152-pound rail on the main track and thirty-six miles of main line 155-pound rail. The application of heavier rail over the years indicates the progressive policy of the road in meeting the needs of heavier tonnage and heavier power.

It is interesting to note, in this connection, that the Bessemer since about 1930 has used a cross section of a steel rail in its trade-mark. However, at the time the road adopted the 100-pound rail in 1896-97 a similar trade-mark was originated by a man named E. H. Utley, according to Freeman H. Hubbard's book *Railroad Avenue*, who later became vice-president and general manager.

The difficulties the Bessemer encountered on what was called the Hartstown Swamp line began shortly after the turn of the century. In straightening the line across a part of Pymatuning Swamp, just north of Hartstown, Pennsylvania, what seemed to be a bottomless sinkhole was encountered. The sinkhole was constantly swallowing filling material, using 15,000 carloads up to the time the track was put in service in 1909. By 1916, 25,250 cars of filling material had been unloaded on the Swamp Line.

Since then additional filling went to lay the foundation for a second track, for raising the grade and further stabilizing the embankment. By 1946, 32,649 carloads of filling material had been used. All ore traffic flows over the line, which is the southbound main track at this point.

Other difficult main-track problems, as they concerned curves and grades, have been met and ironed out. One was the Porter Cut-off, which in its eleven miles required over 2,500,000 cubic yards of fill.

In the years, many high summits have been eliminated, always with an eye to reducing the grades over which the great ore trains move. On all new line the rate of grade was reduced on curves to offset the resistence of the curve, something that was done by early engineers, who performed miracles as far back as the days of the Pittsburgh, Shenango & Lake Erie Railroad Company before 1900.

Realizing that the ore route from Lake Erie to the steel mills was a vital economic artery, the Bessemer built solidly and well the great Allegheny River Bridge, completing it while World War I roared to a climax. This bridge was one of the first in which silicon steel was used. The bridge was engineered for very heavy traffic, having an E-75 loading, which is somewhat heavier than the general specifications of modern bridges. E-75 loading means it was designed for single locomotive axle loading of 75,000 pounds.

The original wooden floor of the bridge was removed in 1934 and replaced by a T-Tri-Lok floor constructed of three and one-half inch steel tees placed close together and locked in place by steel crossbars. The whole was then filled with concrete. Steel plates are used for sidewalks and H-beam posts for supporting the pipe railings, thus, except for the track ties, all wood has been eliminated in the structure. The tracks are GEO construction and are fully ballasted.

Down through the ages, a bridge has been a gauge of civilization. Perhaps nothing could better exemplify the rock solidness of the Bessemer than this Allegheny River Bridge, built to conquer a river, to carry endless rolling wheels coming from their rendezvous with the ore boats at Conneaut. It stands as a gateway to the steel mills, as it spans the Allegheny between River Valley and Blacks Run. Here the ore trains are already slowing for their approach to XB Tower at North Bessemer, close down to the flaming stacks of the steel mills.

Across the Allegheny River Bridge in 1919 rolled 6,734,280 gross tons, 12,462,451 tons in 1942. And in between millions and millions of tons counted off the rail lengths at the Allegheny crossing. Between World War II and Korea many million more tons of the red ore that can be beaten into a plowshare or a sword came down the Bessemer line.

Conneaut Harbor

Conneaut Harbor is important. The red ore that first moved from mine to dock by rail is again loaded to the hopper car for the final stage of its journey. And this transfer from the grimy bellies of the ore boats to the bellies of the ore cars is another of those things that have made the United States great. We can sum it up in one word. *Machines!* The ability to produce has made us great as a nation. We strive constantly to do things faster and better. We have an example at Conneaut Harbor, the great Ohio ore port on Lake Erie.

The first cargo of ore—1,250 tons—arrived at Conneaut on November 6, 1892. It was unloaded in five hours. In 1947, a cargo of 18,962 tons was unloaded from a lake boat in four hours and forty-five minutes.

Before the ore boats began pushing their blunt bows into Conneaut Harbor, it was mostly the home of fishing boats and small craft. The first ore dock went up in 1891-92. It was 1,978 feet long and of light timber construction, built by the railroad, which had brought its track into Conneaut from Albion, Pennsylvania. Brown & King machines were used in combination with ore bridges, which distributed ore either into cars or storage piles back of the dock.

Six Brown hoists were installed in 1892; three in 1893; and four Kings in 1896. Ore at that time was shoveled by hand in the hold of the boat into buckets of about one ton capacity. These were lifted by the hoists, a dog released and the buckets dumped the ore or coal into the car or the stock pile.

In 1897-98, Dock Nos. 2 and 3 were built. No. 2 dock was equipped with what was called a "fast" plant, a new design of ore-handling machines, and No. 3 dock was equipped with a car dumper for the loading of coal into boats. In 1899, Dock No. 2 had twelve machines in its "fast" plant, which, in a test, unloaded a cargo of 6,155 tons of ore in nine hours, establishing a record. This represented really fast work in ore handling, in view of the hand-shoveling necessary.

As boats and cargoes grew in size, constantly improved and

Wabash #24, the new Bluebird, east of Decatur, Ill., enroute to Chicago on the Decatur Division. Courtesy, Wabash RR.

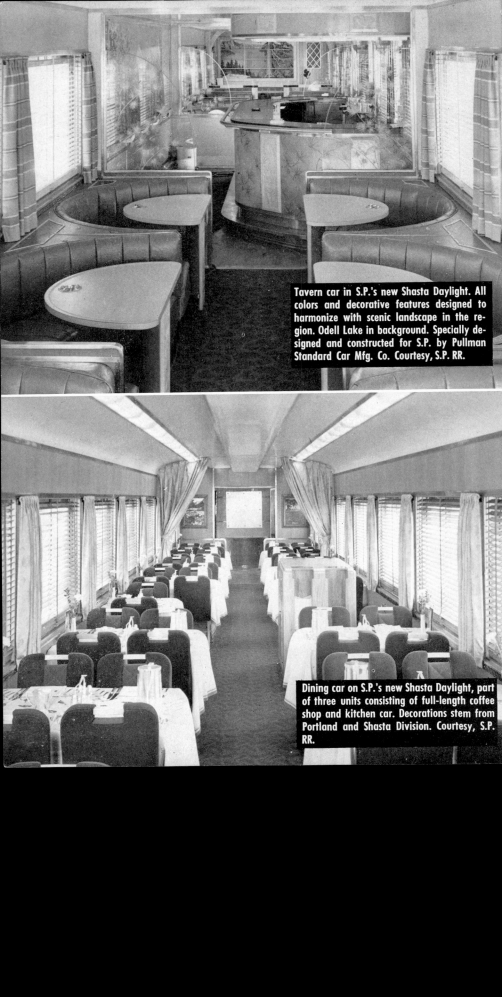

Tavern car in S.P.'s new Shasta Daylight. All colors and decorative features designed to harmonize with scenic landscape in the region. Odell Lake in background. Specially designed and constructed for S.P. by Pullman Standard Car Mfg. Co. Courtesy, S.P. RR.

Dining car on S.P.'s new Shasta Daylight, part of three units consisting of full-length coffee shop and kitchen car. Decorations stem from Portland and Shasta Division. Courtesy, S.P. RR.

View from the cab of a Western Maryland Diesel at Emory Grove, Md., with operator about to hand up orders. Eastward manifest train hauled by two E.M.D. GP-7 1,500 h.p. Diesels. Hagerstown Division. Courtesy, Western Maryland RR.

Returning the empties to the mines. Western Maryland #1407, Class J-1, 4-8-4 type, with seventy-six cars passing Williamsport, Md., at forty miles per hour on the West Subdivision of the Hagerstown Division. Photo by R. H. Kindig.

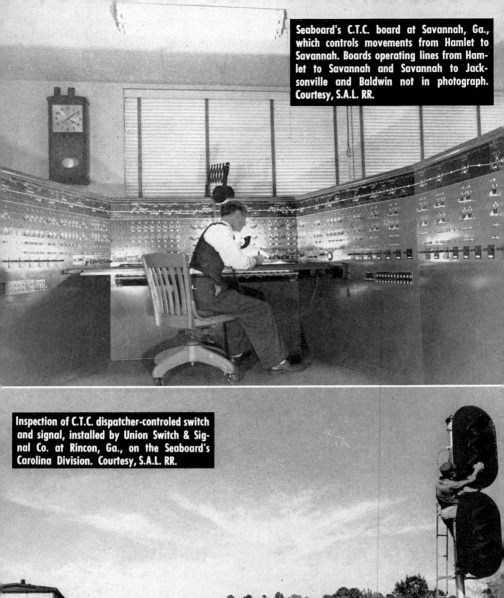

Seaboard's C.T.C. board at Savannah, Ga., which controls movements from Hamlet to Savannah. Boards operating lines from Hamlet to Savannah and Savannah to Jacksonville and Baldwin not in photograph. Courtesy, S.A.L. RR.

Inspection of C.T.C. dispatcher-controled switch and signal, installed by Union Switch & Signal Co. at Rincon, Ga., on the Seaboard's Carolina Division. Courtesy, S.A.L. RR.

Santa Fe's second #22, the El Capitan, with fourteen cars and Diesel 35 leaving Trinidad, Colo., on the First District of the New Mexico Division. Photo by R. H. Kindig.

C.&E.I. #58, northbound Thunderbolt, crack manifest train hauled by Diesel 1408 4,000 h.p. E.M.D. E-7 leaving Terre Haute, Ind. Danville Division. Courtesy, C.&E.I. RR.

Air view of the busy metropolis of Mobile, Alabama, showing the fine port and harbor. Courtesy, Frisco Lines.

Forward end of the Milwaukee's Skytop Lounge Cars used on the Twin Cities Hiawathas showing parlor chairs. Courtesy, Milwaukee RR.

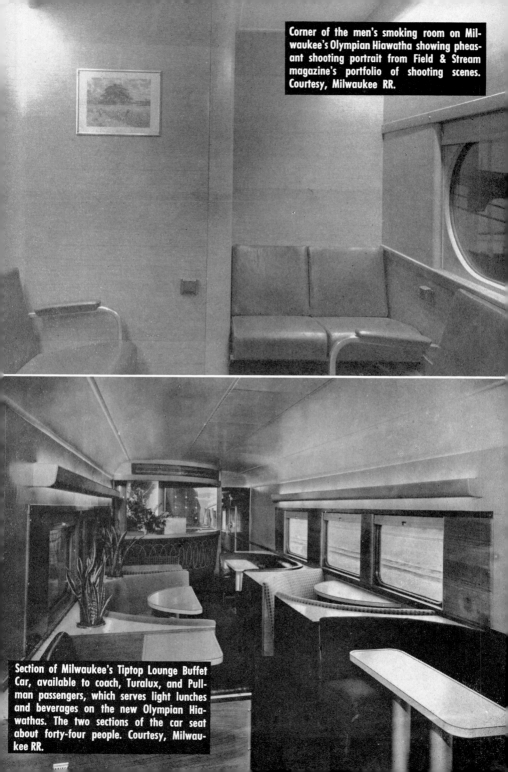

Corner of the men's smoking room on Milwaukee's Olympian Hiawatha showing pheasant shooting portrait from Field & Stream magazine's portfolio of shooting scenes. Courtesy, Milwaukee RR.

Section of Milwaukee's Tiptop Lounge Buffet Car, available to coach, Turalux, and Pullman passengers, which serves light lunches and beverages on the new Olympian Hiawathas. The two sections of the car seat about forty-four people. Courtesy, Milwaukee RR.

Santa Fe #17, the Super Chief, with E.M.D. Diesel 303, climbing Raton Pass on the 1.99 grade at Starkville, Col., on the First District of the New Mexico Division. Photo by R. H. Kindig.

modernized unloading machinery reduced the time for discharging the cargo of red ore. In 1912, 10,636 tons were unloaded in two hours and fifty minutes. In 1942, 17,008 tons went from the hold of the ore boat into the cars in four hours flat.

With the construction of Dock No. 4 in 1888-89 the Pittsburgh & Conneaut Dock Company equipped it with the first Hulett Ore Unloader machines. A Hulett machine has electrically operated clamshell buckets, each of which can take an average bite of seventeen tons of ore and lift it out of the hold to the dumping point.

The original timber dock at Conneaut was replaced by a reinforced concrete structure in 1923-26. This was built back of the old dock, and the channel was widened for the handling of larger boats. This dock was 2,178 feet long and was carried on caissons capable of sustaining the heaviest of ore-handling machines. In 1928, the dock was extended 264 feet.

In 1941-42 more work at the inner harbor was necessary to take care of the new and larger ore boats, which were 640 feet in length. When this work was completed the entire inner harbor was surrounded by modern concrete and steel docks. Docks 2 and 3, however, still had partial timbered portions at the inner ends but these were rebuilt with concrete topping.

Dock No. 4's five modern Hulett machines handle ore-unloading operations. Extensive improvements in tracks and yard have made the Conneaut terminal completely modern, with twenty-eight miles of track exclusive of main-line track.

Just how important Conneaut is can be seen when it is revealed that the Bessemer & Lake Erie is the world's top-ranking railroad for total ore tonnage handled from a single port. It ranks second for total ore tonnage handled from all ports by a single railroad, which indicates the position of the Bessemer & Lake Erie in the great ore traffic.

The average load of ore that went into Bessemer cars in 1929 was 61.15 net tons. This average had grown to 87.70 net tons in 1948, an all-time record for ore.

Some idea of the enormous ore traffic may be gathered by an examination of the following work sheets.

(I)

BUSINESS OF MAY 18, 1950

ORE BOATS

Name	Time Started	Time Finished	Cars Loaded Far'l	N. Bess.	McKp.	Don.	Total	Ore Docked
Fraser	2:35a	9:50a		222				
O. Thompson	10:20a	2:35p		142				
Thomas	7:45p	11:45a		164				
J. Davidson	12:15p	5:10a		122				
(Dock)				40				
		Ore		690				

COAL BOATS

Name	Started	Finished	Cargo	Fuel
Conneaut	6:22a	10:10a	75 Huber, 19 Ford	2 Emory
Halloway	3:05p	10:24p	182 Meek	1 Geist, 1 Sherwin
Huron	11:07p	3:18a	31 Morgan, 62 Huber	2 Emory
Alpena	3:35a	until 5:00a	5 Cashner, 1 Pollock	1 Emory
			6 Huber, 20 Ford	
				Coal ....

OTHER BOATS

Name	Started	Finished	Cargo	Fuel

Remarks

Fuel
4 Elephant
4 Kraus
/8 coal
Total
96
184
95
33
408
Total

		Overtime	
Crews	Tied Up	Hrs.	Mins.
Loop	2:30p		
Puller	2:30p		
Scale	2:30p		
Coal Hill	2:30p		
Loop	10:30p		
Puller	10:30p		
Scale	10:30p		
Coal Hill	10:30p		
Loop	6:30a		
Puller	6:30a		
Scale	6:29a		
Coal Hill	6:15a		
Total			

YARD HELPERS IN CAR DUMP EMPTY YARD

No. Men	Called	Tied Up	Time on Duty	
			Hrs.	Mins.
1	6:30a	2:30p		
1	2:30p	10:30p		
1	10:30p	6:30a		

PILOT ON P & C DOCK CO. CRANE

2	6:00a	2:00p		

SWITCH TENDERS

1	6:30a	2:30p		
1	2:30p	10:30p		
1	10:30p	6:25a		

163

Fri., June 2, 1950—3:35 P.M.
  CC-44

Steamer	Due	Date	Est. Start	Unloading Finish	Est. No. of Cars
Dunlap	Working	6/2		8:00p	200
Norway	8:00p	2	8:30p	12:30a	136
Sylvania	4:00a	3	4:00a	8:00a	71
Cowle	6:00a	3	8:30a	1:00p	148
Manual	11:00a	3	1:30p	5:15p	143
Billings	3:00p	3	5:45p	9:30p	63
Fairless	7:00p	3	10:00p	4:00a	210
McNaughton	2:00p	4	2:00p	6:30p	199
Voorhees	10:00p	4	10:00p	4:00a	209
Gary	3:00a	5	5:00a	8:00a	168
J. T. Hutchinson	5:00a	5	8:30a	1:15p	185
Watson	1:00p	5	1:45p	6:15p	(117)
Sloan	6:00p	5	6:45p	11:30p	(182)
Paul	1:00a	6	3:00a		58
Olds	5:00a	6			216
Finland	8:00a	6			147
Filbert	11:00a	6			174
Phipps	9:00p	6			156

Coal		
Alpena	8:00p	2
Kling	1:00a	3
D. Z. Norton	3:00a	3
Munson	7:00a	3
Conneaut	6:00a	5
Watson	7:00p	5

Ore	XB	McK	Farrell	Donora	Dock
Gr.13	7466			6000	
Gr.13	10725				
Gr.12	Sp	5000			4573
Gr.13	11717				
Gr.13	3022			6000	
Gr.16	5000				3991
Gr.13	16621				
Gr.13	7447			6000	
Gr.13	16542				
Gr.13	4954			6000	
Gr.13	14617				
Gr.13	14000 est.				
Gr.13	14400 "				
Gr.12		4000			6185
Gr.13	16600				
Gr.13	11347				
Gr.13	13401				
Gr.13	12000				

2100 Huber & Morgan car for car 1500 Ford fuel Emory
4500 Castner, 4600 Castner & Ford car for car fuel Emory
9700 Majestic finish Courtney fuel Valco
4500 Potts finish Platz, 5100 Elephant fuel Elephant
2300 Huber & Morgan car for car, 4300 Ford fuel Emory
13300 Harper

Locomotive Performance

As this is set down, the power on the Bessemer & Lake Erie, with the exception of four Diesel-electric switch engines, is steam. However, early in 1950 orders were placed for fourteen Diesel road locomotive units of 1,500 horsepower each for mainline freight service, with an additional five single-unit 1,500-horsepower Diesel switching locomotives.

The standard locomotive for heavy road service in the latter part of 1949 was the Texas type 2-10-4, a great locomotive, with forty-seven in service. These engines have performed remarkably. They haul not only ore, with which this chapter is principally concerned, but all products of the mines of the region, as well as general freight.

This Texas type power has a tractive effort, with booster, of 109,935 pounds. The weight, loaded, is 907,000 pounds, of which 373,700 is on the drivers. The length over striking plate is 104 feet 6 inches. The tender is 47 feet long, and it has a tender capacity of 23,000 gallons of water and 25 tons of coal.

These 2-10-4's are Bessemer H-class locomotives, and a road engine and two helpers on the rear end out of Conneaut will handle 13,050 tons, or about 110 cars, to Albion in temperatures about 35 degrees. Two H-class engines will handle this tonnage to KO Junction. Here tonnage is reduced to 11,400 tons.

When the cars set off at KO Junction are enough to make a train, crews and engines from Albion haul them to North Bessemer. At Branchton, tonnage is reduced by four cars or to about 10,900 tons.

Normally the running time of an ore train between Albion and North Bessemer is about eight hours.

Northbound runs with empties employ two H-class engines for 150 cars, or 125 cars with one engine. Coal and water are taken at Branchton. Southbound, coal and water are taken at KO Junction and Branchton.

Northbound loads include steel, coal, and cement, with a tonnage of 8,900 tons, pulled by two of the H-class locomotives. Tonnage is reduced to 7,450 tons at Branchton for the 1 per cent grade to Harrisville. Here trains can fill out to 10,000 tons and one H-class engine can handle the train through to Albion.

The table that follows gives the record of a normal ore train run between Albion, Pennsylvania, and North Bessemer with steam power. Note the tonnage reduction at KO Junction and Branchton, which we have already referred to.

RECORD OF RUN OF NORMAL ORE TRAIN
June 22, 1950
Weather 80 deg.—Good Rail
Conductor, L. W. VanDusen; engineer, H. A. Engle
Engines 625 and 647

Leaving Albion: 109 ore, 12,044 gross tons, 13,025 rating tons.

Set off 13 ore at KO Junction account heavier grade; leaving there with 96 ore, 10,589 gross tons, 11,453 rating tons.

Set off 4 ore at Branchton account heavier grade; leaving there with 92 loads, 10,152 gross tons, 10,980 rating tons.

9 tons resistance used per car.

The capacity of cars was 55 90-ton; 33 70-ton; 21 50-ton—total 109.

There were 9,510 short tons of ore in the 109 cars.

Station	Time	Speed	Remarks
Albion—called	10:00 A.M.		
RX Tower (south end Albion Yard)	10:42	12	
Springboro	10:56	39	
Conneautville	11:02	34	
Dicksonburg	11:11	23	
Harmonsburg	11:24	14	
Meadville Jct.	11:30	30	
Hartstown	11:41	40	
KO Junction Yard	11:55 12:38 P.M.	19	Set off 13 ore. Took water on both engines. Made walking and running inspection of train.
KX South End (south end KO Jct. Yard)	12:46	12	
Greenville (North Main Street)	12:56	14	
KY	1:16	26	
Fredonia	1:26	36	

167

Station	Time	Speed	Remarks
Coolspring (Porter Cut-off)	1:30	42	
Filer	1:50	24	
Grove City	1:56	35	Speed limit over crossing.
Reed	1:59	25	
Harrisville	2:09	30	
Branchton Yard	2:14	19	Set off 4 ore. Took coal
	2:51		and water. Made walking and running inspection of train.
Claytonia	3:02	29	
Euclid	3:12	22	
Queen Jct.	3:15	33	
Butler (yard limits)	3:48	20	Speed limit over crossing.
BD Tower	4:03	40	
Houseville	4:25	16	
Curtisville Yard	4:45	15	
SU Tower (south end of yard)	4:48	29	
Deer Creek	4:55	40	
River Valley	4:58	30	Speed limit over Allegheny River Bridge.
East Oakmont	5:03	24	
XB Tower (north end Bessemer Yard)	5:10	18	
Tied up	5:41 P.M.		

On duty 7 hours 41 minutes. Running time between terminals 6 hours 59 minutes.

It was necessary to yard this train on two tracks: final terminal time 41 minutes. Had train been yarded on one of the long tracks in ore yard, which would have held entire train, final terminal time would have been approximately 18 minutes.

General Superintendent's Office
Greenville, Pa.
June 27, 1950

Note: In computing tonnage the resistance figure given is added to the total weight of each car.

The tonnage leaving Albion with steam power was 13,025 tons for 109 loads. Tonnage was reduced at two points—KO Junction and Branchton.

In the following table of Diesel locomotive performance, the tonnage was practically the same—12,983 tons with 110 cars. *But there was no tonnage reduction.*

168

DIESEL LOCOMOTIVE PERFORMANCE
July 22, 1950

Units 701A-701B-705A-705B called Albion 2:30 A.M.; tied up North Bessemer 10:10 A.M. On duty 7 hours 40 minutes. Weather 52 deg. Good rail.

Albion: Got train off main track; leaving had 110 loads, 11,993 gross tons, 12,983 rating tons.

North Bessemer: Yarded train on track 38 east.

Conductor reported only one slack action, which was when making release of brakes at Branchton station.

Engineer G. W. Burnett operated engine Albion to Branchton and Butler to North Bessemer.

Station	Time	Speed	Amps	Remarks
RX Tower	3:19 A.M.	11	400	
Springboro	3:37	33	325	
Conneautville	3:42	26	375	
Dicksonburg	3:55	15	560	
Harmonsburg	4:08	12	630	Slowest speed on hill 11 mph; highest amperage 675. No slipping; no sand used.
Meadville Jct.	4:15	25	380	
Hartstown	4:26	37	310	Throttle closed at Patton's Bridge. Dynamic brake applied at Patton's Bridge at 37 mph; released at KO Jct. at 20 mph. Train brakes not used.
KO Jct.	4:36	20	. . .	
KO Jct. Yard	4:39	20	350	
KX South End	4:43	17	520	
Williamsons Rd.	4:48	11	680	
East Ave.	4:55	11	690	
Fredonia Rd.	4:59	11	690	Slowest speed on hill 11 mph; highest amperage 690. No slipping; no sand used.
KY	5:11	20	450	
Fredonia	5:22	28	350	
Coolspring (PCO)	5:27	40	190	
Cornell Viaduct	5:30	32	325	
Kimble Viaduct	5:39	22	425	
Filer	5:51	19	455	
Grove City	5:57	34	300	
Reed	6:00	23	410	Slowest speed on hill 20 mph; highest amperage 450.
Carter	6:08	23	410	
Harrisville	6:12	19	460	Dynamic brake applied at first road crossing south of Harrisville at 23 mph; released just south of Branchton road crossing at 13 mph. Made
Branchton	6:18	16	. . .	
UN Tower	6:21-6:49			
Hallston	7:06	26	355	

169

Station	Time	Speed	Amps	Remarks
Claytonia	7:09	16	525	6-pound brake pipe reduction at
Euclid	7:25	14	525	Wick at 31 mph, increased to 11
				pounds, graduated off at Branchton
				station at 16 mph. Moved via
				northward track Branchton to
				bridge 1, Butler.
				Slowest speed on hill 10 mph; highest
				amperage 725.
				Note: This movement was made
				on a reverse track, apparently mak-
				ing no difference as speed was
				same as though used normal track.
				Slipped several times, Sherwin to
Queen Jct.	7:30 A.M.	30	...	Euclid; used sand intermittently.
				Dynamic brake applied 1 mile south
				of Euclid at 20 mph, released at
				Calvin yard 1000-foot board at 12
				mph. Made 5-pound brake pipe re-
				duction at Tasa Mine, released at
Oneida	7:39	29	...	Sunbury undergrade. Made a 6-
Calvin	7:45	13	150	pound reduction at old Oneida, fol-
Butler	7:56	12	175	lowed by a 2-pound reduction, re-
Nigger Cut 8 deg.				leased at 16 mph ½ mile north of
curve	8:04	24	390	Calvin yard 1000-foot board.
BD Tower	8:11	33	315	
Rockdale	8:19	12	630	
West Saxonburg	8:34	10	700	
Houseville	8:45	10	700	Slowest speed on hill 9 mph; highest
Ivywood	8:51	24	375	amperage 750. Dynamic brake ap-
				plied ½ mile south of Ivywood at
				28 mph, released 1 mile north of
				Culmerville at 30 mph.
Culmerville	8:58	27	...	Made 5-pound brake pipe reduction
				at Refractory at 36 mph, released
Curtisville	9:04	14	...	at Red Hot Coal Co. track at 32
				mph.
SU Tower	9:08	17	...	Dynamic brake applied in south end
				of Culmerville cut at 16 mph, re-
				leased at Republic Jct.
				20-mile slow order Curtisville to south
				switch of Russellton storage tracks.
Republic Jct.	9:15	24	...	
Deer Creek	9:18	36	...	Made 5-pound brake pipe reduction
River Valley	9:22	28	375	½ mile south of Russellton ac-
East Oakmont	9:27	19	475	count slow order, released just north
Milltown	9:31	13	580	of Republic Jct.
XB Tower	9:35	9	750	
				Slipped several times moving through
				XB Tower cross-over.

General Superintendent's Office
Greenville, Pa.
July 25, 1950

The next table covers Diesel performance between Albion and XB Tower, North Bessemer, as in the earlier Diesel run between these points, and as compared with the normal run with steam power between Albion and XB Tower. This train has 117 loads or 13,000 tons.

DIESEL LOCOMOTIVE PERFORMANCE
July 22, 1950

Units 703A-703B-704A-704B called Albion 9:30 P.M., July 22; tied up North Bessemer 5:23 A.M., July 23. On duty 7 hours 53 minutes. Weather 64 deg. Good rail.

Albion: Got train off main track; leaving had 117 loads, 11,947 gross tons; 13,000 rating tons.

North Bessemer: Yarded train on tracks 20 and 21 east.

Conductor reported hard run-out in Hartstown swamp and at Deer Creek.

Engineer F. W. DeArment operated engine entire trip.

Station	Time	Speed	Amps	Remarks
RX Tower	10:33 P.M.	14	475	Delayed 4 minutes in Albion Yard
Springboro	10:50	33	325	by yard engine.
Conneautville	10:56	27	375	
Dicksonburg	11:09	15	550	
Harmonsburg	11:22	11	650	Slowest speed on hill 9 mph; highest amperage 680. Sanders used from Wilson's Road crossing to south end of overhead bridge at Harmonsburg. Slipped 3 times at period of maximum effort north of Harmonsburg overhead road crossing.
Meadville Jct.	11:29	26	375	Dynamic brake applied at south end of second curve north of Adamsville at 38 mph; released at KO Yard limit board at 20 mph. Train brakes not used.
Hartstown	11:40	38	300	
KO Jct.	11:50	20	...	
KO Jct. Yard	11:54	20	150	
KX South End	11:58	16	525	
Williamsons Rd.	12:04 A.M.	11	715	
East Ave.	12:10	11	725	

Station	Time	Speed	Amps	Remarks
Fredonia Rd.	12:15	11	700	Slowest speed on hill 11 mph; highest amperage 725. Sanders used moderately from Williamsons Road to Fredonia Road. Slipping prevented except at Williamsons Road and once just south of East Ave.
KY	12:27	20	450	
Fredonia	12:38	30	350	
Coolspring (PCO)	12:43	40	325	
Cornell Viaduct	12:47	33	325	
Kimble Viaduct	12:55	23	425	
Filer	1:07	18	475	
Grove City	1:13	35	310	
Reed	1:16	23	400	Slowest speed on hill 20 mph; highest amperage 460.
Carter	1:24	23	400	
Harrisville	1:28	20	200	Dynamic brake applied road crossing south of Harrisville at 21 mph, released on curve north of Branchton scale at 14 mph. Made 5-pound brake pipe reduction north of Wick at 27 mph, to bridge position, speed increased to 29 mph, let 3 pounds air leak on, started graduated release at 19 mph, 3 pound build up, full release 20 car lengths north of Branchton station at 13 mph. (Observer remarks: "This was as smooth a job of braking as I have seen on this hill. Train crew reported that there was no slack action anywhere on hill.")
Branchton	1:35	12	...	
UN Tower	1:37	22	400	
Hallston	1:46	32	325	
Claytonia	1:49	21	425	
Euclid	2:02	15	550	Slowest speed on hill 10 mph; highest amperage 725. Sanders used from 1/4 mile north of M.P. NB 47 to Euclid station; slipped three times.
Queen Jct.	2:06	33	...	Dynamic brake applied on first curve south of Euclid station at 23 mph, released at Calvin yard limit board at 8 mph. Made 6-pound brake pipe reduction at Jamisonville at 39 mph, released
Oneida	2:15	28	...	

Station	Time	Speed	Amps	Remarks
Calvin	2:24	16	...	on first curve south of old J Tower at 37 mph. Made 5-pound reduction at pump station at 39 mph, added 3 pounds at old Oneida, released at 15 car lengths north of Calvin yard limit board at 10 mph. Applied dynamic brake 20 car lengths north of Butler Tfr. water tank at 14 mph, released at locomotive foreman's office at Butler Tfr. at 8 mph.
Butler	2:34	15	400	
Nigger Cut 8 deg. curve	2:41	27	375	
BD Tower	2:48	34	325	
Rockdale	2:55	14	560	
West Saxonburg	3:11	10	730	
Houseville	3:20	10	730	Slowest speed on hill 9 mph; highest amperage 775. Sanders used from Rockdale to Houseville tank. Slipped near Rockdale once, twice at road crossing north of Houseville and three times just south of Houseville.
Ivywood	3:26	23	...	Applied dynamic brake at Ivywood south road crossing at 25 mph, released in Culmerville cut at 8 mph. made 6-pound brake pipe reduction at Refractory at 37 mph, released at Red Hot Coal Co. track at 30 mph. Applied dynamic brake at Curtisville 1000-foot board at 12 mph, released at Republic Jct. at 28 mph. 20-mile slow order Curtisville to south switch of Russellton storage tracks.
Culmerville	3:34	20	...	
Curtisville	3:44	12	...	
SU Tower	3:48	15	...	
Republic Jct.	3:54	26	...	
Deer Creek	3:57	38	...	
River Valley	4:00	28	125	
East Oakmont	4:06	17	510	Sanders used from East Oakmont to stop in yard. Slipped three times just north of XB Tower.
Milltown	4:10	13	625	
XB Tower	4:15	10	725	

General Superintendent's Office
Greenville, Pa.
July 25, 1950

Freight Cars

On July 1, 1896, the first all-steel freight cars were placed in service on the lines of the Bessemer—the Pittsburgh, Bessemer & Lake Erie Railroad then—in the ore trade between Conneaut and the steel mills. These were of 80,000 pounds capacity, compared with the 60,000-pound capacity of the all-wood cars.

These first steel cars were the hopper type and they were built by a steel company to demonstrate the practicability of all-steel cars for railroad service. The steel hopper cars served a rugged apprenticeship for a year on the toughest of all rail hauls before being accepted. As a result of the year's experimental runs, 400 cars of a slightly modified design were built and placed in service. Two hundred more cars were built on the same order, but these differed to the extent that pressed steel parts took the place of structural shapes. In 1899, an order was placed for 700 steel gondola cars of 80,000 pounds capacity, built to the pressed steel design.

The Bessemer's car fleet constantly increased, keeping pace with the ever-expanding facilities at Conneaut and the growing output of the Pennsylvania coal mines. Car sizes increased. The forty-tonner became obsolete. In fact, by 1931 the size of the hopper car had more than doubled. They now had a 90-ton capacity.

In 1935, the Bessemer acquired its first light-weight Cor-Ten steel hopper cars. These had a ninety-ton capacity. Since 1935 all cars purchased have been of the Cor-Ten steel construction. Of all the freight cars owned, the Bessemer and Lake Erie acquired 75 per cent since the beginning of 1935.

On January 1, 1950, the Bessemer owned 13,100 freight cars, as follows:

> 10,416 hopper cars
> 1,523 gondola cars
> 987 box cars
> 149 flat cars
> 25 covered hopper cars

Of the total hopper cars owned, 5,927 were ninety-ton capacity, with 82 per cent acquired after the beginning of 1935. Of all freight cars owned, 75 per cent were acquired subsequent to January 1, 1935.

Now let us take a look at some tonnage figures, in particular as they concern a statement made at the opening of this chapter dealing with daily tonnage per mile on the Bessemer.

The average tons per mile for all commodities—expressed as net ton-miles per loaded car-mile, which gives consideration to the distance each ton of all commodities handled was transported—amounted to 76.0 in 1949, a decrease compared with the record high of 1948 of 77.5. This was the thirteenth consecutive year that the Bessemer surpassed all Class 1 railroads nationally in the average load per car-mile.

These high averages have been attributed to the large capacity cars owned by the Bessemer and Lake Erie Railroad.

I never cease marveling at the performance and records of the American railroads, large and small, year in and year out, in good times and bad, in peacetime and wartime. They are astounding, and so little appreciated by so many people. It is obviously impossible to set down even a small part of the worthwhile achievements of the railroads, even over a short period.

Many books could be written that contained nothing but interesting facts concerning United States railroads. The Bessemer alone, for instance, is a participating carrier in over 1,100 freight tariffs.

The Bessemer has over 3,700 established routes in official territory.

The Bessemer storehouse at Greenville, Pennsylvania, stocks over 17,500 different items, which were purchased in thirty-two states.

Loss and damage claims cost the Bessemer only five cents on each carload of freight.

These and many more are things that go toward making a small railroad great.

We associate passing tracks with the usual railroad main line, but on the Bessemer they are practically nonexistent as such.

This is because all trains are freight, except two passenger each way over a portion of the line, and, further, because the freight traffic is consistently the same.

In writing about railroads and railroad men over the years, you come to quickly recognize those qualities that make railroads great, that make their leaders great. And I point with pride to the Bessemer & Lake Erie.

CHAPTER XVII

THE SHASTA DAYLIGHTS

Two New Southern Pacific Streamliners

Folklore, atmosphere, arts and crafts, and landmarks were all taken into consideration when the color and design staff of the Pullman-Standard Car Manufacturing Company, working in close co-operation with the Southern Pacific, set about styling the cars of the new Shasta Daylights, which operate between San Francisco, California, and Portland, Oregon.

You have only to ride one of these trains to know how completely the artists and the decorators have caught the tonal quality of the country in their applied treatment of the interiors.

The exteriors are the same orange, red, and black as previous Daylights, a combination famous on the Coast. The brush strokes within have produced such striking and yet restful colors as Cascade blue, Oregon cedar, summit green, canyon tan, and Shasta yellow. You cannot forget these Shasta Daylights, a brief splash of color against a mountain side, or the completely relaxing effect of the interiors.

The two fifteen-car Daylight streamliners, which went into service on July 10, 1949, are pulled by Diesel-driven locomotives of 6,000 horsepower, built by the Electro-Motive Division of General Motors. These big engines handle the trains beautifully, as they swing across this matchless Shasta route—past Lassen Peak, Shasta Dam's Lake, Pit River, into Sacramento River Canyon, and around the wooded curve that brings you face to face with breath-taking Mt. Shasta. You have left then the Cascade Mountains, Odell Lake, and the Willamette River approach to Portland, Oregon, the "Rose City."

The enormous windows bring the scenic land of northern California and Oregon almost, it seems, within arm's length, while "breathing" devices prevent fogging of the glass.

The Shasta Daylights have the same refinements generally as previous Daylights, except that the superstructures are built of aluminum instead of steel. Lightness has been gained without the sacrifice of strength. The average reduction in weight per car adds up to about 5,300 pounds, or around forty tons for the train.

The foundation of your house is the most important part of the structure. Of equal importance is the sound construction of the unseen welded steel underframes of the railroad car. The Pullman-Standard people know how to build in strength as well as develop grace of contour.

The consist of each Shasta Daylight is identical and includes a combination baggage-postal car; a chair car, seating forty-six, which provides news agent's space; three full chair cars, each seating forty-eight; one chair car, seating thirty-eight, which contains the dining crew's dressing room and toilet; a triple unit, consisting of a coffee shop and a diner, both seating sixty-six, separated by a kitchen car which serves both; three chair cars of forty-eight-seat capacity; a tavern car, seating fifty-four; another chair car, seating forty-eight; and a parlor-observation car remodeled from an existing car and seating thirty-two.

The general lighting is fluorescent. All cars, except the baggage-postal car have radio and public-address equipment. Electric power for passenger-carrying cars and for air conditioning is supplied by equipment with the Waukesha label. An axle-driven generator is located beneath the baggage-postal car. Heat for the kitchen range and the hot water supply is furnished by propane gas.

A feature to which we will return after a little is the motor-driven luggage elevator at the vestibule end of the chair cars.

The baggage-postal car is carried on six-wheel type trucks. The same type trucks are located at the articulations of the triple-body unit. All trucks are equipped with Timken roller bearings.

Each car has a journal-box heat indicator and alarm, vastly reducing damage that might result from overheated bearings. Westinghouse high-speed air-brake equipment is of the electro-pneumatic type that has been engineered into the Daylights, as well as all modern speed liners. A device that has done much to eliminate flat spots on car wheels is the appliance that prevents brake grab and sliding wheels. Each car is equipped with two hand brakes.

In boarding the train, you observe that the window sash openings seem much higher than is usual, and you find this is true. You do not, perhaps, appreciate what it means until you are in mountain country when you can look upward at the close-bordering peaks. There is very little that you miss in the scenery line when you ride the Shasta Daylights.

All cars of the train have fully automatic Vapor temperature controls located at the end of each car. Automatic thermostat devices provide for an even, comfortable temperature at all times regardless of the weather outside. When heat is needed steam is allowed to move into the radiators, and when cooling is desired the air-conditioning system automatically turns on without manual adjustment as the train moves.

Each chair is supplied with five individually controlled heating zones. These have separate thermostats which anticipate and modulate the heat in each zone. For instance, the sunny side of the car requires less heat than the shady side, therefore the separate thermostats on each side automatically perform their opposed functions, which results in absolute comfort for everyone.

Probably in no field have the specialists so consistently performed scientific magic as in the modern train, and nowhere up and down the train is there anything to which the passenger is so keenly tuned as the temperature. In particular, this is true in California where a person has only to turn the corner to step from sweltering heat to too-cool shade.

On the Daylights when the temperature in a car drops a fraction of one degree below the comfortable thermostat setting, this diminutive gadget sends an electric impulse to turn on the heat valve a little, and a little more warmth flows into the aluminum-finned radiators, raising the temperature just a shade, or to the desired point. On the other hand, when the temperature in the car gets above the comfortable setting, the thermostat sentry flashes a message to the air-conditioning equipment, and that goes to work.

Each car is equipped for radio reception. Conveniently placed speakers bring entertainment to the passengers without blare or distortion. Multichannel radio tuners, for both A.M. and F.M. reception, are located in several of the cars to offer a wide selection of programs over the route of the Daylight. To facilitate train announcements, the radio system is linked with a public-address system which may be controlled from a majority of the chair cars, or from the desk of the train conductor.

Forty-eight-seat chair cars have five speakers in the ceiling, while the forty-six- and thirty-eight-passenger cars have four. Four speakers are located in the tavern car, parlor-observation, and in the diner and coffee shop sections of the three-car articulated dining unit.

The modern train is designed, from the rails up, to provide the passenger with the utmost in riding comfort. Gone are the jerky starts, the buckling stops, the lurching motion of a boat in a heavy sea. Today's speed liner represents the final word in passenger train advancement. It has more than just eye-filling beauty. The trucks of the Shasta Daylights have all-coil springs, bolster anchors, and shock absorbers; the draft gear is designed to practically eliminate all lost motion between cars, and the power of the Diesel locomotive is more than sufficient under any circumstances, which makes for "soft" train handling at all times, and a low center of gravity not only aids the train balance on curves but is a factor in maintaining higher sustained speeds.

Interior Features

A pleasing feature of the Shasta Daylights is the generous employment of murals. People who have not attempted train travel these later years are immediately impressed by the manner in which the designers have worked highly decorative pictures into the general scheme of things.

Let's take the bar front and canopy in the tavern car on the Daylight as an example, also a section of the back bar. The panels show animal life of the Northwest, and the back bar detail includes an illustrated transparency in full natural color, made from a photograph of Timberline Lodge. It is amazing what the Pullman people and the Southern Pacific staff have accomplished on this train. Many of these interiors seem to catch and to hold the beauty of the natural scenery outside of the car windows.

Dodge Venetian blinds are used in the tavern car and in the coffee shop and diner of the triple-articulated unit. Other car windows have shades.

The spacious men's and women's lounges are done in the same general color schemes as are used in the main coach compartment in which they are located. One series of chair cars is done in Odell blues and Oregon cedar; another in Summit green, pine brown, and cedar; a third in canyon tan; and a fourth in Shasta yellows, brown, and cedar red.

The very attractive diner has blue-green carpeting with a forest-leaf pattern. The drapery is in gold and the seat coverings are in two tones of autumn red. The table linen is in gold with autumn leaves in reds and browns, a very unusual and striking pattern. The upper walls and bulkheads are done in cloth-backed California oak veneer as a natural background for the general fall coloring. Four full natural-color murals are used on the bulkheads. These were made from Kodachromes and colored by hand.

The author has been on all of the modern trains but this Shasta Daylight diner is among the most striking and pleasing combinations we have seen.

The coffee shop of this three-car unit has a still different color key. It is gay and informal in character. Browns, Cascade blues, and cedar reds predominate. The carpeting has three tones of Redwood brown in a fern pattern. Attractive combinations of seats done in blue and cedar blend with drapery in the same tones. Exceptionally large murals are in blue tones. These cover the entire ends of the room, giving largeness to the general effect.

The interior walls and ceiling of the eighty-foot parlor observation car are in four tones of blue. Foam-rubber seats are upholstered in henna or blue. These revolve and recline. You marvel at the softness of the patterned, three-toned carpet and learn that it is laid on a pad of sponge rubber.

Scenes of the world-famous Shasta Route have been used in the six murals. Card tables for eight persons, a writing desk, and magazine table are set off from the main parlor section, which has seats for twenty-two persons. The observation circle at the rear has settees and lounge chairs for ten, together with reading tables. The forward end of the car includes rest rooms next to the luggage elevator.

These luggage elevators, so far as we know, are individual to the Southern Pacific. They are operated from an enclosed switch box on the outside of the car, and they make possible the loading or unloading of luggage without cluttering up the vestibule. Pieces are tagged for putting off at intermediate points. Luggage going through to final terminals is tagged to the taxi stand, at the passenger's request, and handled by the redcap direct from elevator door. At the taxi stand the passenger surrenders the check given him on the train by the car porter and pays his redcap fee. When not in use, the panel in the outside wall of the car closes over the elevator, which serves as a storage space for luggage but is available to the passenger at any time.

All passenger-carrying car doors of the Daylight are electro-pneumatically operated, as in practically all of the modern trains. Oscillating lights are installed on the front end and rear end of these trains. The rear light, flashing red, goes into operation automatically with a brake application. The white flasher in the front of the Diesel is used in approaching stations and crossings, and at other points where a visible warning would make for greater safety for motorists or people near the tracks.

Maximum comfort and relaxation in the chair car is obtained

through the use of very soft foam rubber and the rotating-reclining design of de luxe coach seats. An Arm-Kap reclining mechanism adjusts and locks the chair in various positions. A new Hammok-Suspension provides a flexible panel to serve as a universal adapter which lends soft, firm support to the body. Seat builders have performed miracles in turning out chairs that can be adapted to the various desires and human forms by the flick of a finger.

Frequently in this book we have made mention of the use of double-glazed, breather-type windows. We do this to emphasize the fact that these always crystal-clear windows add so much to the passenger's enjoyment. You really are not conscious that glass separates you from the constantly changing panorama and the striking scenic beauty.

The Shasta Daylights cover the 718 miles between San Francisco, California, and Portland, Oregon, in fifteen and one-half hours. Northbound, the ferry connections for the Daylight, train No. 10, leaves the foot of Market Street, San Francisco, at 7:45 A.M.

Four miles away across San Francisco Bay, the train leaves Oakland Pier at 8:10 A.M. Wheeling north to Portland it makes eleven intermediate stops. The scheduled arrival at the northern city is 11:15 P.M.

The average speed for the 714-mile rail trip is approximately 47.5 miles per hour. And this is remarkable considering the mountain country traversed.

The Daylights have long been famous on the Coast, and the new Shasta Daylights are doing much to maintain Southern Pacific standards in modern transportation in the land in which it pioneered soon after the march of the Forty-Niners.

Shasta Daylight Success Story

One year after the inauguration of the brilliant new Shasta Daylights cold figures proved that the Southern Pacific had scored again. An average load of 408 revenue passengers (including children) had been carried in each direction in the twelve-month period. And this on a train with a passenger-seating capacity of 442.

More startling still were the figures which revealed that during the first nine days of July, 1950, the average load southbound was 555 passengers, and 502 northbound. This on an all-reserved seat train. On July 9, 611 passengers set a record. "On and offs," or passengers riding only part way which made room for others, made this figure possible.

The Shasta Daylights hit the jackpot in a highly competitive bus and airplane territory, with a bus fare even lower than the Shasta's $12 flat (excluding tax) for the 718 miles, or about 1.7 cents a mile, one-way coach fare. Round trip the coach rate is $21.60, or about 1.5 cents a mile with an eighteen-day return limit. Established special rates, which cover both the rail and seat charge, cover the twenty-two parlor car seats.

The success of the Shasta Daylights was founded on low fares, a beautiful train, the right sort of a schedule, plus some breathtaking scenery. When a traveler can ride this kind of a train for less than two cents a mile he is saving money by leaving his car in the garage. And one man said, when asked why he rode the Shasta Daylight instead of flying, as had been his custom, "My time isn't worth $22.15, when I can loll on the Shasta." He was referring to the fare differential.

We opened this chapter with a description of the train to first highlight these Shasta Daylights, and to show what the Southern Pacific, along with other railroads over the country, are offering the public in modern railway transportation. It is the policy of the S.P. to buy a *train* for this kind of a run, rather than just a fleet of cars and locomotives. A train like this Daylight carries through a theme which stresses the character of the country it serves. The Southern Pacific prefers even to turn away passengers on peak days rather than break into this beautiful train by adding cars that would be out of harmony with the general scheme of things.

The Shasta's success story involves fine equipment, the right schedule, an attractive fare, and the kind of scenery that has made the Cascade mountain area famous. Not every railroad is so blessed as to scenery and population centers, and simply reducing fares would not provide a solution to passenger train losses. In fact, the Southern Pacific does not believe that the salvation of railroad passenger traffic necessarily lies in general and widespread fare reductions. The road feels that, if anything, basic fares are too low, considering costs of operation. But the S.P. does know that to get the volume it needed to make the Shasta story a success story it had to offer lower fares.

What about the intermediate passenger on the Daylights? Does he get under the wire of the low fare? An important point is that they are highly selective with regard to points of applicability, and are quoted specifically between San Francisco and Oakland, California, on the one hand, and Portland, Oregon, on the other. The same pro rata rate is not offered to intermediate passengers, except that the special San Francisco–Portland rate, *in toto*, is blanketed back on the north to Eugene, Oregon, 124 miles south of Portland, and on the south, to Redding, California, 236 miles from San Francisco, at which point it coincides with the fare built up on the basic mileage rate structure. We will illustrate that. An intermediate passenger on the Shasta Daylight ordinarily pays the basic mileage fare. But if he journeys from San Francisco to Eugene, the basic fare exceeds the special rate from San Francisco through to Portland; hence he pays the latter.

By this means the Southern Pacific believes it has preserved the basic fares, while at the same time the road can offer lower rates between points where sufficient volume can be generated to build up a train load which will more than offset the lower revenue per passenger-mile. It is the opinion of the S.P. people that the most profitable field for the railroads lies in daylight trains on runs sufficiently long to attract the motorists, and in this the Shasta fills the bill nicely.

Train travelers like service, in addition to luxury, and they get it on the Daylights in the form of a personable passenger agent. He is a trained S.P. man and he is there to serve you. This agent is particularly helpful to the more timid passengers, perhaps enjoying their first train trip, who are faced with the dubious business of arranging for space on connecting trains.

Let us say that a Mrs. Smith is making an emergency trip north from San Fransico and she will want Pullman space on the Great Northern's overnight train from Portland to Seattle. Being informed of the needs of Mrs. Smith, the agent wires ahead from Dunsmuir, California, 425 miles south of Portland, giving the name and type of accommodations desired. At Eugene, Oregon, 124 miles out of Portland, the agent will receive advice concerning space assigned to Mrs. Smith. This is noted on the lady's ticket folder.

Everything is now taken care of and Mrs. Smith has only to board the Great Northern train, which is waiting at Portland, and fifteen minutes later she is on the final leg of her journey to Seattle. Because of the tightness of the connection she will pay the Great Northern conductor for the space acquired through the efforts of the S.P. passenger agent.

The Daylights were naturals for the vacationing traveler in the summer months, but pleasure travel dropped in midwinter and the road looked to the expense-account travelers to pick up the slack. It took a little time for the canny traveling man to overcome a natural suspicion of a daylight scheduled coach train, but it wasn't long before he discovered that, in addition to being a daylight coach run, the Shasta Daylight was a luxury train offering accommodations at a price a thrifty person cannot afford to ignore.

CHAPTER XVIII

SEABOARD C.T.C.

Underground Lines

Permanence, safety, sureness provided by the underground C.T.C. lines are here, with the Seaboard Air Line Railroad pioneering. The fall of 1948 found 248 miles of main-line control wires between Hamlet, North Carolina, and Savannah, Georgia, underground and tied in for a complete installation, marking another milepost of railroad achievement and advancement.

Between Hamlet and Savannah, the Seaboard has two widely separated single-track lines. The original line is the one by way of Columbia and it is with this line that we are concerned in this chapter on underground C.T.C. lines. The line was constructed as the most direct route, but it included some sections of heavy grades. Part of these were in the Sand Mountains, just south of Columbia.

Between Hamlet and just north of Waynor, South Carolina, the track runs through generally hilly country, with rolling grades up to 1 per cent. Curves are numerous, some of them ranging up to four degrees.

The Seaboard's second line, built sometime later, swings to the coast, passing through Charleston, South Carolina, and it is 14.5 miles longer than the Columbia route, but reaching out to the coastal plain, it is predominantly flat, and consequently completely adapted to the movement of freight.

Thus we find the line via Columbia carrying the road's through passenger trains, while the freights move over the Charleston route. This is a situation similar to the one existing on the Santa Fe, in which passenger trains use the mountain route and the freights the flat-country route on their main east-west lines.

From Waynor to Savannah, on the Columbia line, the Seaboard runs through open country and is consistently straight and level. For example, the track is tangent for fourteen miles between the curve two miles north of Waynor and a point two miles south of Denmark, South Carolina. Between Fairfax and Garnett, the line is tangent for twenty-five miles. From Waynor to Savannah, the grade is level to slightly rolling and as a result this hundred miles is high-speed territory, with a maximum permissible speed of seventy-five miles per hour for modern streamlined passenger trains pulled by Diesel-electric locomotives, and seventy miles per hour for passenger trains with conventional equipment and handled by steam locomotives.

The Columbia line carries such famous name trains as the Sunland, the Silver Meteor, the Silver Star, and the Palmland. Other trains consist of an express train daily, a local freight, perishable pick-up jobs, and some extra freights. In the winter season, additional passenger trains include the Orange Blossom and other trains, totaling seven passenger trains each way daily.

This gives the Seaboard's Columbia line a total number of trains daily varying from fourteen to twenty-four or more.

Before coming onto the fast-wheeling track south of Waynor, passenger train speed is limited in numerous places, and the maximum speed at any point is seventy miles per hour.

So we have the general picture of the Seaboard's fast-stepping speed-queen route across South Carolina into Georgia from North Carolina, with thirty-three C.T.C. controlled passing tracks in between, Osborne, North Carolina, and Meinhard, Georgia, with car capacities ranging all the way from fifty to ninety-two.

A distance of 248 miles is a long way to dig a ditch and lay a cable. A lot of eyebrows went up when the Seaboard began to talk about this underground cable installation, just as folks used to lift an eyebrow when they first hung wires on poles and sent messages over them. This cable was to perform the work of two line wires, i.e., to carry voice communications and D.C. codes and act as carrier for centralized traffic control, meaning that voice communications in each direction could be carried on at the same time that the train dispatcher was flipping switches and pushing buttons at the big C.T.C. cabinet in Savannah to set up meeting and passing points for the speeding trains.

Now if anyone had bragged, along about this time, that they had had a hand in digging a ditch 2,700 feet long and placing therein 2,700 feet of cable in *fourteen minutes*, elapsed time, from start to finish, the listener would have been entirely justified in expressing strong doubts concerning the veracity, as well as the sanity, of the person so elaborating on such a deed. But such a ditch *was* dug and a full reel of cable laid, on this pioneer project, in the time set forth.

In one day 60,900 feet of ditch was dug and a corresponding amount of cable laid, with the work train out a total of six hours and twenty minutes. On another day 52,295 feet were laid in seven hours and fifteen minutes. On a day when the train was out on three trips, for a total of five hours and forty-five minutes, 32,250 feet were laid. At first glance, it might seem incredible, but it was simply another example of railroading the modern way.

The work train outfit that was used to "plow in" the cable consisted of a steam locomotive, a caboose, the plow, a car of cable, and cars to house the signal crew. Because it was a single-track line, considerable time was lost clearing the main track to allow trains to pass.

First, we will concern ourselves with this underground cable, making history on the Seaboard. The cable was made up of two No. 10 solid copper wires, twisted at a pitch of five and one-half inches. The reason for having the wires twisted was to keep the circuit balanced to the ground. Each wire was covered with a 3/16-inch thickness of polyethylene, and these insulated conductors enclosed in an overall layer of Flamenol, 4/64-inch thick, making the finished cable 6/10-inch in diameter. The cable was made by the General Electric Company. It had no other protective covering other than the Flamenol itself. The cable was buried to a depth of eighteen to twenty-two inches.

189

As a general rule, the cable was placed on the east side of the main track about a foot beyond the edge of the stone ballast, which placed the cable about six feet from the nearest rail.

The cable reels contained about one-half mile of cable. No joints were made in the cable. At the ends of the reel lengths, the two ends were brought in through a riser into a cast-iron box where the wires were connected to terminal posts. These boxes were located just above the ground level and painted yellow as a special identification.

Upon coming to wooden trestles, the cable was run in one-inch pipe for protection, and this pipe was supported by chains, spaced about twelve feet apart. Chains were used instead of rigid straps to allow flexibility, thereby minimizing the effects of train vibration. On a long steel viaduct in Columbia, the cable was run as an open aerial construction supported from a "messenger" by the usual rings.

The specially designed plow which performed the miracle of laying the cable has a flat nose three inches wide, which tends to pull the point down into the ground to a depth of twenty-four inches. As the plow is pulled forward, it forces dirt to each side and up. The cable, unwinding from the reel, is fed into a funnel and tube down through the plow to lay the cable at the bottom of the plow furrow.

The plow is pulled by a steel wire cable connected to a steel I beam, which extends outward from a flat car. This beam works between a set of guides and it can be extended or pulled back by a crank, and so can tow the plow at any desired distance up to about twelve feet. A special rack on the flat car holds the reels when paying out the cable. A small hand-operated crane, bolted to the floor of the car, is employed in picking up the reels and setting them on the rack.

The plow moves forward at about the pace of a man walking. It is guided and held upright by two men at the handles. The loose dirt is centered in a ridge over the trench by a drag board, pulled by ropes attached to the plow. Angle irons are bolted to the bottom of this drag in such a position as to pull the dirt to the center. One man rides this drag.

Power to operate the plow comes, of course, from the loco-motive attached to the flat car. The cable reel sits on the car at an angle of about forty-five degrees. Except for a few hundred feet through Denmark, where there are numerous turnouts and crossings, the cable was plowed in for the entire 248 miles.

For the greater part of the distance between Hamlet and Savannah, the soil is sandy loam or red clay. In some sections, however, some gravel was encountered, but the plow pulled through with no trouble, except when it struck old buried ties or logs. In these instances, the sheer pin, which attached the steel wire pull cable to the plow, was broken.

Largest Signal Control Board

The C.T.C. dispatching machine at Savannah, Georgia, con-trols the entire 248 miles over the Hamlet-Columbia-Savannah line. This control board is the largest ever constructed. This board in itself reflects the spirit of progress of the South and its fine railroads.

Previous to the installation of C.T.C., train movements over this line were authorized by timetable, train order, and manual block. There were no automatic blocks in use. The new system was planned primarily to provide track-circuit signal protection.

The station-leaving signals operate to two positions, and they govern from siding to siding. Thus, in this respect, the system is the equivalent of track-circuit-controlled absolute-manual block. The project includes power switch machines at the sid-ings, which, together with the signals at these siding switches, can ordinarily be controlled by coded line equipment from the control machine in the dispatcher's office at Savannah.

The aspects of these signals when controlled by the dispatcher authorize the train, in the conventional manner, to: (1) con-tinue on the main track, (2) enter the siding, or (3) leave the siding and go to the next town. In this respect, the system is similar to centralized traffic control.

The track circuits between sidings are the coded type, and a novel feature is that these track circuits are normally de-energized. They are "turned on" to feed through from one track circuit to another throughout an entire station-to-station block, when lining up to clear a signal. The track circuit feed, throughout a station-to-station block, is in the direction opposite to the train movement to be made.

Having run a train through a station-to-station block, the next operation is to check for track occupancy, broken rails, etc., in such a block, and then return the track circuit to the normally de-energized condition. These operations, including the sending of track-occupancy indications to the control machine in the dispatcher's office, can be termed "clearing out" the station-to-station block.

Automatic Block Change-over

A special feature of the Seaboard's Hamlet-Savannah installation is that if the C.T.C. code circuit from the dispatcher's office fails, the system automatically changes over to a form of approach-clearing, station-to-station automatic block. When the C.T.C. line fails, the line relays at the field stations affected by the break are released and stay down. This change from normal operates the station-disconnect relay which in turn operates a special relay that establishes connections by means of which an approaching train automatically clears its own signal.

When the system is operating as automatic block, the power switch machines at the sidings are each controlled locally by trainmen. On the instrument house near each power switch there is a small cast-iron controller case, the door of which is locked with a regular switch padlock. If a westbound train, for example, on a siding is to use a switch, a trainman opens the door of the case. Inside of each case there is a panel with two keyholes which standard switch padlock keys fit. To cause the switch to operate from normal to reverse, or, in other words, to line it for the train in the siding to pull out, the key is placed in the right hole and turned clockwise. Or to operate the switch from the reverse to the normal position the key is used in the left hole.

A single-channel Type-H Western Electric Company carrier is in operation on two wires of the pole line through this territory. This channel is normally used in through telephone service. In case of trouble on the buried cable, including the three-channel Type-C carrier operated over the wires of the cable, the C.T.C. carrier will be automatically transferred from the cable to the H carrier on the wires of the pole line.

This automatic transfer is under the control of a pilot voice frequency which continuously checks the integrity of the Type-C carrier. This pilot frequency, which is at 2,390 cycles in both directions, is generated and received by Union Switch & Signal Company carrier equipment and is carried over the same channels of the Type-C system as are used for the C.T.C. carrier.

If trouble develops in the buried cable or this Type-C carrier on that cable in the section between Savannah and Swansea, for example, stoppage of the pilot carrier will automatically transfer the C.T.C. carrier apparatus at Savannah and Swansea from the Type-C carrier to the Type-H carrier on the pole line. However, at Swansea the terminal equipment would function to continue to handle the C.T.C. carrier on the buried cable between Swansea and Hamlet, the northern line terminal.

A word here about the Type-C carrier. This system is primarily for telephone service, being designed for modulation of the channel frequency by voice frequencies. Therefore, the Union Switch & Signal Company carrier apparatus, employed for the transmission of C.T.C. codes, must be in the voice range —that is, between 250 and 2,750 cycles per second.

This distinguishes the Seaboard installation from earlier C.T.C. carrier systems in which frequencies have been ten kilocycles and thirty kilocycles.

Equipment Housing

The equipment housing is vital because of the extremely intricate nature of the facilities and every precaution is taken to guard it. Savannah maintains the relays, carrier apparatus, and other equipment in steel cases in a large room on the ground floor of a new modern fireproof, temperature-controlled building. The dispatcher's office is on the second floor of this structure above the relay room.

Where carrier equipment is located at field stations, it is located in a six-by-sixteen concrete house, solidly built and supported on a durable foundation. Here is located apparatus that includes relays, line-coding equipment, and batteries. At other field stations the equipment is housed in sheet-steel structures five by seven feet. Underground cables run from instrument houses at sidings to the switch machines and the signals.

At the ordinary power-switch locations, the storage batteries will keep the switches and signals in operation even if the commercial A.C. power fails. However, the carrier equipment for C.T.C. line coding and for communications circuits requires A.C. power constantly. Accordingly, at nine field stations, which are also carrier repeater stations, an emergency stand-by source of A.C. is required. These have a small gas-engine-driven generator, rated at 1,500 watts, 110 volts. These machines are the light-weight portable type, built by Onan & Sons, Minneapolis.

These units are compact and very reliable. And if at any time the incoming A.C. power fails your gas-engine generator will start automatically and quickly take over the load.

Only until one has made a personal examination of such completely adequate signaling facilities can they begin to appreciate the remarkable job a railroad like the Seaboard has done in carrying out its modernization program. Nothing is left to chance, with the result that every function is performed with clocklike precision.

At certain sidings not needed for passing trains the existing hand-throw switches were equipped with electric locks. Also electric locks were installed on all the main-track switches lead-

194

ing to spurs. When a train on the main line wants to make a move into one of these sidings or spurs, the locomotive or a car is stopped on a short-track circuit located immediately in approach to the facing-point of the switch. Then a trainman operates the electric lock and then opens the switch.

When a train on a locked siding is ready to depart, a member of the crew obtains permission by telephone to remove the derail from the track. The dispatcher then sets the signals governing the block at stop and coded track circuit energy comes to the switch location from both directions from the respective signals at the entrance of the station-to-station block in which the switch is located. Thus track codes to release the lock will not be at the switch unless signals governing into the block are at "stop," and the entire station-to-station block is unoccupied. On each end of every locked siding there is a dwarf signal. After the switch is unlocked and thrown, the signal clears to govern the direction in which the train is to move on the main track.

CHAPTER XIX

FRISCO LINES

Springfield Yard

The St. Louis–San Francisco Railway Company completed in the summer of 1950 new freight terminal facilities at Springfield, Missouri, that included a "saucer" yard, Diesel shop, a division office building, and other supporting facilities for a total expenditure of $5,000,000. This work vastly expanded the efficiency of this important marshaling yard, which is strategically located at an important crossroad of the Frisco Lines.

One of the things that makes the United States great is its vast network of steel rail, linking the industries and the resources of the nation. Each railway system has its place in the scheme of things in the general pattern. We will look for a moment at the Frisco Lines, with 5,000 miles in Missouri, Arkansas, Oklahoma, Texas, Kansas, Tennessee, Mississippi, Alabama, and Florida. Springfield, Missouri, is a crossroad for general east-west and north-south lines, reaching from St. Louis into the lower Texas Panhandle, and from Kansas City to the western limits of Florida at Pensacola.

The first line of defense in an economic world beset with financial quagmires is efficiency and modernization. The railroads had many problems during and following World War II, which were met and solved through the medium of free enterprise, plus courage and ingenuity.

The Frisco railroad was faced with problems in the form of inadequacies, such as the old yard setup at Springfield, and it didn't help when the Diesels came along to bog the yard down with longer trains. Something had to be done, and it was, to the tune of $5,000,000, as indicated in the opening paragraph of this chapter.

Before the new yard was built, switching at Springfield was done principally at North Yard. North Yard was built in the early 1870's, and it was enlarged in 1899 and 1902. The yard had eighteen tracks, which ranged from forty-five to sixty-five cars in length. The layout as a whole was obsolete to begin with, and the comparatively short length of the tracks made immensely difficult the marshaling of cars with the growing density of traffic. The day came when it was necessary to "double" incoming trains into the yard. Worse was the fact that all switching operations had to be stopped when trains pulled in or out.

Conditions became so bad that switch engines averaged less than four hours work during each trick, and even then complete switching was impossible. Many trains leaving Springfield had to be reswitched somewhere along the line. There was only one possible solution, and that was a new yard.

One million cubic yards of grading was required as a preface to the construction of the new layout, which is a saucer-type facility that permits switching moves to be carried on simultaneously from both ends. It also incorporates such modernization features as a control tower, floodlighting, radio communications, conveniently placed paging and talk-back speakers, and a pneumatic tube between the yard tower and the new office building.

Other facilities included a new icing dock, a car repair yard, and the 350-foot long, four-level Diesel shop. Everything bore the stamp of such last-word modernization as the perimeter heating in the office building, claimed to be one of the first installations of its kind in the country.

The new yard, when completed, comprised a total of 30.6 miles of trackage in thirty-two tracks, extending in an east-west direction. The eleven eastbound and the eleven westbound classification tracks were arranged with ladder tracks at each end, permitting switching from both directions. Flanking the classification tracks on the north were the three westbound receiving tracks and on the south the three eastbound receiving tracks.

The maximum capacity of individual tracks in the westbound yard is 158 cars, and in the eastbound receiving yard 155 cars, for a total capacity of 936 cars on receiving tracks and 1,574 cars on classification tracks. Individual classification tracks hold from 52 to 94 cars.

Extending the length of the yard on the north side is an engine running track 8,900 feet in length. The 2,360-foot icing track is located between the eastbound receiving tracks and the adjacent classification tracks. Here is located a 320-foot high-level ice dock.

Connecting with the ladder tracks at each end of the classification yard are two drill tracks. For a distance of about thirty cars back from the end of the yard the east drill tracks descend toward the yard on a grade of 0.35 per cent, while those on the west end descend toward the yard on a grade of 0.25 per cent, the two grades being joined in the yard tracks by sweeping vertical curves. Thus, the saucer effect is achieved. The transverse grade of the yard is 0.5 per cent descending toward the north side.

The main lines of the Frisco system radiate in four directions from Springfield. Northeast, they reach to St. Louis; north, to Kansas City; west, to Monett, Missouri; and thence to Wichita, Kansas; Fort Smith, Arkansas; Tulsa, Oklahoma City, and Enid, Oklahoma; and on to Texas points. Southeast, the Frisco reaches out to Memphis, Tennessee; Birmingham and Mobile, Alabama; and into Pensacola, Florida.

About twelve through trains pull into Springfield yard in each twenty-four-hour period. These trains bring in about 1,500 cars, and there are about the same number outbound. Of the incoming cars, about 200 are delivered to local freight houses, industries, and stockyards, and these sources offer a like number for return to go into the make-up of departing trains.

To enhance the flexibility of the Springfield yard the ladders of the classification tracks are extended across the corresponding receiving tracks by means of No. 8 crossovers. This permits the receiving tracks to be used for switching purposes. Between the two drill tracks at the east end of the yard is a 200-ton, 72-foot Fairbanks-Morse track scale, arranged so cars from either classification yard may be weighed without interfering with switching operations.

Extending across the yard at about its midway point is a four-by-four-foot concrete box with suitable inlets, which takes care of surface drainage. Subsurface drainage is taken care of by two longitudinal lines of six-inch perforated corrugated pipe, with laterals about 700 feet long, which discharge into the concrete drainage box.

The four light-repair tracks have a total capacity of 125 cars. Located between the tracks are concrete runways, 16.8 feet wide, so designed that their edges can be used as jacking pads at any point. The service and supply buildings house a journal lathe; air-brake and tool rooms; lumber, paint, and material storage space; an oil storage room; a waste room; a blacksmith shop; a garage for shop trucks; and wash, locker, and toilet facilities for employees.

Night illumination of the yard is amply taken care of by the seven 100-foot floodlight towers at suitable locations. Each of the towers carries seven to ten 1,500-watt floods. On a number of them banks of light are placed back to back or, perhaps, at an angle, depending on the area to be lighted.

Supervision from Tower

Sixty feet in the air, on the south edge of the yard and midway in its length, we find a fourteen-by-fourteen-foot office from which an assistant-general yardmaster supervises the operation of the yard. From here he has a perfect view of the entire facility, while at his hand is the nerve center of the yard, by means of which he can communicate with those handling the switching operations.

This tower office is enclosed on four sides with Thermopane vapor-proof nonglare glass. There is an asphalt-tile floor and the ceiling is of an acoustical material. The room is air conditioned, and the heating is by electric unit heaters. A walkway, protected by an iron railing, extends entirely around the office at floor level. Beneath the office is another floor, which houses a toilet, the rectifiers, transformers, and other communication equipment.

The man in the tower office has at his command sixty-three talk-back speakers and five pairs of paging speakers. The talk-back speakers are located principally along the ladder tracks and at other points where a need for communication with switch crews is likely to occur, such as at the entrances to the yard, the ice dock, near the car-repair tracks, and at the stockyards. We also find the talk-backs in the offices of the general yardmaster, the terminal superintendent, and the trainmaster, and in the telegraph office.

A conversation may be initiated at any of the talk-back locations by pushing a button on the mast of the speaker, causing a corresponding indicator lamp on the console in the tower to light. On the other hand, if the tower wishes to talk to a particular man it is accomplished by turning the proper key switch and pressing a foot switch and calling the man's name. If the location of the man is unknown he can be summoned to a talk-back speaker by calling his name over one or all of the paging speakers.

Radio communication is used not only in the yard but also in directing the activities of switching locomotives working in the outlying areas of Springfield. When this happens, the switch crews are under the direction of the general yardmaster. In addition to radio hookups in the tower and in the general yardmaster's office, this new and long arm of modern communication for yard work reaches stations in the yard office on the south side of the city; it goes to another yard office on the north side and to the office of the road's telephone engineer in the general office building.

The radio circuit may be used as an intercommunication system between various offices without going out over the air. In the summer of 1950 seven switch engines at Springfield were equipped with radio sending and receiving apparatus.

Color for Efficiency

Color enters largely into our lives, and to a greater degree than many people suppose. Color, at Springfield, enters into the general yard office building interiors in connection with the functional use of colors. This is probably the first time that a decorative scheme has been employed as a means of furthering efficiency.

Certainly, this is opening up a new field in modern railroading endeavor.

Each of the four walls of each office in this building is a separate color, chosen on the basis of the direction the office faces, the function of the office, and the size of the room. Particular attention was given the matter of selecting the color on the wall which is faced by the employees occupying the office to be sure that it would be soft and friendly to the eyes.

In all, sixty-two colors were used throughout the building. Several colors were used in the corridors to increase the apparent width and decrease the apparent length.

This modern office building is 40 by 140 feet, of brick and concrete construction, having a finished basement and two upper stories, and with provisions for the addition of a third floor in the future. The usual unsightly clutter of heat, vent, and electrical pipes is missing, these facilities having been hidden in sheet-steel mullions between windows, and in a space that also houses the structural columns.

Venetian blinds and permanent visors control daylight and the direct rays of the sun. The principles of solar heating were applied in the use of the visors.

Located at West Springfield, this example of a new kind of office structure has attracted attention far and wide. We have spoken of its perimeter heating system, which consists of heating with continuous hot water radiation completely around the building on each floor. A continuous heating cabinet encloses not only the fin-tube radiation but all telephone, buzzer, inter-communicating, and electrical conduits. These conduits are thus easily accessible at all times at any point.

A short distance from the new office building there is a two-story restaurant building, its architecture harmonizing with the office structure. The first floor is used entirely as a restaurant, the second floor has bedrooms for the accommodation of out-lying crews.

Diesel Shop

Yesterday's roundhouse, with its stall for the iron horse, was a gloomy and a noisy place. Today's Diesel shop is well lighted, it is heated, and generally a pleasant place to work. It is not a storage place for motive power as the roundhouse was at times, but rather a repair and servicing base.

The Diesel shop at the Springfield Yard has a width of 127 feet and a length of 354 feet. The building has four levels and a floor area of 48,000 square feet. The window areas are glazed with corrugated actinic glass to block out heat rays and prevent sun shadows inside the building.

The main building has one through track and four stub tracks. The through track and the stub track next to it are for general service. One of the three remaining stub tracks is a truck release track and the other two are for heavy overhaul work. All tracks are served by a drop pit except the through track. This pit is twenty-four feet wide and ninety-eight feet long, with a depth of eighteen feet. In it is installed a drop table for removing trucks. Each of the pit tracks is equipped with body supports to hold up Diesel units when trucks are removed.

Diesel shops the country over hold to a similar pattern in general. They are amazing examples of efficiency and co-ordination. Service and repairs are made on an almost produc-tionlike basis.

A thirty-ton overhead crane, with a five-ton auxiliary crane, operates in a seventy-five-foot crane bay the entire length of the shop. It serves the two heavy-repair tracks and the truck-release track. The through track, located on the north side of the building, and the two adjacent tracks are built over inspection pits 214 feet long and 4 feet deep. They are served by adjacent elevated platforms and depressed working areas so that upper and lower engine work may be carried on at the same time. Lubricating oil, treated water, steam, and air are available at both the platform and the lower levels.

At the end of the lower stub tracks, on a level with the elevated platforms, are located an office, a storeroom, a parts-cleaning and parts-reconditioning shop, an electrician's shop, and an air-brake room. At the basement level are the "heavy" storeroom, water-treating facilities and pumps, and the "lube" oil room in which is stored approximately 69,000 gallons of oil in ten-gallon tanks.

About half way between the shop level and the oil-room floor are a wash-and-locker room, store department facilities, and a part of the shop facilities. A ten-ton freight elevator operates to and from this level to handle heavy parts for use on the upper levels. The different elevations in the building are connected with numerous ramps and stairways. On the south side of the building are two additions housing a large wheel lathe and a large lye cleaning vat.

The Diesel-shop building is equipped with thirty-two powered ventilators.

A feature of the Diesel shop is its communication system, which employs twenty-two dial-type telephone sets, strategically located throughout the shop. With the aid of paging speakers, men can be brought to any of these telephones. This is a vastly important factor in the efficiency of the shop.

Near the Diesel shop there is a building used for reclaiming lubricating oil. In the basement there are three settling and used-oil storage tanks, and such other tanks as are necessary for blending and refortifying the reclaimed oil. On the second floor there is a testing laboratory, which also houses two oil retorts, filters and tanks for holding the reclaimed oil. Pipe lines extend to the lubricating-oil tanks in the basement of the Diesel shop.

A fire-protection system liquid foam is installed in the reclaiming plant and in the oil storage room.

Two 55,000 Diesel fuel-oil storage tanks are located northwest of the Diesel shop. The unloading facilities consist of two spur tracks on which ten cars can be spotted for gravity unloading into a 10,900-gallon underground sump tank. From here the oil is pumped into cross-connected storage tanks set at the same level. Oil is pumped from the storage tanks into two 20,000-gallon tanks located along the Diesel shop servicing tracks.

Many railroad pages have been turned since the North Yard chapter was started, there in Springfield, Missouri, early in 1870. The man in the glass-walled tower today looks out over a yard plant at a crossroad of the Frisco Lines, the new saucer yard, standing ready for what tomorrow may bring.

CHAPTER XX

RIO GRANDE COAL HAUL

Geneva Steel

Geneva is a big name in the West, and it will be bigger. In the East it is Gary, Pittsburgh, Youngstown; in the West—Pueblo, Colorado; Geneva, Utah. The names are synonymous when it comes to steel. You think of them in connection with flame-spouting chimneys and iron-roofed buildings.

Geneva is the West's largest steel mill, and it is located thirty-eight miles south of Salt Lake City, Utah. It sprang up in the middle of fruit orchards and vegetable patches under the shadow of the mighty Wasatch Mountains in air clear as crystal. Steel is usually associated with vast, smoke-fogged industrial areas and waterways and ore boats.

Geneva is different. Geneva is new. Gary came into being around the turn of the century. Geneva, some forty years later, went into production to aid the West Coast war effort. Geneva, the whistle stop on the Rio Grande, became Geneva Steel. From blue prints in 1941 to a great steel plant in 1943-44, with three 1,100-ton blast furnaces, nine 225-ton open hearth furnaces, a 45-inch slabbing and blooming mill, a 132-inch continuous plate mill, a 26-inch structural mill, and various complementary facilities, including 252 by-product coke ovens.

The plant was operated for the government by the Geneva Steel Company, a new U.S. Steel subsidiary. It turned out plates and structural shapes for the building ship fleet in Pacific Coast yards.

Geneva Steel, even though a fair-haired boy in the government book, had a lot of trouble getting the things it needed

205

before it could start steel rolling down the rails. Such things as locomotives and cars, any old kind of locomotives, were as scarce as hen's teeth.

Geneva Steel ended up with a dozen twenty- and thirty-year-old steam locomotives of various makes, about every one tottering between the back shop and the junk yard, but they had to do. Rolling stock was also a desperate problem. Every road in the nation was staggering under its load of war traffic, and no road was letting go of anything with eight wheels and drawbars.

Geneva had a coal mine at Horse Canyon, Utah, served by the Carbon County Railroad. Many folks never heard of the Carbon County Railroad, but it was mighty important to the Denver & Rio Grande Western and Geneva Steel, all eleven miles of it. The Carbon County Railroad was the steel link between the Geneva Mine at Columbia, Utah, and Columbia Junction on the eighteen-mile Sunnyside Branch.

Somewhere in the East, agents for the Carbon County Railroad found 600 aged coal hopper cars that were about ready for the scrap pile, but they had to do. And they were started in service, with the Rio Grande operating them in special trains at reduced speeds. En route, they received careful inspections. These old cars and the old locomotives did their bit in putting Geneva on the map. They have been replaced now—the locomotives with modern Diesels, and the cars with high-side hoppers than can keep pace with modern main-line traffic.

In 1948, Geneva produced 800,000 net tons of finished steel and semifinished steel. And for every ton of steel produced there had to be two tons of iron ore, one ton of coke, and a half ton of limestone. Raw materials had to move in, and steel had to move out to distant fabricating plants. The hauling problem had to be solved by the two railroads that served Geneva—the Denver & Rio Grande Western and the Union Pacific.

Little has been written of the fine service rendered by these railroads in connection with Geneva, but they did a heroic job, and at no time failed to maintain the tradition of American railroads. Since this is a Rio Grande chapter, we will concern ourselves here mainly with the Rio Grande story.

We will go back a little to the early production of pig iron in the West, which, surprising enough, dates back to 1852. Like Geneva, it was produced in Utah. Columbia Steel started to make pig iron commercially for West Coast steel plants at Provo, Utah, in 1924.

Neither the Rio Grande nor the Union Pacific had any particular knowledge regarding serving big steel, but they learned at Geneva. Both roads knew about copper mines and smelters and the resulting heavy traffic, but waiting on Geneva was something else again. It meant engineering layouts and operations designed to cope with a different kind of heavy traffic, a traffic of the magnitude and precise regulation incident to meeting full-fledged steel production.

In the East, the famous ore boats bring to Gary and other lake terminals the red dust of the Mesabi, but at Geneva the red ore travels by rail across sagebrush deserts, 225 miles, from Iron Mountain to Geneva over the Union Pacific. Also large quantities of this ore are hauled from Provo, Utah, by the Rio Grande across Utah and Colorado to the Colorado Fuel & Iron Company in the Pueblo district.

Geneva uses fifteen to twenty carloads of limestone and dolomite per day, and this originates at Geneva Steel's Keighly quarry, near Payson, Utah, thirty-three miles from the steel plant. This quarry is on the Tintic Branch of the Rio Grande, which joins the main line at Springville, six miles south of Provo. Denver & Rio Grande Western freight trains working out of Provo haul the rock, either by special pickup moves or by what are called "tramp" assignments, meaning by other than solid through trains. It is handled in hopper cars.

For the reason that Utah coal is "just on the border line between coking and noncoking," Geneva blends it with a small proportion of a "coky" variety of coal from Oklahoma, which strengthens the coke structure. This is hauled from the Rio Grande's eastern gateways at Pueblo and Denver in mixed trains.

Geneva uses about eighty-five cars of coal a day. This originates for the most part at the Horse Canyon mine, and is hauled out to Mounds, on the Rio Grande main line, in seventy-ton hopper cars over the Carbon County Railroad, which we have mentioned. The Rio Grande then moves it to Geneva. Though the haul is shorter by half than the U.P. red ore movement from Iron Mountain, the Rio Grande encounters far more severe grades and curvature.

To meet the operating problem, the D.&R.G.W. worked out a solution that proved satisfactory. Never was there a stretch of track so much written about or so much photographed as that between Helper, Utah, and famous Soldier Summit, the Rio Grande right of way over which this coal from Horse Canyon moved on to Geneva.

This black-diamond haul over Soldier Summit involves whipping the heaviest westbound grade on the Rio Grande main line—2.4 per cent, Helper to Kyune, a distance of seven miles, 2 per cent for eighteen miles more. At the start of the run, the coal move generally is downhill to Mounds. On the head end there is a four-unit, 6,000-horsepower Diesel, capable of handling up to 105 loads, or a tonnage of 8,500 to 10,000 tons.

At Mounds, tonnage is reduced to 7,200 tons, or eighty cars. The same road engine handles the train to Helper, with a maximum grade of 1 per cent for the twenty-three miles. At Helper, where the Soldier Summit pull begins, a Diesel helper of 6,000-horsepower is cut into the coal drag. A second helper works at the rear of the train. This is the heaviest steam power on the Rio Grande, a 2-8-8-2 type simple articulated steam locomotive of the L-131 class, with a tractive force of 131,800 pounds.

The road Diesel whistles off and the train of Geneva coal starts its crawl over the hump. The grade drops at Soldier Summit, twenty-nine miles to Thistle. Going down, coal trains fill out to ninety cars, and they hold at this number so that full utilization of the dynamic braking on the four-unit Diesel may be realized. The retainers are turned up to "light" position, and no inspection stops are necessary.

Retainers are returned to normal at Thistle and the coal drag goes through to Geneva. Here it heads into the plant receiving track. Now we see the advantage of Diesel power and the way it is applied to modern precision railroading.

Bessemer and Lake Erie's new 4-unit E.M.D. 6,000 h.p. freight Diesel crossing the Allegheny River Bridge at River Valley, Pa., with 110 loads of ore totaling 11,000 tons. Courtesy, B.&L.E. RR.

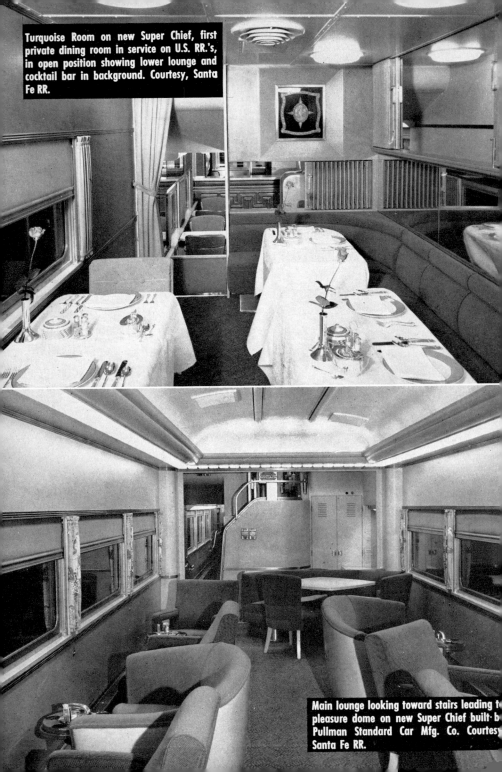

Turquoise Room on new Super Chief, first private dining room in service on U.S. RR.'s, in open position showing lower lounge and cocktail bar in background. Courtesy, Santa Fe RR.

Main lounge looking toward stairs leading to pleasure dome on new Super Chief built by Pullman Standard Car Mfg. Co. Courtesy, Santa Fe RR.

Frisco Diesel #2010 new E.M.D. E-8 hauling #4, the Will Rogers, approaching Bristow, Okla., with seven cars on the Southwestern Division. Photo by Preston George.

Frisco #1522, 4-8-2 type of the famous Frisco's 1500 class, with an eastbound reefer block running between Sapulpa and Tulsa, Okla., with thirty-three cars. Southwestern Division. Photo by Preston George.

S.P. Extra 6253 west approaching Dunsmuir, Calif., running along the Sacramento River with Mt. Shasta in the background. C.T.C. territory. Shasta Division. Courtesy, S.P. RR.

S.P. officials ride their freight trains. Second 632 Oakland-Portland Fast Freight arriving at Crescent Lake with business car on head end. Shasta Division. Courtesy, S.P. RR.

K.C.S. #2 new Southern Belle leaving Pittsburgh, Kansas on first district. Northern Division. Courtesy, K.C.S. RR.

Frisco's C.T.C. machine at Springfield, Mo., which handles train movements from Pacific, Mo., to Monett, Mo. Note the unique timetable drum over the dispatcher's head on the left. Courtesy, Frisco Lines.

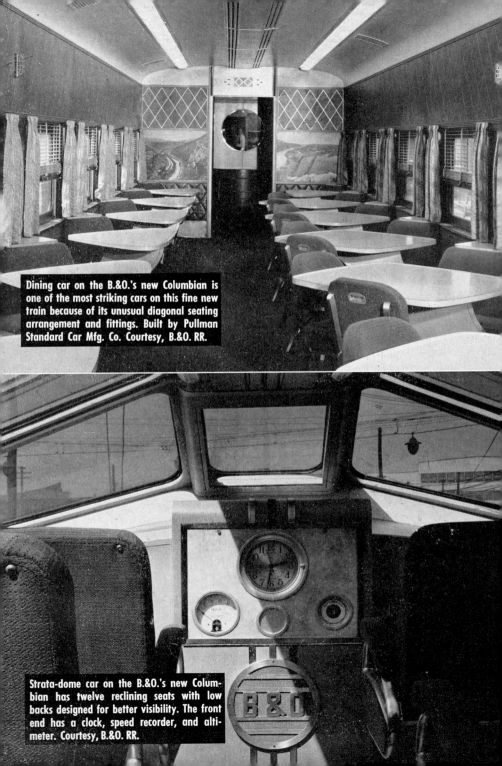

Dining car on the B.&O.'s new Columbian is one of the most striking cars on this fine new train because of its unusual diagonal seating arrangement and fittings. Built by Pullman Standard Car Mfg. Co. Courtesy, B.&O. RR.

Strata-dome car on the B.&O.'s new Columbian has twelve reclining seats with low backs designed for better visibility. The front end has a clock, speed recorder, and altimeter. Courtesy, B.&O. RR.

Rear end of the new B.&O. Columbian's observation lounge car built by the Pullman Standard Car Mfg. Co. Courtesy, B.&O. RR.

The cocktail lounge is found in the forward end of the observation car on the B.&O.'s new Columbian #25, and its furnishings have received many fine comments. Courtesy

B.&O. #25, the Columbian, fine new all-coach streamliner built by the Pullman Standard Car Mfg. Co., at Takoma Park, Md., on the Baltimore Division. Courtesy, B.&O. RR.

Immediately that the road Diesel brakes its coal train in at Geneva, it is cut off and run around the train to pick up the caboose, which is coupled on behind a train of 100 to 120 empties. The Diesel then backs on and the train line is hooked up and the brakes tested. In about an hour from the time it pulled in through the switch it pulls onto the main line for the eighty-two-mile run to Helper.

Eastbound, Thistle to Soldier Summit, the grade lifts for twenty-nine miles at 2 per cent. The Diesel takes the long train up the hill without a helper. Upon arriving at Helper, the bad order cars are switched out and replaced, and the train proceeds to Columbia Junction behind the same road Diesel, climbing the ruling 1.76 grade on the branch without the service of helper power.

The coal trains are handled between Columbia Junction and Helper by two crew turns out of the latter point daily. These are known as DPC-1 and DPC-2, having been so designated for the Defense Plant Corporation, original owners of the mine. The runs are about twelve hours apart. Generally, if DPC-1 brings down full tonnage to the main line at Mounds, where the tonnage is reduced, DPC-2 will come down with a lighter train, filling out at Mounds with the loads left by the DPC-1.

Two crews handle two turns between Helper and Geneva every twenty-four hours. Sometimes they set out commercial coal at Provo, Utah, for other destinations.

The time sequence of the coal runs includes departure from Columbia Junction at 2:00 P.M., the arrival at Helper at 4:00 P.M. The train leaves Helper at 8:00 P.M., pulling into Geneva at 4:00 A.M. in the morning. The Geneva departure, as has been pointed out, is about an hour later, or at 5:00 A.M. The train is due into Helper at 10:00 A.M. Upon call, a turn works out of Helper to Columbia Junction, starting a new sequence.

Around 800 hopper cars are employed in the Geneva coal movement, about 300 of these are the new-type seventy-ton cars, which were purchased by the Carbon County Railway. These are equipped with a type of brake-shoe key that will not shake out when the car is turned over by the Geneva unloading apparatus. The new cars are also equipped with the Lewis type empty-and-load brakes. Geneva Steel in its early days had a lot of trouble with brake shoes and keys being buried in its furnace charges, while the railroad was plagued with bad-order cars.

The Rio Grande spent about $284,000 in preparing its Sunnyside branch for the increased load it had to carry. A change of line near Mounds reduced the grade against loaded movements from 0.70 per cent to 0.50 per cent, and against empty movements from 1.76 to 1.33 per cent. Relocation work at Columbia Junction reduced the empty movement from 2.54 to 1.78 per cent. Also, a Y and two interchange tracks were constructed at this point.

The old branch rail dated away back to 1912, and this was replaced with ninety-pound relay rail, with six inches of gravel ballast between Mounds and Dragerton, a mile north of Columbia Junction.

To meet the needs created by the Geneva Steel plant, the Denver & Rio Grande Western enlarged its Provo, Utah, yard, revamping the leads and laying additional track. This provided facilities for handling limestone loads and empties, for plant loading at Geneva and took care of such coal setouts as might be made. To handle the traffic in and out of Geneva, beside the solid through coal movements, tramp assignments again operate between Provo and Salt Lake City's Roper Yard, forty-four miles away. These assignments deliver empties into Geneva for loading, haul out the finished steel for movements to the North and West, and handle coal and limestone loads and empties.

The Denver & Rio Grande Western's biggest single source of income is Geneva Steel, and the road is most happy to serve it. If ever a railroad deserved the support that industry can offer economically, it is the Rio Grande, which operates trains over some of the roughest terrain in the United States. It has, further, battled through some very rough financial hills on a road that seemed destined for the poorhouse. It suffered bankruptcy but it never lost the will to fight, and in the year 1950 it was physically in a position to look the world in the eye and accept every challenge.

The road that drove through the Rockies, instead of dodging around them, is writing a new story of conquest in the West, and this time it has to do with the birth and growth of a new industrial giant, slowly uncoiling in a region that once was a part of Utah's sagebrush deserts.

CHAPTER XXI

SANTA FE

Today's Super Chief's New Kind of Dome Car

New world standards for rail travel were set by the Santa Fe when, on January 28, 1951, two of the most outstanding and modern cars ever built went into service on the Super Chief. A completely new design of dome-lounge car, featuring the Turquoise Room, and a new diner appeared in the make-up of the road's famous train, as well as all new sleeping cars.

The dining car is completely new, it is roomier, it is richly appointed. Its color schemes catch the unmatched tints of the romantic Southwest. It rightly maintains the high standards set by the Santa Fe dining service long ago. It is a place of good food, of ease and relaxation, this Santa Fe diner, but the dome car is the star of the show.

The ultramodern diner has a larger and more complete stainless steel kitchen, and it is equipped with Carbofreezer refrigeration units which utilize dry ice for the cooling medium, providing for the better keeping of meats, vegetables, and other food and eliminating possibility of contamination.

Because it is a complete innovation, the Santa Fe's new dome car attracted vast throngs at its preview showings. By January, 1951, people in the United States were fairly well acquainted with the average dome car, either through personal contact on train trips or from pictures in railroad advertisements, but the features of the Super Chief's dome-lounge were so entirely new and startling that the public turned to it as they would have to a new comet.

Everywhere you heard people saying, "Have you seen it?"

You caught the words, "Turquoise Room" and "Pleasure Dome." Many travelers have come to expect new and better things of their favorite railroads. Some Santa Fe travelers were wondering when they were going to be able to ride through the enchantment land of the Southwest under a glass roof. And then, at the peak of the modern trend, it was announced. One man we know said, "I canceled plane reservations to ride the Super Chief. I am making up a dinner party for the Turquoise Room."

Private parties up to ten persons can be served in the Turquoise Room. When not reserved for private use, all passengers may enjoy this room for relaxation and refreshments, served from the lower lounge. Turquoise, the traveler's stone, gives the room its name, as it influences the decorative treatment of blue, which is blended with gold and silver coloring.

No fine club could offer more than this Turquoise Room on the beautiful all-room Super Chief. It is destined to be one of the most popular sections of the train.

The dome car has three levels, the first of which is the lower-lounge level; then comes the main-lounge level, the level on which the Turquoise Room is located; and finally the dome level —upstairs under the stars.

The lower lounge, under the dome, is a smart cocktail room seating ten in an intimate, congenial setting. The main lounge, forward, has a specially designed diagonal seating and extra-wide windows. An alcove in the end of the lounge has a writing desk, which is convenient and private.

The Pleasure Dome, reached by a stairway from the main lounge, has glare-proof windows and deep-cushioned swivel chairs, a feature which at this writing is not incorporated in other dome cars, but it is something that is vastly appreciated by the Santa Fe traveler.

Later, we are going to ride the Super Chief out of Chicago, but first, to appropriately set the stage, we will examine the decorations and appointments of this new dome car, into which the Pullman-Standard Car Manufacturing Company put such painstaking efforts.

We return to the Turquoise Room. Side and end walls have gold-tinted Vinylite treatment, as well as the accordian-type sliding panels covered with the same material, which separate the room proper and the passageway. These panels form the upper part of the partition; the lower part being solid. The panels may be opened or closed, according to the desire of those occupying the room.

Golden-tint plate mirrors line the side wall above the banquette seating arrangement. Gold-colored textured draperies frame the windows. The portiere covering the door separating the Turquoise Room from the lower lounge is of the same material. The service plate was specially designed and fits in with the decorative treatment of the room. The color of the carpet is turquoise. On the forward-end wall there is a full color reproduction of a genuine turquoise medallion, encased in a modern shadow box, incorporated in the structure of the wall.

The lower cocktail lounge is in modernistic design. The bar front is covered with Vinylite material in a cherry red of quilted design, accomplished by the use of brass-colored, oval-shaped snap-on moldings, typical of the Southwest. A considerable portion of the side wall is covered with flesh-tinted mirrors, adding to the beauty and warmth of the room and giving it a feeling of spaciousness. The cherry-red tone is carried out on several of the stainless, semibarreled designed chairs and window draperies. Exposed wall surfaces are covered with Vinylite material in a contrasting color. The floor is covered with a *tête-de-Negre* colored carpeting with a lighter pattern.

The main lounge is spacious for lounging and it has a new and unique arrangement of furniture. Located at the forward end of the room is a specially designed diagonal seat for card playing with pull-up chairs. Further seating consists of two modern sofas, several lounge chairs, and a built-in seating arrangement. All seating permits the occupants a direct view from the wide windows without having to face the person across the car, which was characteristic of the older type lounge-car arrangements.

A warm and friendly color scheme is carried out in the room.

214

The upholstery is arch green and terra cotta, walls are of beige, and the ceiling a creamy yellow. Window draperies are of California seashells design in Southwest colors which blend with the room scheme. The same color scheme is carried out in the observation dome.

Thus the car has four completely separate rooms, plus the writing desk alcove. The service is the same high standard as is traditional on the great name train of the Santa Fe. Today's Super Chief service includes push-button radio, music, and train announcements in your private room—when you want it! You have barber, valet, shower bath, news bulletins, stock reports, newspapers, magazines, and distinctive train stationery.

A great train, a modern train is this Super Chief, with its striking Turquoise Room, and a stairway leading to the stars, as are the Chief, Texas Chief, and new Kansas City Chief, plus many others on the Santa Fe.

Upstairs on the Super Chief

This is June. The air has that softness that stirs the urge to look at far horizons. You want to board a train and go somewhere—just for the ride. You turn over in your mind place names. Western place names—Dodge City, Wagon Mound, Santa Fe! The Atchinson, Topeka & Santa Fe brings to mind Cyrus K. Holiday, the Harvey Girl, the famous Nellie Bly Special, the run of Death Valley Scotty's "Coyote Special." Santa Fe—"The Main Line West," the magazine advertisement read.

That's it! You're going to the Coast on the Santa Fe. But on which train? There is the Grand Canyon Limited, the California Limited, the El Capitan, the Chief—the Super Chief. You hesitate a moment. Here is one of the great name trains of the world, the Santa Fe's Super Chief, but it is extra fare. Perhaps you have the money but are a wee bit on the thrifty side, or perhaps that extra fifteen dollars is going to require a little extra scrimping on something else, as is the case with the majority of folks.

And then you suddenly remember that in January of this 1951 the Santa Fe added all new cars to its consist, and that one of these was a dome car—the Pleasure Dome, the folder read. Your brief mental debate ends there. The Indian country —brown pueblos, ancient villages, red cliffs, timeless mountains —from a seat "upstairs" on the Super Chief!

Chicago, 7 P.M.

You are on the new Super Chief. You hear the final "All-ll aboar-r-d!" there in the Dearborn Station, and the famous light-weight-car streamliner starts its feather-soft glide down the shining rails into the West. You are in the new diner and you glance at your water glass, your coffee cup—there is not a ripple, which means that, from the crimson-splashed nose of the powerful Diesel ahead to the dull-glowing tail sign, there is perfect balance and co-ordination between roadbed, trucks, couplers, and motive power.

When boarding the Super Chief you noticed that the dome car was behind the dining car, and there was pleasant anticipation when your eye caressed it. You had thought of hurrying there at once, but there was the matter of establishing yourself in your roomette and you assure yourself that there is plenty of time for you to enjoy it later.

Your timetable tells you that Fort Madison, Iowa, is the first scheduled stop, 232.9 miles from Chicago, although the train will stop to pick up revenue passengers at Galesburg, Illinois, 177.5 miles from Chicago.

No. 17, which is the number of your westbound Super Chief, is past Nemo, Illinois, before you finally go to the dome car. Entering the car with the famous Turquoise Room is like entering an exclusive club. It is hardly like being on a train at all— these sofas facing the wide windows, the general seating, the convenient smoking stands. People are reading, playing cards, or sitting relaxed with a cocktail.

You move up the thick-carpeted stairs and slip into a deep-cushioned swivel chair, feeling like a privileged guest in a strange land of make-believe.

This is part of the prairie country of the state, flat under the enormous sky. Downstairs you were not aware of this night landscape, but in the dome a peculiar intimacy is unfolded; you are on a plane between the earth and the stars. In the distance farm house lights make golden punctuations. As you watch, one winks out; the countryside is going to sleep.

Ahead, the beam of the headlight is a silver blade, probing the gloom. Fairy lights leap at you. A town rushes past—Media. Then you are coming down to the Mississippi—great waters, caught with shafts of light. There is a song of steel under the wheels and you are crossing the 3,347-foot Mississippi River bridge at Fort Madison.

This is Missouri now. Kansas City is only two hours and a half away when you finally leave the dome. You are not going to forget the dome car and your first experience, surrounded by glass, there under the eaves of the night sky.

The Super Chief picks up a sleeping car at Kansas City—ten roomettes, six double bedrooms, and two compartments—which was ready for occupancy at 9:30 P.M. In the morning, somewhere in the vastness of Kansas, passengers will go to the dome car, finding you already there. You wanted a look at Dodge City, and so you were up and through breakfast early. You wanted, in particular, to see Dodge from the dome—the Dodge of the trail drivers and the buffalo hunters.

The time is 7:53 A.M. No. 17 is stopping and you are glad to have a few short minutes to look closer at the Dodge City of today, while your mind paints a Frederick Remington picture of the Dodge City of yesterday.

Those boarding the train here are passengers for New Mexico, Arizona, and California. The Super Chief soon is speeding west again.

Mighty Kansas is part of the breadbasket of America, of which you have read so much. You are intensely interested in the yellow sea of golden wheat, the towering grain elevators, the long sidings filled with cars for the wheat move. Where the hoofs of a million Texas longhorns raised an almost perpetual cloud of trail dust in their northward march, you look now at ripening grain. You watch a reaper, and beyond, in the midst of things, you see an Ab Blocker cowboy.

You see a row of cottonwoods and a road turning a section corner at a schoolhouse. There is a third dimension to this panorama from the dome car, a deep perspective that allows you to see beyond the "fence row" of fleeting telegraph poles. You look back, turning your chair, and far ahead. You see that splash of red when your Diesel comes off a tangent, and silver cars and things one hundred miles away. You are not thinking much about that extra fifteen dollars right now.

You are a modern adventurer, riding a blunt-nosed steed on the race track of the Santa Fe at almost one hundred miles an hour. It is almost impossible to believe that you are climbing into the sky. Last night, at Fort Madison, you were a bare 500 feet above sea level. Now, in the morning, you are moving into Colorado and approaching 4,000 feet, which explains the clearness of the air. It is like crystal. Your eyes have the power of field glasses in bringing detail close. You have a particular awareness of this from your seat in the dome of the Super Chief. From the picture window of your Pullman the landscape is moving, but from the dome, looking ahead, it stands still. It is like watching a passing train, which, if you are close, becomes a blur. But watching its approach from a point dead ahead it does not appear to move, it simply enlarges.

No one who has seen the Rockies, approaching them from the prairie states, will forget that picture, or the small emotional teapot inside that was set to brewing at about the same time.

The Rocky Mountains do not arise brazenly to smite the beholder with their magnitude and grandeur. The Rockies are as coy and subtle as a beautiful lady. They approach you with complete diffidence and modesty, and yet never have they failed to awaken in the observer an immediate feeling of humility and insignificance.

The Rockies reveal themselves as God might, quietly but in a wondrous manner—from the sky.

Perhaps it is only a blue backdrop; perhaps there are cotton-batting clouds, away off there in the west. Then there is a white-lace edging across the sky, dainty and fine.

That is the snow-capped roof of America—the Rockies.

The Super Chief reaches La Junta, Colorado, at 9:42 A.M. If you wish to impress a traveling acquaintance with your knowledge of things Western, refer to this place as *La Hoon'-tah*, not as La *Jun*ta. From here on you are warned to watch for these trick Spanish pronunciations. *La junta* means "the junction." You will eventually come to a place in California written El Cajon', which you will call *El Kah-hon'*, with the *a* broad, and not under any circumstance El Ca*john,* or you will identify yourself as the rankest sort of a tenderfoot.

Your Super Chief reaches Trinidad, Colorado, and begins the climb over Raton Pass. Trinidad has an elevation of close to 6,000 feet and No. 17 snakes up a 3.5 per cent grade to Raton Tunnel at 7,622 feet. This is New Mexico now, and the high noonday sun pours its brightness hard down on some of the most colorful scenery out of doors. No artist has ever been able to quite imprison on a piece of canvas the true color or the immensity of New Mexico's mountains and high plateaus.

You, in this dome car of the Super Chief, from high up on a corner of the Culebras, are riding into a land of enchantment, as this track of the Santa Fe continues to flirt with the eastern ramparts of the Rockies. You pass Wagon Mound and glide on toward the Glorietas and some of the most tempestuous scenery anywhere. This country cannot begin to be appreciated until it is viewed from your dome. You ride through it surrounded by all of the luxury the Super Chief affords, and you count that fifteen dollars extra fare one of the best investments you ever made.

This, you are told, is the Indian Detour country, where, if it is your pleasure, you may arrange for a motor trip through old Santa Fe and other points of extreme interest. (The main line of the Santa Fe does not pass through the city of Santa Fe, which is the state capital.)

No. 17 comes off the Glorietas, dropping to Albuquerque in

the late afternoon. It then climbs to the Continental Divide, which is at a slightly less altitude than Glorieta Pass. Your Super Chief comes into Gallup, racing daylight through the Western twilight. Gallup is the center of the fabulous Indian country. This is the land, too, of the conquistadors and the padres of old Spain, the land of pathfinders and traders. You feel an intangible kinship for this part of America. Its vastness and its color does something to you. To the north and to the south lie limitless frontiers, some of them unscarred by the foot of the white man.

The sun falls away behind kaleidoscopic cliffs and there is immediately a splash of gold on other cliffs and mountain peaks, and you sit tensely forward, braced against the impact of such titanic splendor.

You enjoy your late dinner, listen to the radio for a little, perhaps, read the paper, and some time after the Winslow, Arizona, departure at 9:22 P.M., you discover that your feet are carrying you back to the dome car. You have read *Under the Western Stars* and similar stories of the West with their intriguing names, and your expectations of experiencing some new thrill in the dome receives something of a setback. You do not become excited when you mount the steps and settle into a seat. You are not emotionally provoked as at a man-made spectacle. This is like entering a candlelit cathedral for a service at which you will conform more closely to the rites if you kneel.

The night is silver. The moon is a gold pendant on the bosom of the sky. The stars are sprinkling diamond dust over the dome from the canopy of heaven. Nowhere are stars so low and bright as on these high Arizona plateaus. Something draws scratches, bright, and intense in their transience—sparks from the Almighty's anvil. All of your life you have looked up at the stars but never before have you felt yourself so much a part of them.

You lose sight of train sounds and movement. You hear a voice exclaim, "Wonderful!" but it is in another world, not in the seat adjoining.

An abyss opens and the rush of wheels echo to the famous Canyon Diablo bridge. Off on the right a white-tipped cone is caught by the moonlight in some unreal realm—San Francisco Peak, 12,611 feet.

This is timber country now—Flagstaff, Arizona—the pines are silvered. Williams, Arizona, is only a sprinkle of lights. Off there a few desert leagues across the top of Coconino County is the Grand Canyon of the Rio Colorado, Bill Williams Mountain, a mountain valley, a winding road, car lights.

Your Diesel is lifting the train to Supai. Now you are dropping. Blue vistas are before you—moonlight vistas such as you never before dreamed of. Johnson Canyon, more lights—you are not sure whether they are of heaven or earth. Your silver comet, the Super Chief, almost seems to have become a part of the celestial parade as it turns a mighty arc. Ash Fork in the valley has its bright eyes on the streamliner, swinging the great horseshoe curve at Gleed. The air beacon on old Bill Williams Mountain seems to wave an *adiós* to the palefaces in the dome.

Seligman, Arizona, at 12:35 A.M. Past midnight, past your bedtime. But in this world time has no meaning. As these strange Westerners say, "There is always *mañana*—tomorrow." Still, you can't go to bed yet, you must ride this dome down the roller coaster—126 miles of 1.42 per cent descending grade to the Colorado River, Yampai to Needles.

Westbound or eastbound, the Super Chief crosses the great Mojave Desert while night's curtain is drawn. However, early risers at Barstow, California, are repaid by the glorious vistas of morning on the desert—the weird Joshua trees, the blue line of the San Gabriel Mountains, Old Baldy, San Antonio Peak, 10,080 feet, carrying a great snow cone in winter months, the San Bernardino Mountains, and notched El Cajon Pass.

Dropping down this much photographed El Cajon grade, your Super Chief reaches San Bernardino—"Santa Fe Town," so-called, with its shops—at 7:03 A.M. Then it is orange groves, and Pasadena at 8:12 A.M. Los Angeles Union Station at 8:45 A.M.

Your eastbound Super Chief, No. 18, leaves Los Angeles at 8:00 P.M., Pacific time. No. 18 makes an operating stop at 2:05

A.M. at Needles, California; then crosses the Colorado River and goes into Mountain time at Topock, Arizona. Another operating stop of two minutes is made at Seligman, at 6:07 A.M.

You are retracing now the journey you made across northern Arizona at night. It is like attempting to review a dream—nothing seems quite the same as you try to remember it. It is a new world now, a land of immensity, of beauty, of this strangely rarefied air that enables you to look back from your dome seat at San Francisco Peak, almost one hundred miles away. There is the Painted Desert country near Holbrook, and the Petrified Forest, for those who will revisit and live for a little in this wonderland.

Winslow, Arizona, is another operating stop, and your Super Chief is at Gallup, New Mexico, for another of these brief and expertly executed operational pauses. Albuquerque at 1:25 P.M. You are looking back of beyond from the dome, at far horizons which you will not forget. The color and the clouds are photographed in your mind. At Las Vegas, New Mexico, you are thinking back to the Land of the Pueblos. You have lived a thousand years in a day on this road of the Santa Fe, which means "Holy Faith."

You are climbing Raton; you are gliding into Kansas in the evening. You have your last look at Dodge City at 11:15 P.M., Mountain time, you leave Dodge at 12:18 A.M., Central time. Your Super Chief pulls into Kansas City at 5:35 A.M. From your dome seat, you look at Fort Madison and the Mississippi at 9:35 A.M.

Chicago, Dearborn Station, 1:45 P.M.

CHAPTER XXII

CHICAGO & EASTERN ILLINOIS

Red Ball Trains

A railroad that runs freight trains as second sections of passenger trains; a railroad with 80 per cent of its motive power less than three years old; a railroad that has doubled the ownership of its boxcars in one year, 1950 over 1949—that is a lot of railroad. A railroad deserving of a place in a book of modern railroading.

A railroad with a central switchboard for direct transfer to *forty* different railroads. An old railroad with young ideas. The Chicago & Eastern Illinois.

The main line of the Chicago & Eastern Illinois extends southward from Chicago to Evansville, Indiana, on the banks of the Ohio River, a distance of 287.2 miles. For 162 miles, Chicago to Clinton, Indiana, it is double track. From Clinton to Evansville, it is single track, but with that able traffic master, centralized traffic control, installed by the Union Switch & Signal Company, providing vastly added track capacity.

From Dolton Junction, 16.9 miles south of Chicago, to Clinton the road has automatic train stops, giving almost iron-clad security on this speedway. The C.&E.I. was the first railroad in the United States to employ automatic train control. This was voluntarily installed in 1914; it is now replaced by the most modern type. The road has installed radio in all yard engines in the new and excellent Wansford Yard, just north of Evansville, and it is also included in the equipment of terminal locomotives in the Evansville terminal. Train radio experiments are in progress as this book is written.

A railroad is no better than its freight terminals, and the Chicago & Eastern Illinois have fine flat yards in Yard Center, immediately south of Dolton Junction, Illinois, and Wansford Yard. Yard Center is the road's classification and receiving yard on the Chicago end. It receives its cars from the various belt railroads around Chicago and from its eastern, western and northern connections.

The C.&E.I.'s Red Ball manifest trains make up here for their flight south. Wansford Yard, on the other end, has a capacity of 2,000 cars daily and can probably handle 50,000 cars per month. In the fall of 1950, it was handling from 1,400 to 1,900 cars daily and about 32,000 monthly.

Wansford Yard consists of four receiving and departure tracks, with a capacity of 145 cars, and sixteen classification tracks, divided into two yards of eight classification tracks each. Wansford has a ten-car icing platform, a track scale, four rip tracks, and a turntable. It has a new yard office and a telegraph office. The old steam engine house has been made over into a Diesel shop for light running repairs.

The classification tracks hold from forty-nine to fifty-seven cars each. The yard is floodlighted from towers. The yardmaster's tower has polarized windows and it is equipped with the usual radio and loud-speaker facilities, such as you would expect to find in an up-to-date yard, providing communication between tower and switch engines and all key points. The C.T.C. machine into the Evansville terminal is operated from the yard office in the tower; the territory extends from Wansford to Union Track Junction.

The yard is laid completely with 112-pound rail. No. 8 turnouts are used on all switches and leads.

The Chicago & Eastern Illinois links at Evansville with the Louisville & Nashville, and a unique method of handling the cars in the transfer is used. One month the C.&E.I. performs all of the switching and transfer work, and the next month the L.&N. does it. In this way, only loaded trains are taken from one yard to the other. Both roads switch their own passenger trains in the Evansville terminal. In the city the C.&E.I.-owned Evansville Belt performs the switching.

Before we take a look at the fast freights we will briefly review the main line, the tonnage, and the motive power. Ingle, Indiana, eleven miles north of Evansville, is the top of the northward .88 per cent ruling grade. The southbound ruling grade is .87 per cent at Miller, Indiana, thirty-five miles north of Evansville. Two-unit Diesels handle all freight trains on the system.

Beside its 123 miles of C.T.C., the entire main line has color-light signals, or 97 per cent of all signals. The road has forty interlocking plants, twenty-eight of which are used jointly with foreign roads. Passing tracks in C.T.C. territory average 105-car capacity. The lightest main-line rail is 110-pound, except from Findlay Junction to Thebes, on the Central-Southern Illinois line. This is ninety-pound.

The Chicago & Eastern Illinois reduced its 130 steam engines to 87 Diesel units. All of the following Diesel power is covered in the General Motors' Diesel chapter. Breaking down the eighty-seven units, we have thirty-eight A and B unit Electro-Motive F3's; three Electro-Motive 2,000-horsepower E7's; twenty-six of the Electro-Motive GP7's, and fourteen of the 1,200-horsepower Electro-Motive switchers. In addition the road owns three switch engines of 600 horsepower and three branch-line switchers. The C.&E.I. was one of the first railroads to take the GP7 road switcher to its heart, confident that it was a great piece of power. The road gets 90 to 95 per cent utilization in yard power.

The Chicago & Eastern Illinois has every reason to be proud of its southbound manifests, Nos. 57 and 51. They are typical of the spirit of this progressive road in their conquest of time and distance. They might be called feature trains of the freight service, dogging the heels of the road's crack passenger trains.

Let's go along with No. 57 out of Yard Center, in the Chicago area—only it is not No. 57 yet, but *Second No. 7*. No. 7 is the road's crack speed liner to Atlanta, Georgia. Our manifest, carrying meat from the Chicago packing houses, does not as-

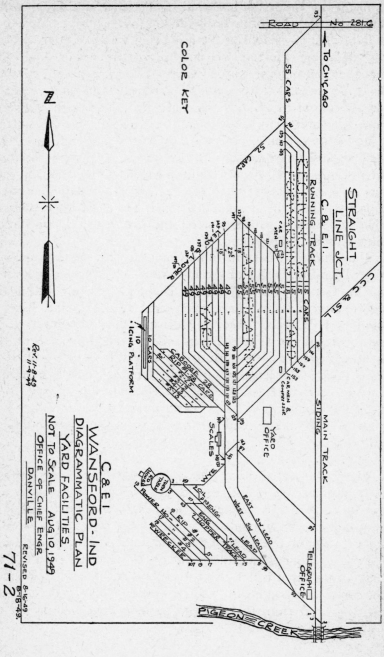

STRAIGHT
LINE JCT.
C. & E.I.

C & E I
WANSFORD-IND
DIAGRAMMATIC PLAN
Yard Facilities.
Not To Scale Aug 10, 1949
OFFICE OF CHIEF ENGR
DANVILLE
Revised 8-16-49
8-18-43.

71-2

Rev. 11-8-49
" 11-9-49.

COLOR KEY

N

ROAD No 281.6

To CHICAGO

55 CARS

52 CARS

RUNNING TRACK

55 CARS

115 CARS

LADDER

CABOOSE 28
R.I.P. 28 CARS

MAIN TRACK

SIDING

YARD
OFFICE

CARMEN &
COMPRESSOR

CAR
MEN

CARMEN

SCALES

10 CARS

ICING PLATFORM

10 CARS

EAST SW LEAD

WEST SW LEAD

SW LEAD

OIL STORAGE

POWER HO. R.I.P. #1

R.I.P. #2

HOPPER HOUSE

TURN TABLE

WRECKER

TELEGRAPH
OFFICE

PIGEON CREEK

sume identity as No. 57 until it reaches Brewer, Illinois, 126 miles south of Chicago. From Brewer it shows up on the time-table as a second class train—No. 57. As No. 57 it streaks on to the Evansville gateway over the Evansville Subdivision. This train is allowed to run fifty-five miles an hour. Beside meat, No. 57 carries miscellaneous fast freight for the Louisville & Nash-ville and the Nashville, Chattanooga & St. Louis connections for points south.

No. 57 arrives at Brewer (Danville Yard) at 12:30 A.M. The train crews change, the train is completely inspected and makes its departure at 1:15 A.M., arriving at Wansford Yard, Evans-ville, at 7:00 A.M. It completes the run of 266 miles in nine hours. Cabooses on this manifest are run right through from Yard Center to Wansford. All cars that are to go south are blocked, that is, placed together, at the head end and at Wans-ford are taken in one cut directly to the Louisville & Nashville yard preparatory to leaving Evansville.

Train No. 51 leaves Yard Center at 1:05 P.M., running as Second No. 3, which has passed Yard Center at 1:03 P.M., or two minutes before. It runs to Brewer as the second section of the passenger, where it becomes No. 51. This manifest arrives at Brewer at 4:30 P.M. and departs at 5:15 P.M. It arrives at Terre Haute, Indiana, at 6:25 P.M., stops at Vincennes at 8:15 P.M. to deliver cars to the Baltimore & Ohio interchange; then heads for Wansford, arriving there at 11:00 P.M.

Both Nos. 57 and 51 carry many automobile parts to Evans-ville. They are fine, exciting trains, a part of the great American network of modern fast freight lines.

Northward, Train No. 58, of the manifest fleet, leaves Evans-ville at 11:30 A.M.; leaves Princeton, Indiana, at 12:30 P.M., after picking up perishables from the Southern Railway; does the work at Terre Haute; then goes on to Brewer, arriving at 4:45 P.M. After an hour and a quarter inspection, it pushes on north to Yard Center, pulling in at 10:30 P.M.

Train No. 56 leaves Evansville at 4:30 P.M., Princeton at 5:20 P.M., Vincennes at 6:30 P.M., Terre Haute at 9:05 P.M. and Cayuga, Indiana, at 10:30 P.M. Arrival at Brewer is at 12:05

CHICAGO & EASTERN ILLINOIS RAILROAD

Office of Superintendent Transportation
Chicago, Illinois

Revised Nov. 1, 1950

FREIGHT TRAIN SCHEDULES

SOUTHBOUND

Train #55

Leave Brewer	6:35 P.M.
Leave Terre Haute	8:30 P.M.
Arrive Evansville	2:00 P.M.

Train #51

Leave Yard Center	1:05 P.M.
Arrive Brewer	4:30 P.M.
Leave Brewer	5:15 P.M.
Arrive Evansville	11:00 P.M.

Train #57

Leave Yard Center	10:00 P.M.
Arrive Brewer	12:30 A.M.
Leave Brewer	1:15 A.M.
Arrive Evansville	7:00 A.M.

Train #61

Leave Yard Center	12:01 P.M.
Arrive Villa Grove	9:30 P.M.

Train #63

Leave Yard Center	7:15 P.M.
Arrive Villa Grove	12:15 A.M.

Train #163

Leave Villa Grove	3:15 A.M.
Arrive Salem	7:00 A.M.
Leave Salem	8:35 A.M.
Leave Thebes	5:00 P.M.
Arrive Chaffee	7:00 P.M.

NORTHBOUND

Train #52

Leave Evansville	2:00 A.M.
Leave Vincennes	4:30 A.M.
Leave Terre Haute	7:15 A.M.
Arrive Brewer	11:00 A.M.

Train #58

Leave Evansville	11:30 A.M.
Leave Princeton	12:30 P.M.
Arrive Brewer	4:45 P.M.
Leave Brewer	6:00 P.M.
Arrive Yard Center	10:30 P.M.

Train #56

Leave Evansville	4:30 P.M.
Leave Princeton	5:20 P.M.
Leave Vincennes	6:30 P.M.
Leave Terre Haute	9:05 P.M.
Leave Cayuga	10:30 P.M.
Arrive Brewer	12:05 A.M.
Leave Brewer	2:35 A.M.
Arrive Yard Center	6:45 A.M.

Train #62

Leave Mitchell	1:15 P.M.
Arrive Villa Grove	6:00 P.M.
Leave Villa Grove	8:00 P.M.
Arrive Yard Center	1:00 A.M.

Train #64

Leave Mitchell	7:45 P.M.
Arrive Villa Grove	11:00 P.M.
Leave Villa Grove	12:01 A.M.
Arrive Yard Center	6:00 A.M.

228

SOUTHBOUND		NORTHBOUND	
Train #65		Train #164	
Leave Yard Center	10:50 P.M.	Leave Chaffee	8:00 P.M.
Arrive Villa Grove	1:55 A.M.	Leave Thebes	9:00 P.M.
Leave Villa Grove	2:30 A.M.	Arrive Salem	9:20 A.M.
Arrive Mitchell	8:00 A.M.	Leave Salem	11:10 A.M.
		Arrive Villa Grove	3:30 P.M.

Note: Local Freight Operation shown on other page.

C. H. Fischer
Superintendent of Transportation

A.M. It leaves Brewer at 2:35 A.M. and reaches Yard Center at 6:45 A.M. for first-morning delivery in Chicago. Dead time in Brewer is used so as not to arrive in Yard Center too early.

The two-unit Diesels handle 7,000 tons and make the time of fast trains from Danville and Villa Grove (on the St. Louis line) into Chicago. From Evansville, northward to Vincennes, they pull 4,200 tons; from Vincennes to Terre Haute 4,500 tons; and from Terre Haute to Danville 7,000 tons. These freights usually average slightly lighter southbound, due to the commodities they handle.

The heaviest grade on the railroad is 1.28 per cent. On the Salem Subdivision to Thebes, Illinois, and Chaffee, Missouri, the sharpest curve is only 6.30 degrees. There is no helper district on the entire Chicago & Eastern Illinois road.

Coal produces the heaviest traffic on the C.&E.I. This is from the Illinois, Indiana, and Kentucky coal fields. No. 2 commodity is grain; No. 3, iron and steel; No. 4, petroleum products; No. 5, automobile parts. Three of the top soya bean counties in the world are served by the road. Evansville is the leading refrigerating manufacturing city in the world.

The Chicago & Eastern Illinois has three river terminals on the Ohio and two on the Mississippi. These are at Evansville and Mt. Vernon, Indiana; Joppa and Thebes in Illinois; and St. Louis, Missouri.

Major improvements scheduled as this is set down include a

CHICAGO & EASTERN ILLINOIS RAILROAD
Office of Superintendent of Transportation
Chicago, Illinois

Nov. 1, 1950

LOCAL FREIGHT OPERATIONS
(As of November 1, 1950)
Subject to change without notice

Villa Grove to Yd. Center	Daily	Cissna Park Mon., Wed., Fri. Does Momence Switching.
Hoopeston Switcher	Daily	Goes to Alonzo when necessary.
Danville to Yard Center	Daily except Sun.	
Yard Center to Danville	" " "	To Brothers Mon., Wed., Fri.
		To Judyville Tues., Thurs., Sat.
Danville-Villa Grove Turn	" " "	To Jamaica Mon., Wed., Fri.
Evansville-Mt. Vernon, Ind. and return	" " "	
Danville to Locust St.	Mon., Wed., Fri.	Handles Brazil Branch
Locust St. to Danville	Tues., Thurs., Sat.	
Locust St. to Wansford	Daily except Sun.	
Wansford to Locust St.	" " "	Handles Sullivan County Mine Branch when necessary
Salem to Villa Grove	" " "	
Villa Grove to Salem	" " "	
Mt. Vernon, Ill. Switcher	" " "	West Frankfort to Mt. Vernon and return Tues. through Fri. Ties up Salem Sat. and runs Salem to W. Frankfort on Mon. Takes tonnage to Kell for No. 164
Mitchell to Hall	Mon., Wed., Fri.	
Hall to Mitchell	Tues., Thurs., Sat.	

C. H. Fischer
Superintendent of Transportation

new yard at Chicago, a new bridge over the Wabash River at Clinton, Indiana, a new bridge over the White River at Decker, Indiana, and a new communications system, which will include Teletype facilities. Double track will be built from Spring Hill to Dewey, Indiana, through Terre Haute. This will relieve congestion in that great industrial center.

Terre Haute is the home of Tony Hulman, Chicago & Eastern Illinois director, to whom this book is dedicated, but he is equally well known in Evansville and all over the Hoosier State.

Blue-chip Shippers

A railroad, on every possible occasion, should pay tribute to those shippers who patronize it, and, further, dedicate itself to returning to them the finest possible rail service, for their contributions to industry mean the difference between a bright and shining rail and rust.

At Evansville, we find such blue-chip shippers as Chrysler, Servel, Seeger Manufacturing Company, General Foods, International Harvester, Swift, International Steel, Cooks Brewery, and Fendrich & Company, makers of the world-famous La Fendrich Cigar. These great firms are served by the Chicago & Eastern Illinois Railroad.

Terre Haute blue-chip shippers include the Bledsoe Coal Company, Commercial Solvents, Hulman Company, Continental Can, Great Lakes Steel Corporation, Charles Pfizer Company, Terre Haute Brewing Company, Wabash Fibre Box Company, and Princeton Mining Company.

The road's new Diesel shops and operating headquarters are located at Danville, Illinois. Here are located such blue-chip shippers as the Consolidated Products Company, Hegeler Zinc Company, the Lauhoff Grain Company, Sugar Creek Creamery, Hyster Company, Electric Steel Foundry Company, and Paxton Grocery Company.

Valued customers at Chicago Heights include the American Manganese Steel Company, Armour & Company fertilizer plant, American Locomotive Company, Calumet Steel Company, Columbia Tool Steel Company, Flintkote Company, Gold Seal Asphalt Roofing, Inland Steel Company, International Minerals & Chemicals, Victor Chemical Company, Montgomery Ward & Company, and the Thrall Car Company.

I only regret that I cannot name all of the fine coal shippers, oil companies, and other industries that are all up and down this fine railroad but space does not permit.

CHAPTER XXIII

VIRGINIAN ELECTRIC POWER

6,800-Horsepower Locomotive

In 1925, the Virginian Railway Company began to use big electric locomotives to haul trains over the heavy grades of the Appalachians between Mullens, West Virginia, and Roanoke, Virginia. The electric system was 11,000 volt, 25 cycle single phase, which operated two-speed induction-motored locomotives of 6,000 horsepower, with constant-speed at fourteen and twenty-eight miles per hour.

These big electric locomotives were entirely satisfactory for heavy-tonnage movement on the maximum ruling eastward grade of 2.07 per cent just as long as the business was confined to this kind of haul, but in the course of time a new sort of freight movement developed. This was what was called time freight, and it demanded a different type of power.

It was decided that a variable-speed locomotive would be the most practical when it came to supplementing the electric locomotives in service. The basic operation for which motive power is designed is the eastbound movement of 3,000 tons per locomotive from Elmore, West Virginia, to Clark's Gap, the high point of the line, with a fill-out here to 9,000 tons, which becomes the tonnage to Roanoke.

Early in 1948, the Virginian Railway purchased from the General Electric Company four motor-generator locomotives for the same sort of hauling problem, and for operation with the older locomotives, single or doubled. These locomotives are double enders of two units, developing 6,800 horsepower. The two units, or two halves, of the locomotive, are exact duplicates, permanently connected at the inside ends. Each locomotive half has four two-axle swivel trucks, making a total of eight for the locomotive. A vestibuled walkway provides a passageway the length of the locomotive between the two cabs.

Normally, a road locomotive and a pusher handle a 6,000-ton train from Mullens to Clark's Gap, as has been revealed. These are eastward loads. Westbound empties are hauled by a single locomotive between Roanoke and Mullens, a distance of 134 miles.

The traction motors used in the Virginian's electric locomotives are duplications of the type in widespread use on large Diesel-electric locomotives, which have become pretty well standardized, and this results in better service when the power reaches its terminal and, of course, a cheaper service.

The motor-generator locomotive is provided with a large number of running control steps available through the relatively fine generator-field control and various combinations of series and separate excitation of traction motors. This permits accurate control of acceleration and regenerative braking. The acceleration control makes for ease of operation when doubled with the older constant-speed locomotive, and the regeneration control greatly reduces and, with certain tonnage and grade combination, even eliminating the need for the application air brake.

When used alone the newer locomotives can be operated over portions of the line at speeds up to thirty-five miles per hour. Speed does not matter in the movement of tonnage trains, but it is important in the handling of time freights. A saving of an hour and twenty minutes over the electrified section of the road has been effected with the new electric power, and this includes the time required for meets and other operating delays. It may be pointed out here that, except for nineteen miles of double track east of Mullens and ten miles at Norfolk, the line is single tracked.

Because of the simplicity of inspections, these locomotives can be turned in fifteen minutes. If it should become necessary to change out a truck it can be done in an hour and one half. On these electrics, sand is used only for starting on heavy grades

233

and a weight-compensating feature, which allows for weight shift on the two axles of a truck during acceleration.

The average mileage for all electric motive power reaches about 60,000 per year. About 25 per cent of the power used in pulling trains is returned to the line by regeneration. This is the power that in a Diesel is devoured by grids in the roof of the locomotive, as we mentioned in our Electro-Motive chapter.

Power for the locomotive comes from overhead wires, taking alternating-current energy at 11,000 volts, single phase, 25 cycles. This A.C. power is converted to D.C. power on the locomotive by step-down transformers and synchronous motor-generator sets. The direct-current power is distributed to sixteen series-wound, axle-hung traction motors, geared to the driving axles by single-reduction gearing.

These double-end locomotives are built for running in either direction. The cabs and cab underframes are fabricated from steel sheets, plates, and shapes for welding. The cab weight and apparatus is carried through center sills and span bolsters to the truck center plates. There are no loading pads.

Each cab is divided into three compartments, or sections— the nose section, the operator's section, and the apparatus section. The section devoted to major equipment has hatchways in the roof for the removal of major equipment for repair and maintenance. The nose section has a removable plate, fitted to the outside front end for the same purpose. The nose is reinforced with collision posts for the protection of the crew and equipment.

All locomotive trucks are duplicates and interchangeable. Spare trucks, complete with traction motors, can be employed to replace any truck on any of the four locomotives. All cables, sand pipes, air-brake hoses, et cetera, running between cabs and trucks, are so arranged that they can be disconnected and coupled up again easily and quickly.

The journal boxes have roller bearings. The axle-hung traction motors have coil-spring nose suspension. The wheels and gears are steel, pressed on solid forged-steel axles. The two complete cabs weigh 262 tons, and the eight trucks, complete with motors,

234

weigh 176 tons. The complete locomotive weight is 500 tons, complete with principal components.

A general summary of the Virginian's newer type of electric locomotives follows:

Wheel arrangement	2(B–B+B–B)
Total weight, lb.	1,033,832
Weight on drivers, lb.	1,033,832
Number of driving axles	16
Weight per driving axle, lb.	62,500
Continuous rating	
Horsepower at rail	6,800
Tractive force, lb.	162,000
Speed, m.p.h.	15.75
Adhesion, per cent	15.7
Starting tractive force at 26 per cent adhesion, lb.	260,000
Maximum operating speed, m.p.h.	50
Length overall between knuckles	150 ft. 8 in.
Total wheel base	133 ft. 10 in.
Rigid wheel base	9 ft. 0 in.
Width overall	11 ft. 1 in.
Height over pantograph, locked down	16 ft. 3 in.
Driving wheel diameter	42 in.
Number of traction motors	16
Gear ratio	70/17
Contact line voltage (nominal)	11,000
Phase	single
Cycles	25
Air-brake equipment—straight and automatic	8-EL
Number of air compressors	4
Total capacity of air compressors, c.f.m.	600
Type of control—electropneumatic	PCL
Electric braking	Regenerative

The most desirable use of the traction-motor and generator characteristics is made by selective operation of the traction motors as either self- or separately-excited machines. This permits optimum use of power for motoring or for regenerative braking at reduced traction-motor field excitations.

Driving-wheel slippage is held to a minimum by permanent parallel connections of all traction motors. Selective weight-shift compensation is provided for further protection against wheel slippage on starting, especially with heavy trains. This weight-shift compensation is obtained by reducing the field excitation and consequently the voltage of the traction generators supplying power to the traction motors geared to the leading axles of each truck.

Located conveniently in the operator's cab are the master controllers, push buttons, valves, instruments, gauges, and indicating lights. Strong and rigid support is provided for all control devices, wiring, and power cables. Special attention in the locomotive design was given to the desirability of having all devices located conveniently for inspection and maintenance, something that often is sadly neglected.

The high- and low-voltage 25-cycle apparatus is protected by a primary protective relay. This relay detects electric grounds, overload, and short circuits. It has two trip positions. The first of these opens the auxiliary circuits and removes the auxiliary load from the main transformer. If this fails to clear the fault, the relay automatically goes to full-trip position and opens the oil circuit breaker, thus de-energizing the entire locomotive.

The traction motors are protected by high-speed circuit breakers and overload relays. The auxiliary apparatus is protected by the usual thermal and magnetic devices.

Putting Electricity to Work

Steam power, as a direct means of locomotive propulsion, apparently is riding into the sunset, while the Diesel, the modern work horse of the rail, is in the ascendancy. In between, there is the electric locomotive. The electric engine had done a lot of railroading before the Diesel was thought of, although Dr. Rudolph Diesel completed the first workable Diesel engine just two years after America's first electrified train service began on the seven-mile Nantasket Branch of the New York, New Haven & Hartford Railroad in 1895.

In railroad service, the first Diesel-electric was a switch engine, installed in 1925 by the Central of New Jersey.

Many factors have combined to keep the electric locomotive from being generally used on United States railroads, but that is something we will not go into here. Suffice to say that in the early part of 1949, eighteen Class I railroads were operating 2,643 route-miles and 6,432 miles of track by means of centrally generated electric power. Every Diesel electric, of course, is a self-contained electric powerhouse, delivering voltage to the same sort of traction motors employed in the driving of the Virginian's newer motor-generator locomotives.

It may be interesting to briefly touch on some of the equipment of these motor-generator type of electric engines, built by General Electric for the Virginian Railroad down there between Mullens and Roanoke.

The locomotive's main transformers have double-winding primaries, 11,000/22,000 volts. This makes them suitable for operation on the existing 11,000-volt contact system, or, by reconnecting the windings, on a 22,000-volt contact system if the Virginian should at some future time wish to go to this voltage.

Power is fed to transformers from overhead wires, and the low-voltage windings of the transformers have taps at 557, 795, 995, and 1,550 volts for supplying auxiliary loads and running the main motor-generator sets. Each transformer delivers power to a five-unit four-bearing main motor-generator set.

A complete motor-generator set consists of a single-phase synchronous motor, two traction generators, a main exciter, and a regenerative exciter. The synchronous-motor stator of the main motor-generator set is spring mounted to isolate the 50-cycle vibration.

The set is started by using one of the traction generators as a starting motor. The starting power is supplied from the battery-charging generator of the auxiliary motor-alternator set in the nose of the locomotive. The main set is thus accelerated to about 460 r.p.m. The synchronous motor is then automatically connected to the 995-volt tap of the main transformer and the set further accelerated to within a few revolutions of synchronous speed.

Partial field is then applied to the motor to pull the set into synchronism and the motor connections are automatically transferred to the 1,550-volt running tap of the main transformer. The entire starting cycle takes approximately one minute.

The main motor-generator sets, traction motors, and transformers are ventilated by vertical-shaft, 125-cycle, three-phase, induction motor-driven blowers. These blowers are special axial-flow units and have self-contained centrifugal air cleaners incorporated where required.

Cooling air is admitted to the cab through special grill-covered roof hatches. The air then enters the blowers from which it is distributed through ducts to the various apparatus units at the pressure and volume required for proper ventilation. All apparatus, including the main motor-generator set, is ventilated by external blowing.

These electric locomotives are equipped with three pantographs, two on one cab and one on the other. Space has been provided on the roof of the second cab for the installation of a fourth pantograph if desired. Normally the locomotive is operated with two pantographs raised. The third is for emergency use.

It is a fascinating sight to watch the Virginian's big electric locomotives taking the slack out of one of those coal trains and getting under way. Silent power flows to the traction motors and the cars begin their march with no fanfare from a stack, but with an amazing freedom of apparent application to the job at hand.

Electric locomotives have been serving some eighteen American railroads a good many years, and while there is no trend toward further electrification, these big electric engines still have their place in the world of modern railroading.

CHAPTER XXIV

THE NEW COLUMBIAN

The B.&O.'s All-coach Feature Train

Immediately following the close of World War II the Baltimore & Ohio Railroad began the complete modernization of its passenger equipment, which was part of the road's gigantic improvement program. If railroad critics had been more than passingly interested in the railroad industry when it began the enormous task of rebuilding after the war, the Baltimore & Ohio could have supplied a splendid example of how a railroad tackles the complete revitalizing of its plant and rolling equipment after it has worn itself threadbare carrying troops and war materials.

Politicians cared only for votes until Korea; then their cries went out for help, and only for the fact that the railroads of America, in spite of postwar shortages and readjustments, had begun to get back to full strength and were proving the tradition of free enterprise was the black situation relieved as the home transport went into action.

There were no railroad fleets in moth balls.

This chapter deals with a crack new train, the Columbian, and not with blood-soaked Korea, and there, perhaps, seems to be no parallel. But there is. If Korea had been within reach of American railroads the war equipment would have been delivered, so far as it was available, and the track and communications and modern motive power and terminal facilities that make possible the new Columbian and all of the other crack trains would have been determining factors in this war movement.

After World War II the B.&O. rebuilt part of its modern passenger car equipment in its own shops. About forty cars came from the shops of the Pullman-Standard people. As this is written more passenger equipment is being modernized in the road's Mt. Clare shops.

In view of the shortages after World War II, it would have taken a long time to put these streamliners into the main line if the B.&O. had had to wait their turn in taking new car deliveries. Instead, the Baltimore & Ohio took the bull by the horns and, in effect, said to the shop force, "Let's go!" And the Mt. Clare shops went to work rebuilding the coaches and special cars that later became streamliners.

The program, for one thing, emphasized roller bearings and they were applied to passenger cars in a constant flow, until by the end of 1949, 107 passenger cars had been so equipped. The mileage per hotbox increased from 500,000 miles in 1941 to an average of 9,328,000 miles per hotbox in June, 1949.

The new Columbian was the first train to feature the dome car between Chicago and Washington. The Baltimore & Ohio calls it the Strata-Dome, and it is part of a luxury coach streamliner that, once you have inspected it, will make you ask, "Is this an extra fare train?"

It is not. You pay the regular coach fare, but you enjoy de luxe features that are amazing.

You do have to make your seat reservation in advance but at no additional cost. We lose sight of a lot of the old-fashioned virtues in this modern world, but the B.&O. has revived some of the things that passengers, over the years, felt had been relegated to the limbo of the lost. Trains like the new Columbian have, happily, revived them—if they were ever lost on the Baltimore & Ohio.

For instance, there is the friendly courtesy, immediately apparent from the time you make your first approach to ticket office or train. There was a time when passenger trainmen were notoriously gruff, brusque, and close to insulting, and it never sold a passenger a return-trip ticket. A smile is a universal lan-

Westward Ore Extra hauled by Western Maryland's E.M.D. 4,000 h.p. Diesel meets the eastward local hauled by engine 761, Class H-7, east of Emory Grove on double track. Hagerstown Division. Courtesy, Western Maryland RR.

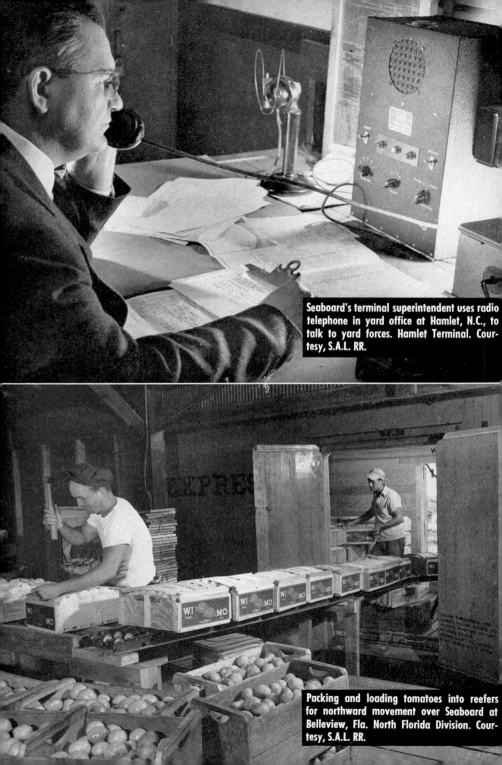

Seaboard's terminal superintendent uses radio telephone in yard office at Hamlet, N.C., to talk to yard forces. Hamlet Terminal. Courtesy, S.A.L. RR.

Packing and loading tomatoes into reefers for northward movement over Seaboard at Belleview, Fla. North Florida Division. Courtesy, S.A.L. RR.

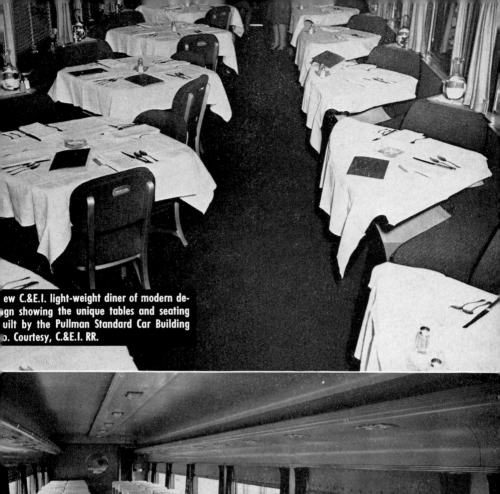

ew C.&E.I. light-weight diner of modern de-
gn showing the unique tables and seating
uilt by the Pullman Standard Car Building
o. Courtesy, C.&E.I. RR.

aterior of new C.&E.I. light-weight coach
owing Sleepy Hollow seats, individual
ghts, and wide windows. Courtesy, C.&E.I.
R.

K.C.S. #41, morning fast freight out of Kansas City, with E.M.D. Diesel #71 at Grandview, Mo. Note empty strawberry cars deadheading south on head end. Photo by Preston George.

Roadway equipment of modern railroads of today is completely mechanized. Here is Seaboard's spike-driving machine near Maxville, Fla. North Florida Division. Courtesy, S.A.L. RR.

Rio Grande #7, the Prospector, starting the fifty-mile climb to the Moffat Tunnel west of Denver on the Pueblo Division. Photo by Les Logue.

Rio Grande Extra 560 east, E.M.D. 6,000 h.p. F-7 freight Diesel in Byers Canyon near Sulphur, Col., with sixty-four cars. Pueblo Division. Photo by R. H. Kindig.

B.&O. National Limited, #2, crack train from St. Louis to Washington, Baltimore, and New York, arriving in Washington terminal. Courtesy, B.&O. RR.

Frisco #4506 east, 4-8-4 type, with a solid train of oil at East Tulsa, Okla., on the Cherokee Subdivision of the Southwestern Division. Courtesy, Frisco Lines.

Southern Pacific's beautiful Lark #76, at Chatsworth, Calif., on the Los Angeles Division with engine 4433, 4-8-4 type, Class GS4. Photo by R. H. Kindig.

S.P. #3, the Golden State, crossing Cienega Creek, on the westward track between Marsh and Vail, Ariz., on the Rio Grande Division, Mescal Subdivision. Courtesy, S.P. RR.

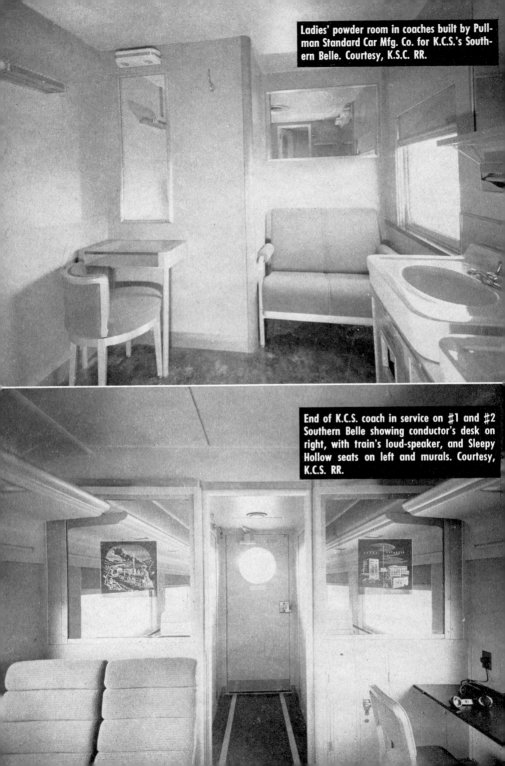

Ladies' powder room in coaches built by Pullman Standard Car Mfg. Co. for K.C.S.'s Southern Belle. Courtesy, K.S.C. RR.

End of K.C.S. coach in service on #1 and #2 Southern Belle showing conductor's desk on right, with train's loud-speaker, and Sleepy Hollow seats on left and murals. Courtesy, K.C.S. RR.

guage, and little courtesies are remembered longer than most folks imagine.

And on the new Columbian there is the matter of the homey sort of cooking that goes with meals at home. When you enjoy good food in a hotel, restaurant, or on board a train it makes an impression that is not soon forgotten. "Say, that B.&O. certainly serves good food." You pass the word along.

And then there is the matter of on-time performance. Sometimes railroad men refer to this sort of dependability as running "on the advertised." In other words, the timetable reads, "Ar. Chicago (Grand Cent. Sta.) . . . . . 7:20 A.M." And when your train pulls in on the dot it can mean a lot in the day's tight-packed schedule.

The new Columbian is a gleaming symphony in blue, gray, and gold. This is a striking color combination that leaves its imprint on the observer. I consider it one of the outstandingly beautiful trains in the United States. The arrangements are not overdone, and there is a comfortable but substantial look about the interiors. A lot of thought went into the layout. Nothing has been omitted throughout and yet there is no feeling of overcrowding, or congestion as you walk through such cars as the cocktail lounge or the colorful coffee-shop section.

You look at a new train, after a while, with a very critical eye and find yourself searching for something different. All modern streamliners have a "train of tomorrow" look. The new Columbian is no exception, and there is something in the Strata-Dome car that emphasizes this. That is a panel in the front glass dome section that is bound to fascinate the traveler. The eye of the passenger in the Strata-Dome keeps returning to it curiously.

There are instruments on the panel which include a speedometer, an altimeter, and a clock. The figures on the dials indicate how high you are above sea level, how fast you are going, and the time of day. Panoramas may unfold but those instruments will remain mighty intriguing to the veteran rider as well as to the newcomer to the modern streamliner.

The Strata-Dome seats twenty-four in relaxing comfort. Downstairs there is a lounging room with seats for eleven, a smaller lounging section seating six, a men's washroom, and a women's room with primping facilities, and a toilet annex. Forward in the car there are seats for eighteen. To the rear of the underdome section there are seats for twenty-four, plus the porter's seat, and a locker. The passenger ascends to the Strata-Dome from this rear portion.

Trains like the new Columbian do not soon grow old and run down in appearance. The newness built into them remains. This is largely because of the materials used and the care with which these crack liners are maintained. Stainless steel and other modern metals keep them young. With the advent into the picture of the two re-equipped eight-car trains under the Columbian banner there was a 15 per cent passenger increase, with the earnings of the all-coach train close to five dollars per mile.

Improvements in any line draw patronage and at the same time provide an unbeatable advertising medium. Improvements plus such tradition as that of trains of the B.&O. like the Capitol Limited, the Royal Blue, the Ambassador, the Shenandoah, and right on through the entire aristocratic fleet. All with a reputation as fast feature trains.

It was believed that the appeal of the Strata-Dome would draw occupants largely in the daytime. Surprisingly enough, there were many passengers who liked the starlit panorama, the twinkling town lights, and the shadowy hills under the velvet cloak of night. The tracks of the Baltimore & Ohio pass many great steel mills, which offer a spectacular show against the blackness. This observation-roof idea is doing much to draw passenger business and it is one of the things people like to talk about afterward, which is a fine advertising medium.

The coffee-shop section of the new Columbian provides a feeling of complete peace with the world. You drop in for a snack or your favorite beverage and find radio or recorded music in the background; your enjoyment grows under the influence of the pleasant color tones, the richness of the furnishings, the opportunity to relax with friendly fellow travelers. You are entitled to the coffee-shop service, for your coach ticket includes this feature.

Something the ladies like and talk about is the luxury of the women's lounges, with their full-length mirrors, satin-finish chrome, gleaming porcelain, and blue Marbelle flooring. Fluorescent lights, which are individually controlled, are directed over each mirror. The chairs are upholstered in foam rubber and are remarkably comfortable. For each lounge there are two toilet annexes.

Except that these lounges are more compact, your club or favorite hotel could offer no more in the way of sparkling cleanliness and beauty. Freshening up in such surroundings is a pleasure. The facilities are vastly appreciated by the women passengers.

Individual tastes differ, but one of the things about these coach trains on the B.&O. that this writer likes are the coach compartments under the Strata-Dome, mentioned in an earlier summary of this car's accommodations. These semiprivate coach compartments are a new feature, a striking feature of coach travel, which today is elevated to those Pullman standards which have existed through the years.

The coach compartments are designed to accommodate family groups and persons traveling in parties. They have large, comfortable sofa-type seats and smoking accessories. Here groups may settle themselves behind low partitions, a little apart from the other passengers without having their privacy immediately trespassed on by passageway traffic.

The new Columbian's dining car offers an unusual arrangement in which every diner enjoys comfort and freedom of movement through the easy-access wall seats and the legless tables that are suspended from the walls. All seats are built in, except ten chairs along the aisle, and all seats are set at about a forty-five degree angle. Tables for two occupy one side of the car, with tables for four on the opposite side.

The dining room takes up about half of the car; the remaining area is occupied by the modern, stainless steel kitchen and the pantry. Kitchen equipment, of course, includes mechanical refrigeration. There is also a large refrigeration unit immediately behind the dining-room partition. Another refrigeration unit is located at the steward's end of the car.

Dining-car passengers enjoy recorded programs of music or, possibly, special radio broadcasts. You anticipate mealtime on the B.&O., and you remember it.

Glamorous and strictly informal is the atmosphere of the congenial cocktail lounge on board this new Columbian. There are cheerful color tones and smart furnishings. You can play cards, enjoy a drink, have a part in the friendships that so easily spring up amid informal surroundings. We might say that this car could offer the highlight of your trip on some trains, but speeding through on this train every car will leave something with you.

Beyond the cocktail lounge there is a stewardess-nurse's room. There are accommodations here for women and children requiring, perhaps, special attention. This kind of service is particularly appreciated by women traveling alone, or women with children. Your stewardess-nurse is trained for her job, and on the Baltimore & Ohio they have covered millions of miles in serving the traveler.

This feature train offers service for babies, including bottle-warming and feeding facilities, and also a new type of basinette built to fit nicely into the couch seat beside the mother.

In addition to the usual porter service, the new Columbian put on a maid service. Because she is able to enter them at any time, the maid keeps the washrooms clean, when, otherwise, the lounges are bound to become littered. The maid makes her inspection every hour. The result is freshness and cleanliness always.

When I am not riding the head end I like the lounge cars. In particular, I like the observation-lounge on the Columbian. I like the overstuffed chairs set facing the wide windows where you can sprawl out and watch the scenery. Or you can settle down on one of the deep-cushioned sofas. There are also comfortable seats facing the curved rear windows. Of course, there are the newspapers and magazines, and a writing desk.

Like all cars of the train, the observation-lounge has the last word in heating and air conditioning. Regardless of the weather, temperatures are maintained at exactly the right degree for personal comfort.

I would like to return for a moment to the service. It is one of the things that will sell the railroads, and I keep repeating it. And you find it on your coach train just as you expect it on your extra-fare train. The biggest mistake any railroad or any concern can make is to disregard what I call the little people. They are often sensitive, retiring, some have an inferiority complex. They are easily hurt. I am glad that the railroads today are giving service to the men and women who ride the coach trains. It is, of course, good business.

Take your stewardess-nurse. She is there to help you. She will mail your letter, attend to the sending of your telegram, aid elderly people and the tired mother, supply information, indicate points of interest, give first aid. She is there to help make a "happy train." Cultivate her acquaintance early on your journey; she is a jewel.

If you have never known the luxury of a Sleepy Hollow train seat you will find it hard to imagine how complete is its comfort. It tilts back, it has a footrest, it will mold itself to the shape of your body so completely that you will feel as though you were sitting on a cloud.

In days gone by the day coach was simply a place to sit down when you were riding. It got smelly, and there were cinders and insipid drinking water; it was either too hot or too cold; it shook and jerked and swayed like mad. When it stopped it tried to stop all at once, and it started the same way. You looked at a box full of tools that reminded you of wrecks, and when you staggered down the steps at your destination you were sooty and frazzled, and everyone commiserated you on the rigors of your eighty-mile journey.

Those were the "good old days." The modern traveler aboard the modern train, if he remembers those days at all, does so with a shudder. In this chapter, together with other chapters concerning coach travel, we have reviewed feature cars that could have been cut out of some of the de luxe trains of the country for exhibition purposes. We haven't mentioned the coach car itself, but a lot of accessories that are available to you, a coach ticketholder.

A new Columbian coach compartment has fifty-six individual reclining seats of the Sleepy Hollow type, along with all of the fine material and workmanship specifications which went into the make-up of the feature cars we have described.

Nothing was so horrible as the cotton-mouth feeling of thirst that used to afflict the coach passenger, something the old-fashioned cooler did little to alleviate, except in providing moisture. In comparison, in a nook of the passageway at the women's-lounge end of the coach there is an electric water cooler. And that is not all. It is not filled with just any faucet water, but contains crystal-clear drinking water from the Baltimore & Ohio's own Deer Park Spring.

There are times when you will put a drink of cold water before such things as rubber-cushioned trucks, shock absorbers, truck speed governors, roller bearings, and Diesel-electric locomotives, but aboard this train you have them all—and your drink of ice-cold spring water.

There is a train telephone system on the new Columbian by means of which the conductor and engineer can converse regarding routine checks, which further the safety of the train.

The coach includes fluorescent general lighting and an individually controlled light at each seat. There are generous luggage racks, Venetian blinds, stainless steel doors, and electropneumatic operating devices.

The Pullman-Standard Company can be proud of the part it played in making the Columbian the success that it is. It has demonstrated forward-looking design and craftsmanship and the last word in modern engineering. The diagonal seating which we have mentioned in the dining car represents a Pullman-Standard innovation.

The new Columbian, in a given period since its inauguration, carried 12 per cent more passengers than it did in the same period the preceding year. There is no getting away from the fact that fine trains draw patronage.

CHAPTER XXV

GENERAL MOTORS DIESELS

The Famous 567 Series

Wherever steel rails reach in the nation the big, blunt nose of the General Motors Diesel-electric locomotive is a familiar sight. It is instantly identified, and it seems to reflect the power that is behind it. There have been many improvements since the earlier Diesels began their conquest in a new railroad world, and it is my purpose to review here something of the progress accomplished, as represented in some of the Electro-Motive main-line power.

The General Motors Diesel story began away back in 1922 and was covered in my book, *Railroads of Today*; also in an earlier book, *Railroads at War*, when I wrote the early history of these Diesels, which now have come to play so great a part in modern railroading.

In the spring of 1949, the Electro-Motive Division of the General Motors Corporation, of La Grange, Illinois, announced three new main-line Diesel locomotives, designed to increase train tonnage and speed up the schedules of trains in both freight and passenger service. We will, first, identify these locomotives as the F7, the FP7, and the E8.

The F7 and the FP7, for freight and heavy-duty passenger service, supplant the F3 general-purpose locomotive brought out in 1946. The new E8 model succeeds the E7 high-speed passenger locomotive.

The F3 is a great piece of motive power and it made a record for itself on the head end of some of the best-known name trains in the country. And it still is a valiant locomotive, performing well and faithfully.

When Diesel power began crowding the steam locomotive a lot of railroaders called these new engines the "big growlers" and muttered that they were not all they were cracked up to be. True, the early Diesels had their shortcomings and there were bugs to be ironed out, but even in those days they had the ability to handle tonnage. They were constantly improved until only respect was employed in conversations concerning them. The Diesels have proved themselves everywhere, but nowhere have they done a finer job than in the difficult Tehachapi Mountains in California. The story of this fabulous grade is told in an earlier chapter.

The Diesel made possible the use of the dynamic brake, used first on freight Diesels; then on the modern high-speed passenger Diesel. It has performed wonders in today's railroading. For the nonrailroad reader, we might explain that the dynamic brake performs a service comparable to that of an automobile or truck employing a lower gear when descending a heavy grade. That is, it reduces the need for train-brake application to a minimum, thus effecting a saving in wear and tear on wheels and brake shoes.

In dynamic braking the traction motors are turned into generators, thus aiding in retardation. On straight electric locomotives this power is turned back into the line. On a Diesel this current is dissipated by means of grids in the roof of the locomotive.

Another feature of this latest Diesel is the automatic transition, successfully used in high-speed passenger locomotives, and made basic equipment in the new freight power.

Earlier Diesels had the fault of being limited as to water capacity for train heating, but this has been increased, which lengthens the mileage between necessary water stops and makes for faster passenger-train schedules.

Fast passenger schedules do not always mean constant speed in the higher brackets, but rather a reduction in stops and slowdowns, which can play havoc with a fast schedule.

The General Motors people are always forward looking when they bring out a new locomotive, in that it is so designed that it can be operated with older units, which permits inter-changeable use and protects the railroad's investment in older Electro-Motive Diesels.

The new traction motors and generators developed by Electro-Motive utilize silicon insulating materials and other new methods of application of insulation. This, plus improved cooling, permits higher load factors, and these are translated into greater tractive force. The new motors and generators were built to last longer, to give top service longer between major overhauls.

With a steam locomotive the observer sees all of the major moving parts, threshing away there under the boiler, straining, crashing, threatening. The Diesel, on the other hand, has silent, powerful driving units geared to the driving axles. These electric traction motors perform, in substance, what is accomplished by the drivers of a steam locomotive, and, though they make less fuss about it, they are at the same time subjected to heavy burdens, as the electric power that flows into them from the direct-driven generators on the big Diesel motors is, in turn, transmitted through gears into the axles and so becomes the tractive force that pulls the train.

The new type injector perfected for Electro-Motive Diesels has broadened the range of fuels which may successfully be used. Before, Diesel locomotives required fuel of at least 55-cetene rating. With the new General Motors injector it was possible to use cheaper fuels of as low as 40-cetene rating. An important by-product of the new injector is the reduction of peak-shock-cylinder loads for all qualities of permissible fuel, with resultant longer life.

Because of the improvements in the Electro-Motive traction motors and generators, the maximum continuous tractive force of the F7 unit is increased to 52,400 pounds, as compared with 42,500 pounds in the F3. Horsepower rating of the Diesel engine remains at 1,500 for propulsion alone. Top speed remains at 102 miles per hour, as in the F3, but, with greater tractive force, the F7 is able to haul heavier tonnage.

The F7 can haul 25 per cent more tonnage up a 1 per cent grade at continuous rating, and 30 per cent more tonnage at short-time ratings for two hours. Since there are few grades in the country which require more than two hours to climb with the heaviest train permissible with present drawbars, the effect of this is that most railroads will be able to increase tonnage 30 per cent with the new motive power units.

We have referred to the dynamic brake. On the F7, 23 per cent greater tonnage than formerly can be safely controlled, which means decrease in the use of air brakes on grades and a resultant savings in brake shoes, wheels, and air-brake equipment. This has been done by increasing the capacity of the brakes from 540 to 600 amp.

Electro-Motive engineers increased the pulling ability of the F7 by developing hot-pressed silicon and glass insulation for coils in the traction-motor armature, and by designing a new kind of insulation for field coils. Another factor was greatly improved motor cooling. It was found that the elimination of organic material in insulation, through the use of this hot-pressed silicon and glass, reduced deterioration caused by heat. Silicon, glass, and mica are unaffected by cold or moisture or heat, and through the employment of these for insulation a greatly increased service life of the new motors is anticipated.

Further, these improvements are something that can be built into existing Electro-Motive traction motors as these locomotives go in for repairs.

In the past, the human element has entered into the handling of Diesel locomotives to a certain extent, and sometimes damage to equipment resulted from the improper handling of the various shifts as a Diesel got under way or reduced speed. General Motors successfully used automatic transition on high-speed passenger locomotives over a period of years. This automatic transition became standard equipment on the F7 heavy-duty locomotives.

Without automatic transition, the changing of connections between traction motors on the F series locomotives to give variations in performance for varying requirements in starting, accelerating, and maintaining speed with heavy loads had been a manual operation performed with a control lever by the engineman. As a locomotive gathers or reduces speed, automatic performance of the different shifts relieves the engineman of the responsibility for making them in a manner that will contribute the most to the train handling.

Another pronounced improvement in the F7 is the increase in capacity of the steam generators for train heating. Train heating has been something that the engine builders had to learn by the trial and error formula, for they did not have a titanic steam boiler at their command to draw from under unusual extremes. Instead, the Diesel locomotive units were equipped with generators that performed satisfactorily in average cold weather but which ran into trouble in extreme subzero conditions. This was true, in particular, when there were extra cars added to the train and which were sometimes a mixture of old and new cars.

The new F7 Diesels are equipped with 2,500-pound steam generators, for the A units, while the B units can be equipped with either 2,500-pound or 4,000-pound generators. Thus a two-unit F7 locomotive may have a total 6,500-pound capacity, or an increase of 1,900 pounds over the older F3 maximum. The total capacity of a four-unit F7 locomotive can be 14,500 pounds, as compared to 10,600 pounds in the four-unit F3.

The F7 Diesel has the same length, height, and weight as the F3, plus the wide range characteristics made possible by eight optional gear ratios and variations in number of units that can be coupled or uncoupled to fit the locomotive capacity to the size of the train. The range is broadened, however, by the increase in the tractive force of the more modern locomotive.

The F7 was General Motors' contribution to modern railroading, in that this is a versatile freight and heavy-duty passenger locomotive, operating as a single unit of 1,500 horsepower or in combinations of 3,000, 4,500, or 6,000 horsepower.

The F7 looms large as the most effective tool available to American railroads in the mighty struggle for traffic against competitive services. For here is a locomotive that already is achieving new levels of performance in both freight and passenger service.

The field for heavy passenger service has been considerably broadened by the new General Motors FP7 lead unit, which provides increased train heating capacity and longer distance between water stops.

The FP7 is basically the same as the F7-A, with car body extended four feet to permit installation of a 2,500-pound steam generator, together with 1,750 gallons of water if dynamic brakes are not required, or 1,150 gallons of water if dynamic brakes are installed.

This extra water supply of 1,750 gallons is made possible for the reason that the tank can be installed in the roof space which otherwise would be occupied by the dynamic brake grids. It might be pointed out that the dynamic brake, so essential to mountain operation, is not required on divisions or railroads operating in predominantly flat country. With a locomotive made up of four units, the maximum water supply, without dynamic brakes, would be 7,100 gallons; thus it follows through that the supply would be reduced 600 gallons per locomotive unit when dynamic brakes were used.

Your Diesel locomotive is designed to use different gear ratios, which the manufacturer indicates in his specifications. For combination freight and passenger use most railroads order gear ratios based on desired top speeds ranging between sixty-five and eighty-nine miles per hour. With these FP7 units of 1,500 horsepower, it has been indicated that a three-unit 4,500 horsepower combination General Motors locomotive can be geared for a maximum speed of eighty-three miles an hour and still have a continuous tractive effort of 96,000 pounds.

An A unit, for those unfamiliar with Diesel locomotives, is the unit which contains the cab. The B unit has no cab and consequently no operating controls, and it must always be used in conjunction with an A unit. Two A units may be employed, back to back, and, to provide greater power, one or two B units may be used behind an A unit, or between two A units. Or even three B units may be used behind the A unit.

While the FP7 was built for heavy passenger service, the locomotive can, with the proper gear ratios, be used for combination freight operation, with the ability to haul heavy tonnage.

Ranked high in its field is the General Motors E8, a piece of motive power that by every standard of measurement broadens the application range of Electro-Motive streamliner locomotives, which have delivered millions of miles of the finest sort of service on America's fastest scheduled runs.

Because of improvements in traction motors, with their 25 per cent increase in continuous tractive effort, this modern sleek giant of the rails can haul heavier trains over longer grades without helpers, and that is a money-saving service, as well as a time saver.

This E8 has a six-wheel truck, which some believe gives it smoother operation in the higher speed range. The middle wheels were designed to aid in the weight distribution only. The E8 is a rugged piece of equipment, both in looks and performance, and these trucks are masterful and smooth in modern high-speed work.

The E8 is especially suited to single-unit passenger work because it has *two* Diesel engines, turning out 1,125 horsepower each, making a 2,250-horsepower locomotive. It also has two steam generators, thus providing a 100 per cent factor of safety in both propulsion and train heating.

Like all of these General Motors locomotives, this piece of motive power is designed for the maximum of interchangeability because of its standardized parts, which provides the utmost simplicity of maintenance. We are going to come back to this feature later because it is of the greatest importance. The motorist, years ago, in particular, knew the satisfaction and the peace of mind that came with the knowledge that his car was one that could be serviced and supplied with necessary parts anywhere in the country that repairs might be needed.

These 2,250-horsepower E8 units can be coupled to form single- or double-end control combinations to meet every motive power requirement, right up to 6,750 horsepower. The E8, of course, has a B unit for use in various desired combinations such as we mentioned previously.

Modern railroading certainly achieved distinction in having placed at its command such a high standard of motive power as this six-wheel truck passenger hauler.

Dynamic brakes are applicable with this passenger power, and the roof hatch containing the grids is interchangeable with the F7 locomotive. If dynamic brakes are not employed, as was pointed out in connection with the FP7, the hatch may be used for a 600-gallon water tank, which on the E8 would bring the total water capacity to 1,950 gallons per unit.

Road-switching Locomotive

One of the great locomotives that the Electro-Motive Division has produced, the General Purpose GP7, is not only a real work horse when it comes to handling freight, in the yard or on the main line, but it can get out and wheel passenger trains of the local or mixed variety. It can do more with its 1,500 horse-power than any railroad has a right to expect. As a unit, it combines the power and the versatility of the F7. It has a complete look of competence, with the muscles under its hood to back up its sturdy appearance.

In 1935 General Motors Diesel switchers began setting the pattern for this type of service. These doughty locomotives have established records for hard work, long life, high availability, and low operating and maintenance costs.

There was a distinct need for a general utility type piece of power—something more than just a switch engine. A design finally came off the drafting boards that gave every indication of being an outstanding contribution to the railroads' needs.

The GP7, in the first place, introduced a new and simplified electrical control system which provides instant response to the throttle for ease and speed in switching. Starting tractive effort is under the control of the operator. Acceleration is velvet smooth.

The engineer of this locomotive is one of the first to appreciate what it offers for he is the man who works closest to it. The cab is especially designed for single-control operation in either direction, but dual controls may be installed when required. The narrow hood provides excellent visibility for the men in the cab. Doubly insulated against noise and heat, the GP7 cab provides positive ventilation in summer and individual temperature control for both engineer and fireman in winter, which in itself is a great feature.

Many demands are made on a road switcher, including all sorts of emergency calls. There is that excursion train and that helper job, or perhaps motive power is needed for a snowplow. Or it may be needed for a branch-line passenger train.

With 1,500 horsepower, 125 tons, this locomotive offers a choice of six different gear ratios, making it possible to meet a wide range of services. Fitted to meet certain conditions at the time of delivery, the GP7 can quickly be tailored to perform other than the work originally planned by simply changing gears and pinions.

Perhaps this general purpose locomotive is wanted for passenger work, and, consequently, will need heating facilities; in that case, space ahead of the cab is provided for a 2,550-pound steam generator with 800-gallon water supply. This space also contains a toilet.

The GP7 can meet many and varying traffic conditions. It can be equipped to multiple with other GP7's, for additional tractive effort, and with any other General Motors locomotive for emergency service when required.

The Diesel engine is the same as the engine in the F7 road type locomotive, with 1,500 horsepower driving the main generator, which also is the same powerhouse as we find in the road locomotive. The four-wheel trucks also are interchangeable with the F7. They are designed for maximum stability and good riding quality, even on secondary branch lines, and to perform perfectly on the sharp curves in yards.

One of the most important Electro-Motive developments is the outside swing hanger suspension used on both the six-wheel and four-wheel roller-bearing trucks. Placing the swing hangers outside the rails practically doubles the distance between them, thus providing greatly increased stability on curves, which makes for better riding and reduced body roll. These latest and finest trucks are used on this road switcher, which indicates that the best of everything has gone into it, with the result that it is making a name for itself as a remarkable piece of motive power.

There are many special features that go to make this road switcher the kind of power that railroad men like to work with and that yard and main-line operating forces like to have at their command.

A great feature is accessibility, which is one of the highlights of the GP7, of all parts and equipment. Cab heating and ventilation is taken care of by means of forced air circulation, including ducts and diffusers for defrosting all cab windows. People look at a Diesel switch engine and wonder what kind of heating arrangements it has, if any. Heat for cold-weather operation in the cab of the GP7 is obtained from two engine radiator sections that have individually operated shutters for controlling air from the outside. And, as we have mentioned, engineer and fireman have precise control of heat on each side of the cab.

In doing freight roadwork, a head brakeman rides the cab. To provide for this member of the crew, a third seat is available, it being optional equipment. The cab has no divisions, making it easy for the engineer and fireman to call signals or engage in conversation. Upholstered armrests on window ledges on each side provide comfortable arm- or backrests when leaning out of the windows.

Ample space is provided at one end of the locomotive for the oil cooler, cooling water, oil filter, fuel filter, and fuel pumps, which are conveniently grouped for checking, servicing, or other attention. Air filters in hoods protect the engine and generator from dirt and snow. Headlights are twin sealed-beam, with bright and dimmer switch in the cab at a convenient location.

A feature of the main generator is its separate compartment housing. This has a "blizzard hatch" to draw warm air from the radiator, thus keeping the temperature well above freezing; it also prevents an accumulation of ice and snow in the air filters.

The many modern features of this work-horse switch and road engine reflect the vast experience of Electro-Motive in building the Diesel. The years that were behind created a vast reservoir of experience from which to draw when the GP7 went onto the drafting boards.

The GP7 does well in transfer service—those trains of freight being moved from one road to another—it can be used to handle work and supply trains, or to buckle on behind a snowplow. It performs well in hump switching service, and it will handle any assignment in local freight and passenger work.

We watch and admire the powerful Diesels on the long freight train and we look with keen pleasure at the colorful passenger Diesels, but our glance at the Diesel switch engine is brief almost to the point of being contemptuous. We see no glamour there, and yet there is perhaps more concentrated modern railroading wrapped up in a locomotive like the ubiquitous road switcher than in anything of like dimensions around the railroad plant. It is powerful and compact. It is built to do not alone one job well but many jobs.

A railroad would not get far without the services of the humble switch engine. It is the drudge of the road, unheralded, unsung. In a slightly older era it was the "yard goat" in some railroad vocabularies. It shuffles back and forth, performing endlessly the humble duties attendant to assembling and disassembling freight trains and passenger cars. It pulls in cars from sidings, which previously it had distributed. It works the clock around, except for a bit of servicing now and then. It clasps hands with cars from every state and every clime.

A great breed, the Diesel switcher, it really does its share of work.

In the fifteen years after 1935 General Motors Diesel switchers put in more than 50,000,000 hours of service, and they have set many records for long life and high availability, and it follows out that this means low maintenance costs. To accommodate the wide range of railroad service demanded, General

Motors, already with a strong pattern, set their engineering sights on the highest possible goal for switching motive power. Standardization has been one of the things that raised this company's motive power to the position it holds in the railroad world today.

The standardization, we might say, starts in the lowly switcher —in the heart and core of the locomotive—the Diesel engine, which we will return to shortly. For ten years General Motors' 125-ton, 1,000-horsepower switcher performed the toughest assignments in every field of heavy switching service. Then there was introduced to modern railroading the same rugged switcher, but with the horsepower increased to 1,200, utilizing the surplus power of the twelve-cylinder 567 series engine and so providing power for a 20 per cent increase in speed with the same tonnage rating. This new locomotive, therefore, was even more adaptable to fast transfer service and opened up a wider field in freight application.

An eight-cylinder 567 series Diesel went into a new addition of General Motors' switchers—an 800-horsepower, 115-ton switching locomotive. This power handles just about all of the work performed previously by the 1,000-horsepower locomotive at a considerably lower initial cost and, of course, lower operating cost. It has the same generator and traction motor as the 1,200-horsepower switcher and it works in many types of hump operation.

Now we come to the six-cylinder switch engine—600 horsepower, 100 tonner—with a decade of outstanding service. Transmission in this modern version of a veteran included a new generator, interchangeable with the 800- and 1,200-horsepower locomotives, and new silicone-insulated traction motors. This yard engine is a bruiser for work in a field that demands economy of operation. Remember, it is still a 567 series job, still that famous Diesel that powers all General Motors locomotives, only with less cylinders.

Now we come to a tandem job—a two-unit 2,400-horsepower transfer locomotive which delivers an astonishing 81,600 pounds continuous tractive effort at 8.7 miles per hour with a ratio of

65:12. This unusual switching locomotive is made up of two 1,200-horsepower power plants, *permanently* connected. The lead unit is the same as the 125-ton switcher. This duplication follows out in the booster unit, except that the latter has no cab, simply an extension of the hood.

Right straight through we find the same standard equipment employed in every piece of General Motors' motive power, except as to size of the main generator, one size of which is used with the sixteen-cylinder engines and the other with the twelve-cylinder engines.

For extra heavy transfer and humping operations, a three-unit combination of this type locomotive is available, which simply involves permanently hooking on a second booster unit.

General Motors—Diesel Pioneer

The General Motors Company is the father of the Diesel. They pioneered and developed it, and they are today the leading manufacturers of Diesel-electric locomotives, built by the Electro-Motive Division at La Grange, Illinois. Working from the ground up, General Motors achieved a power plant in which the co-ordination between the Diesel engine where the power is conceived and the electric drive, the force that turns the wheels, is marvelously smooth.

For the man who looks at the Diesel locomotive in action, without any clear notion of what is transpiring inside, a few words will tell the story. A Diesel engine drives a main generator, directly connected to it. Electric power flows from this generator, through suitable controls at the hand of the engineer, to direct-current traction motors, geared to the driving wheels. Simply, a Diesel converts mechanical energy into electrical energy.

General Motors uses only two generator sizes. One is used in the F7 and GP7 units, the other is used in the E8 road engines and the 600-, 800-, and 1,200-horsepower switchers. When used in road engines, the generators are equipped with alternators, built into the main units, to provide A.C. current for the induction motors which drive traction motor blowers and engine cooling fans. In the road locomotive the generator is force ventilated.

Many people wonder how the throttle for the mechanical energy (the Diesel engine) is co-ordinated with the electrical energy (the generator). Like the rest of the modern Diesel, these controls have been simplified and made foolproof to an amazing degree.

Let's take a look at the locomotive controls.

A highly selective load regulation system completely synchronizes the engine and transmission system. It ties the generator output, or voltage, directly to the fuel injection system of the engine, thereby assuring a constant horsepower output at each throttle position regardless of locomotive speed.

Now something called transition takes place, and that has been a baffler for many railroad enthusiasts. Transition is the process of connecting, or reconnecting, the traction motors to the generator in combinations which will give the best locomotive performance throughout the speed and load range. The various connections are accomplished by electropneumatic switches and contactors. These are operated by compressed air controlled by electrically actuated valves. Transition is designed for ease of operation and to avoid the possibility of operating errors that might cause damage to electrical equipment. This transition is fully automatic on the F7 and GP7 engines, and also fully automatic when running forward on the E8, and semi-automatic backward.

The finest machine in the world, proud of its newness, becomes absolutely worthless once part failure takes place. The ability to replace and repair quickly marks the degree of success of the organization which built the machine. A parts department, nationwide in scope, has given General Motors' railroad customers the kind of service modern transportation must have to keep trains moving on the high green.

The parts department can become a nightmare if frequent

changes in design and model, over the years, burden the department with a vast number of parts. The greater variety of parts and part sizes, the greater the cost. There could be no better example of consistency in engine design than is found in the General Motors great 567 Diesel. Beside being a clean trim-lined piece of machinery, a dependable piece of machinery, it offers an interchangeability of parts, from the flashing stream-liner motive power right down to that 100-ton switcher, that has inherently been interlocked in its design from the beginning of the 567 series.

All models of this 567—six, eight, twelve, and sixteen cylinder —have the same bore and stroke. And that is eight and a half inches by ten inches. The result is that all wearing parts are completely interchangeable.

The two-cycle principle is used in the General Motors engine, and that is the ultimate in simplicity of design. In the two-cycle engine the piston takes a power smash on every down stroke. The two-cycle gives more power in a more compact engine.

Fuel is introduced into the cylinder with a unit injection sys-tem that combines with a high-pressure fuel pump, a metering device and spray nozzle in a single unit, doing away with trouble-some high-pressure lines. A Root's type displacement blower provides excess air for clean, efficient combustion at any speed or altitude. The pistons are the oil cooled, floating type, free to rotate in the cylinder, resulting in more uniform wear and longer life.

Needless to record is the fact that the materials and the work-manship that goes into the famous 567 is of the highest stand-ard.

The Diesel body structure employs the bridge-type design and practically all of the weight above the trucks is carried on the rigid side frames. These bodies are built to stand a squeeze of 800,000 pounds, applied to the couplers, without any permanent deflection. This not only meets the requirements for passenger cars but protects locomotive crews as well as train passengers.

Switcher design is different. Here the underframe is the back-bone. This supports the entire weight of the power plant and auxiliary equipment. The weight is built into the structure to obtain the desired drawbar pull without slipping the wheels. A switch engine is constantly taking and delivering blows, and it must stand up in this grueling service. Massive underframes consist of heavy, rolled steel components, welded into a structure capable of withstanding the most severe buff and drag stresses.

The fabulous General Motors Diesel has achieved distinction through the number of units delivered to the railroads from 1934 through 1949. This includes a total of 3,364 freight units, 1,893 switchers, and 1,456 passenger units. In terms of horsepower, it ranks as follows:

Year	Total Horsepower (Cumulative)
1934	600
1935	11,100
1936	45,900
1937	129,300
1938	222,000
1939	385,300
1940	610,600
1941	925,050
1942	1,209,450
1943	1,470,850
1944	2,145,850
1945	2,799,300
1946	3,458,800
1947	4,822,600
1948	6,676,200
1949	9,077,300

General Motors' Diesel-electric locomotives have provided *two billion* unit miles of railroad service, as of the latter part of 1950, and the fleets continue to grow in this era of modern railroading which has given the nation better trains and better locomotives.

262

CHAPTER XXVI

NEW D.&R.G.W. FLAT YARD

Streamlined Facilities

The demands of modern railroading are constant and imperative. The railroad that lags is lost. The voice of the shipper is raised against delay; the trucker is a thundering competitor in the modern scheme; rival rail lines are shouting up their wares —new power, better cars, faster schedules. Speed and improved communication facilities are featured in the stories of the day. Everything is machine and push button.

In Denver, Colorado, the yardmaster has under his hand banks of little switches for directing incoming trains to the yard track desired; he has a microphone, paging speakers, and talk-back speakers at his command. There is a streamlined yard office building and a streamlined tower for the streamlining of freight classification and train movement over the lines of the Denver & Rio Grande Western.

Requirements at Denver do not demand a hump yard, and an eighteen-track yard of the flat-switching type amply takes care of the work at this important point. Everything about this Denver yard is smart and symmetrical. It has provided important operating advantages for the Denver & Rio Grande Western, including the speedier handling of industrial business in the area—in particular, the time required to deliver stock cars to the stockyards—and the advancing of the departure time of trains of connecting roads. On one road the time has been advanced an hour; on another by four hours and thirty minutes, a very considerable saving in the rush of 1950 railroading.

The new yard makes possible maximum tonnage for all departing trains, with a decrease in train-miles and a very considerable decrease in helper-miles. The yard has brought about a reduction of per diem payments, and also eliminated a number of switch-engine shifts.

The present yard replaced two small freight yards, and in addition to its eighteen tracks in the classification yard it has tracks and servicing facilities that include an engine run-around track, rip tracks, a Y track, a scale track, hold and team tracks, a modern icing station, and service track with car-repair and Diesel-locomotive servicing facilities, two electrical substations, communication facilities, and a new modernistic yard office.

The yard slopes down from the south to the center on a 0.19 per cent grade, and from the north the slope toward the center from the north end is 0.4 per cent. This saucer shape was adopted partly to give sufficient grade to the yard tracks to prevent cars from rolling out of the yard after being switched. The yard is well drained, with runoff water carried under the yard through two forty-eight-inch corrugated metal culverts.

After the grading for the new yard was completed the entire trackage area surface was covered with seven inches of pit-run gravel having a maximum size of three-quarter inch. The portion of the yard upon which trackage was not constructed was covered with pit-run gravel to a depth of four inches.

The eighteen tracks comprising the body of the yard range from 4,600 to 1,700 feet in length, with a total car capacity of 1,200. The tracks were built on fourteen-foot centers, with the exception of two eighty-car icing tracks, built on each side of the 3,600-foot icing dock. The length of the yard, throat to throat, is one mile. The yard was arranged to permit future expansion to more than double the present capacity. Two 3,000-foot yard-entrance tracks were built at the south end and one 5,000-foot lead at the north end.

The two long icing tracks were built with 110-pound rail, the next four tracks with 100-pound rail and the remainder of the yard tracks with 90-pound rail. The rail and all of the other track material, except the spikes, were second-hand material.

A scale track, 1,150 feet long, was built just west of the run-around track with the scale track at the center of it. This track gives a weighing capacity of eleven cars. For holding peach diversion cars, two hold tracks, 2,000 feet long, were constructed between the yard and the main track, and these latter tracks can also be used as team tracks for the small amount of unloading that may be necessary.

One of the outstanding features of the new yard is its modern icing facilities. This plant was built near the mid-point of the yard length between the main track and the longest yard track. The plant includes an icehouse with a storage capacity of 16,000 tons, an icehouse office building, a long ice dock, two Link-Belt Rico Master car-icing machines, two salt-storage houses, and an ice-machine track.

The icehouse is a three-room building, 96 feet by 290 feet, and it is constructed entirely of fire-retardant and rot-resistant treated wood, with the exception of the concrete floor and the asbestos-cement siding. Because it would be impossible to get ice out of the three rooms in sufficient quantities to ice two peach trains simultaneously, a daily storage room, 12 feet wide and 9 feet high and running the entire length of the ice structure was built on the ice-track side. With the added space thus made available, ice can be taken out of the house continuously.

During periods between trains, a readily available reserve supply can be built up, thus allowing the crews in the main icehouse to work steadily. Two spiral chutes descend from the storage room to tunnel conveyors which move the ice laterally and on up inclined conveyors to the ice dock.

This ice dock, built between the two icing tracks, is 6 feet wide, 6 feet high, and 3,600 feet long. The two Rico Master car-icing machines run on a track laid between the dock and the second ice track. The machines take ice from a conveyor on the ice dock, crush it, and elevate it to the top of the machine and chute it down to cars standing on either track. Salt is automatically mixed with the ice to the proportion required. This salt is stored at both ends of the dock.

The ice used at this Denver yard icing plant is taken from ponds in the mountains, being harvested in cakes cut twenty-three inches square, the ice thickness being between sixteen and twenty inches thick. Generally the ice is delivered in January in whatever types of cars are available. The ice cakes are unloaded opposite each of the three big storage rooms, and an inclined conveyor in the center of each room delivers them at the proper elevation.

South of the ice plant, a small one-story office building houses the ice inspectors, and also provides a tool and storage room.

Modern Yard Office

Your modern yard office, in contrast to the yard office of yesterday, stands out as an architectural triumph. It is, perhaps, the least publicized of all the present-day railroad plant facilities. Like the old-time railroad depot, the freight house had nothing to recommend it except its convenient location as concerned the property. It was dingy, gloomy, and poorly ventilated and lighted.

Today the yard office building is clean lined and trim, and the one at the Denver yard is particularly attractive and business-like in line and make-up. It was constructed adjacent to a main road at the south end of the new yard. It is two stories, with a basement and tower, built of brick and terra cotta. The building is seventy-five by thirty-five feet. The four-story communication tower is twenty feet square, located on the southeast corner, looking over the yard. The basement of the yard office building contains signal and communication facilities, a compressor for the pneumatic-tube system, and a heating plant.

Office space is provided on the first floor for the yardmaster, the engine dispatcher, and their associated personnel. Heating is by hot-water radiation and convection, and the locker room by unit heaters.

The tower observation and control room is thirty-six feet above the ground. It provides a clear view of the entire yard, and houses the controls for the paging and talk-back speakers, as well as a radio and yard-track indicator. The latter is connected with equipment in the north throat of the yard, which, by means of a control machine in the yardmaster's office, flashes any number from one to eighteen, indicating the proper track for an incoming eastbound train to head-in on, thus averting the necessity of calling the dispatcher before entering the yard.

A pneumatic-tube system serves the telegraph office and all other principal locations, in keeping with the practice in nearly all modern yards across the country.

The mechanical forces have facilities adjacent to the three rip tracks which include a small office building and shop equipped with gas, electricity, and hot and cold water. In the rip-track area are convenient electric outlets for the use of electric tools and welding machines. Compressed air is distributed at a pressure of ninety pounds per square foot over the rip-track and yard areas for testing on these tracks and for charging train lines before departure.

Lighting facilities include four 117-foot towers, equipped with five to nine floodlights to the tower. Towers are located at each end of the yard and others on each side midway down its length. These floodlights are arranged to illuminate the main body of the yard, but with the highest degree of intensity concentrated on the leads, the ice dock, and the areas surrounding the yard office and rip tracks.

Through two transformer substations power is furnished the icehouse and associated facilities, and the yard office and adjacent area requiring power and lights.

Servicing of Diesels is performed in the vicinity of the rip tracks. Here we find a 70,000-gallon fuel-oil storage tank, with fuel outlets, water hydrants, two sand towers, sand-storage space, and oil pump house. A small building is provided for lubricating oil storage, while another building takes care of caboose supplies.

Because the new yard lies within the limits of a C.T.C. system, changes were necessary in the control machine to conform with the revised main-track and new yard layouts. These changes involved the installation of eleven power switches at the north end of the yard and five power switches at the south end of the south leads.

I have the greatest admiration for a road like the Rio Grande that has so adequately modernized facilities which make for speeding the movement of freight. Many times we do not realize how important such a modernization program can be until an emergency arises. Then, instead of jamming up the railroad, traffic is taken in stride. Minutes, hours, days are saved; a nation can be saved through our modern transportation system and such completely adequate facilities as we have examined in this flat yard of the Denver & Rio Grande Western.

Such a railroad invites the attention of shippers, just as a streamlined train invites passengers. There is no room for indifference and outmoded practices in the modern railroad picture.

On the average, about four westbound through trains, for a total of some 295 cars, make up and depart from this Rio Grande yard daily. The eastbound traffic volume is approximately the same as the westbound. Most of these freight trains have written a place for themselves through their speed and dependability—trains like the Ute, which make connections that aid in the rapid movement of merchandise to and from the big eastern, mid-continent terminals and the Pacific Coast.

Through yards like the one just described, the time used in interchange and in all yard operations has been reduced to an absolute minimum. Nothing is left to chance any more. Shouting and lantern waving no longer serve the railroad to any great degree. Shoe leather and tempers are saved in this new era. The engineers have provided for every emergency. We have an example in the amplifier equipment. Somewhere something has happened and everything is dead. There is no excitement, no scurrying hither and yon, desperately hunting the trouble. The yardmaster simply flips a switch and cuts in a corresponding spare unit.

Where underground cables are employed, terminal junction boxes are located every 600 feet to facilitate testing and trouble hunting. A spare cable is run to each speaker stand in the yard. If a short circuit develops or there is other trouble, the spare can be connected up in a very short time.

The communication equipment is operated on 110-volt A.C. which normally is obtained from a commercial line. However, if the current goes off the yardmaster simply turns a key and so starts up a 1,500-watt, 120-volt A.C. Onan gas-engine set as a means of supplying power for communications and electric lights in the office.

This yard is typical of the Rio Grande—pep and thorough railroading ability. President Wilson McCarthy, Executive Vice-President E. A. West, and General Manager A. E. Perlman know their modern railroads and how to run one in that manner.

CHAPTER XXVII

SEABOARD PERISHABLE MOVE

The Orange Goes to Market

There is no comparable service anywhere to the railroad's perishable move. It operates with clocklike precision, day in and day out, in good weather and bad, over thousands of miles of track. It starts in the soft semitropic regions of the South and Southwest, between the oceans, and carries to such great market and distribution centers as New York, Chicago, and Boston. Every safeguard is thrown around the flight of today's orange and grapefruit that it may bring edible sunshine to your breakfast table tomorrow.

We are going to travel with a box of oranges (or grapefruit) from a place called Winter Haven, midway down the great sunshine land peninsula of Florida, to New York City and see, firsthand, something of the thoroughness and efficiency of the Seaboard Air Line Railroad in this perishable movement.

We are at a packing plant in Winter Haven in the fabulous central section of the state. The sunshine fruit is brought from the groves to the beginning of these endless belts which carry it in a yellow stream through the operations that grade it for size and quality. It flows then to the coloring rooms. The citrus fruit, arriving at the plant from the groves, has different shadings, and these coloring rooms give it a uniform golden hue.

The fruit now moves on to the busy packing shed and is placed in the familiar boxes for shipping—one and three-fifths bushels to a box. In the meantime, the traffic manager or shipping clerk has placed with the agent of the Seaboard Air Line an order for one or more refrigerator cars, depending on the volume of business on this particular day. Before this car, or cars, arrives at the packing plant it is pre-iced. This pre-icing is generally done in the Seaboard yards at Wildwood, sixty-four miles to the north, and involves the loading of approximately 9,600 pounds of ice into the bunkers at the ends of the car.

Our box of oranges is loaded into the car along with 499 others. The boxes are braced securely, the doors are closed and sealed and the bill of lading signed. This reefer is now ready to go into Train No. 80, the Marketer.

Our car, which we shall call FGE No. 25,500, becomes a part of the northbound Marketer, starting for a New York City warehouse. As the train moves northward, additional cars are picked up from packing plant sidings in this great citrus belt. Or there may be cars of other kinds of perishables, starting their northward flight.

At Wildwood these cars that have come up from the Winter Haven area are consolidated with other cars of perishables that have already arrived from loading stations on various sections of the Seaboard Air Line. With the train made up, the famous Marketer quickens its pace as it roars on to Baldwin, Florida, 109 miles away.

No prima donna could receive more solicitous care and attention than our box of oranges. It is watched over almost every minute, its temperature is taken, and the shipper instructs the railroad, through the modern and alert communications systems, as to just what is to be done concerning icing and other matters.

Baldwin is nineteen miles south of Jacksonville, and it has facilities for such icing of our 500-box load of oranges as it may require. Some cars move under one form of refrigeration and some under another. The extent to which ice is replenished is, of course, dependent on the season of the year and the section of the country through which the train is traveling. It follows that a warm southern clime requires more refrigeration than colder northern latitudes. It is because of these climatic changes that infinite care must be exercised in this rush of the perishable train. The type of refrigeration required for citrus fruits is different from that employed, for example, for a car of green corn or celery.

The Marketer and our box of oranges, upon leaving Baldwin, Florida, heads for Savannah, Georgia, with a rush of wheels and a breathless clicking of rail joints. The train is reclassified at this point and cars that are to move to Atlanta and thence to points west go into Train No. 89. Our perishable cars that are consigned to Savannah for diversion are reconsigned here to the final destination.

We wrote in the opening chapter of the overnighters—the manifest trains of the country that are giving the shipper the finest possible fast freight service. The Seaboard Air Line operates six of these overnighters over distances of from 325 to 418 miles. Two of these trains, Nos. 72 and 80, operate from Jacksonville, Florida, to Hamlet, North Carolina.

Our car FGE No. 25,500 required no icing at Baldwin, but at Hamlet, the next terminal north of Savannah, and 554 miles from Winter Haven, Florida, where our box of oranges began its journey, the bunkers require some 5,000 pounds of ice. This service is performed by the railroad, under its contract with the shipper and as expressed in the terms of the bill of lading, that the shipper, receiver, and consumer may be assured that the fruit, at its final destination, will be in the same perfect condition as when it started its journey.

And this means that the orange or grapefruit, or their juices, placed before you on the breakfast table in New York, Chicago, Boston, is exactly as fine and tasteful as it would be if it was served to you in Winter Haven.

Remember, this is precision railroading, and the detention time for re-icing and checking of waybills at Hamlet is the absolute minimum required. The Marketer again gets the green and storms away for Richmond, Virginia, 254 miles distant. At Hermitage Yard, in Richmond, the Seaboard delivers our box of oranges and its fast-wheeling perishable train over to the Richmond, Fredericksburg & Potomac Railroad.

A locomotive of the latter road handles the train over its tracks to Potomac Yard, Virginia, across the Potomac River

K.C.S. #77, fine Merchandise Special, climbing 1.25 grade up Rich Mt., Ark., with seventy-five cars and 4-unit E.M.D. Diesel #56. Note radio. Photo by Preston George.

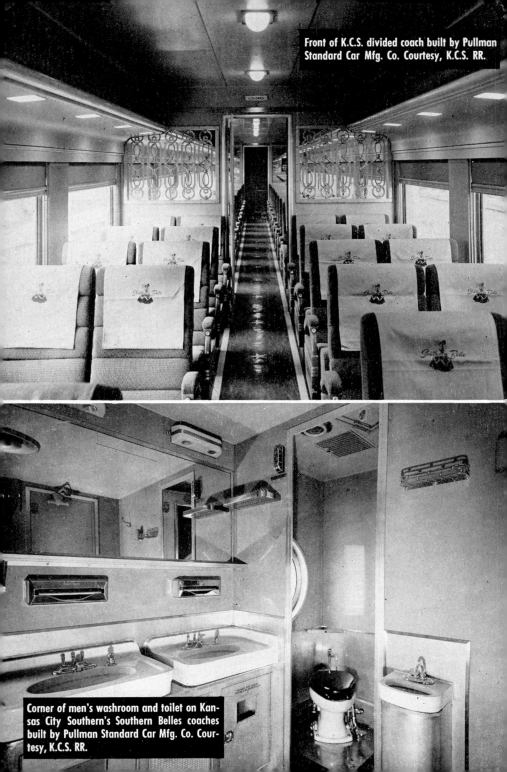

Front of K.C.S. divided coach built by Pullman Standard Car Mfg. Co. Courtesy, K.C.S. RR.

Corner of men's washroom and toilet on Kansas City Southern's Southern Belles coaches built by Pullman Standard Car Mfg. Co. Courtesy, K.C.S. RR.

Southern Pacific second #806 solid train of potatoes climbing the 2-per-cent grade above Caliente, Calif., on the Tehachapi Subdivision of the San Joaquin Division, about to enter tunnel #1. Courtesy, S.P. RR.

View of Southern Pacific's new Taylor Yard at Los Angeles with car rolling down through retarders. Towers on left and right. Courtesy, S.P. RR.

Operator working Union Switch & Signal Co.'s retarder in tower of S.P.'s Taylor Yard at Los Angeles. Note switch list and teletype. Courtesy, S.P. RR.

Looking toward apex of hump in S.P.'s Taylor Yard with cars coming through retarders. Hump signal in background. Entire installation built by Union Switch & Signal Co. Courtesy, S.P. RR.

Cars are given side inspection as well as underneath from pit on hump of Southern Pacific's new Taylor Yard at Los Angeles on division of that name. Courtesy, S.P. RR.

Communications control panel being worked by hump yardmaster at Southern Pacific's Taylor Yard, Los Angeles. Courtesy, S.P. RR.

Santa Fe #7, the Fast Mail, hauled by Diesel 306, new E.M.D. E-8, climbing Cajon Pass on the westward track between milepost #38 and #39 west of Victorville, Calif., on the First District of the Los Angeles Division. Photo by R. H. Kindig.

Santa Fe #105, the Scout, with engine 2917, their great 4-8-4 type, with fourteen cars at Heman, Okla., on the First District of the Plains Division. Note 160-car passing track in foreground. Photo by Preston George.

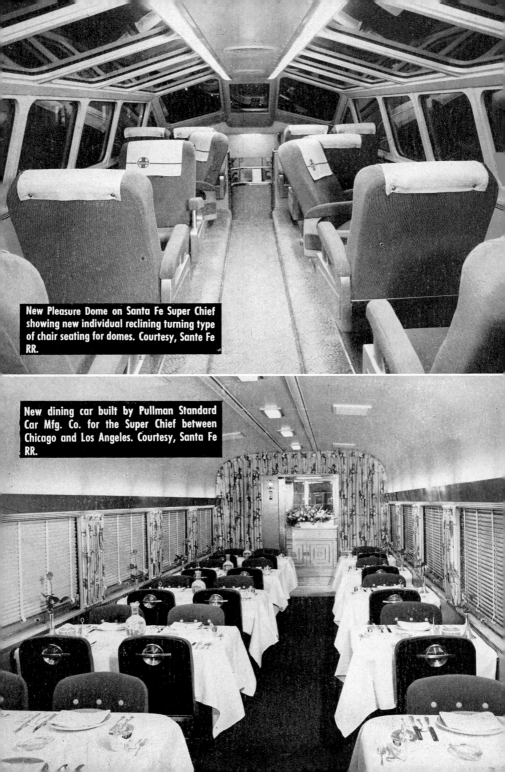

New Pleasure Dome on Santa Fe Super Chief showing new individual reclining turning type of chair seating for domes. Courtesy, Sante Fe RR.

New dining car built by Pullman Standard Car Mfg. Co. for the Super Chief between Chicago and Los Angeles. Courtesy, Santa Fe RR.

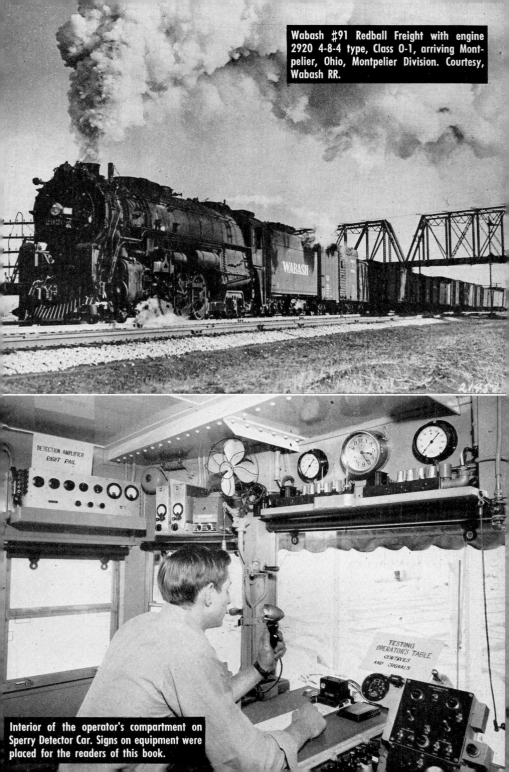

Wabash #91 Redball Freight with engine 2920 4-8-4 type, Class 0-1, arriving Montpelier, Ohio, Montpelier Division. Courtesy, Wabash RR.

Interior of the operator's compartment on Sperry Detector Car. Signs on equipment were placed for the readers of this book.

The Frisco's fine Meteor #10 leaving Newburg, Mo., on the Eastern Division hauled by Diesel #2005 E.M.D. passenger Diesel. Courtesy, Frisco Lines.

from Washington, D.C. Here the Baltimore & Ohio Railroad takes charge of our box of oranges and car FGE 25,500, and we highball over the B.&O., bound for Jersey City. Here the cars are run onto lighters, which move across the harbor to piers in New York City.

With others, our box of oranges is unloaded and placed on the floors of warehouses, where, during the early morning hours, it is sold at auction. It is taken away by the buyer and resold almost immediately and made available soon thereafter to the hotel and restaurant buyers, to the home buyer and housewife.

Part of the contents of this box of oranges is ready to serve, a scant five days after it left the sunshine of Florida's orange grove at Winter Haven.

This great perishable movement was accomplished by the finely timed schedules of three railroads and their steel links between southern grower and northern consumer. It was done on a freight rate of ninety-eight cents per box, including the refrigeration service that insured the delivery of the fruit in A-1 condition.

Now we will break this down a little further. Our box of oranges numbered 216. An average box of grapefruit holds ninety-six. The railroads involved in this top-notch transportation job received about one cent for each grapefruit and around one half a cent for each orange.

Few people realize how much value received they get for each dollar invested in their rail shipments, whether it is iron ore or liquid sunshine. From origin to destination, this Seaboard Air Line perishable move covered 1,159 miles. It involved the finest kind of roadway, the best in rolling stock, modern motive power and the last word in signaling and communications.

The cost for one ton (approximately twenty-two boxes) hauled one mile was less than two cents.

Manifest Name Trains

The Seaboard's manifest freight trains are all named, and they move in all directions. No one appreciates this high-speed service more than the shipper, and the perishable shipper, in particular.

We will take first this name freight, known all up and down the Atlantic Coast—No. 80, the Marketer, with which the reader is already familiar.

No. 80 operates in sections, the number governed by the demands of the perishable movement, which builds to a peak and then recedes. The Marketer carries most of Florida's citrus crops. It leaves Tampa at 1:00 A.M. and Miami at 9:00 P.M. The two trains, one from the east coast and the other from the west coast of Florida, consolidate at Wildwood in the morning, arriving there at 7:05 A.M. No. 80's departure from Wildwood is at 8:15 A.M.

It is at Baldwin, junction point and the beginning of the line that by-passes Jacksonville, at 1:00 P.M. The fast-traveling train makes Savannah at 6:00 P.M., with a departure at 9:30 P.M. It pulls into Hamlet, North Carolina, at 6:00 A.M. the next morning. It is there an hour and a half, while the Norfolk-Portsmouth cars are cut out. It leaves Hamlet, a very important point on the Seaboard, at 7:30 A.M. The Marketer reaches Hermitage Yard, Richmond, at 6:00 P.M. and is taken over, as indicated earlier in the chapter, by the Richmond, Fredericksburg & Potomac.

The Pioneer, No. 84, is among the most important of the road's manifests. It leaves Montgomery, Alabama, eastbound, every morning at 9:30 A.M. with cars from the western connections. It is split at Baldwin that night, leaving there at 12:30 A.M. for a Tampa arrival at 7:30 A.M., and a Miami arrival at 9:30 P.M.

The Cavalcade, No. 74, is another West Georgia-Florida crack freight. It pulls out of Columbus, Georgia, at 3:30 P.M., arriving at Baldwin at 4:00 A.M. the following morning. As there is no hurry to get the connections into Tampa and Miami before late that night and the next morning, it does not leave Baldwin until 12 o'clock noon, with arrival at Tampa at 9:00

P.M. and Miami at 1:00 A.M., ready for following-morning delivery.

Two of the fastest southbound manifests are the Capitol, No. 27, and the Migrator, No. 87.

The Capitol leaves Richmond, Virginia, with direct connections from Potomac Yard (Washington), New York, Philadelphia, Baltimore, and other Northern cities, including Boston. This train, No. 27, pulls out of Richmond at 1:00 P.M. It arrives at Hamlet, North Carolina, at 8:00 P.M. The Capitol is classified and inspected there in the remarkable time of fifty minutes. It reaches Howells, the great yard in Atlanta, at 7:00 A.M., for first-morning delivery. Leaving Howells at 8:30 A.M., No. 27 reaches Birmingham, Alabama, at 3:00 P.M. This is really moving freight.

No. 87, the Migrator, leaves Hermitage Yard, Richmond, at 6:00 P.M. and arrives at Hamlet at 3:00 A.M. It picks up cars here and is ready to leave at 4:30 A.M. No. 87 reaches Baldwin, down there south of Jacksonville, at 9:00 P.M. that night.

Northbound out of Birmingham we have No. 82, the Courier. This is the Seaboard's heavy-products fast freight, the kind of a freight we do not usually immediately classify in the manifest class, but they do down on the Seaboard. This train is the Seaboard's "Steel King." It leaves Birmingham at 12:30 A.M. and arrives at Atlanta at 7:00 A.M. It pulls into Hamlet at 5:00 A.M. the following morning. Leaving Hamlet at 8:00 A.M. it arrives at Portsmouth, Virginia, at tidewater, at 11:00 P.M., with direct connections for the Norfolk gateway and the Pennsylvania at Cape Charles.

This great manifest network of the Seaboard is a pulsing part of the new industrial South, a strong link in its teeming domain. We have seen the tight linkage between the citrus grove and its packing house and the distant warehouse and market stalls. The grower and the consumer are no further apart than the length of a steel rail. This is a result of the organization and the leadership of Seaboard men—the kind of men who determined and fashioned the by-passing of the crowded Jacksonville terminal

275

district as a means of saving countless precious hours of train time for north-south main-line traffic.

Henry W. Anderson, of Richmond, is chairman of the Seaboard's special board of directors, which includes well-known businessmen from all along the line. The Seaboard's executive committee is composed of six members, of which Chairman Anderson and President Legh R. Powell, Jr., are members. Mr. Powell is a fine railroader. G. B. Rice is another fine all-round traffic expert, solicitor, and railroader whose hard work and grand personality have brought a great deal of business to the Seaboard.

The railroad has excellent freight and passenger traffic departments, headed by experts in this line; a fine new industry department; a fine public relations department; and an able operating Vice-President in C. H. Sauls. I have known Mr. Sauls personally for twenty-five years and I know his ability as among the top-ranking railroad men of the country.

CHAPTER XXVIII

SAFE RAILS

Sperry Men Guard the Track

On the land, on the sea, and in the air, the name of Sperry has won a place in the minds and the hearts of men. Elmer A. Sperry—the late Dr. Elmer A. Sperry—wrote a glowing page on American history. Born in 1860, he died in 1930, and in his lifetime Dr. Sperry took out, all told, 400 patents, most of which were concerned with transportation.

Sailors remember Dr. Sperry for the Sperry Gyro Compass, a requisite of modern navigation; flyers depend on the flight instruments which were pioneered by him. Railroad men know him best for his rail testing devices and the little detector car which made its first appearance in November, 1928, when Car No. 102 arrived at Montpelier, Ohio, to fulfill a contract with the Wabash Railroad for rail test service between Montpelier and Clarke Junction, Indiana.

Detector car No. 102 and its companion unit, motor car No. 501, have grown into a fleet of modern, self-driven rail cars of standard size, equipped to take care of such field personnel as a chief operator and his assistants, including a steward, who actually live out on the line.

Sperry supplies a service—a protective service through which the railroads of the country throw up an added shield of safety armor by employing the Sperry people to put their electrical robot detective to work in running down possible lurking fifth-column saboteurs, in the form of tiny imperfections, lurking in the rail structure. Sperry is the G-man.

The Sperry Rail Service offers an additional safeguard against track failure, something like the doctor who checks up on the physical structure of the railroad employee. Safe rails and a sound body are necessary to the high-speed movement of modern trains. In 1947, the railroads performed 46,000,000,000 passenger-miles of service. To accumulate such mileage, a train passenger traveling fifty miles per hour twenty-four hours a day, would have to ride this train for about 1,600 years before he could expect to be in an accident.

There are train accidents, of course, but few really serious accidents. Man failure enters into most of these, and this is rare. Rail failure? In view of the number of miles of main-line track, it is so small as to be almost negligible. One of the reasons for this fractional hazard is the alertness of the Sperry car and its operators. In twenty years, 2,000,000 miles of track were tested on 124 railroads. Constant research and inspection car improvement by Sperry has effected continually increased efficiency.

In 1930, Sperry tested 31,000 miles of track; in 1946, 176,000 miles. The tracks of more than one hundred roads are tested annually.

Before examining a modern Sperry Rail Service car, let us go back to No. 102, the first car, and its companion unit, the motor car, which provided the motive power. In this, a gasoline engine, mounted at the front end, was geared to the wheels. It contained living accommodations to the extent of two bunks, a small washbasin and toilet facilities. The detector car contained a gasoline-driven generator, a recording table, and the interior detection equipment. The brush carriages, suspended between the wheels of the car, were raised or lowered manually by means of levers. A searching unit was suspended from each carriage. Lead weights on the brush carriages were used to maintain contact pressure against the rails. This car also had a bunk hung above the generator.

Both cars were equipped with manually operated brakes, independent of each other, and as a result a high degree of co-operation was required to effect a smooth stop. Since the cars were not equipped with standard couplers or air brakes, and were not capable of sustained light runs at traffic speed, the double

278

unit was shipped by flat car when it went from one testing district to another.

Old No. 102 has long since gone the way of aged equipment, but the basic principle—induction testing—has not. Greatly refined, this principle has remained the same—the most efficient and successful method of rail testing known. Today, twenty Sperry induction type detector cars are busy on American and Canadian railroads. Each car tests almost 10,000 miles of track each year.

A Sperry detector car has a motor compartment forward and behind it a well-equipped galley. Next is a dining and lounge room. Sleeping quarters, with upper and lower berths, are in the mid-section of the car, adjoining are toilet and shower facilities. The generator compartment includes cabinets, a work bench, and paint tank. At the extreme end of the car is located a recording table and functional apparatus. An operator sits at the recording table, watching the operation of the pens as they tell the unfolding story of the rails and a possible lurking saboteur.

The crew of the detector car are constantly on the alert, never relaxing when the car is on patrol. One occupies the small cabin in front, operating the electric drive which propels the car from power originating in a gasoline marine engine. Another sits at a desk watching the tape which crawls slowly downward as the car moves. A third may be stationed in the recording compartment and ready to jump from the back of the slow-moving car to examine a spot in the rail when a jog occurs in a line made by one of those recording pens.

Throughout the day it is start and stop, almost continuously. Seldom is a mile traversed that a stop is not made and one or two Sperry men are there over the rail with a paint gun to make an indication mark. Most stops are for but a minute or two, but if there should be a dangerous rail section this portion will be daubed with red paint. But before this danger mark is placed a searching unit will be used to recheck the findings registered on the tape.

In making a hand test, a delicate meter wired in circuit with the hand-searching unit reveals the exact extent of the hidden defect.

The detector cars waste little time between dawn and dusk, and for that reason they are staffed so the operators can take rest periods. The car has a small library and a radio, and some have tiny darkrooms for picture developing, as the constant traveling gives the staff opportunity for picture taking. Nightly layovers provide an opportunity to go to movies. Diversions are helpful, relieving the monotony of the long duty tours. Aside from the night stops, the cars are constantly on the move, except when it is necessary to shop for food or take on other supplies.

A gasoline engine drives a main generator, which delivers current up to 4,500 amperes at two to three volts to the main brush carriage. An extra generator supplies current for supplementary pre-energizing brush carriages.

A car steward is employed for cooking and the maintenance of the living quarters. It can be seen that, with the limited accommodations and space, railway supervisors and other railroad employees traveling with the detector car must be limited. As lonely as the life of a Sperry man out on the line may seem, the list of applicants is always long. It is a fascinating job, and the big yellow car, creeping along, is not without moments of tension and excitement, for train schedules have to be watched closely and at times there must be flag protection.

Waste time must be avoided so far as possible and the Sperry detector car receives every possible help from the Operating Department. Sometimes a trainmaster and dispatcher will cooperate by arranging to run trains around the working detector car in double-track territory.

We are going to consider Sperry's new Ultrasonic Detector Car, but before we do we will make clear the terms "inside" and "outside" the joint bars.

Joint bars are those drilled bars or plates which are bolted to the rails at the rail joint. In using the sentence, "Testing between the joint bars," we desire to convey the fact that the Sperry detector car tests the rail outside the limits of these joints —that is, the induction detector car.

The Ultrasonic Detector Car tests the rail ends within the length of the joint bars, i.e., the bolt-hole section. It is at this point that defects are apt to occur, such as bolt-hole cracks. Little rail gangsters can lurk around these unseen web sections.

A dirty rail is difficult to test, and the car must be run over it several times. In hand testing, the rail is thoroughly cleaned In sections where flange oilers are in operation, the railroad is asked to shut them off a couple of days before the Sperry car arrives.

The rail test service finds the little cracks and fissures before they have become enlarged and consequently dangerous.

New Ultrasonic Detector Cars

Sperry's pioneering research in the field of rail testing employed the induction method over twenty years ago. This method tests the rail *outside* the joint bars. Now, in this modern railroad day, Sperry has introduced the "ultrasonic" method for testing *inside* the joint bars. It brings to the railroad complete end-to-end testing of rails in the track.

As of April, 1950, five of the Sperry Ultrasonic Detector Cars were in use in commercial tests on American railroads.

This new service provides the railroad with a means of detecting bolt-hole cracks and head-and-web separations in the rail—*inside* joint bars and at railroad crossings, station platforms, switch points, and frogs.

The Ultrasonic Detector Car consists of a standard inspection car modified by the addition of an auxiliary electric drive used to propel the car during testing; a device which automatically spots the car in testing position; a swivel mounted out-rigger seat for the operator; a gasoline-driven generator set and the ultrasonic detection equipment.

This equipment is of special design, developed particularly for application to the testing of rail inside of track structures. Improvements, undoubtedly, will be made rapidly as research progresses and in view of long experience gained under varied conditions on different railroads.

At each joint, the operator moves the hand-held searching unit along the rail surface and observes the shielded viewing screen of the detection equipment for indications of defects. The type, location, and size of any defects are accurately indicated by the pattern on the screen.

Through the employment of the new Ultrasonic service for testing *inside* the joint bars and the addition of new auxiliary equipment to the induction cars for improved performance *outside* the joint bars, Sperry now provides the railroads with high accuracy end-to-end testing of rails in track.

What is this ultrasonic principle, you ask? It has, of course, to do with sound, and sound has been used by the railroads as a testing means for many years.

A familiar example is the well-known hammer test, which had an extremely limited field of application. More recently, scientists have been investigating the behavior of "silent sounds," that is, those sound vibrations lying within the frequency range from inaudible up to 5,000,000 or 10,000,000 cycles per second. One of these investigations led to an invention known as the ultrasonic reflectoscope, which has many applications in locating hidden defects in metal, and has recently been adapted for testing rail in track within the limits of the joint bars.

The ultrasonic reflectoscope is an electronic instrument designed for the nondestructive testing of materials by means of high-frequency sound vibrations. Its principal elements include a searching unit, a cathode ray tube, and a cathode ray screen. The searching unit consists of an "X-cut" quartz crystal designed to vibrate at a desired frequency. This unit sends out a beam of pulsed high-frequency vibrations into the material under test, and if these vibrations encounter a crack or the opposite side of the material, they are reflected back to the instrument. The initial pulse and its reflections are presented on the cathode ray screen of the instrument in their correct time sequence.

A hood covers the operator of the Ultrasonic Detector Car and the detector equipment. This hood makes for better screen visibility on sunny days and protects from the weather on stormy days. The control switchboard for the car is located within easy reach of the operator. About ninety joints, for an average, can be tested per hour.

In the past no quick means was offered of determining whether new rail was developing fatigue cracks inside the limits of these joint bars, but with the ultrasonic equipment checks could be made of a sufficient number of joints to secure an immediate answer.

CHAPTER XXIX

FRISCO FAST FREIGHT

The Staff of Life and a Steel Rail

The joint storage capacity of the great terminal elevators at Enid, Oklahoma, Wichita, Kansas, and Kansas City, Missouri, is 131,343,500 bushels of wheat. Freight cars haul this wheat—great fleets of freight cars. Without freight cars, the wheat would rot and America would starve. For the ten years between 1940 and 1950 the average annual wheat production in the states of Oklahoma and Kansas alone was 258,813,000 bushels. It takes the grace of God, men skilled in wheat production, and American machinery to raise wheat in that quantity. It takes a steel rail, a boxcar, and transportation know-how to move that kind of a crop.

The railroads begin storing empty boxcars in April and May, readying for the wheat surge that will come with the harvest. By the time the harvest gangs attack the golden grain thousands of cars are waiting. Wheat goes by wagon or truck down the road to the county elevator at the siding. These local elevators hold from 10,000 to 15,000 carloads of wheat. When the cars are loaded they start for the big terminal elevators; eventually the wheat moves on to the flour mills, again by freight car.

The Frisco plays an important part in the wheat movement. As flour or export wheat, much of it goes to the Gulf ports and to the four corners of the world. A great deal of the wheat handled by the road passes through the St. Louis gateway en route to the big flour mills at Buffalo.

In the old days the railroads would have their surplus steam power put in shape to handle this move, but from 1948 the

Diesels took over the wheat haul without fuss or feathers. Enid, Oklahoma, to me, is the most interesting of all the wheat centers. It is served well by the Frisco, and also by the Santa Fe, as is, of course, Wichita and Kansas City. Enid, there on the prairies, with its bulging wheat elevators against the sky—Enid, the county seat of Garfield County, a part of America's wheat empire, the breadbasket of America.

Let us take a look, for a moment, at the wheat tonnage when it starts to roll. From Enid to Hallett, Oklahoma, eighty-three miles, the four-unit Diesel will handle 7,500 tons, or 5,900 tons if it is a three-unit locomotive. From Keystone, Oklahoma, to West Tulsa a three-unit Diesel will take 12,000 tons; a four-unit, 14,000 tons. They are real trains, there on the Frisco.

Expert handling of the wheat move is only part of the fine service that the Frisco renders its many shippers. The road operates a crack fleet of merchandise trains, which are given every consideration all over the railroad. Two fast Red Ball freight trains operate daily in each direction between Kansas City and Birmingham.

The Packer Special, Train No. 131, handles packing-house products and perishables, moving from the Middle West and the far West territories to the Southeast. No. 131 leaves Kansas City at 9:47 P.M. It arrives at the Springfield Yard at 4:10 A.M. the next morning. It is switched and ready for departure at 5:40 A.M. It pulls into Yale Yard, Memphis, at 3:40 P.M., with a departure at 5:00 P.M. that afternoon. It reaches Birmingham at 3:00 A.M. The total distance is 737 miles, and the time—twenty-nine hours and thirteen minutes.

No. 131's companion train is No. 135. This fast freight leaves Kansas City at 9:45 A.M., arriving at the Springfield yard at 5:00 P.M. It leaves there at 7:00 P.M., arriving at Yale Yard, Memphis, at 6:35 A.M. It pulls out at 8:00 A.M., arriving in Birmingham at 5:30 P.M. that afternoon, the second day. The time is thirty-one hours and forty-five minutes.

In the reverse direction, manifest train No. 134 departs from Birmingham at 7:30 P.M., arriving in Kansas City at 4:00 A.M. the second day. No. 136 leaves Birmingham at 5:00 A.M. and pulls into Kansas City at 5:20 P.M. the first day. This train handles Florida perishables and miscellaneous freight from the Southeast to the West and Southwest.

These trains also handle phosphate received from the Seaboard. Manifest schedules are also in operation between Pensacola, Florida; Mobile, Alabama; and Amory, Mississippi, to connect with manifest trains 134 and 136 for the handling of traffic at Memphis, St. Louis, Kansas City, and all points on and beyond the Frisco Lines.

No. 835, from St. Louis to Memphis over the River Division, is commonly known as the Ford Special. It departs at 9:00 P.M., arriving at Turrell, Arkansas, at 4:30 A.M. and Yale Yard, Memphis, at 6:30 A.M. From there south it will be at Amory at 11:30 A.M. and Pensacola at 11:45 P.M. that night.

No. 37, often referred to as the Frisco Flash, between St. Louis and the Southwest is scheduled to depart from St. Louis at 6:30 P.M., arriving in Springfield at 12:50 A.M. It is there just twenty minutes, leaving at 1:10 A.M. It arrives at Monett, Missouri, at 2:45 A.M., stopping fifteen minutes for inspection and to change crews. It is scheduled for arrival at Tulsa at 7:30 A.M., and with a departure at 8:30 A.M. It arrives at Sherman, Texas, at 3:30 P.M. that afternoon, where it connects with the Southern Pacific for Houston and Galveston, Texas. It pulls into Dallas and Fort Worth at 9:00 P.M. The 725-mile run is made in twenty-six hours and thirty minutes.

The Kansas City connection with No. 37 is manifest No. 39, leaving Kansas City at 8:40 P.M. and arriving at Tulsa at 7:00 A.M., a distance of 262 miles, covered in ten hours and twenty minutes.

Comparable manifest schedules are operated eastbound. These handle perishables and other commodities. We have Advance No. 38 from Fort Worth to Kansas City, leaving at 5:00 A.M. and arriving in Kansas City at 2:00 A.M. the first day—574 miles in twenty-one hours. The section to St. Louis arrives there at 7:00 P.M. the next day—736 miles in thirty-eight hours.

No. 30, handling perishables and other traffic from the West through the St. Louis gateway, leaves Fort Worth at 8:30 P.M.

and arrives in St. Louis at 3:00 A.M. the second morning. This run is made in thirty hours and thirty minutes.

This is pretty much the story of the great Frisco Lines fast freight service, and the pattern is the same all over America in this day of modern railroading.

The following train schedules indicate in a condensed form the operation of the Frisco's fast freight fleet.

FRISCO LINES
MANIFEST FAST FREIGHT TRAIN SCHEDULES
As of July 1, 1950

30-130

Leave Fort Worth	9:30 P.M.
Leave Dallas	7:30 P.M.
Arrive Sherman	12:00 A.M.
Leave Sherman	1:30 A.M.
Arrive West Tulsa	9:00 A.M.
Leave West Tulsa	10:00 A.M.
Arrive Afton	12:40 P.M.
Arrive Monett	3:15 P.M.
Leave Monett	4:00 P.M.
Arrive Springfield	5:30 P.M.
Leave Springfield	6:30 P.M.
Arrive St. Louis	3:00 A.M.

130

Leave Afton	2:30 P.M.
Arrive Kansas City	11:59 P.M.

31

Leave St. Louis	12:01 A.M.
Arrive Springfield	8:00 A.M.
Leave Springfield	10:30 A.M.
Arrive Monett	11:59 A.M.
Leave Monett	1:00 P.M.
Arrive West Tulsa	7:00 P.M.
Leave West Tulsa	11:15 P.M.
Arrive Sherman	9:15 A.M.
Leave Sherman	11:00 A.M.
Arrive Fort Worth	4:30 P.M.

32

Leave Oklahoma City	9:15 P.M.
Arrive West Tulsa	12:15 A.M.
Leave West Tulsa	2:00 A.M.
Arrive Monett	8:30 A.M.

Leave Monett	9:15 A.M.
Arrive Springfield	10:30 A.M.
Leave Springfield	11:15 A.M.
Arrive St. Louis	7:00 P.M.

33

Leave Kansas City	9:40 A.M.
Arrive Afton	5:00 P.M.
Leave Afton	5:45 P.M.
Arrive West Tulsa	8:30 P.M.

35

Leave St. Louis	11:00 A.M.
Arrive Springfield	7:30 P.M.
Leave Springfield	9:00 P.M.
Arrive Monett	10:30 P.M.
Leave Monett	11:55 P.M.
Arrive West Tulsa	6:00 A.M.

37

Leave St. Louis	6:30 P.M.
Arrive Springfield	12:50 A.M.
Leave Springfield	1:10 A.M.
Arrive Monett	2:45 A.M.
Leave Monett	3:00 A.M.
Arrive West Tulsa	7:30 A.M.
Leave West Tulsa	8:30 A.M.
Arrive Sherman	3:30 P.M.
Leave Sherman	4:30 P.M.
Arrive Dallas	9:00 P.M.
Arrive Fort Worth	9:00 P.M.

Advance 38

Leave Fort Worth	5:00 A.M.
Arrive Sherman	8:45 A.M.

287

Leave Sherman	9:30 A.M.
Arrive West Tulsa	4:00 P.M.
Leave West Tulsa	4:50 P.M.
Arrive Afton	7:10 P.M.
Leave Afton	7:40 P.M.
Arrive Kansas City	2:00 A.M.

Regular 38

Leave Fort Worth	8:30 A.M.
Arrive Sherman	12:30 P.M.
Leave Sherman	1:30 P.M.
Arrive West Tulsa	8:30 P.M.
Leave West Tulsa	10:00 P.M.
Arrive Afton	1:55 A.M.
Leave Afton	2:50 A.M.
Arrive Kansas City	11:59 A.M.

39

Leave Kansas City	8:40 P.M.
Arrive Afton	3:30 A.M.
Leave Afton	4:00 A.M.
Arrive West Tulsa	7:00 A.M.
Leave West Tulsa	2:30 P.M.
Arrive Sherman	6:00 A.M.

131

Leave Kansas City	9:47 P.M.
Arrive Springfield	4:10 A.M.
Leave Springfield	5:40 A.M.
Arrive Yale (Memphis)	3:40 P.M.
Leave Yale	5:00 P.M.
Arrive Birmingham	3:00 A.M.

134

Leave Birmingham	7:30 P.M.
Arrive Yale (Memphis)	4:45 A.M.
Leave Yale	5:45 A.M.
Arrive Springfield	6:00 P.M.
Leave Springfield	7:00 P.M.
Arrive Kansas City	4:00 A.M.

135

Leave Kansas City	9:45 A.M.
Arrive Springfield	5:00 P.M.
Leave Springfield	7:00 P.M.
Arrive Yale (Memphis)	6:35 A.M.
Leave Yale	8:00 A.M.
Arrive Birmingham	5:30 P.M.

136

Leave Birmingham	5:00 A.M.
Arrive Yale (Memphis)	5:15 P.M.
Leave Yale	8:30 P.M.
Arrive Springfield	8:00 A.M.
Leave Springfield	9:15 A.M.
Arrive Kansas City	5:20 P.M.

156

| Leave Neodesha | 2:50 A.M. |
| Arrive Fort Scott | 8:45 A.M. |

157

| Leave Fort Scott | 5:00 A.M. |
| Arrive Neodesha | 10:30 A.M. |

169-338

Leave Fort Scott	2:15 A.M.
Arrive Joplin	7:00 A.M.
Arrive Monett	10:30 A.M.

236-136-836

Leave Pensacola	1:00 A.M.
Arrive Boligee	9:05 A.M.
Arrive Aliceville	10:30 A.M.
Arrive Amory	1:15 P.M.
Leave Amory	1:45 P.M.
Arrive Yale (Memphis)	5:15 P.M.
Leave Yale	8:00 P.M.
Arrive Turrell	9:15 P.M.
Arrive St. Louis	7:00 A.M.

238 (Irregular operation)

Leave Birmingham	9:30 P.M.
Arrive Amory	2:15 A.M.
Leave Amory	7:00 A.M.
Arrive Yale (Memphis)	1:00 P.M.

239 (Irregular operation)

Leave Yale (Memphis)	1:00 P.M.
Arrive Amory	3:35 A.M.
Leave Amory	4:00 A.M.
Arrive Birmingham	9:00 A.M.

330

| Leave Ellsworth | 2:00 P.M. |
| Arrive Wichita | 8:00 P.M. |

| Leave Wichita | 9:00 P.M. |
| Arrive Monett | 11:05 A.M. |

331

Leave Monett	1:15 P.M.
Arrive Wichita	2:45 A.M.
Leave Wichita	5:00 A.M.
Arrive Ellsworth	12:30 P.M.

339-166

Leave Monett	6:00 A.M.
Arrive Joplin	8:15 A.M.
Arrive Fort Scott	11:20 A.M.

430

Leave Quanah	5:00 P.M.
Arrive Oklahoma City	3:00 A.M.
Leave Oklahoma City	4:00 A.M.
Arrive West Tulsa	8:00 A.M.

431

| Leave West Tulsa | 12:30 A.M. |
| Arrive Oklahoma City | 5:00 A.M. |

437

Leave West Tulsa	10:30 A.M.
Arrive Oklahoma City	2:30 P.M.
Leave Oklahoma City	8:00 P.M.
Arrive Quanah	5:00 A.M.

630

| Leave Enid | 3:30 A.M. |
| Arrive Beaumont | 10:00 A.M. |

631

| Leave Beaumont | 6:00 A.M. |
| Arrive Enid | 1:05 P.M. |

632

Leave Avard	9:00 A.M.
Arrive Enid	11:59 A.M.
Leave Enid	6:20 P.M.
Arrive West Tulsa	11:59 P.M.

636

| Leave Avard | 9:00 A.M. |
| Arrive Enid | 11:40 A.M. |

637

Leave West Tulsa	11:30 A.M.
Arrive Enid	5:00 P.M.
Leave Enid	7:00 A.M.
Arrive Avard	10:00 A.M.

639

| Leave Enid | 5:30 A.M. |
| Arrive Avard | 8:00 A.M. |

731

| Leave Monett | 2:00 P.M. |
| Arrive Fort Smith | 9:00 P.M. |

732

Leave Paris	9:00 A.M.
Arrive Fort Smith	5:15 P.M.
Leave Fort Smith	9:30 P.M.
Arrive Monett	5:30 A.M.

735

Leave Monett	11:50 P.M.
Arrive Fort Smith	6:00 A.M.
Leave Fort Smith	10:00 A.M.
Arrive Paris	7:00 P.M.

736

Leave Madill	8:00 A.M.
Arrive Hugo	11:59 A.M.
Leave Hugo	2:20 P.M.
Arrive Hope	9:30 P.M.

737

Leave Hope	9:20 A.M.
Arrive Hugo	4:00 P.M.
Leave Hugo	12:15 A.M.
Arrive Madill	6:15 A.M.

833

| Leave St. Louis | 7:00 A.M. |
| Arrive Yale (Memphis) | 10:00 P.M. |

834

| Leave Yale (Memphis) | 10:00 A.M. |
| Arrive St. Louis | 11:59 P.M. |

Advance 835

Leave St. Louis	5:00 P.M.
Arrive Turrell	4:30 A.M.
Arrive Shelco	5:30 A.M.
Arrive Yale (Memphis)	6:15 A.M.

Regular 835-135-235

Leave St. Louis	9:00 P.M.
Arrive Turrell	4:30 A.M.
Arrive Yale	6:30 A.M.

Leave Yale	8:00 A.M.
Arrive Amory	11:30 A.M.
Leave Amory	12:01 P.M.
Arrive Aliceville	2:45 P.M.
Arrive Boligee	3:40 P.M.
Arrive Pensacola	11:45 P.M.

836

Leave Yale (Memphis)	8:00 P.M.
Arrive St. Louis	7:00 A.M.

CHAPTER XXX

COAL TERMINAL ON THE B.&O.

Staten Island Installation

The Baltimore & Ohio Railroad moves millions of tons of coal every year. From deep in the bowels of the earth come the black diamonds, priceless in economic value, to fill the grimy hopper cars of the B.&O., which go slogging away to inland cities and to the tidewater in an endless parade.

A very considerable amount of this coal was delivered in New York, and to speed the handling upon its arrival the Baltimore & Ohio constructed facilities at Howland Hook, Staten Island, New York, which placed it in a position to make a stronger bid for the delivery of coal to waterfront industries, to utility plants, and to barges moving to points in New England.

These facilities include a modern coal-dumping and barge-loading installation which performs the work handled before that by a high-level timber pier at St. George, Staten Island, that proved inadequate. The new facility cost close to $500,000. It involves two elevated tracks on which hopper cars are unloaded by means of their pockets, two Robbin car shakeouts to speed the unloading process, an inclined apron conveyor and loading chute for transferring the coal from big hoppers beneath the unloading tracks to barges, and yards for loaded and empty cars.

Howland Hook is located on the Staten Island Rapid Transit Lines, a subsidiary of the Baltimore & Ohio. Coal arriving at this point moves from mines on the B.&O. in West Virginia, arriving over the rails of the Reading and Central of New Jersey, on both of which the B.&O. has trackage rights. All traffic for Staten Island leaves the main line of the Jersey Central at

Cranford Junction, New Jersey, where it crosses a drawbridge over the Arthur Kill, a channel which separates the west side of Staten Island from the New Jersey mainland.

Looking at this unloading tower, you see a gaunt skeleton structure with two towers about one hundred feet apart. One is an unloading tower which supports the two unloading tracks, the two car shakeouts, and, in winter, a pair of car-cleaner plates. The other tower carries a seventy-one-foot boom which has a telescopic loading chute attached at its outer end. Here also are located the rigging and electric motors for moving the boom. The tower has its own apron conveyor.

This conveyor receives coal from the inclined conveyor, some 120 feet long and 54 inches wide, that brings the coal up from the hoppers beneath the unloading tracks, pouring it into the boom conveyor and so moving to the telescoping chute that delivers it to the holds of the vessel below.

The length of the telescoping chute can be changed to suit the depth of the barge or other ship in the process of being loaded. The chute operator occupies a place in a cab at the outer end of the boom. He controls a discharge gate at the bottom of the chute, which can drop the coal straight down or cast it out at an angle. This chute discharge gate can be rotated horizontally through 180 degrees. The gate can also be interchanged with a belt trimmer, also rotated through 180 degrees, making it possible to deliver the coal in remote nooks and corners of the vessel or barge with a minimum tendency to degrade it in the process.

The yards for loaded and empty cars are situated south of the unloading tower. The loaded yard consists of four tracks, in line with the tower, having a total capacity of fifty cars. The yard tracks slope toward the unloading point on a descending grade of 1 per cent. The cars are spotted in the yard with their brakes set and they are brought to the unloading point with a car puller.

The arrangement of turnouts at the lower end of the yard is such that one unloading track may be served from three or four yard tracks. The second unloading track is served by two yard tracks.

Now let's look into the aspects of the unloading process in this coal transfer production line. If the coal is not frozen the unloading is accomplished in from three to five minutes, depending on the size of the car, of course, and the grade of coal.

When the car is in position at the unloading point the hoppers are opened and a machine termed a car shakeout is lowered into place. It grips the top edges of the sides of the car and goes to work. It consists of a steel frame on which is secured an eccentrically mounted flywheel, driven by an electric motor through V-belts. The eccentric motion of the whirling flywheel sets the car to vibrating with force and rapidity, shaking loose any clinging coal and causing it to run freely.

These car shakeouts are supported by cables from small overhead cranes operating on tracks at the top of the unloading tower. The operator, stationed in an enclosed cab above the between-space of the cars, can spot these shakeout frames anywhere along the tops of the cars.

In extremely cold weather, with the coal frozen, it becomes necessary to use heavy car-cleaner plates in addition to the shakeout apparatus. There is a plate for each of the two unloading tracks, and this plate is notched to accommodate the center sills of hopper cars. They are equipped with spring snubbers. The plates weigh about 8,000 pounds and they are dropped repeatedly into the frozen coal, breaking up the mass to a point where it will run from the pockets.

The receiving hopper under each car has a feeding mechanism which moves the coal to the main inclined conveyor. After being unloaded the car on either track is shoved from the unloading tower by the next loaded car as it is spotted. The empty car then rolls down an incline to a kickback trestle, and, upon being reversed, moves by gravity into a two-track empty yard of fifty-six-car capacity.

As the cars are taken from the loaded car yard and emptied and room is made for another cut, a call goes to the main yard nearby for more cars.

From the time that the coal starts its journey underground in the West Virginia mountains until it is aboard ship at Howland Hook it almost never ceases its march to the tidewater. Unhurried, continuous is its flow, timed to the march of wheels down the rails, a black river, loosed by grimed men to supply the needs and the fires of industry.

The new slip at Howland Hook is 825 feet in length and 300 feet wide. It was dredged to a depth sufficient to accommodate vessels as large as the Victory type. The bulkhead along the slip is of concrete, but it is faced with a treated-timber fender system. On the east side of the waterway a timber tie-up dock has been provided for loaded and empty barges.

After empty barges have been worked into position at the coal dock they are handled by workmen who maneuver them after loading gets under way. Through the use of capstans the barges can be moved in either direction, which makes possible even loading.

Compared with coal-handling methods of but a few years ago the coal-loading facilities mark an advancement in keeping with all rail operations in an era that is writing railroad history.

The Baltimore & Ohio Railroad has spent millions in improving coal-handling facilities alone. The road has had a substantial part in the development of the Gauley-Sewell coal field in West Virginia, and the tonnage from this region alone may reach 7,000,000 or 8,000,000 tons yearly.

The Baltimore & Ohio built its own facilities for handling lake cargo coal at Lorain, Ohio, spending some $4,500,000. It entered into a joint project with the New York Central for coal handling at Toledo, Ohio, built at a cost of $18,500,000.

The B.&O. bought 12,500 new hopper cars to augment its earlier fleet. All part of its multimillion dollar improvement program.

Let's take a look at the way the coal business has grown along the lines of the Baltimore & Ohio in the past fifty years. For the fiscal year ending June 30, 1900, 6,845,415 tons of bituminous coal came out of the ground. In 1910 the production

294

along the B.&O. lines had grown to over 23,000,000 tons. In 1948 it was almost 42,000,000 tons.

About a quarter of the road's total freight revenue is derived from coal traffic. Black diamonds, indeed!

Strange as it may seem, coal is the most important economic mineral known to man. And in spite of oil it is estimated that future demands will increase. If it does the Baltimore & Ohio will provide the equipment to handle it with the same speed and efficiency we have seen at work at Howland Hook.

The installations here can handle up to 128 carloads of coal in an eight-hour day.

CHAPTER XXXI

THE C.&E.I. STORY

Road at 101-Year Peak

The Chicago & Eastern Illinois Railroad, in 1950, saw the highest net income peak in the history of its 101 years of operation.

The answer to that stems from the traffic department and the support given the road by its blue-chip shippers. But the best efforts of the Traffic Department and the patronage of all of the shippers in the world would have been to no avail if the Chicago & Eastern Illinois had not had the facilities to operate in the modern way. And that means sound track, the best in signaling, crack manifest and passenger trains, and complete efficiency.

In 1947, the C.&E.I. employed some 5,000 people. In 1950, this was reduced to 3,600, largely because of mechanized maintenance of way equipment, the long trains, and Diesel power. The road's passenger out-of-pocket net in 1950 was ahead of 1949 with 16 per cent less volume of business. This is a fine showing and it reflects good management.

Many line changes were necessary to bring the Chicago & Eastern Illinois main line to the standard necessary for the fast operation of a speedliner fleet and a manifest fleet, but these improvements were accomplished. The road remodeled eight passenger stations in 1949 and four in 1950 and is building a new one as this is written.

It must be remembered that the C.&E.I. does not have the resources of many larger railroads; it cannot jump in and do things in a hurry. It has to pinch pennies; it often has to plan improvements years ahead. The success of the road lies in an inherent ability to welcome opportunity the moment that its knock is heard, to make opportunities through its own initiative.

Here is an example. They set off head-end cars handled by passenger trains at key points, and distribute the contents with their own trucks. This saves valuable time, otherwise taken in unloading express at the station platform, and vastly improves the service to the shipper and consignee. It makes the railroad a little money and at the same time builds up good will and a reputation for fast service. The only strictly head-end work is now performed by No. 1.

Here is another example of what a railroad can do for the "Good-Will Department." Credit it to a modern, wide-awake Traffic Department.

The Dixie Flagler does not operate every day. The Chicago & Eastern Illinois put in a southbound train, running as far as Evansville, on the days the Florida streamliner does not run. Also, northbound, the road has a fast train from Evansville to Chicago on the days the Dixie Flagler is not scheduled. This latter train leaves Evansville two hours earlier than the Flagler on old No. 2's departure time. In this manner the C.&E.I. have provided an excellent streamlined train service to fill the gap. People at Chicago and Evansville, as well as those in intermediate cities, benefit immeasurably from this arrangement. It is good business, a good-will builder, something every railroad needs.

The Dixie route to Florida consists of linking six railroads. The roads are: the Chicago & Eastern Illinois to Evansville, Indiana; the Louisville & Nashville, to Nashville, Tennessee; the Nashville, Chattanooga & St. Louis, a historical and beautiful line and a completely up-to-date railroad, Dieselized and with C.T.C., to Atlanta, Georgia; the Central of Georgia to Albany, Georgia; the Atlantic Coast Line to Jacksonville, Florida; and the Florida East Coast to Miami. These roads not only represent the shortest route to Florida's "Summer Land," but provide excellent service. The Dixie Flagler, as has been indicated, offers service every third day, second day in winter, and the Dixie

Flyer is the daily year-round train, with evening departure from Chicago.

No. 7, the Georgian, provides overnight service between Chicago and Atlanta, via the C.&E.I., the Louisville & Nashville, and the Nashville, Chattanooga & St. Louis. This train also carries sleeping cars to New Orleans, connecting the Louisville & Nashville to and from the Crescent City at Nashville.

Nineteen new coaches, parlor, and dining cars have augmented the road's passenger equipment during this book's preparation. The road operates four dining cars and serves excellent food.

The new streamlined Meadowlark, Nos. 11 and 12, in the local field, runs from Chicago to Cypress, far down in the southern tip of Illinois. This train leaves Chicago at 5:10 P.M., arriving in Cypress at 12:50 A.M. (midnight), for a total of 345 miles. Cypress is thirty-three miles from Thebes, Illinois, which is across the Mississippi River from Chaffee, Missouri, at which point the Chicago & Eastern Illinois interchanges with the Frisco.

The C.&E.I. has trackage rights over the double-track line of the New York Central from Pana to East St. Louis, Illinois. Pana is twenty miles from Findlay Junction, Illinois, where the line branches off for Chaffee. Only freight service is operated over this line today and there is no car limit that the C.&E.I. cannot handle over this part of the Big Four, Pana to East St. Louis.

Diesel Club

What is no doubt unique in the history of both American railroading and Diesel clubs was inaugurated on the Chicago & Eastern Illinois in October, 1949. This is a club entirely in one railroad. It is known as the Danville Railroad Diesel Club of the C.&E.I.R.R.

Danville was chosen as headquarters of the club for the reason that all heavy Diesel repairs are made in the shops in Danville, a famous railroad town to begin with. Danville is a central division point on the road and so convenient for engine crews.

Membership of the club includes roadmen, shopmen, and supervisors, and so serves as a clearinghouse for information on all problems involving Diesel operation. The club, also, serves to familiarize the men of one shop craft with the work of men engaged in another craft, making for greater understanding of one another's problems, together with a better mutual understanding. Officers of the club are elected from various ranks of employees. The president is an electrician; an enginehouse foreman is vice-president; the secretary is a sheet-metal worker, and the sergeant-at-arms is an air-brake foreman. There is an advisory committee and a topic committee.

The membership is about 130, and the average attendance at each meeting is 65 to 70. Sixteen members have not missed one of the meetings. There are two evening meetings a month, from 7:00 P.M. to 9:00 P.M. To take care of additional roadmen and shopmen on the second and third tricks, two afternoon meetings are held each month, from 1:15 P.M. to 2:45 P.M. There are no dues and all costs are absorbed by the railroad, which furnishes the clubroom.

The club has a sound moving picture outfit, a blackboard, and a bench for the study of parts. A lending library contains Diesel literature for loaning to members. A file of visual aids to education includes films from the University of Illinois, the National Safety Council, and various manufacturers. Electro-Motive has contributed a complete set of slides.

Meetings are usually opened with an educational movie, followed by a short business meeting. A paper generally is then presented by a C.&E.I. man, or, perhaps, by a guest speaker. Possible Diesel failures are reviewed and studied. If it is available, a film on the general subject of the failure in question is shown, and the case history is given. For example, if the failure in question involved an improperly installed cylinder head, the movie would show the proper application.

Questions are submitted at one meeting and discussed and answered at the subsequent meeting. The answer to each question is prepared by a specialist on the road in the line of work which the question involves. Rules for the club were laid down after an examination of returned questionnaires, also new subjects and the kind of pictures preferred were decided upon through the questionnaire method. The self-improvement aims of the Diesel Club members were indicated by the almost unanimous vote for educational films, with travel pictures second.

White-collar men and men in overalls get together at the Chicago & Eastern Illinois Diesel Club for a common purpose—greater knowledge. It speaks well for the caliber of our railroad men.

The Chicago & Eastern Illinois is blessed with a board of directors who are extremely capable and who have an interest and a pride in the property, which has obtained an enviable position among the smaller railroads in its acceptance of modern trends. President C. M. Roddewig is a man of exceptional qualifications, with a close knowledge not only of his own road but others, as well. He spends a great deal of his time out on the line and so has a firsthand knowledge of matters in the field.

H. R. Sampson, traffic vice-president, is one of the ablest traffic and rate men on any railroad in the United States. He has traffic representatives and Chicago & Eastern Illinois officers in some thirty-six off-line cities, as well as those on the railroad. The present superintendent and former chief engineer, A. W. Schroeder, performed an able job in the construction of the new Wansford Yard. He has further worked tirelessly toward the end that every possible improvement be made over the entire railroad main line and its branches, maintaining a standard that has contributed much to an A-1 condition of the property so necessary to train movement the modern way.

CHAPTER XXXII

SOUTHERN BELLE

Speed Liner of the Kansas City Southern

Before the first new Southern Belle left Kansas City on Sunday afternoon, April 3, 1949, it was christened with a bottle containing water from the Gulf of Mexico and the Mississippi and Missouri rivers, as symbolic of the joining of Kansas City with the five Gulf ports of the Kansas City Southern lines. At about the same time a Southern Belle at New Orleans and another at Port Arthur were traditionally christened with champagne. So began the initial runs of the road's proud new streamliners.

Twenty-four million dollars was invested in the Southern Belle trains and their equipment. The Kansas City Southern, at the close of World War II, prepared to play an ambitious part in modern railroad development and orders were placed almost immediately, but work stoppages and material shortages delayed the inauguration of this new service until the spring of 1949, when with a bow and a smile the Southern Belle went waltzing down the rails.

The original Southern Belle trains were placed in operation in 1940 and they performed faithfully and well the job of transporting thousands of servicemen to and from training centers and then on to points of embarkation, as well as providing service to the general public.

Previous to making the first regular runs, a Southern Belle train was exhibited in forty cities and towns over the system and 61,218 visitors passed through the new cars. The Southern Belles were designed with an eye to utility and comfort as well

301

as attractiveness. Two factors in particular went into their creation—the well-being of travelers and more efficient operation.

When the new passenger service was begun a new low-fare plan went into effect, reducing chair-car fares between all stations on the Kansas City Southern and on the Louisiana & Arkansas from 22 to 44 per cent, depending on the number of tickets purchased at a given time.

The low-fare plan works like this: Tickets are issued for 2, 4, 10, 30, 100, and 200 rides, good in either direction within a thirty-day period. For instance, a two-trip ticket might be used by one person for a round trip, or for two one-way trips, or it might be used by two persons for a one-way trip each, while a 100-ride book of tickets might be used for a party of fifty on a round trip, or a party of one hundred on a one-way trip. This "Thriftrip" plan provides a very economical way to travel, and it is less than the cost of driving a car. Certainly it is a travel bargain in a day of climbing prices.

The motive power of the Southern Belle is an Electro-Motive F7 Diesel-electric locomotive, consisting of two units of 1,500 horsepower each. This is the culmination of years of experience and research by the General Motors people, and it includes improvements that make for faster acceleration and more climbing power on grades. It can, in fact, pull up to 30 per cent more tonnage than earlier Diesels of the same size.

The Kansas City Southern was one of the first roads to use the Diesel electric on passenger trains. They began hauling the Flying Crow trains in the late thirties. The new Diesels are all equipped with the latest type of radiotelephone equipment, permitting the engineer to talk with operators in wayside stations and making for speedy communication between the speeding train and the dispatcher through the medium of land circuits.

The new Southern Belle trains operate on an eighteen-hour schedule between Kansas City and New Orleans—a reduction of three hours and forty-five minutes, compared with the previous time. This streamliner service has been extended to the

Port Arthur–Beaumont–Lake Charles area by means of connections at Shreveport.

The two Southern Belle trains, Nos. 1 and 2 respectively, leave Kansas City and New Orleans at 4:00 P.M. and arrive at their respective terminals at 10:00 A.M. the following day. Departure of the connecting train from Port Arthur is at 4:20 P.M., while the arrival time there from Kansas City is at 9:30 A.M.

No. 9, a third Kansas City–New Orleans train was placed in operation on approximately the former Southern Belle schedules. No. 9 leaves Kansas City at 9:40 A.M. and arrives in New Orleans at 7:30 A.M. No. 10, northbound, leaves New Orleans at 9:30 P.M. and arrives in Kansas City at 7:45 P.M. Besides their regular Pullman sleepers, these trains provide special sleeping-car service between Shreveport and New Orleans and between Shreveport and Baton Rouge, enabling travelers between those cities to retire as early as 9:30 P.M. and occupy the sleeper until 8:00 A.M.

Besides placing in service the best available in passenger power and equipment, Nos. 15 and 16 hauls mail and express plus berries and perishable fruits in season.

Equipment

The superstructure of Southern Belle passenger cars are all Alcoa aluminum, built on steel underframes. An interesting sidelight reveals that these aluminum trains are operating in a territory closely identified with the conception and growth of the aluminum industry. Arkansas supplies most of the domestic bauxite, or aluminum ore, while a large percentage of the petroleum coke and soda ash, essential to the manufacture of aluminum, originates in the great refineries on the lines of the Kansas City Southern.

The cars of the Southern Belle are equipped with high-speed, electrically controlled brakes, with speed governor controls and decelostats to prevent wheels from slipping. The cars have roller bearings, stabilizers to prevent rolling on curves, and vertical snubbers to eliminate bouncing movement.

The decorative treatment used in the chair cars, diners, and tavern-lounge-observation cars is provided by murals etched in Plexiglass, backed by mirrors and edge-lighted by invisible fluorescent tubes, causing the etching to appear as delineations of light. This is a novel and striking feature that draws immediate attention. In the chair cars the etchings portray the historical, cultural, and industrial background of the cities for which they are named. They are Kansas City, Texarkana, Shreveport, Alexandria, Baton Rouge, and New Orleans. Background reviews of these cities are included in another Kansas City Southern chapter.

The Southern Belle chair-car seats, by the touch of a button can be adjusted to ten positions, from near straight-back to positions for resting, relaxing, lounging, or sleeping, as well as in-between positions. The footrest, located at the bottom of the seat ahead, is adjustable to four positions. The chairs can be swung to almost any angle. Four passengers may group together, or the chair may be turned to obtain the most view from the big picture windows. Lighting is adjustable to individual desires. There are ample baggage racks above. Color combinations are pleasant and the tones restful.

Before these Sleepy Hollow seats were manufactured by the Heywood-Wakefield people, Transportation Seating Division, of Gardner, Massachusetts, Harvard professors went deeply into the general shape of the human form by taking eight measurements of 3,867 persons in an effort to determine the posture requirements of the average man and woman.

The chair cars, which include the regular and divided types, were built by the American Car and Foundry Company, builders also of the dining, tavern-lounge-observation, and mail-baggage-dormitory cars. The four regular-type chair cars seat sixty passengers each, and the two divided-type seat sixty-two passengers each.

Sleepers are the latest product of the Pullman-Standard Car Manufacturing Company. They were the first in the Kansas

Santa Fe Diesel 227, 4-unit E.M.D. F-7, climbing 1.60 grade on the westward track west of Victorville, Calif., with seventy-five cars and no helper on First District of Los Angeles Division. Photo by R. H. Kindig.

B.&O. Cincinnati #94 leaving Garret, Ind., hauled by engine 5587, class T-3D, 4-8-2 type, with 6,100 tons. Courtesy, B.&O. RR.

Seaboard's ice plant at Baldwin, Fla., on the North Florida Division icing perishable trains enroute north. Courtesy, S.A.L. RR.

Sperry Detector Car #119 testing under the famous Hanging Bridges in the Grand Canyon of the Arkansas on the Rio Grande's first sub-division of the Pueblo Division. The car is westbound.

Sperry Ultrasonic Detector car with operator testing rail within joint-bar limits on the Western Maryland RR.

Virginian Time Freight #72 hauled by engine #505 2-8-4 type, Class BA, passing Suffolk, Va., on the Norfolk Division. Photo by H. Reid.

Virginian Extra 737 west, Elmore-Gilbert Turn with 140 loads and 10,500 tons at Shannon, West. Va., on the Guyandot River Branch of the New River Division. This engine, 2-8-8-2 type, was formerly Santa Fe #1797, used during the war on Raton Mountain. Courtesy, Virginian RR.

Operator's station on Sperry Car. Control board in front of operator is used for signaling rear operator for raising and lowering brush carriage, etc. Operators interchange positions at intervals to prevent fatigue.

Sperry Car #123 testing on Western Pacific RR. with section forces on following motorcars.

Sperry Detector Car tapes during actual test. Left tape is used as aid in interpreting indications received on standard tape.

Main brush carriage of Sperry Detector Car. This unit is used to introduce test current into rails. Detector or searching unit mounted on independent wheels may be seen at center of brush carriage.

S.P. Ogden Fast Freight Extra 6145 east with new E.M.D. F-7 6,000 h.p. Diesel crossing Great Salt Lake Trestle at Colin, Utah, on the Salt Lake Division. C.T.C. territory. Courtesy, S.P. RR.

S.P. Extra 6123 west rounding the 10-degree horseshoe curve at Caliente, Calif. C.T.C. Territory on the San Joaquin Division. Courtesy, S.P. RR.

View of five of the eight major wheat-storage elevators in Enid, Okla., looking east along the Frisco's Main Line. Photo by Preston George.

Frisco #4502, 4-8-4 type of this railroad's great class, with #30 eastbound manifest train near Spencer, Okla., on the Oklahoma Subdivision of the Southwestern Division. Photo by Preston George.

S.P. Los Angeles–San Francisco Fast Freight #913 at milepost #335.17 west of Acate, Calif., on the Coast Division. Courtesy, S.P. RR.

Southern Pacific #99, San Francisco Daylight, passing Chatsworth, Calif., on the Ventura Subdivision of the Los Angeles Division hauled by engine 4439, 4-8-4 type, Class GS-4. Photo by R. H. Kindig.

City Southern area to employ the lengthwise and crosswise bedroom arrangements. Each car has four bedrooms and fourteen roomettes. All compartments are equipped for full comfort, which includes wardrobes, toilet facilities, circulating ice water, and individual speakers for radio and wire-recorded programs.

A bedroom accommodates two people but they are so arranged that by folding the partition back there are accommodations for four, making it an excellent arrangement for families or for businessmen who want a conference room. Roomette doors may be locked at night, or left open, since a zippered curtain permits leaving the door ajar. The roomette is the answer for those desiring the advantages of a completely private room at low cost.

The bedroom-roomette cars carry the names of the three deceased presidents of the three primary railroads that went into the making of the present Kansas City Southern Lines. They were Arthur Stilwell, William Buchanan, and William Edenborn. Other cars of this type were also named for Job Edson, Leonor Loree, Harvey Couch, Colonel Fordyce, and Stuart Knott—all of whom served as presidents of the road and held other high posts.

There is an intimate appeal in the arrangement and decorative treatment of the dining cars of the Southern Belle trains. This is acquired by dividing the cars into three dining rooms, each separated by ornamental grills and adjustable portieres. Each diner accommodates thirty-six passengers at tables arranged both in the conventional manner and diagonally against serpentine settees, with the diagonal tables for two opposite conventional tables for four.

Old Plantation and Mountain Lodge are dining car names, and the cars carry out something of the atmosphere suggested by the names.

The tavern-lounge-observation car is a distinct addition to the Southern Belle. As the last car of the train, it has a rounded end, with a bar of modern design separating the tavern and lounge sections. Chairs and settees are deep cushioned, tables are provided for drinks and sandwiches. Near the bar is the compact panel-built combination radio and reproducer of wire-recorded music. Programs can be heard throughout the train. The names of the two cars are Good Cheer and Hospitality.

On the head end, the mail-baggage-dormitory car is built entirely of steel. In addition to the most efficient facilities for the handling of mail, baggage, and express, there is full equipment and accommodations for taking care of the post-office personnel, including wardrobes, steam cookers, and refrigerators. At the dormitory end we find every facility for the comfort and convenience of the dining-car crews.

People like the Southern Belle, they like the "Thriftrip" ticket plan, and they like the service of the Kansas City Southern. The Flying Crow is a little closer to the people and the towns along the line; it is highly regarded by those making shorter trips and they find the train comfortable and convenient. Trains Nos. 9 and 10, air conditioned, streamlined, Diesel powered, have a place in the travel scheme and leave little to be desired. They are excellent modern trains.

The Southern Belle is the de luxe train, the name train, offering new travel thrills for some; top service and dependability for the veteran traveler; a way to enjoy speed, relaxation, and a new frontier for others. The old fascination of railroading clings to most of us, along with the urge to visit faraway places, and you could not chose a destination more enchanting and colorful than this fabulous Gulf country and the one and only New Orleans, rich in tradition and gracious entertaining.

CHAPTER XXXIII

WESTERN MARYLAND

Fast Freight—Speed and Service

Primarily a fast freight link between the Eastern seaboard and the Midwest, the Western Maryland operates at Port Covington, Baltimore, a tidewater terminal that is not only one of the finest in the country but is scheduled for very considerable expansion. The Western Maryland has still wider access to Eastern seaboard traffic through its connection with the Reading Railroad. As its line extends westward, important branches tap the rich bituminous coal regions of West Virginia and Pennsylvania.

An indication of the manner in which the Western Maryland is playing the modern railroad game is the fact that, despite a comparatively new fleet of 1,400-series fast freight engines, this hustling freight road has turned to Diesels for all operations east of Hagerstown. The fine steam fast freight haulers will be used in stand-by service and during peak periods.

The Western Maryland's Diesel fleet has been expanded to sixty-seven units.

Another forward step by the Western Maryland's progressive management has been the installation of centralized traffic control on the high-speed Lurgan Subdivision. This line, a veritable fast freight race track, carries the heaviest load of Western Maryland traffic.

C.T.C., the magic push-button dispatcher, was a "must," for this manifest artery handles the freight of the line's four principal connections, together with important "origin" traffic. The installation operates on both single and double track between Antietam Street, Hagerstown, and Plainfield, Pennsylvania. The automatic territory from Plainfield to Lurgan will be merged into the new facilities. Existing color light signals will be employed wherever possible. Where it is necessary, new high, light-weight signal bridges will be erected. These put the signal lights directly over the tracks.

President Eugene S. Williams, in the latter part of 1950, announced a plan to modernize and expand the road's tidewater facilities at Port Covington in Baltimore Harbor to the tune of $12,000,000. These improvements include the erection of another large covered merchandise pier, an extension of the ore pier, and the installation on this pier of a heavy-duty crane. Other installations will include the building of a new Diesel shop, the establishment of open storage yards, and the laying down of considerable additional trackage.

We have mentioned the Port Covington Terminal in an earlier book, and again cannot pass up the opportunity to call attention to this great Western Maryland facility. Twenty-three ocean-going vessels can berth at this terminal at one time. If its total floor space was contained in one structure it would make a two-story building a mile in width and nearly two miles and a half long. It is a big factor in this Baltimore port, far up the miles of ice-free Chesapeake Bay, which is destined for even greater prominence in both land and water commerce of America. Baltimore now ranks second among the nation's ports in foreign tonnage.

Baltimore and Port Covington and the broad Patapsco River mouth and the blunt-bowed freighters that push up the Chesapeake searching for Western Maryland docks play a vital role in the road's destiny, as they also supply, in part, at least, the ingredients that make for the roaring manifest trains. Tidewater had a part in the tradition that resulted in the trade-mark of this fine road's 700-odd miles of main track. Tidewater and a steel rail are tightly woven into the fabric of the nation and its fabulous transportation system, and fast freight is more and more playing a major role in the modern scheme of things.

We opened this book with the chapter, "The American

Freight Car," and we have carried the theme predominantly through the pages. We see the freight car on lonely sidings, at busy loading docks, in pulsing freight yards; slogging along in drags, speeding through the night in a Red Ball train. The freight car carries American food and American arms.

We see a particular freight car down on the very outskirts of the great Port Covington Terminal. A trundling switch engine grumbles up and couples on. This and other freight cars are gathered from here and there and pulled to the yard and built into a train—a manifest train. WM No. 1, a part of the most famous of the Western Maryland's fast freights, roars west behind its powerful Diesel, leaving the tidelands and the low country for the climbing hills of the Blue Ridge and the more rugged Alleghenies. It carries cars for Hagerstown and Cumberland, Maryland; Connellsville, Pa.; and Pittsburgh and Youngstown and Cleveland, and other points. PCS-1 is on her way for second-morning delivery in Chicago from Baltimore and Philadelphia.

WM No. 3 rolls west and block signals flash as its cars race the clock for distant off-going junctions. In faraway New England, New York, and New Jersey other freight cars are joined in trains, and the famous CSD—Central States Dispatch—which carries the proud banner of "97" starts its westward flight. Maine, New Hampshire, Massachusetts send their freight-car emissaries; little Rhode Island and Connecticut send cars of potatoes, cars of cloth, cars of machinery. Cars hurrying for a rendezvous at famous Maybrook Junction; cars from Harlem and Staten Island—the night is full of them—join the iron-lunged parade. Diesels are on the move. The Central States Dispatch is rolling. This is another of the 97's, rushing through on the Reading for Rutherford, Pennsylvania, where it will become Western Maryland No. 97, bound for Cherry Run and a meeting with the 97's of the B.&O.

Meanwhile, WM 6 is driving through the gorges of the Alleghenies, fighting for escape from the mountains. There are parts aboard for a vast ordnance plant, for a plane factory, for a Connecticut arms' manufacturer, hemp for a ropewalk, machine tools for a concern in Providence, and these are but a few of the fleet of fast freight trains that daily operate on Western Maryland's busy tracks.

Neither time, tide, nor fast freight waits.

The Western Maryland and other railroads have set new records in trainloads and train speeds in 1950, and they are 14 per cent above the peak of the World War II years and about three times better in tonnage and speed over what they were in 1920.

The Western Maryland has an A-1 Operating Department, as a railroad famous for its fast freights must have, and it has a top Maintenance of Way Department, which gives the Red Ball trains the rail and the roadbed to hold their pace. The road has modern railroad shops at Hagerstown, with facilities for handling every type of construction and repair. Port Covington has repair shops and up-to-date marine equipment. Its traffic department knows its business. More and more ore is moving this way, especially from South America and Africa, and the indications are that it will bulk large in future years.

The Diesel locomotive, with all due respect to the great fast freight steam locomotives that have performed so heroically for American railroads, is a marvel at handling the manifest train. It is particularly fine at pulling the manifest because of its ability to move tonnage on mountain roads without helpers and it makes long hauls without the necessity of taking on coal and water.

The Diesel is a champion in an era of modern railroading that is as truly blazing a trail to new transportation heights as did the Berkshires and the Northerns and the Mountain types. It is just that the Diesel is the railroad's motive power answer today, exactly as the gasoline engine in the automobile outmoded the faithful and often brilliant performer, yesterday's steam-driven automobile.

With this up-to-the-minute motive power, centralized traffic control and excellent facilities of every type, the Western Maryland is truly railroading in the modern manner. It is significant that five times in the last nine years the road was singled out for national safety honors, which included the E. H. Harriman

Memorial Gold Medal for its 1949 performance. That spells efficiency!

The Western Maryland has its roots deep in the beautiful Potomac Valley, of Maryland, in the coal fields of West Virginia, in the soil of southern Pennsylvania—iron roots that carry the rushing manifest from the great piers at Port Covington to an inland empire, and, in return, bring almost every commodity under the sun to the bottoms at tidewater.

This road has a very able president, Eugene S. Williams, who has a fine board of directors, and C. N. Zarfoss, the road-traffic vice-president, is an outstanding traffic expert and heads a fine department. G. R. Haworth, operating vice-president is one of this country's leading operating men.

CHAPTER XXXIV

THE S.P.'S TAYLOR YARD

Modernized in 1949

Constructed in 1925 when Los Angeles, California, was less than a quarter of its 1950 size, Taylor Yard, the Southern Pacific's freight classification yard on the northern outskirts of the city, was modernized at a cost of $2,500,000 in 1949.

Taylor Yard formerly had a rider-operated hump, but it had become outmoded and was badly congested during World War II and in postwar years. The reconstruction of the plant included the installation of retarders, power switches, communication systems, loud-speakers, Teletype machines, floodlights, and car-inspection facilities. A new hump was built and the yard tracks regrouped.

While the track layout was undergoing the remodeling process a new Diesel repair shop of the most modern type was built, also an ultramodern laboratory. The new Taylor Yard covers an area of about 240 acres and reaches a length of two miles and a half.

To relieve the congestion in this key switching center during reconstruction, an advance blocking of cars was made at division points as far as 370 miles away. For example, southbound cars on the Coast Route for points beyond Los Angeles were switched into blocks at division points far to the north.

Los Angeles is like no other city in the world for the mushrooming growth of its population, and keeping pace closely has been this miracle city's industrial expansion. And no other like shipping center has so few railroads to serve its needs. In Los Angeles, including all of its great suburban area, there is only the Southern Pacific, the Santa Fe, and the Union Pacific, with the Southern Pacific handling about half of the freight, 60 per cent of which is terminal freight and 40 per cent of the freight passes through.

The Southern Pacific has three principal lines reaching out from Los Angeles: (1) the Sunset Route east to El Paso, Texas, and New Orleans, Louisiana, with the Golden State Route, which turns off at El Paso to connect with the Rock Island at Tucumcari, New Mexico, for Chicago; (2) the San Joaquin Valley Route heading north by way of Bakersfield, California, to the San Francisco Bay area, and also going to Sacramento and on north to Portland, Oregon, and from Sacramento east to Ogden, Utah; and (3) the Coast Route to San Francisco by way of Santa Barbara, Watsonville Junction, and San Jose.

The sprawling city of Los Angeles reaches from the Pacific Ocean to the foothills of the San Gabriels, a distance of about twenty-five miles, taking in a vast and evergrowing industrial and harbor area. About 600 cars daily are delivered to industries, warehouses, docks, and other points. Before the modernization of Taylor Yard, switch crews had to reswitch cars at outlying points, as required, to make their setouts. But now thirteen industrial classifications are made at Taylor Yard. This not only expedites deliveries but saves time for industrial switch engines.

The Southern Pacific delivers about 500 cars daily to other railroads in Los Angeles and receives about the same number from them. Previously, a good deal of this switching of interchange was done at various outlying points, but now the cars are classified in Taylor Yard.

The Taylor Yard facilities are confined between a huge bow in the Los Angeles River and San Fernando Road. There was no opportunity for expansion of trackage to the east, where the crowded tracks threaded on into the city proper, and there was only the west with room for extension of the yard track system.

In this west-north section, the receiving unit and part of the departure unit was enlarged from sixteen to twenty-four tracks, an increase in car capacity from 1,204 cars to 2,021 cars. This was accomplished by the extension of sixteen tracks and the con-

313

struction of eight new ones. Also added were two 2,400-foot drill tracks and a 3,100-foot engine track.

To increase the length of the classification section of the yard, the old hump was removed and the new one constructed 215 feet farther west. This done, the entire classification unit was revamped, increasing the distance between track centers to fourteen feet, adding five tracks, changing the grades, and replacing the ladder tracks with a group arrangement, which generally facilitated operations and reduced the number of retarders required.

When the work was completed the classification tracks had a capacity of 1,237 cars against the former 958 car capacity. Modernized, Taylor Yard can classify about 2,700 cars per day, while the limit of the old hump yard was around 1,500 cars every twenty-four hours.

Before Taylor Yard was revamped, yardmasters supervised operations, and they had to chase down switch crews and give orders by word of mouth. And then modern railroading moved in to the tune of $2,500,000, and it was worth every dollar of it.

Today Yardmaster J. C. Herron sits behind glass in a three-story concrete tower, like a skipper in a pilothouse, and is king of all he surveys. There is a panel in front of him, a microphone, a loud-speaker, a telephone. Every man working under him is no farther away than his microphone and loud-speaker. This is railroading the modern way.

The yardmaster communications includes talk-back loud-speakers on seven-foot pipe posts at various locations, some 150 to 200 feet apart throughout the yard area where men are normally working; also there are paging speakers on forty-five-foot poles, spaced about 90 feet apart, having a range of several hundred feet. When a man hears his name called, he goes to the nearest talk-back speaker to answer.

In addition to the yardmaster's tower, located adjacent to the yard office, there is the hump-master's tower; also three control towers, part of a more or less standardized arrangement in all retarder yards.

You will find the pattern the same, generally, wherever freight cars congregate in terminals across the country. Retarder yards are production lines where long lines of freight cars move continuously at walking speed to a place where they are cut off and dropped into a kind of freight car sorting rack for redistribution to the four winds.

Under normal conditions, Taylor Yard makes up and sends on their way about ten eastbound trains over the Sunset Route, while six head over the San Joaquin Valley line and six depart over the Coast Route.

To expedite departures, switches and lead tracks at the east end of the classification unit were rearranged so that as many as four tracks can be pulled simultaneously. Thus, two or more switch runs to interchange points or industries can couple onto their cuts of cars and depart without interfering with each other or with yard operation. Also, the blocks on various tracks can be pulled and assembled into complete road trains, ready for departure, on the long tracks in the departure unit, without interfering with other operations.

Manifest road trains, for the most part, are made up on the five long tracks located along the north side of the receiving unit at the west end of the entire layout. These tracks have capacities up to 108 cars.

Before Taylor Yard was made into a retarder yard, thirty to forty-five minutes were required for car inspectors to walk the length of a train arriving in the receiving unit to make their inspections. Now these duties are performed as the cars are pushed over the single-track lead from the receiving unit to the hump. Inspection pits and towers are located on each side of this track, and provide both top and undercar inspection. When an inspector notices something wrong he reports in on an intercommunication system to a tagger, who is stationed between the inspection point and the hump, and this man tacks a card on the car for the instruction of repairmen.

Consists of trains heading toward Los Angeles are transmitted ahead by Teletype from the last division point. Taylor Yard immediately prepares switch lists in the yard office, and these are transmitted to the hump-master's cabin at the crest of the hump and to the three control towers.

The control towers house the operations of the various groups of retarders and the switches, which are power operated. The yard, of couse, is floodlighted. With this illumination the tower operators may check occupancy of the entire yard to its far end. The main floodlighting units are on five steel towers, with three at the west end and two at the east end of the yard. The towers are 100 feet high. The long-range floodlights have either 1,000- or 1,500-watt lamps.

The lighting system is automatically turned on and off in the evening and morning, being under control of astronomical time switches.

Yard communications include two-way radio between the yardmaster's office, the hump-master's cabin, and fourteen locomotives used in yard service.

The revamping of Taylor Yard was accomplished only after the handling of an enormous amount of dirt. Making the task more difficult was the fact that much of the work had to be done piecemeal so as not to interfere too much with the normal yard operation. The project involved moving 125,000 cubic yards of dirt. To grade an area for nine additional tracks, 12,000 cubic yards had to be moved. New icing and repair track facilities required the movement of 10,000 yards. And there was a fill to take care of parking for mechanical forces. Eight thousand cubic yards of old ballast was taken from beneath the tracks at the west end of the classification yard and used to build up the east end of these tracks.

The grading was done by three tractor-scraper combinations and six Turnapull dirt movers, which handled 32,000 cubic yards in thirty days and 93,000 cubic yards in sixty days respectively.

The subgrade under Taylor Yard is largely sand. The ballast in the yard tracks is gravel, with No. 3 crushed rock ballast placed eight inches under the main leads and twelve inches under the retarders. The rail is the 132-pound head-free section on the main leads and 90-pound on the body tracks. Other leads have 110-pound rail. The turnouts are No. 9 with sixteen-foot, six-inch points, and self-guarded manganese No. 9 frogs. The ties on the main leads are creosoted gum, and, under the retarders, creosoted fir, twelve inches by twelve inches.

The Southern Pacific has a fine president, A. T. Mercier; a most able executive vice-president, R. D. Russell; its operating vice-president, J. W. Corbett is one of my great favorites; and W. W. Hale and C. E. Peterson, freight- and passenger-traffic vice-presidents know their jobs and head fine departments.

CHAPTER XXXV

WABASH INDUSTRIAL DEPARTMENT

Smokestacks and Rolling Wheels

The smokestack of industry and the steel rail march hand in hand. One could not exist without the other. The traffic demands of the factory make business for the railroad. The manufacturer turns the raw material, brought to his loading dock by the freight car, into the finished product that goes back into the freight car for delivery to the merchant. They—the industrialist and the railroad man—are meshed gears, working toward the same ultimate goal, the kind of economy that will allow both a fair margin of profit.

The Industrial Department of the Wabash system is one of the most important on the railroad. This is the tonnage producer that keeps the wheels rolling. We don't hear too much about this industry segment of the railroad, but we see its results every time a freight train roars by, for on board of that train are products of the factories, or raw materials going to these factories.

General Industrial Agent H. H. McIntyre, of the Wabash, while operating in a division of the Traffic Department, is actually the wheel in the before mentioned Industrial Department. In fact, all departments and all officers, from President A. K. Atkinson on down, contribute to the activities of this department, in one way or another, being individually and specifically alive to its needs.

H. H. McIntyre took charge of the Industrial Department in 1938, and he was the first college-educated and railroad-trained engineer to head this division of the Wabash road. The advantages of such a combination were soon obvious. His education and training brought outstanding benefits to the railroad, and, more important, to its clients. And now the entire personnel of the Department dealing with prospects are engineers both by profession and vocation.

Industrial development, which has become so vital a part in modern railroading on the Wabash, stems to a great extent from private enterprise, and the development of private enterprise has been achieved through the operation of this railroad's energetic and carefully schooled industrial agent. To keep pace with the requirements of industrial expansion from 1940 on, the Department has experienced a healthy growth.

The industrial department on a railroad is fundamentally laid down along the lines of a chamber of commerce, engaged in drawing to the city it represents new industries, or tourist trade, or any other factor which will contribute to the continued well-being of the locality.

A railroad's industrial department searches out the location for new industries. They may be warehousing, manufacturing, or product distribution. The department undertakes to find tenants along its lines for any vacant properties that may exist. The poorest advertisement in the world for a community is an idle smokestack. Further, it fattens neither the coffers of the local municipality nor the railroad cash drawer, hence the quicker a fire is built under the boilers the better for all concerned.

That is the reason for the industrial department—to see that there are no smokeless smokestacks along the railroad, while at the same time it looks to the development of new sites for industrial prospects. Being national in scope, the industrial department is qualified to advise communities adjoining its property as to the best means of directing their efforts toward the securing of firms interested in examining new locations in their particular vicinity.

Ordinarily, an industry seeking a site undertakes first of all to find the place where it can most efficiently and economically assemble its raw materials in relation to markets, labor, and transportation. From these fundamentals it branches out in innumerable angles, most of which are peculiar to the individual

319

industry. Such factors as recreational facilities, water facilities, taxes, and so on are all worked out and then brought together in a brief for the consideration of industrial executives.

Representatives of the road's Industrial Department are constantly searching for raw materials, for vacant buildings, or for advantages of any kind that may exist along the lines of the railroad so that through their knowledge they will be in a position to bring to the attention of industrial executives interested a full review of the possibilities.

Railroad representatives are constantly in touch with local and state chambers of commerce and municipal authorities. Through the years the work of the Department has been found so effective and so confidential that this office has served as a clearinghouse for industrial information of all sorts.

When the details of location are worked out the Department begins a survey for track layouts and such other matters as the situation may demand in regard to the railroad's interests. This teamwork creates and lays the groundwork for future close relationship with the shipper, and at the same time indicates the road's realization that only through an understanding of one another's problems can unity of purpose be achieved.

We recently came across a fine example of just one phase of the Department's work, i.e., that dealing with vacant buildings along the railroad. An old brewery in a medium-size city went out of business and, through the work of the Industrial Department, a grain and grain-products processor was interested in examining the plant with a view of adapting it to his use.

This old brewery appeared to offer the necessary layout for a factory beginning, and, starting from scratch, this industry developed into one of the top thirty traffic producers of the railroad.

In another city, a fertilizer company was shown the advantages in a certain area where an abandoned brick plant was located. In a few years this industry also had become one of the thirty top railroad customers.

Now let's move into a larger St. Louis area, where the Wabash Railroad found itself with practically no desirable industrial sites

Southern Pacific new Shasta Daylight #10 climbing the 2.2 grade as it rounds wonderful Cantara Loop in C.T.C. territory on the Black Butte Subdivision of the Shasta Division. Courtesy, S.P. RR.

Virginian Extra 128 east, with 6,000 tons of coal climbing the 2.07 grade at Covel, West Va., on the New River Division. Note the 116-ton Class G-3 gondolas. Courtesy, Virginian RR.

The Virginian RR.'s fine coal pier #2 at Sewalls Point, Va., showing the dumping car on top of pier. Courtesy, Virginian RR.

Seaboard #94 leaves Yeoman Yard, Tampa, Fla., South Florida Division, with thirty-five loads of phosphate rock on the head end in specially designed covered hopper cars used in phosphate trade. Courtesy, S.A.L. RR.

The Seaboard's Silver Comet, crack Birmingham and Atlanta–New York streamliner, #34, at Ragland, Ala., Georgia Division. Courtesy, S.A.L. RR.

The Frisco has modernized many passenger stations. Here is the Miami, Okla., depot on the Afton Subdivision of the Northern Division before reconstruction started. Courtesy, Frisco Lines.

The new remodeled station at Miami, Okla., after construction was finished. Note the excellent train order signals. Courtesy, Frisco Lines.

Mining of the most important and valuable phosphate rock near Bartow, Fla., on the South Florida Division of the Seaboard. Courtesy, S.A.L. RR.

Top view of Seaboard's seventy-ton covered hopper-bottom car used for transporting phosphate rock. Built by the Pullman Standard Car Mfg. Co. Courtesy S.A.L. RR.

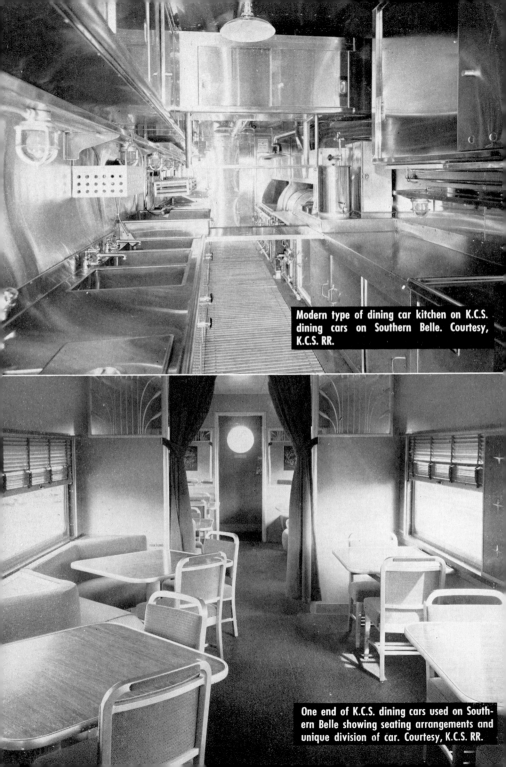

Modern type of dining car kitchen on K.C.S. dining cars on Southern Belle. Courtesy, K.C.S. RR.

One end of K.C.S. dining cars used on Southern Belle showing seating arrangements and unique division of car. Courtesy, K.C.S. RR.

Interior view of Seaboard's automobile box-car showing loading devices. Four automobiles can be carried in one of these cars, which are built by Pullman Standard Car Mfg. Co. Courtesy, S.A.L. RR.

The Seaboard and other railroads have special cars for the handling of cement. Here is one being loaded at Tampa, Fla. South Florida Division. Courtesy, S.A.L. RR.

SEABOARD
8221

CAPY   140000
LD LMT 156000
LT WT   54000   JTN 4-47

B.&O. #7628, 2-8-8-4 type, Class EM-1, drifting down the 2.19 grade at Strecker, Md., with coal train on the west end of the Cumberland Division. Courtesy, B.&O. RR.

New Electro-Motive F-7 used in pusher service on the B.&O. St. Louis #94 being assisted from M.&K. Jct. to Terra Alta, West Va., on the Cumberland Division. Courtesy, B.&O. RR.

left. However, the company had made a survey of various sites, which originally had been prepared for certain government projects during the war. These sites, now available, were brought to the attention of one of the world's largest industries and they proved to be acceptable.

This alertness on the part of the Wabash's Industrial Department resulted in a development at Robertson, Missouri, near the Lambert Municipal Airport and just sixteen miles northwest of downtown St. Louis. Five years later several other large industries had located in this area, and in 1950 this section gave every indication of becoming one of the most desirable industrial areas around St. Louis.

Previously, the Wabash had occupied a relatively poor position in regard to industry, but this was changed to one extremely favored. The work and co-operation of the railroad with the initial industry resulted in the opening up and the development of like expansion and growth in other sections of the country.

Teamwork by all departments on the railroad is required to carry on this industrial development, and a little education among employees in this connection is often of tremendous value. We found fine teamwork on the Wabash and the Ann Arbor Railroad, with every officer and facility available where it was needed and when it was needed.

The Wabash system serves a territory lying between the Niagara frontier and the Missouri River. The opportunities in this territory for industrial development are many, and the railroad, with its highly specialized Industrial Department, is in a position to aid materially in its future expansion.

Improved Facilities

The bringing of factories to an area immediately produces a demand for increased tracks, for more cars, for better communication facilities. It means also the expansion of yards for house tracks, for team tracks, for holding and inspection tracks, and receiving and classification tracks.

The Wabash, located in the so-called Heart of America, has found it necessary to modernize its plant, through constant improvements, that it may remain in a position to provide the best in service. During 1949, for example, improvements made involved a gross expenditure of almost $17,000,000.

Twelve miles is not a great distance, but twelve miles of grades and curves can slow trains on a fast main line. And a fast main line is a requisite of modern railroading. Between Baylis and Kinderhook, Illinois, there was a piece of track that required straightening and leveling, it being on the main Wabash freight line between Kansas City and Decatur. This is under construction at this writing, and it involves extensive grading and bridge construction work. The finished cost will be $1,500,000.

Another improvement in the making involves the removal of the St. Louis Avenue Yard, which will be replaced by a new $1,000,000 yard in a new location in North St. Louis. This is to serve a number of important industries and the city's new $3,-000,000 wholesale produce terminal. The new yard will have thirty-eight tracks capable of handling 780 freight cars. The tracks and their capacities are: housing tracks for 108 cars, team tracks for 220 cars, holding and inspection tracks for 84 cars, and receiving and classification tracks for 368 cars.

This yard relocation became necessary for reasons of obsolescence of the existing yard through the growth of the numerous industries served and by the abandonment of the present "Commission Row." A new wholesale produce market is now being erected at North Market and Second Streets and will result in great savings to the produce people through a vast increase in the efficiency of local distribution. The Wabash will install direct rail lines to the rear of the new buildings.

We are going to run down a few of the Wabash Railroad's improvements, an indication of the enormous sums required to keep pace with the times.

A new concrete and steel freight house was constructed at Detroit to handle the consolidation and forwarding of automobile parts and accessories.

Yard capacity at Moberly, Missouri, was increased from 549

to 839 cars, involving construction of 3.9 miles of additional yard tracks and relocation of 8.8 miles of tracks.

A Teletype system was installed between the following cities: Chicago and St. Louis; Kansas City and St. Louis; Chicago and Montpelier, Ohio; Decatur, Illinois, and Detroit.

During the postwar years, 1946 to 1950 inclusive, the Wabash spent $62,250,000 for major improvements.

The Wabash acquired thirty-nine freight Diesels, eleven passenger Diesels, and forty-four Diesel switch engines.

Ten major fueling stations were required for servicing these engines, and a complete Diesel repair shop was constructed at Decatur, Illinois. Probably by the time this book is published the Diesel service and repair facilities will have been finished at Moberly, Missouri, and on the Buffalo Division.

During the postwar period the Wabash acquired twenty-seven new passenger cars and modernized fifteen coaches. The new cars included seven streamlined light-weight cars for the City of Kansas City, six streamlined light-weight cars for the Blue Bird, ten light-weight sleeping cars for Wabash overnight runs and the streamliner, City of St. Louis, and four new light-weight coaches for the latter train.

During this postwar period a total of 3,822 freight cars were purchased, rebuilt, or constructed in company shops. These are listed as follows:

500	50-ton steel gondolas
50	70-ton steel gondolas
918	50-ton steel hoppers
60	70-ton covered hoppers
1,728	50-ton steel boxcars
	(Material ordered for 500 additional 50-ton steel boxcars)
415	40-ton steel boxcars
110	50-ton steel boxcars with BF equipment
1	drop-well car
40	steel cabooses.

AB type air-brakes were installed on 6,479 freight cars.

The Wabash undertook the reconstruction of 299 bridges, 76 crossing protection installations, plus many other improvement projects. They laid 297.7 miles of new rail. This included 146 miles of 115-pound rail, 11.7 miles of 131-pound rail, and 31.2 miles of 132-pound rail. The rest was 112-pound.

Forty items of road maintenance-of-way machinery were acquired, and 90.3 miles of C.T.C. were installed.

Worn out and obsolete units retired in 1949 included 794 boxcars and 26 cabooses.

Yes, President Arthur Atkinson, a fine all-round railroad man and Operating Vice-President George H. Sido, a great operator, and L. E. Clarahan, a most able traffic vice-president, are constantly at it.

CHAPTER XXXVI

VIRGINIAN COAL MOVE

From Tipple to Tidewater

This is coal—black diamonds from deep in the hills of West Virginia—starting for coal pier No. 2, of the Virginian Railway Company at Sewalls Point on Hampton Roads. A coal train, blasts up the grade from Page to Silver Gap over a 2.04 per cent grade behind engine 736, one of the recently converted 240-pound boiler pressure U.S. Railroad Administration 2-8-8-2 type Mallets, having a tractive effort of 114,000 pounds. Coupled in ahead of the caboose are two lighter Mallets, their black throats echoing the chant of the mighty road engine.

Looking back around the curve we see coal-peaked cars of the Virginian, straining at their iron-locked fists. Here are huge gondolas, the largest coal-carrying cars in the United States, having a net capacity of 105 tons. These are the G3C and G4C class cars, with six-wheel trucks—cars, we'll say, like this VGN 19146 that is to be our special protégé on this journey to the tidewater.

VGN 19146 received its black load at a tipple at Robson, some four miles from D.B. Tower, at the west end of the system. Here it was picked up by a "mine run" job to be made into a train at Page. These cars have dual AB air brakes and are equipped with steel wheels.

Locomotive 736 is a veteran of World War II and was purchased from the Norfolk & Western Railway by the Santa Fe for Western war haul, and now has come back to its native coal country through purchase by the Virginian. These great engines seem to appreciate being home in the Virginias, their fireboxes stoked with fine West Virginia coal.

325

Our drag out of Page is sixteen cars per locomotive. At Silver Gap we pick up five more cars for each engine, a total of fifteen, and drop down a 1.1 per cent grade through Lively; then start up a 1.75 per cent hill past Cirtsville and Sweeneyburg, to Harper, 5.5 miles. Harper is just another hump between the creeks, riverbeds, and ridges which make up this part of West Virginia.

At Harper we get eight more cars for each engine and drop down a 1.1 per cent slope to Surveyor; then there are a few miles of 1.6 per cent up through Jenny Gap. We roll through Slab Fork and on down grades varying from 1.65, 1.06, and 1.57 per cent to Elmore classification yard. The run has required about five hours for this rugged run over a fine piece of railroad. All is C.T.C. rail.

Everything is classified at Elmore, which is always a beehive of activity. The receiving yard consists of five tracks, each holding 140 cars. Then comes the hub with a classification yard of eleven tracks, taking from 45 to 60 cars. Trains are made up here for the run to tidewater. If there are cars for the Norfolk & Western at Roanoke, Virginia, they are blocked together; if there are cars for the Southern Railway connections at Altavista or Meherrin, or the Seaboard at Alberta, or the Atlantic Coast Line at Jarratt, they are blocked near the head of the train in the order in which they will be dropped, so far as possible.

Out of Elmore, our power is one of the new EL2B's, electric engine 127, and the train consists of 3,000 tons for this one great locomotive. This great piece of electric power steps from Elmore to Clark's Gap, fifteen miles, in less than fifty minutes, or at an average speed of nineteen miles per hour up a 2.07 grade. The older EL3A electric-type locomotive would have moved the same tonnage up the hill at fourteen miles an hour, and they have been doing this since electric power was first employed in the coal haul in 1925.

The new motor, the EL2B develops 260,000 pounds starting tractive effort, against 231,000 pounds tractive effort for the EL3A. At fourteen miles per hour they have 162,000 pounds tractive effort. Take note of the pulling power of this new

326

locomotive that can haul a 3,000-ton train up a 2.07 per cent grade for fourteen miles at nineteen miles per hour.

At Clark's Gap our coal drag is filled out to 9,000 tons. This extra tonnage represents an accumulation of coal cars that have been brought to the summit by a "hill run" and left there for our train. The train is inspected before leaving the Gap.

A word here about these new motors, which have a rating of 8,000 horsepower—11,000-volt A.C. generating D.C. They put 25 per cent back into the power line and powerhouse with their regenerative braking. This is a lot of current—the best this author has ever seen on any electrified railroad.

The engineer starts the train very easily, even though the cars and wheels are cold. The temperature is about twenty-five degrees, yet no tonnage has been reduced. Dropping down from Clark's Gap, the regenerative brake is used immediately. Snow is falling lightly; the grade is 1.25 per cent descending as far as Rock; then 0.5 to .015 ascending to Princeton.

Princeton is the headquarters of the New River Division. Here superintendent Berkely Mills has his office. The Princeton car shops turn out these husky coal cars, the great burden bearers of the Virginian, cars of the big hopper type and gondola giants like our VGN 19146, packing its 105 tons behind us, out of the hills to Pier 2 at Sewalls Point. At Princeton, too, are the storehouses of the road and the principal locomotive shops.

We roll through Princeton and drop down the 1.5 per cent grade to the New River and East River bridges where our 125-car train crosses over the main line of the Norfolk & Western, which parallels the Virginian here, twice in two states and over two rivers, the New and the East, all in the same short period of time. Quite a train. Quite a railroad. The place is Glen Lyn, Virginia, and I only hope that some of the readers of this book may one day have the opportunity of seeing this operation on these railroads.

At the foot of the grade is Rich Creek at milepost 320, and we roll by the big powerhouse at Narrows. Here the electric power is generated for these great electric locomotives. At Klotz, milepost 307, the fine limestone ballast used over the entire system is mined and crushed.

Out of Rich Creek the grade is 0.2 per cent ascending, as we make our run for the crest of the Alleghenies. The nine and one-half miles approaching Merrimac is 0.6 per cent ascending. At Merrimac we cross the main ridge of the Alleghenies, passing through a 5,176-foot tunnel, the longest on the road.

Breaking out of the Merrimac Tunnel, we go into regeneration again and drop down a 1.5 per cent grade for seven miles. This is the heaviest grade the westward drags of empties have to face. From milepost 270 to milepost 260 at Kumis the grade is 0.9 per cent, and from there to Roanoke it is seventeen miles 0.6 per cent descending.

At Roanoke we say good-by to Motor No. 127. Our train is inspected and a 900-class AG backs down onto our VGN 19146 and the train. These 900's are Lima-built Mallets with a 2-6-6-6 wheel arrangement. This engine is similar to the Chesapeake & Ohio H8 class Allegheny, except that it is a trifle lighter as it does not have to carry as much sand and does not have the valve pilot. The 900 AG has a 26,500-gallon tank, with an eight-wheel rear truck on the tender. The engine's tractive effort, maximum, is 110,200 pounds.

As we are about to leave Roanoke another AG 900 class is coming in from the east with 145 empties, which the electric motor will haul back to Elmore. The old motors of the 100 type, EL3A, are given the same tonnage up to Clark's Gap, and also Clark's Gap to Roanoke, as the new EL2B's but require about thirty-five to forty minutes longer for the run.

Our locomotive out of Roanoke is 901 and our tonnage is 12,500, right up to the maximum allowed for this portion of the Norfolk Division. From Hardy, east of Roanoke, through Stewartsville to Goodview, a distance of six miles, the grade is only 0.2 per cent against us. It is a little difficult to imagine climbing the Blue Ridge slope on a 0.2 per cent grade. We pass through the Clevilas Tunnel to Huddleston, fourteen miles, 0.6 descending; then it levels off to 0.2 per cent. All grades of the Virginian are compensated.

328

We make the run to Victoria, 123 miles, in five hours and thirty minutes. Here the engine is serviced, the train inspected, and filled out with 1,500 tons. We pull out with 148 cars, all loads. We had taken water at Seneca on the Second Subdivision and filled the tank at Victoria so are able to go all the way to Morgan, seventy-two miles, with our heavy drag. With this one stop, and with the slow running through Norfolk, we make the run to Sewalls Point, 120 miles, with this heavy train in the same time it took to come from Roanoke to Victoria, i.e., five hours and thirty minutes.

This is the end of the run for our coal drag and for VGN 19146 and the 105 tons of coal it has brought out of the hills. It will move from the receiving yard to No. 2 coal pier and will be caught up quickly and dumped for trans-shipment through the modern and efficient facilities that make Sewalls Point famous. In a matter of a few hours, VGN 19146 will, with some 145 other empties, be rolling back toward the coal fields behind a cannonading 900 AG Mallet, and a deep-laden coal ship will be wallowing in the ground swells of the Atlantic, bound for some distant dock.

They're great, they're tremendous—these coal trains of the Virginian, rolling from the Pocahontas and New River fields of southern West Virginia to the tidewater.

Probably the most important of the many great coal-producing branches of the Virginian is the Kopperston, fifty miles back in the West Virginia hills from Elmore. Kopperston is reached from Simon Junction on the Guyandot River. Here a single Mallet handles 6,500 tons over a river grade. The Guyandot River Branch is another fine one from Elmore to West Gilbert, so is the Winding Gulf from Elmore to Willabit. We must never forget the important producing branch lines of any coal-hauling railroad.

THE VIRGINIAN RAILWAY COMPANY

Typical movement of a coal train between Elmore, W. Va., and Roanoke, Va. (131.6 miles), as evidenced by Transcript of Train Sheet below:

Third Subdivision

August 27, 1950, Ex. 126E (Electric), Engr. J. L. Brinkley, Conductor R. F. Pritchard, reported 7:30 P.M.

Departed	Elmore	8:20 P.M. with 38 loads o mtys 2980 tons
	Clarks Gap	" 98 " " " 8960 "
	Matoaka	10:00 P.M
	Princeton	10:39 P.M.
	Whitethorne	12:18 A.M.
Arrived	Roanoke	1:55 A.M. August 28, 1950

November 12, 1950, Ex. 128E (Electric), Engr. J. F. Teaford, Condr. A. D. Burcham, reported 7:30 P.M.

Departed	Elmore	8:15 P.M. with 38 loads o mtys 2970 tons
	Clarks Gap	" 113 " " " 8920 "
	Matoaka	9:45 P.M.
	Princeton	10:30 P.M.-10:38 P.M. Met X 126 W.
	Whitethorne	12:19 A.M.
Arrived	Roanoke	1:55 A.M. November 13, 1950.

Office of President,
Norfolk, Virginia,
November 22, 1950.

THE VIRGINIAN RAILWAY COMPANY

Typical movement of a coal train between Roanoke, Va., and Victoria, Va. (123.4 miles)—Second Subdivision—as evidenced by Transscript of Train Sheet below:

Sept. 20, 1950, Ex. 903 East-Engineer F. C. Brown, Conductor
J. C. Meador reported 4:40 A.M.

Departed	Roanoke	5:30 A.M. with 145 loads 13,511 tons
	Altavista	7:33 A.M.-8:10 A.M.
	Seneca	8:37 A.M.-9:12 A.M.—coal and water
	Brookneal	9:41 A.M.
	Phenix	10:11 A.M.
	Cullen	10:28 A.M.
	Abilene	10:40 A.M.
	Meherrin	11:14 A.M.
Arrived	Victoria	11:50 A.M. with 145 loads 13,511 tons

Sept. 29, 1950, Ex. 906 East-Engineer Hutchinson, Conductor Love
reported 3:45 A.M.

Departed	Roanoke	4:35 A.M. with 131 loads 13,503 tons
	Altavista	6:31 A.M.-7:24 A.M.
	Seneca	8:00 A.M.-8:25 A.M.—coal and water
	Brookneal	8:49 A.M.
	Phenix	9:16 A.M.
	Cullen	9:34 A.M.
	Abilene	10:00 A.M.
	Meherrin	10:28 A.M.
Arrived	Victoria	11:00 A.M. with 131 loads 13,503 tons

Office of President,
Norfolk, Virginia,
November 22, 1950.

THE VIRGINIAN RAILWAY COMPANY

Typical movement of a coal train between Victoria, Va., and Sewalls Point, Va., (Norfolk) (125.1 miles) First Subdivision, as evidenced by Transcript of Train Sheet below:

Sept. 20, 1950, Ex. 906 East-Engineer J. R. Sheffield, Conductor Wright reported 2:00 P.M.

Departed	Victoria	2:27 P.M. with 145 loads 14,574 tons
	Kenbridge	2:48 P.M.
	Dundas	3:03 P.M.
	Alberta	3:19 P.M.
	Adsit	3:44 P.M.
	Purdy	3:57 P.M.
	Jarratt	4:09 P.M.
	Joyner	4:31 P.M.
	Sebrell	4:43 P.M.
	Sedley	5:32 P.M.
	Suffolk	6:51 P.M.
	Carolina	7:42 P.M.
	Tidewater	7:48 P.M.
Arrived	Sewalls Pt.	8:25 P.M. with 145 loads 14,574 tons

Sept. 29, 1950, Ex. 907 East-Engineer Pool, Conductor Otey reported 1:30 P.M.

Departed	Victoria	2:05 P.M. with 133 loads 14,544 tons
	Kenbridge	2:25 P.M.
	Dundas	2:36 P.M.
	Alberta	2:48 P.M.-3:48 P.M.
	Adsit	4:12 P.M.
	Purdy	4:23 P.M.
	Jarratt	4:34 P.M.
	Joyner	4:56 P.M.
	Suffolk	6:34 P.M.
	Carolina	7:13 P.M.
	Tidewater	7:19 P.M.
Arrived	Sewalls Pt.	7:48 P.M. with 133 loads 14,544 tons

Office of President,
Norfolk, Virginia,
November 22, 1950.

THE VIRGINIAN RAILWAY COMPANY

Typical movement of coal empties—Sewalls Point, Va. (Norfolk) to Elmore, W. Va. (380.1 miles), during a period of car shortage, composed of cars dumped over Sewalls Point Coal Piers between 12:01 A.M., and 7:00 A.M., on the date of departure from Sewalls Point, Va., and placed at the mines for loading the following day, as evidenced by Transcript of Train Sheet below:

First Subdivision

Sept. 5, 1950, Ex. 907 W., Engineer Martin, Conductor Bowden reported
8:00 A.M.

Departed	Sewalls Point	8:30 A.M. with 0 loads 163 mtys 4,411 tons
	Tidewater	9:00 A.M.
	Carolina	9:19 A.M.
	Suffolk	9:58 A.M.
	Walters	10:23 A.M.
	Sedley	10:37 A.M.
	Sebrell	11:05 A.M.
	Joyner	11:18 A.M.
	Jarratt	11:39 A.M.
	Purdy	11:52 A.M.
	Adsit	12:02 P.M.
	Alberta	12:21 P.M.
	Dundas	12:36 P.M.
	Kenbridge	12:45 P.M.
Arrived	Victoria	1:05 P.M. with 0 loads 163 mtys 4,411 tons

Second Subdivision

Sept. 5, 1950, Ex. 902 W., Engineer Stump, Conductor Cromer reported
2:30 P.M.

Departed	Victoria	2:50 P.M. with 0 loads 163 mtys 4,411 tons
	Meherrin	3:31 P.M.
	Abilene	3:53 P.M.
	Cullen	4:04 P.M.
	Phenix	4:14 P.M.
	Brookneal	4:35 P.M.
	Seneca	5:26 P.M.-5:40 P.M.—coal and water
	Altavista	6:15 P.M.
Arrived	Roanoke	8:10 P.M. with 0 loads 163 mtys 4,411 tons

333

Third Subdivision

Sept. 5, 1950, Ex. 128 W. (Electric), Eng. J. F. Teaford, Condr. O. L. Wolfe
reported 9:15 P.M.

Departed	Roanoke	10:00 P.M. with o loads 138 mtys 2,984 tons
	Whitethorne	11:38 P.M.
Supplied	Klotz 10 empties	
	Princeton	1:56 A.M.
	Matoaka	2:30 A.M.
Arrived	Elmore	3:25 A.M., Sept. 6, 1950.

Office of President,
Norfolk, Virginia,
November 22, 1950.

THE VIRGINIAN RAILWAY COMPANY

Typical movement of Westbound Time Freight No. 71 between Sewalls Point, Va. (Norfolk), and Dickinson, W. Va., (457.7 miles) as evidenced by Transcript of Train Sheet below:

No. 71 Symbol J
First Subdivision

November 10, 1950, Engine 508, Engineer Martin, Conductor Otey

Departed	Sewalls Point	9:00 P.M. with 12 loads 5 mtys 708 tons
	Tidewater	9:13 P.M.
	Carolina	9:19 P.M.-9:27 P.M.
	South Branch	Picked up 10 loads o mtys
	Suffolk	10:16 P.M.-10:29 P.M. picked up 2 lds 7 mtys
	Jarratt	11:43 P.M.-11:58 P.M. Del. 2 loads to ACL
	Alberta	12:35 A.M.-12:50 A.M. Del. 2 loads to SAL
Arrived	Victoria	1:30 A.M. with 20 loads 12 mtys 1,356 tons

Second Subdivision

November 11, 1950, Engine 505, Engineer M. Brown, Conductor Connell

Departed	Victoria	3:00 A.M. with 48 loads 16 mtys 3,087 tons
	Altavista	6:48 A.M.
Arrived	Roanoke	8:30 A.M. with 48 loads 16 mtys 3,087 tons

Third Subdivision

November 11, 1950, Engine 128 (Electric), Engineer R. L. Hart,
Conductor T. J. Henretta

Departed	Roanoke	9:55 A.M. with 50 loads 17 mtys 2,990 tons
	Ellett	11:05 A.M.
	Merrimac	11:18 A.M.
	Whitethorne	11:33 A.M.
	Princeton	1:33 P.M.-1:42 P.M. Met train No. 4
	Matoaka	2:17 P.M.
Arrived	Elmore	3:10 P.M.

Fourth Subdivision

November 11, 1950, Eng. 701, Engr. J. S. Middleton, Conductor W. C. King,
Pusher engine 705, Engineer F. Fanning

Departed		Elmore	5:16 P.M. with 49 loads 14 mtys 3,358 tons
		Gulf Jct.	5:22 P.M.
		Maben	5:36 P.M.
		Slab Fork	6:10 P.M.
		Surveyor	6:30 P.M.-6:51 P.M. water
		Harper	7:10 P.M.
		Pax	7:30 P.M.
		Oak Hill Jct.	7:53 P.M.
		Page	8:14 P.M.-8:45 P.M. coal and water
	NYC	DB Tower	9:10 P.M.-9:15 P.M. Jct. stop
Arrived		Dickinson	10:30 P.M.

Office of President,
Norfolk, Virginia,
November 22, 1950.

335

THE VIRGINIAN RAILWAY COMPANY

Typical movement of Eastbound Time Freight No. 72 between Dickinson, W. Va., and Sewalls Point, Va. (Norfolk) (457.7 miles) as evidenced by Transcript of Train Sheet below:

No. 72 Symbol Z

Fourth Subdivision

August 28, 1950, Engine 724, Engineer Ira Stone, Conductor G. Meador

Departed	NYC	Dickinson	5:10 A.M. with 42 loads 34 mtys 2,918 tons
		DB Tower	5:55 A.M.-6:02 A.M.

Cut in pusher engine 714, Engineer T. P. Long

	Page	6:27 A.M.-7:10 A.M. coal water & set off 18 mtys
	Hamilton	7:19 A.M
	Oak Hill Jct.	7:42 A.M.
	Pax	8:01 A.M.
	Harper	8:27 A.M.
	Surveyor	8:38 A.M.
	Slab Fork	8:57 A.M.
	Maben	9:12 A.M.
	Gulf Jct.	9:38 A.M.
Arrived	Elmore	9:50 A.M.

Third Subdivision

August 28, 1950, Engine 127 (Electric), Engineer R. L. Hart, Conductor T. J. Henretta

Departed	Elmore	12:10 P.M. with 47 loads 0 mtys 2,609 tons
	Herndon	12:41 P.M.
	Clarks Gap	with 89 loads 0 mtys 6,431 tons
	Matoaka	1:42 P.M.-1:52 P.M. Met train No. 71
	Princeton	2:32 P.M.
	Rich Creek	3:12 P.M.
	Pembroke	3:44 P.M.
	Whitethorne	4:12 P.M.
	Merrimac	4:32 P.M.
	Ellett	4:45 P.M.
Arrived	Roanoke	5:35 P.M.

Second Subdivision

August 28, 1950, Engine 505, Engineer Foor, Conductor W. E. Roberts

Departed	Roanoke	8:15 P.M. with 43 loads 3 mtys 2,065 tons
	Altavista	9:37 P.M.-9:46 P.M. Del. 4 loads Sou. Ry.
Arrived	Victoria	11:40 P.M. with 39 loads 3 mtys 1,875 tons

August 29, 1950, Engine 509, Engineer C. E. Sheffield, Conductor Mumford

Departed	Victoria	12:20 A.M. with 38 loads 3 mtys 1,825 tons
	Alberta	12:50 A.M.-1:45 A.M. Del. 11 loads SAL pick up 2 loads
	Jarratt	2:15 A.M.-2:56 A.M. Del. 6 loads 1 mty ACL
	Suffolk	Set off 3 loads
	Carolina	4:53 A.M.
	Tidewater	4:56 A.M.-5:16 A.M. Set off 5 loads to Fords
Arrived	Sewalls Pt.	5:35 A.M. with 15 loads 2 mtys 784 tons

Office of President,
Norfolk, Virginia,
November 22, 1950.

THE VIRGINIAN RAILWAY COMPANY

Typical movement of a train handling coal empties between Sewalls Point, Va. (Norfolk) and Victoria, Va. (125.1 miles) as evidenced by Transcript of Train Sheet below:

Sept. 18, 1950, Ex. 902 West-Engineer J. R. Sheffield, Conductor Wright reported 10:00 P.M.

Departed	Sewalls Pt.	10:30 P.M. with 0 loads 165 mtys 4,502 tons
	Tidewater	11:13 P.M.
	Carolina	11:23 P.M.
	Suffolk	12:04 A.M.
	Jarratt	2:10 A.M.—Departed 3:06 A.M.
	Alberta	4:00 A.M.
Arrived	Victoria	4:55 A.M. with 0 loads 165 mtys 4,502 tons

Sept. 19, 1950, Ex. 906 West-Engineer Clark, Conductor White reported 10:30 P.M.

Departed	Sewalls Pt.	11:00 P.M. with 0 loads 142 mtys 4,541 tons
	Tidewater	11:43 P.M.
	Carolina	11:50 P.M.
	Jarratt	4:07 A.M.
	Alberta	4:55 A.M.
Arrived	Victoria	5:45 A.M. with 0 loads 142 mtys 4,541 tons

Office of President,
Norfolk, Virginia,
November 22, 1950.

THE VIRGINIAN RAILWAY COMPANY

Typical movement of a train handling coal empties between Victoria, Va., and Roanoke, Va. (123.4 miles) as evidenced by Transcript of Train Sheet below:

Sept. 19, 1950, Ex. 900 W-Engineer Montgomery, Conductor
J. Booth reported 5:30 A.M.

Departed	Victoria	6:05 A.M. with 0 loads 164 mtys 4,478 tons
	Cullen	7:46 A.M.
	Phenix	7:59 A.M.
	Brookneal	8:22 A.M.
	Seneca	8:48 A.M.-9:02 A.M.—coal and water
	Altavista	9:39 A.M.-9:50 A.M.
	Huddleston	10:19 A.M.
	Moneta	10:44 A.M.
	Goodview	10:59 A.M.
Arrived	Roanoke	11:45 A.M. with 0 loads 164 mtys 4,478 tons

Office of President,
Norfolk, Virginia,
November 22, 1950.

THE VIRGINIAN RAILWAY COMPANY

Typical movement of a train handling coal empties between Roanoke, Va. and Elmore, W. Va. (131.6 miles) as evidenced by Transcript of Train Sheet below:

Third Subdivision

November 8, 1950, Ex. 126W (Electric), Engr. J. T. Shirley, Sr., Condr. B. B. Brown, Sr. reported 7:00 P.M.

Departed	Roanoke	7:30 P.M. with 130 mtys o loads 2,992 tons
	Whitethorne	9:10 P.M.
	Princeton	11:05 P.M.
	Matoaka	11:35 P.M.
Arrived	Elmore	12:10 A.M., November 9, 1950

November 12, 1950, Ex. 128W (Electric), Engr. H. H. Mounts, Conductor T. R. White reported 2:45 A.M.

Departed	Roanoke	3:15 A.M. with 141 mtys o loads 2,991 tons
	Whitethorne	5:01 A.M.
	Princeton	6:49 A.M.
	Matoaka	7:21 A.M.
Arrived	Elmore	7:55 A.M., November 12, 1950

Office of President,
Norfolk, Virginia,
November 22, 1950.

CHAPTER XXXVII

SPERRY RAIL SERVICE

Locating Sick Rails

The modern railroad, with its higher speeds and heavier trains, presents a problem that can only be answered by a rigid, periodic inspection of the rail over which the streamliners and the Red Ball freights move in their headlong conquest of time and distance.

In an earlier chapter, "Safe Rails" we told a little of the story of the Sperry G-Men and the Sperry Rail Service, together with the highly specialized rail-testing cars—the Sperry Ultrasonic Detector Car and the larger Induction Detector Car; the first having the appearance of a complicated motor car, such as section men use, and the other looking like a baggage-mail car with windows in the ends. These cars play a major part in the rail-testing program of the railroad employing this service, which is made available by the Sperry Company.

Probably the least glamourized department of the railroad is that concerned with the track—the Maintenance-of-Way Department. The track forces, the unsung, almost unnoticed by the public at large, men who keep the roadway safe for modern traffic.

The credo emphasized by William T. Faricy, president of the Association of American Railroads, on the occasion of the yearly presentation of the Harriman Medals "for the utmost progress in safety and accident prevention," was "Safe roadway, safe equipment, and—safe-thinking and methods." Mr. Faricy further stated, "Men wearing the proud emblem of the railroad industry will never be satisfied as long as a passenger or an employee gets killed or injured."

Progressive, modern railroading is built around safe rails! The modern railroad bends every effort toward providing not only a fast passenger train and a fast freight train, but toward laying the foundation of *safe* trains. The steel rail is the backbone of America in peacetime and in days of crisis, and because it is, it must be sound.

Because American railroads know the importance of safe track, the growth of the rail service offered by the Sperry people has been phenomenal. A periodic presentation of statistics concerning the condition of the track is a regular function of the Sperry Rail Service.

Years ago railroads relied upon track walkers for track inspection, and the track walker, of course, had to depend on his keen eye for any visual indications of rail cracks or other flaws. But by the time the flaw was large enough to be noticed by the track walker it was large enough to be dangerous, for by then the inner defect had broken through the surface.

The transverse fissure, potentially the most dangerous, generally grows slowly in a plane normal to the length of the rail and spreads outward from a nucleus until it attains a size sufficient to weaken the effective strength of the rail. Large or small, a transverse fissure is a potential danger spot.

The elimination of accidents caused by rail flaws depends on the ability of the railway maintenance forces to locate such flaws. A steel rail, like a man or a machine, can get tired. This happens when interior forces deteriorate. In a rail internal fissures figure in the start of deterioration. Metallurgists know this as "sub-molecular disintegration within the steel" and fatigue failure of the railhead may result. Thus can be seen the importance of locating this sick rail and replacing it.

Locating the sick rail is the job of the Sperry Service. Once it is located, the track gang will immediately move in.

The detector car inspects track at a rate of about twelve miles per hour. An operator, sitting at the tape printer, surrounded by instruments and gauges, has contact with the man at the motive power controls at the forward end through the car's communication system. The operator on duty is relieved at the end of each hour to avoid fatigue, an indication of his on guard attentiveness to duty.

The railroad personnel assigned to a detector car should be a maintenance-of-way representative and a trainmaster. These men will save time and the resultant saving of many dollars.

The maintenance-of-way man can be valuable in the following ways:

1. Notify division offices as to the amount of replacement rail needed.
2. Issue advance orders concerning the disconnection of flange oilers several days before arrival of the detector car.
3. Have all rail which is not to be tested staked out in advance.
4. Issue advance orders to have dirty rail sanded and washed before the test starts.
5. Make advance arrangements on each successive division regarding division personnel needed and the approximate time of the arrival of the car.

The division trainmaster can reduce chargeable time still further by:

1. Having detector car and work train crews called at least thirty minutes before testing is scheduled to commence.
2. Assigning a crew member to pick up orders before starting time.
3. Scheduling the start for each testing day to take maximum advantage of traffic.
4. Sending a motor car ahead of the detector car to pick up orders during the testing period.
5. Obtaining accurate figures on trains and making use of the flag when trains are running late.
6. Having trains run around the detector car when testing in multiple-track territory.
7. Assigning the duty of gathering rail data to the section foreman, or other qualified representative, who will stay with the replacement crew.

Sperry's *Service and Operating Specifications and Data Sheets*, printed in booklet form, always goes to the railroad concerned with the contract. The Sperry Service co-operates with the railroad in every way possible that greater efficiency may be developed.

The Sperry service specifications for testing rails in track (Induction and Ultrasonic methods) follow:

1. DESCRIPTION OF SERVICE
    a. Sperry supplies a service including:
        1. Testing rails and sections of rail in track using Detector Cars owned and operated by Sperry. Testing is conducted in accordance with a standard form of contract and Sperry Standard Practice Instructions (for use of Sperry Personnel).
        2. Operating Specifications, supplied to the railroads with the contract, consisting of suggested procedures to be followed by Sperry.
        3. Operating Data Sheets, supplied to the railroads with the contract, consisting of suggested procedures to be followed by the railroads.
        4. Daily Reports of Detector Car operation, time distribution and defective rails detected.
        5. Service Failure investigation and follow-up with report to the railroad.
        6. Statistical Reports on detected and service failures including graphic charts, showing efficiency of railroad's testing program.
        7. Technical Information relative to rail defects, their origin and growth, and their relation to the most effective rail testing programs.
        8. Research and Development of Detector Cars, assuring that Detector Cars operated by Sperry Rail Service will consistently find more and smaller transverse defects, and more longitudinal defects than any other type of rail testing equipment.

We are going to run down the Operating Specifications and General Information for Testing Rails in Track (Induction Method), as indicated in Sperry's specification No. 01-206, without making a complete notation of each item or attempting a chronological list of the items. Full specifications and general information may be obtained from the Sperry Rail Service, Danbury, Connecticut.

To obtain the maximum performance from the Induction Detector Car and for the most efficient handling by the railroad the Sperry Rail Service offers the following information:

Detector cars are self-propelled and provide sleeping quarters for Sperry crew only. Railroad personnel desiring a noon meal on the car should arrange with the chief operator a few hours in advance.

Sperry personnel in the field consists of chief operators, operators, and stewards; also traveling supervisors, mechanics, and electricians. The number depends on testing conditions, insuring the completion of the test in the shortest time with maintenance of equipment at its maximum efficiency.

The delivery of supplies, shipments, and mail to the detector car can often be expedited by railroad personnel, to the mutual advantage of both the Sperry people and the railroad.

The Sperry crew take care of maintenance of equipment and repairs, or it is done by traveling service men. The cars carry spare parts to the extent practicable. Any repairs are performed outside of testing hours. However, if emergency repairs become necessary for efficient testing, operators are instructed to make them immediately. Any such delays by Sperry are not charged to the railroad.

An advance notice of the arrival of the car is always given the proper railroad officials, enabling arrangement for the arrival of railroad personnel at the point of delivery.

Testing arrangements are made between the chief operator of the car and the maintenance-of-way representative. They go over arrangements and make certain the proper instructions have gone out to the railroad personnel.

Detection performance is related to the condition of the rail being tested and under average conditions is the detection of defects having a transverse separation of approximately 10 per cent or more of the cross sectional area of the railhead. Longitudinal defects in the head of the rail are usually detected and those in the web of rail are sometimes detected. However, Sperry does not guarantee a specific performance and is not liable for failure to discover or to report any defective rails.

344

An indication caused by burn, shelling, or flow can, in most cases, be interpreted from the car. If they cannot be properly interpreted from the car, they are examined on the ground and, when necessary, hand tests are made. Satisfactory hand tests cannot be made when burn, shelling, or flow is cracked or silvered, and a notation to that effect is made on the tape.

Track structures such as rail braces, spacer blocks, mud rails, frogs, switch points, derails, high spikes, etc., indicate on the tape and are interpreted as such from the car.

Rail welds containing metal other than metal from the rail itself cause indications and are not investigated.

The joint bar condition (type, tightness, etc.) may effect detection in the area adjacent to each end of the joint bar. All rigid and some spring frogs necessitate the raising of the brush carriage to prevent damage to the equipment. The rail, for the distance the brush carriage is raised, is not tested. The brush carriage is also raised, for the same reason, at derails.

When a hand test reveals a transverse separation at one location in a rail, no further tests are made in the rail.

Each day the Sperry crew issue car reports for the day's operation to the railroad representative.

Railroads using the new Ultrasonic Service have determined its accuracy by careful checks. This has been done by marking on the joint bars the location, path, and length of defects detected by the ultrasonic equipment *before* the bars were removed. Then they were taken off and examined and the defects were found to be exactly as charted by this new testing device.

Sometimes there are minor head-and-web separations at the joints which offer no immediate threat. Checks then can be made periodically, and any increase in the length of the separation noted and the rail removed.

Ultrasonic testing is less costly per joint than the visual inspection method, and as techniques and equipment are improved, together with the greater experience gained, the average cost per joint and per mile of track inspected is certain to decrease.

The new Ultrasonic Detector Cars operated by the Sperry Rail Service tested more than 110,000 sections of rail within the joint bar limits during the first half of 1950.

One point where visual rail inspection is difficult is in tunnels, but here the Ultrasonic Detector performs as well as on open track. It has been next to impossible to detect failures at the heel of trailing-point switches, and it is here that traffic may open the fracture to a point where a derailment results. Here again the sensitive pulse of the ultrasonic equipment performs its miracle of detection, the break is caught, and the faltering switch section replaced.

And so we find a new guardian of the steel rail that speeds the sparkling streamliner and carries the flashing wheels of the manifest train. This is railroading the modern way—the safe way, thanks to the Sperry Rail Service and its founder, Dr. Elmer A. Sperry.

CHAPTER XXXVIII

THE SEABOARD'S PHOSPHATE MOVE

The Rock Trains

The world's largest known deposits of phosphate rock are located in Polk and Hillsborough counties, less than fifty miles due east of Tampa, Florida. So far as it can be estimated, the supply appears to be just about inexhaustible. And this phosphate rock is another Florida product that moves over the rails of the Seaboard Air Line Railroad.

Surprising as it may seem to a great many people, the famous Florida citrus and vegetable crops do not provide the big rail movement out of this famous sunshine state. Instead, it is the lowly phosphate rock, which supplies one of the three chief components of the commercial fertilizer known as phosphate.

Phosphate rock, treated with sulphuric acid, becomes acid phosphate, or superphosphate, and then in combination with nitrogen and potash it completes its manufacturing transformation and is returned to old Mother Earth to enrich the soil from which it came. It is practically indispensable as a nutrient in the growth of nearly all agricultural products. The rock also has many other uses.

The rock is mined by several large operators, who first remove the overburden, or upper stratum of soil, then hydraulic machinery gathers up nodules or small lumps rich in bone phosphate of lime. A mill, through a flotation process, removes sand and other impurities. The pure phosphate remaining is dehydrated and the dry rock is ready to be transported to acidulating plants.

Between 8,000,000 and 10,000,000 gross tons of phosphate

347

rock move out of the state of Florida every year. Some of this rock is exported, but the majority of fertilizer plants are in this country.

The two railroads serving the phosphate deposits are the Seaboard Air Line and the Atlantic Coast Line. Solid trains of covered hopper cars leave the mines for the ports of Tampa and Boca Grande, Florida. The rock is handled by elevators and loaded aboard vessels for movement to port cities of the Gulf of Mexico and the North Atlantic Coast then to Europe and Asia. Japan, also, has always provided a market for Florida's phosphate rock.

Rail movements of the rock is either in boxcars or covered hopper cars, depending on the facilities for unloading at the destination. The rock cars on the Seaboard come out of Mulberry, Florida, on train No. 94, rolling northward to Hampton, Baldwin, and Jacksonville on Nos. 88 and 94. At these points the trains are broken up and the cars go into trains for various destinations over the rails of connecting railroads, as well as destinations at points on the Seaboard.

The phosphate rock channels through the classification yards as those at Montgomery, Alabama; Columbus and Macon, Georgia; and Richmond, Virginia. They roll on then to a hundred or more cities in the area east of the Rockies where fertilizer manufacturers operate these acidulating plants.

Upon arrival at the processing plant, the rock is unloaded into bins or silos where it is stored until it moves on to the mixing chambers and is duly incorporated as the number "8" element in a bag of manufactured fertilizer which bears the formula "5-8-5." Translated, this indicates that your sack of fertilizer contains five units of nitrogen, eight units of phosphorus, and five units of potash.

It is interesting to discover the various functions performed by this bag of 5-8-5 that goes into the soil to stimulate the growth of these fresh vegetables that will one day find their way onto our table, via the Seaboard, and other railroads of the nation's network. The first "5," nitrogen, forces the seed and leaf development. The "8," phosphorus, develops strong root

348

stems and hastens maturity. The last "5," potash, promotes resistence to disease.

And the railroad, which provides the cheapest form of mass transportation, plays a vital part in the country's economy through its ability to handle these products of the earth, speedily and with the amazing efficiency that characterizes these roads like the Seaboard.

Tidewater Loading

The Seaboard Air Line placed in operation in 1947 a new elevator for handling phosphate rock at the tidewater area. This loading plant is on Seddon Island, Tampa, Florida. It handles 1,500 tons an hour of phosphate from hopper car to ship's hold. This amazing performance certainly rates a place in the pages of modern railroading.

Sixty tons a minute!

Some ninety cars can be unloaded through the plant without requiring the employment of a switch engine. Once the wheels start turning, there is practically no cessation in the flow of phosphate rock, except as the loading spout and automatic trimmer are moved from hold to hold.

The production of phosphate rock in Seaboard territory and its movement over this road's lines has mounted continuously, with a high in 1949 of 4,529,232 tons, and this is despite curtailment of production and shipping during the second quarter of the year because of labor trouble at the mines.

Every feature of the Seaboard's loading plant at Tampa was designed with the idea of maintaining a steady flow of phosphate rock from car to ship with an absolute minimum of dead time. Factors engineered into the plant include the highest efficiency in the handling of cars, coupled with the work of the traveling loader and the power cargo trimmer, the latter eliminating slow and costly hand trimming.

An electric motor-driven loading tower, supported on tracks above the dock, eliminates the necessity for hauling the ship along the dock as the loading progresses. This tower travels from hold to hold, and it is equipped with a movable boom, which supports a belt conveyor. This boom terminates in a loading spout to which is attached the automatic cargo trimmer. The spout and trimmer can be lowered quickly through any hatch for placing the phosphate.

Serving the elevator is a layout that provides eight covered track hoppers some twelve feet above the normal track levels on the island. These receive the phosphate rock from closed-top hopper-bottom cars. The load tracks serving the plant are constructed on a descending grade to feed the loaded cars to the foot of an inclined approach to the receiving hoppers. The cars are pulled up the incline and over the track hoppers with a cable attached to an electric car-haul engine, operated by an attendant in a tower at the north end of the hopper house. The man stationed here has an unobstructed view of the hauling and dumping operations.

This phosphate loading is typical of the manner in which progressive America performs its day's work. This is a free enterprise in a land where industry looks to the production line for a means to an end. You hear some people complain that labor-saving devices create unemployment. On the contrary, machinery makes employment for the reason that it requires labor to both build and operate these machines.

The hopper cars, as they are pulled through the hopper house, release their loads of phosphate into the track hoppers. The empty cars are then released and they roll on a descending grade through a spring switch and up a gravity kickback, thence back through the switch to an empty-car yard. This yard accommodates about a hundred cars. This arrangement puts all car storage north of the plant, with the result that there is no interference with plant operations because of switching movements, either in placing the loads or in removing the empties.

Additional storage tracks for loads and empties are provided on the Island so that there is no difficulty in maintaining a constant flow of cars through the plant regardless of the size of the ship which is loading.

Let's take a look at the facilities that make possible this remarkable precision loading of phosphate rock at dockside, for the handling of sixty tons of this sort of cargo per minute commands attention.

The material moving from the track hoppers to the ship is handled on four forty-two-inch conveyors. No. 1 conveyor is located directly under the hoppers. It is fed from the hoppers by eight adjustable speed roll feeders. This conveyor discharges onto No. 2 conveyor, which elevates the phosphate rock about 57 feet above the dock where it discharges it into a chute. This chute delivers it onto No. 3 conveyor, which extends horizontally for a distance of some 450 feet at a height of 47 feet above and parallel to the face of the dock. A tripper is provided on this conveyor by means of which the contents of the belt can be discharged at any point within the middle 400 feet along its length, and so unload its rock to No. 4 conveyor, or the boom conveyor on the mobile loading tower.

In conveyor No. 2 there is an automatic weightometer which accurately weighs the material carried over the belt.

All belts travel at 530 feet per minute. Belt No. 1 is powered by a 15-horsepower motor; belt No. 2 by a 200-horsepower motor; belt No. 3 by a 75-horsepower motor; belt No. 4 by a 40-horsepower motor. The roll feeders are powered by 4-5 horsepower variable speed motors, which are operated in pairs for flexibility in operation.

All of the motor controls are electrically interlocked to prevent the flooding of the belts when any one of the motors is stopped or started.

The traverse of the mobile loading tower is accomplished by two 7½-horsepower motors driven through worm gears. The boom on the tower is raised and lowered by a hoisting drum which is directly connected through a gear box to a 30-horsepower motor.

Three motors of ⅓ horsepower, ¼ horsepower, and 20 horsepower are provided on the automatic cargo trimmer to actuate its various movements. Power and interlocking are carried to the motors and controls on the loading tower by means of trolleys supported on the roof of the gallery for the No. 3 conveyor.

Loud-speaker talk-back stations are strategically located along the conveying system to give the plant foreman direct communication with each operator at any time. This has proven to be a great timesaver.

The value of the cargo is determined by the quality of the phosphate rock, which is measured by the percentage of bone phosphate of lime (PPL) present. It is very necessary that the PPL percentage be accurately established, and this requires that a truly representative sample of the material loaded be obtained.

An automatic sampler, located in a building at the point of discharge of the No. 2 conveyor, accomplishes this. Here sample buckets of an endless chain completely cut the flow of phosphate every 16.6 seconds, taking 0.50 per cent of the entire cargo for the original sample. This sample is dumped into a hopper at the top of the building. It is then carried over a magnetic separator to remove "tramp" iron.

Ninety-nine per cent is taken from the magnetic separator and flows into a rotary crusher where it is reduced to particles not exceeding $\frac{3}{16}$ inches in size. One per cent is taken out as a moist sample to determine the moisture content.

The material from the crusher is passed downward through three eight-way rotary splitters to reduce the quantity of retained sample; then through a fine grinder and another eight-way splitter. The material rejected by the splitters is fed to a small bucket elevator which returns the reject to No. 3 conveyor for loading. The final dry sample obtained from a 10,000-ton cargo is approximately thirty pounds of material composed of small fractions of phosphate rock from each 6.9 tons of rock loaded.

In addition to the export shipment of phosphate rock, a large volume moves to widespread domestic destinations, which, generally, embrace a large part of the territory east of the Rocky Mountains. Because of a marked increase in the use of fertilizers in the Midwest in the 1940's the production and movement of Florida phosphate rock has been stimulated.

The following figures indicate the increase in the phosphate rock movement between 1940 and 1949. The drop in 1942, 1943, and 1944 was due to war conditions and reduced export shipments.

Year	Tons
1940	1,440,012
1941	1,597,459
1942	1,284,175
1943	1,393,346
1944	1,516,502
1945	1,704,207
1946	2,378,623
1947	3,358,970
1948	3,763,662
1949	4,529,232

CHAPTER XXXIX

BALTIMORE & OHIO

Line Improvements Speed Freight

Counting from the time of the passing of the last Baltimore & Ohio train until a new span had been slipped into place and the rail laid, there at the White River bridge, near Riverdale, Indiana, the elapsed time was two hours and forty-one minutes. That tells something of the story of your modern-day railroad engineering on the line.

This two hours and forty-one minutes represented the average time required for the replacement of each of five of the six spans of the White River railroad bridge. Span 6 required two hours and fifty-two minutes. The business of the renewal and the construction of bridges is simply part of the day's work for C. E. Sloan, engineer of bridges for the Baltimore & Ohio Railroad, and this chapter is more or less the reporting of Engineer Sloan in connection with this bridge job on the White River's east fork on the main line between Cincinnati, Ohio, and St. Louis, Missouri.

When the engineers turned their attention to the Mill Creek crossing, near the East Fork of White River, they were confronted with the need for at least a small change in alignment, and this led to consideration of a more substantial change. Study showed that, by crossing several hundred feet upstream from the old bridge, the curvature could be reduced to only one degree and fifty-five minutes. The length of track would be shortened about 800 feet, but, in its effect on the grade, the engineers saw, this was going to be more than compensated for by

354

moving the east end of the grade approximately one-half mile farther east.

Having made their decision in connection with the relocation of the Mill Creek crossing, the B.&O. engineers at the same time considered extensive changes at the White River bridge. Because of operating advantages to be gained, the final blueprints included the repairing of old piers and abutments and the erection of new deck-girder spans of modern design, and also the creation of a new grade five feet and five inches above the old grade.

By the time the work at Mill Creek was completed steel for the new White River bridge had been ordered and the work of raising the track and repairing the masonry was well under way, and operating men on the B.&O. began to count the time when it was going to be possible to not only haul heavier tonnage west but discontinue the practice of doubling westbound freights over three-mile Mitchel Hill, with its 1.07 per cent grade.

The old Mill Creek bridge was a short distance west of the bottom of the hill and near the middle of a five-degree thirty-minute curve, which held safe speed down to forty-five miles per hour. This was part of the old Ohio & Mississippi road, which was opened to traffic in 1857.

To mountain railroaders 1.07 per cent may not seem like a heavy grade, but in this case it was so located that tonnage trains could not get a run in approaching it.

It is not recorded what kind of a structure served at White River, but in 1872 this crossing included three Phoenix truss spans, each about 172 feet long. They were supported on two large stone piers and abutments. In 1892, three new limestone piers were added and the trusses were replaced by six through girder spans, each eighty-eight feet and six inches in length. These remained in service until they were pulled out to make room for the spans of the new White River bridge, a part of the B.&O.'s vast improvement program, set in motion following World War II.

The first improvement was carried out at the Mill Creek crossing and consisted primarily of a line change, necessitated by the renewal of the badly deteriorated bridge. The result was a reduction of both grade and curvature on the first mile or so of Mitchel Hill. The second improvement was the renewal of the superstructure and the strengthening of the foundations of the White River bridge, making it possible to remove a bothersome speed restriction.

When the work was done westbound freights were able to handle at least 400 tons more than they had previously.

The girder spans of the White River bridge, possibly because of some peculiarity of original specification or design load, were deficient in the length of cover plates. The lateral bracing was composed of rods extending to seats through holes in the girder webs. Sole plates and masonry plates without pins or provision for deflection were the only measures used for bearing, and this caused a serious deterioration of the masonry. Further, the floor system was not only of poor design but the parts had been badly affected by brine drippings, something that present-day engineers have to take into consideration.

Also the girders were spaced on very close centers and their lateral clearances were far below those of today's standards. The tops of the older stone piers in particular were in need of extensive repairs.

Because of these deficiencies severe speed restrictions of twenty-five miles per hour for passenger and fifteen miles per hour for freight were placed in effect at the White River bridge early in 1949.

The first phase of the work at the White River crossing involved pressure grouting the old masonry. Older units required replacement of some of the face stones and cement-gun work in addition to grouting. The newer piers, which were Bedford Limestone and built in 1892, were in much better condition and accepted an almost negligible amount of grout.

The second phase involved raising the existing bridge to the new grade, building a new bank abutment, and repairing or replacing the bearing courses of the pier abutments. Be it understood, this work was all done under traffic, which because of favorable weather conditions held pretty close to schedule.

The wing walls of the east abutment, which were parallel to the track, were built up to the new elevation with concrete and held together with reinforced concrete ties extending beneath the track.

The wings of the old west abutment were badly bulged and it was necessary to remove part of the fill between them. A new abutment was constructed back of the old one and the breast of it so altered as to make it function chiefly as a pier. A thirty-one-foot six-inch beam span was erected between the new and the old abutments.

The raising of the old spans to the new elevation was carried out in steps, with timber blocking placed to support them. This blocking was arranged so that it could be cut through readily on the transverse center lines to permit removal in halves for placing the new spans directly on their shoes.

Deck-girder spans were selected for this structure because of the smaller amount of steel required, the limitation imposed by the newer group of piers as regarding the lateral clearances of through spans, and, lastly, the location of the bridge at a dip in the grade. Mainly, however, a modern through span would have been too heavy and cumbersome to be handled as a unit in this location, unless it could be rolled into position, which would have entailed great expense.

The work of raising the approaches to the bridge and the spans was completed by maintenance forces about in the middle of November, 1949. The steel work was stored adjoining a construction siding a few hundred feet west of the bridge. The erection equipment arrived on the ground the first of December and the new spans were assembled, including the decks, and placed on top of one another beside the main track opposite the siding.

This work was completed in three weeks. Meanwhile loading platforms for the temporary storage of one new span and one old span at a time were built near the west end of the bridge. Rails, cut to exact length, were prepared so that, when those on the old spans were removed, short pieces could be placed to bring both rails up to the very end of the span on which the derrick car would stand while changing the spans.

The six new girder spans were designed for Cooper's E-72 loading. Each was eighty-nine feet four inches long and, as lifted into place, weighed eighty-two tons with bridge ties and guard rails. The weight of the steel alone was sixty-four tons.

Changing Out the Spans

No type of bridge engineering is so interesting to the layman as that of changing out the spans, and it is a never failing source of wonder that the work can be accomplished without doing more to train schedules than, perhaps, slow them a little at the point of construction. The beautiful timing and precision with which the old spans are replaced makes it all appear very easy, but it is the masterful hand of the engineer of bridges that makes possible this smooth replacement function.

The modern streamliner, waltzing down the line, commands the attention of the general public, but the bridge builder and the track forces make the swift flight of the passenger train and the timesaving Sentinel Service freight movement possible.

We are going to follow along closely the description of the change-out at White River by Engineer Sloan.

In preparing for the changing out of the spans the short length of track over the approach to the bridge, between the storage platform and the west abutment, was corduroyed by placing crossties between the existing ties. This was to prevent settlement of the new fill under the heavy loads on the front truck of the derrick car when carrying a span.

A day or so in advance of the installation of a span it was picked up bodily from the storage piles, loaded on a heavy-duty push car, and moved to the storage platform. It remained here until the day set for the change out.

At the west end of the bridge old Span No. 6 extended over dry ground, and this was the first to go. The work was done on December 28, or about a week after the completion of the new approaches. The span's weight, including the deck, was seventy-six tons. The crane lifted it, turned it about ninety degrees and lowered it directly to the ground for dismantling.

New Span No. 6 then was removed from the loading platform, placed on the push car and moved as near the end of the bridge as possible. Here it was picked up at boom radius of about fifty-three feet, turned transversely to the track, and the push car was removed. The span was set down on the track and the derrick car brought forward. It again picked up the span, this time with a short boom radius, and moved close to the east end of Span No. 7, located between the new west abutment and Pier No. 6. Then the car was blocked, the boom lowered to the fifty-three foot radius and the span was rotated until parallel with the track, then was lowered to the final position on its shoes. Just as simple as that.

All six of the new spans were handled in this manner, using a push car while on the fill, then moving slowly along with the load held at short radius when the derrick car was taking it out across the newly placed bridge spans.

The load on the six-wheel front truck of the derrick car when traveling with the load was about 380,000 pounds. This was increased to about 450,000 pounds when placing the span.

Old Spans Nos. 5 to 1, inclusive, were taken back to the unloading platform on the push car after removal. This car was brought out ahead of the derrick car, the boom of which extended over it for the lift of sixty-four tons with deck removed.

A Baltimore & Ohio locomotive crane, working east of the span being removed, was used to lift out the rails and as much of the deck as could be reached by the boom. The remainder of the deck was dumped into the river to save time. After the old span was removed this crane took out the west half of the blocking, which had previously been sawed through, and then shifted the new shoes to the proper position for receiving the new span.

Because it involved no interference to passenger trains, a period from 10:40 A.M. to 2:25 P.M. was selected for changing the spans. Arrangements with the Operating Department to schedule freight trains outside of this period on change-over days were made.

It was difficult to fix a date in advance for change-overs because of weather conditions. Complications could easily be presented in the handling of the spans through possible high winds, as it was impossible to block the derrick on the new spans to counteract lateral forces that would be set up by wind. On several occasions it became necessary to postpone change-overs.

Following the changing out of Spans Nos. 5 and 4 on December 29 and 30, a period of bad weather set in and Span No. 3 was not removed until January 5, 1950. Then the weather began acting up again, and new Span No. 2 was not put in place until January 11. The next day the last change-over was accomplished. We have listed the time for the replacement of each span in the opening paragraph of this chapter.

With the last spike hammered home, the last nut tightened on this White River bridge job, the Baltimore & Ohio was another step nearer the completion of a mammoth improvement program. When President R. B. White, a great all-round railroader, assumed control in 1941 he bent every effort toward attaining outstanding achievement for his road in this day of modern railroading.

Between 1941 and the close of 1949 the B.&O. spent $258,000,000 on improvements and betterments, an illustration of private enterprise at work on one of the nation's great railroads.

CHAPTER XL

RIVER DIVISION

Frisco River Line versus Barge Line

The Frisco's River Division is one of the most interesting on the system. It is the river-fighting division—in more ways than one—with the steel pacing the old Mississippi, the granddaddy of them all, from St. Louis to Memphis. There isn't much trouble from the flood waters any more, but the old river is there, powerful and brooding, carrying these river boats and their cargoes, seeming to resent this rival carrier of the land.

In all of the world, there are no legends like those of the Mississippi, and the River Division of the Frisco has its share on the 305 miles that reach from St. Louis to Memphis—302 odd from Southeastern Junction, just out of St. Louis, to Yale Yard, fringing Memphis. But here we are not dealing with legends but commerce, something very real in United States economy, with railroad economy.

Memphis is a great distributing point and the River Division handles its large cotton and cottonseed-oil movement. Also along this division there are one or two of the greatest soy bean producing areas in the country. Too, a good deal of corn is grown in this area, as well as some wheat, though not, of course, in anything like the amount grown in the territory of the Western Division.

The division has approximately 380 miles of branch lines, and these provide A-1 service to shippers, with the result that the branches are making money. These include the Caruthersville, Campbell, and Malden Branches, the Wilson and the Piggot Branches. In connection with branches, mixed trains have drawn the attention of railroad writers these later years, and perhaps no mixed train ever wended its lazy way between two more completely fascinating place names than Nos. 265 and 264 on the Frisco, 11.2 miles, Marked Tree to Lepanto, through Tyronza Junction.

The River Division has one of the best operating departments of any division I have ever seen anywhere. All of its employees and officials are top river fighters, having been at it for many years, but, as we have pointed out, trouble rarely comes from that direction now.

In the eighties people shipped and traveled by the river boats, the picturesque stern-wheelers, which splashed their way up and down the Father of Waters, and these river boats performed a real service; they were a part of America and American tradition. But there has come to Old Man River a newer and different river boat. This boat, at the direct expense of the American taxpayer, operates under the title of the Federal Barge Line and in direct competition with the railroads, self-supported, self-maintained, and themselves among the country's biggest taxpayers.

In other words, we have a situation that, were it not serious, might indulge our sense of humor. And that is a condition which makes possible spending the money of a taxpayingbody to keep its competitor in business. Not only does this money enable the competitor to stay in business but to undercut the rate of the railroad, which, though not great, seems to prove attractive to many shippers.

The Federal Barge Line usually takes three days to move its cargo from St. Louis to Memphis. Freight traveling behind modern Diesels delivers the goods from thirty-six to forty-eight hours ahead of the barges. What little the shipper saves on the one hand is immediately wiped out by the slow river move. It is an unfortunate and very unfair sort of competition. It is something to think about.

The Frisco has met and conquered, to a large degree, the problem of quick handling of l.c.l. freight. This less-than-carload traffic is most attractive to the St. Louis–San Francisco Railway, and they have completely mechanized all of the road's principal freight platforms with an eye to expediting its movement.

Unit-load handling equipment is a part of every modern railroad, and the year 1949-1950 saw a real growth in the use of all mechanical freight handling devices, which include "fork" trucks, powered conveyors, gas or electric-powered tractors, and mobile cranes. Many roads are experimenting with portable containers, which, of course, require a lift truck to handle. Not all railroads feel that containers are the solution to handling costs, but they do reduce loss and damage to lading.

At first, only larger freight houses employed mechanized loading units, but the program has been extended to the smaller stations. The Frisco, in connection with its l.c.l. freight, has co-ordinated its rail service with its subsidiary truck service, the Frisco Transportation Company, and this has enabled the road to provide first-day delivery to most all of the principal points on the system and not later than second-morning delivery to the remainder.

Through merchandise cars are loaded by many of the southeast and west connections, quickly moving to break-up points on the line. Here the lading is transferred and loaded in through cars or to Frisco Transportation trucks, and so effecting delivery with the minimum delay. Merchandise cars are also loaded on the railroad to break-up transfers on connecting lines, which enables the Frisco Railroad to effect prompt delivery of the traffic it originates.

This kind of service is appreciated by the shipper, who is finding more and more the economic value of the freight car in a modern railroading world.

The Frisco is a modern railroad of today, and its perfect physical condition is the direct result of the efforts of President Clark Hungerford and Operating Vice-President R. J. Stone. They have left no stone unturned in their efforts to bring the Frisco to the highest possible standard. They have built up the morale in such a way that every man on the road feels that he has an equal chance of bettering himself, according to his ability.

There are few railroads on which you will find more of the younger officials, with all of the younger man's earnestness and ambition. They are proud of the Frisco and proud to be a part of it.

The Traffic Department is ably organized and directed under the fine leadership of Traffic Vice-President T. H. Banister. As we have pointed out before, the Traffic Department, with its finger on the pulse of things in various cities, is vital to the economic health of the railroad.

President Clark Hungerford, a Princeton graduate, Class of 1922, has seen a lifetime of active service, and he brings to the Frisco the experience of twenty-five years service with the Southern Railway. Vice-president Stone also broke in on the Southern, following the receipt of his engineering degree.

Hungerford was paid the compliment of being made a colonel in the United States Army, in charge of the Southwestern region when the railroads were taken over by the government in August, 1950 for a short period because of a strike.

In general summary, we can record that the Frisco has been brought up-to-date on a system-wide basis. In addition to its fine passenger service, it has built up the components that make for a splendid freight service, as we indicated in the Frisco's fast freight chapter.

The Frisco and the men of the Frisco can well be proud of the record it has established, and so face the future with a continued desire to serve in the same railroad tradition.

CHAPTER XLI

VIRGINIAN COAL PIERS

Record Loadings

Sewalls Point, Virginia, great coal port of the Virginian Railway, plays an important part in the movement of the leading freight commodity handled by railroads in the United States. Coal Pier No. 2, there on the tide rim of Hampton Roads, has a capacity of 7,200 tons per hour, which means moving 120 tons per minute through its double car dumpers.

Sewalls Point No. 2 pier is a marvel of American ingenuity, and a fine example of the manner in which coal can be transferred from the coal car to the hold of the ship at dockside in this modern age. The great coal trains that come down from the New River and Pocahontas fields dissolve their black lading like magic at this high-capacity pier. Great 55-, 70-, and 105-ton cars hardly stop rolling before they are dumped and are rolling back into the yard to join rank in 145-car trains of westbound empties.

This is black magic! It is accomplished not as an exhibition of showmanship, it is simply routine—part of the day's work at Sewalls Point.

Let us, briefly, take a look at these Virginian coal piers before we consider their operation. Coal Pier No. 1, with a capacity of 2,500 tons per hour, was modernized prior to World War II. It is equipped with a low-level lorating unit, designed to handle prepared coal at a minimum of degradation by eliminating the dropping of the coal, and so avoiding breakage of the most fragile nature of the commodity.

Coal Pier 2 was placed in operation in April, 1925. Its length is 1,074 feet; the width, 86 feet; the height, 74½ feet. The facilities include two double car dumpers and haulages, each dumper handling two railroad cars of coal up to 70 tons capacity, or one 120-ton car, at one cycle of transfer into pier cars for delivery to the traveling loading towers. The dumpers are equipped with sprinkling devices, modernized with Sealtite deduster machines for allaying coal dust, this service at the option of the shipper at no extra cost. There is also a repair elevator, four traveling loading towers with mechanical trimmers for distributing the coal in the ship's hold, and six 130-ton conveyor cars.

Pier No. 2 will accommodate three small type, or two large vessels on either side for loading simultaneously. The anchorage for vessels served by the Virginian piers is in close proximity to Sewalls Point, thus avoiding movement in the restricted channels of the lower harbor. Sewalls Point, too, is several miles closer to the gateway to the open sea.

Let us take coal car VGN 19146, which came down in a coal train from Page, West Virginia, and which we assumed sponsorship of in a preceding chapter. VGN 19146, with its 105 net tons of coal, has come to the pier from the receiving yard and it is taken over by an electric "mule," which piece of power takes it up an incline to the dumper. As quickly as the dumper lowers VGN 19146 back to the track a car rider boards it and it moves by gravity down an incline track into the yard to be made into a train, outward bound.

Record loadings were made at Sewalls Point as long ago as April 21, 1926 when the S.S. *Lemuel Burrows* was loaded with 11,875 tons of coal in two hours and fifty-five minutes. On July 25, 1927, the S.S. *Chilore* was loaded with 20,027 tons in five hours flat.

Trains handling as many as 165 coal cars of the various sizes move out of the yard at Sewalls Point behind the Virginian's 900 class AG Mallets, bound for Roanoke. At Roanoke the electric motive power takes over the train and hauls it to Elmore, West Virginia. Mullens, a few miles beyond, is the end of the electrified territory. About ten hours will be occupied in getting

VGN 19146 and the other empty cars from Sewalls Point to Roanoke, a little less than 250 miles. The 134 miles, Roanoke to Elmore, will be covered in close to five hours and one half.

It may be interesting to the reader to examine a table of the different type coal-carrying cars, their class and type, and their weights, loaded and empty. Earlier chapters have covered the coal trains and their overall tonnage, and we present here a table for examination of the cars of the Virginian's coal car fleet.

The classification yards, connected with the coal pier yards at Sewalls Point, have an approximate capacity of 5,000 cars. Facilities at this great coal trans-shipment point include a round-house, car repair yards, and other subordinate units that go into making a complete and modern terminal.

The coal piers are equipped with large scales, designed for "motion weighing" of coal in the process of transferring from cars to ships, which is simply another link in the Virginian Railway's chain of service, tying closely together the coal mine, the coal tipple, VGN 19146, of the coal-carrying fleet, the empire of old King Coal and the coal ships, moving in from anchorage at Hampton Roads for their cargoes of black diamonds.

Of the business handled by the Virginian 85 per cent is coal, the remaining 15 per cent is general freight and passenger service. The road maintains an excellent fast freight service, which is represented by trains No. 71 and 72, operating between Norfolk, Virginia, and Dickinson, West Virginia, at which point they link with the New York Central, via the Deepwater Bridge connection.

These trains are limited to eighty cars, with the 500 class 2-8-4 Berkshire-type locomotives used east of Roanoke. This power does a remarkable job at moving the time freights, and the Dickinson connection affords the Eastern shipper a fast reliable route to markets from Columbus and Toledo, Ohio, Elkhart, Indiana, Chicago, and other New York Central points. Other crack trains are the CN-2 and the NC-3. The former is received from the Central and the latter operates for the westbound through traffic.

367

Car Nos.	Class	Kind	Weight in Tons	
			Loaded	Empty
1000— 3199	H3	Hopper	69	21
1000— 3199	H3A	”	76	21
3300— 3670	H7	”	70	21
3850— 3924	G2A	Gondola	66	22
4000— 4468	G1	”	73	21
4500— 4877	G2	”	74	20
5000— 5230	H9	Hopper	70	21
5600— 5698	H-10	”	70	21
5700— 5797	H-11	”	69	20
6000— 6999	H4	”	75	21
7000— 7499	H5	”	95	24
8000—10399	H8	”	80	21
11000—14099	H6, H6A	”	75	21
11000—14099	H6B, H6C	”	81	22
11500—15999	H-8A	”	78	21
19000—21024	G3 & G4	Gondola	144	40
22000—22099	G5	”	71	22
23000—24249	H-12 & H12B	Hopper	77	20
25000—25499	H-13	”	78	21
25500—25999	H-13A	”	77	20
28000—28499	H-13B	”	77	20
30000—30499	G-6, G-6A & G-6B	Gondola	76	22

B. Mills,

Superintendent.

Copy—Bulletin Boards
All Conductors
All Engineers
Trainmasters
Chief Dispatchers
Yardmasters
Mr. C. E. Reynolds
Mr. Harry Leard
Mr. K. M. Cook
Mr. W. D. Davis

TYPES AND CAPACITY OF VIRGINIAN COAL-CARRYING CARS

Chicago & Eastern Illinois #7, the southbound Georgian, passing milepost #24, just south of Glenwood, Ill., en route to Atlanta. Courtesy, C.&E.I.RR.

The Capitol, Seaboard Air Lines crack manifest train #27 from Richmond to Atlanta, passing Neuse, N.C., Virginia Division, with Diesel 4002 built by Electro-Motive. Courtesy, S.A.L. RR.

Partial view of Seaboard's car-washing facilities at Hialeah (Miami), Fla., with the crack Silver Meteor's equipment getting a cleaning up. North Florida Division. Courtesy, S.A.L. RR.

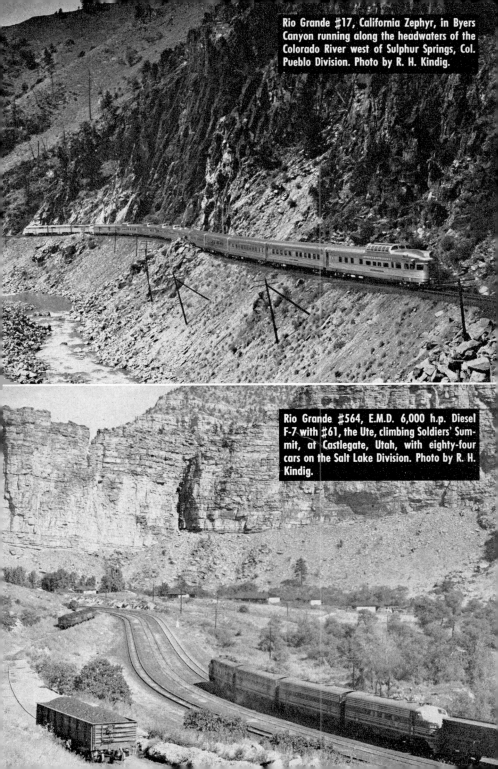

Rio Grande #17, California Zephyr, in Byers Canyon running along the headwaters of the Colorado River west of Sulphur Springs, Col. Pueblo Division. Photo by R. H. Kindig.

Rio Grande #564, E.M.D. 6,000 h.p. Diesel F-7 with #61, the Ute, climbing Soldiers' Summit, at Castlegate, Utah, with eighty-four cars on the Salt Lake Division. Photo by R. H. Kindig.

Rear end of Kansas City Southern's observation car on Southern Belle #1 and #2 in operation between Kansas City and New Orleans. Courtesy, K.C.S. RR.

Observation lounge car on Kansas City Southern's Southern Belle looking forward. Courtesy, K.C.S. RR.

We present a schedule of Nos. 71 and 72 because of their importance to the road in the handling of fast freight.

SCHEDULE 1949—TRAIN NOS. 72 AND 71 BETWEEN NORFOLK AND DICKINSON

	Westbound No. 71	Eastbound No. 72
Norfolk (Sewalls Point) Va.	9:00 P.M.	5:45 A.M.
Suffolk, Va.	10:20 P.M.	4:15 A.M.
Jarratt, Va.	11:50 P.M.	2:30 A.M.
Alberta, Va.	12:45 A.M.	1:00 A.M.
Virso, Va.	3:35 A.M.	10:35 P.M.
Altavista, Va.	5:45 A.M.	8:27 P.M.
Roanoke, Va.	7:15 A.M.	6:45 P.M.
Dickinson, W. Va.	10:30 P.M.	5:00 A.M.

Every morning that I saw No. 72 she was running a couple of hours ahead of time, due to the excellent runs over the Virginian. Again, it is a fast freight writing the story of modern railroading. This kind of quick, reliable service is winning the serious attention of the shipper more and more. When he can practically set his watch by the fast freight's whistle it is a daily reminder that the iron horse, whether steam or Diesel, is the best possible medium of both l.c.l. and heavy-haul service.

The Virginian operates a passenger train each way over its main line daily, and those traveling on these trains are given an opportunity to have a close look at the fabulous coal fields, back in these West Virginia hills. This is an on-time service, the trains being handled by fine Pacific-type steam locomotives. The Virginian owns six of these engines, which have sixty-nine-inch drivers and a tractive effort of 44,460 pounds. Built in 1920, they are maintained in perfect condition and are stoker equipped.

The steam locomotive will be in active service in many parts of the country for a long time, and engines not out on the road will be held for stand-by service, ready to meet any emergency, serving well and faithfully, as this type of motive power has in the past.

CHAPTER XLII

HIGHWAY TRAFFIC IS TOUGH

When the Trucks Roll

This writer has been a railroad rider all of his life. He prides himself on the fact that previous to 1949 he had never driven anywhere in an automobile except for two trips from New York to Boston and one from New York to Maine. Locally, in the last two or three years, his driving has been confined to motoring between New York City and his home in East Hampton, Long Island, a distance of 107 miles, because of the train service on the Long Island Railroad.

With this book in view, we thought it would be well to get behind the wheel and get out on the highways for a look at some of the obviously unfair competition with which the railroads of the United States are faced. We chose an automobile trip in one of the most densely populated areas of the east.

It was with no anticipation whatsoever that your author selected Tuesday, December 27, 1949, to begin a trip that would take him from New York to Baltimore the first night, thence through Annapolis, Maryland, to Washington and Richmond, Virginia, and then Norfolk and back to New York.

We have made it our business to ride the air lines of the United States at intervals to see what kind of competition they offered and what they were doing, and, of course, out of this country we have flown thousands of miles, but, as we have indicated, it was this writer's first attempt at an automobile trip of any length in a long time. We planned to call on our many railroad friends on the Western Maryland and the Baltimore & Ohio office in Baltimore; the Richmond, Fredericksburg & Potomac, and the Chesapeake & Ohio offices in Richmond; Norfolk & Western, Virginian, Seaboard, and Norfolk & Southern offices in Norfolk. And we were hopeful that they would understand our motives and forgive us our temporary abandonment of rail travel in favor of the crowded and abused highways.

There follows a log of the motor trip of this railroad author, New York City to Norfolk, Virginia, and return.

Tuesday

First Day

I left Fifty-third Street and Park Avenue, in New York, at 9:30 A.M. The crosstown traffic was so congested that by the time I reached the West Side highway at Forty-second Street and the Hudson River, I decided to to give up the trip and take a train. I turned around and went back to the Racquet Club on the east side of New York and had a Coca-Cola. I gained a little courage and debated whether to call the whole thing off or make another attempt.

One of the things that influenced my final decision was the fact that I had a new Cadillac, which is the next best thing that General Motors turns out to their Diesels. This fine car has everything in the world, and, in my opinion, has the same quality standard as that great piece of motive power that is known everywhere the rails reach in America—the GM Diesel. Only the Cadillac has no dynamic brakes.

I slid behind the wheel again at 10:30 A.M., determined to see it through. After a wait for traffic at the Holland Tunnel entrance, I finally was about to enter the bore that takes you to New Jersey under the Hudson River. Suddenly an automobile two cars ahead of me became enveloped in flames. It was half an hour before I got out of that line and was allowed to move through the tunnel with traffic.

After leaving the tunnel, there was the Pulaski Skyway in New Jersey. Two detours, two accidents, and 120 miles later at Pennsville, I waited in line about thirty-five minutes before getting on the ferry which crosses the Delaware River to New Castle. (And this was on a Tuesday.)

I am a fast driver, and by making as good time as possible I reached Baltimore, Maryland, at 6:30 P.M. I only climbed out from behind the wheel for a very brief lunch. Practically eight hours of fighting traffic. If I had left New York on either of two good railroads, which provide hourly service from New York to Baltimore and Washington, I would have been in Baltimore in about three hours and a quarter.

Wednesday
Second Day
I left Baltimore in the afternoon, made a business call in Annapolis and arrived in Washington at 6 P.M. On the 120 miles from Washington to Richmond I met fifty-eight northbound trucks. I tallied them. Many undoubtedly were grossly overloaded, perhaps all of them, according to reports. Great behemoths carrying freight on passenger motor roads that rightly belonged to those carriers designed for such traffic—the railroads; in this case the Richmond, Fredericksburg & Potomac.

I was three hours and fifty minutes making this trip between Washington and Richmond. By train the time required would have been approximately two hours and a half, and I would have arrived relaxed and rested instead of tired out.

Thursday
Third Day
I spent the day with officials of the Chesapeake & Ohio and the Richmond, Fredericksburg & Potomac. I drove to Williamsburg for dinner and then went on to Norfolk that night without any traffic difficulty.

Friday
Fourth Day
I left Norfolk in the afternoon in plenty of time to get the four-o'clock ferry from Little Creek to Cape Charles. Realizing that it was Friday afternoon and expecting some traffic, I

372

planned on reaching the ferry at ten minutes past three, which put me there with a leeway of a good fifty minutes.

What happened?

The line of cars was two miles long. I did not get on the four-o'clock ferry, and I did not get on the five-o'clock ferry!

The line crawled and I crawled with it. I got on the six-o'clock ferry.

I arrived at Cape Charles at 9 P.M. that evening and solaced myself with some of their delicious oysters.

Saturday
Fifth Day

I left Cape Charles at 8 A.M. and arrived in New York at midnight. More heavy traffic, more dodging around heavy trucks, and an hour and a half wait to get on the Pennsville Ferry. I had no particular difficulties the rest of the way into the city because this time I was wise and crossed the bridge to Staten Island and took the ferry into downtown New York.

I cannot understand anyone fighting this motor traffic day in and day out. The automobile driver is subjected to danger constantly—the normal danger of traffic, plus the threat of habitually bad drivers and the ever growing number of those great overloaded trucks.

The end of the fifth day left me more than ever convinced that driving an automobile in congested areas is something to be avoided, in particular when good train service is available.

Tests to Determine Highway Damage

The state of Maryland, at this writing, is conducting tests on a one-mile stretch of Route 301 south of La Plata to determine the extent to which heavy trucks damage public highways. Note the use of the word "public." Truckers apparently consider that this allows free and unrestricted use of America's paved roads for their use for profit. True, the trucker pays taxes,

373

including a gasoline tax; so the railroad also pays taxes. But would the trucker finance the construction of a private truck highway in addition to paying taxes?

On this piece of Route 301, day and night, eight trucks of different weights are being driven back and forth over this closed stretch of pavement. The experiment is financed by the United States Bureau of Public Roads. October, 1950, saw the midway point in the test, and it was found that the loaded trucks were opening up crack after crack in the pavement of this test section.

Long before the completion of these tests, it was absolutely determined that heavily loaded trucks do damage highways. Thus it stands that the campaigns against overloading are not merely railroad-inspired attempts to persecute the trucking industry, as has so often been charged, but a true picture of existing conditions.

Truckers are not only responsible for highway damage within the scope of set load limits, but to a greater degree because of flagrant overloading violations. It is clear that the state roads' commission's effort to enforce truck weight laws is the least that can be done to protect Maryland highways against premature and costly deterioration.

Overload Violations

Something which we wish to emphasize is the fact that in these state of Maryland tests the trucks used are not loaded beyond the maximum weight limits set by the state, which are among the most liberal in the nation. Still, these loads were sufficient to start breaks in the pavement.

Scores of overloaded vehicles are picked up at checking points on Maryland's highways every week. But the small fines do not amount to anything. Further, every effort is made by many of the truckers to evade and flout the law. The taxpayer and the pleasure driver in Maryland are being hijacked and browbeaten

374

by the bootleg, or overload, trucker, just as they are eating the dust of the legitimate highway freighter.

Try and imagine what would happen to the railroads if they constantly evaded the laws in this manner. The press and the public would demand that they be prosecuted, and rightly so. The railroads only ask fair play and a modicum of justice.

In July, 1949, a state trooper in Maryland swore out warrants against the owner and loader of an overloaded truck on his own initiative, and he secured convictions against both of them. If a state trooper can perform this kind of duty, certainly the highway commissions of the various states should possess enough enterprise to give these overweight truckers a bad time.

CHAPTER XLIII

HIGHWAY CROSSING ACCIDENTS

Safety Insurance

The suicidal mania of motorists is increasing. They not only drive onto the railroad tracks in front of trains at highway crossings but they drive into the middle of passing trains. It is a trite but true saying that "The most dangerous part of an automobile is the nut at the wheel." They threaten not only their own lives but the lives of those in the car with them, and they endanger the lives of railroad men and destroy railroad property.

The menace of trucks and bad drivers is at times appalling. Often frightful crossing accidents are the result of gross negligence. Even though a railway crossing may be protected by adequate signs, gates, and electromatic wigwag signals, motorists will disregard them and blindly drive into the path of the oncoming train. The headlong rush of a motorist to get somewhere else, often without any particular reason for getting there in a hurry, is one of life's mysteries.

Railroads spend millions to install protective crossing devices across the nation, and they spend more millions for damaged equipment, track, and right of ways. In fact, collision costs represent one of the biggest items on the debit side of the ledger.

Probably the most serious of all offenders, strangely enough, are the heavy oil trucks and trailers. While there have been comparatively few casualties to engine crews where Diesel engines have been involved in this country, there is a very grave menace when a collision occurs between an oil truck and trailer and a passenger or freight train hauled by a steam engine. A fire is almost sure to result, with almost certain tragic consequences.

In November, 1942, this writer was riding in the cab of a fine new passenger locomotive, hauling a crack train on one of the nation's foremost railroads when it was involved in a highway crossing collision. Although no lives were lost, it was an unforgettable experience. I have chosen this collision as an example of the danger and the cost of an accident of this kind.

A man driving a heavy sedan stalled it on a railroad crossing. When he could not get it started, he and a young lady companion got out and left it. They made no attempt to flag the train, and, of course, had nothing with which to flag us anyway in the short interval before the collision occurred. Those things always happen too fast for co-ordinated thought and action.

A big passenger locomotive with all of the heavy equipment that goes to make up a fourteen-car train, traveling at seventy miles an hour, requires considerable distance to stop, even when the full emergency braking power is applied. After the brake handle goes to the last notch, the "big hole," as it is sometimes termed, you wait what seems an interminable time before the train comes at last to a savage, grinding stop on smoking rails.

I never think of this accident that my mind does not bring back the picture of the engineer jamming the throttle closed and grabbing for the brake valve and the sander, doing in a split second everything in his power to stop his train. I can still hear the terrific impact and see the fire fly as it was very definite we were on the ground.

The road foreman of engines, who was firing the engine, was on the seat on the left side in front of me. He shut off the stoker and the water pump. After the warning shout that went across the cab, the fireman headed up on top of the tank, the best place he could think of, I imagine. I stood up behind the boiler head. At such times, you never know which way you're going to go and it doesn't do much good if you do.

The locomotive was a 4-6-4 type, with a heavy trailer truck, which, I am certain, helped prevent the locomotive from turning over. The crossing whistle had been sounded, as it is on

377

every railroad, but it seems that in the rush of modern driving people don't pay much attention to warning signals, if they hear them at all in a car with every window closed.

Our locomotive engine truck was on the ground and part of the automobile was fouling the adjoining track, which called for quick action because a manifest was due. The short flagging of this train and the resultant emergency application of the brakes resulted in flat wheels on fifteen cars. There were many flat wheels on our train and six cars had to be cut out at the next division point.

Now let's examine some of the damage done, in addition. The pilot was torn off completely. All of the steamheat connections had been knocked off between each car and many of the air and signal-line hoses were severed. The westbound main over which the limited was running was tied up over six hours while the wrecking gang rerailed the passenger locomotive and the track men repaired torn-up roadbed.

Because this busy double-track line had to route traffic over one track, freight and passenger service suffered all along the division until everything had been cleared up, which meant the payment of a lot of overtime. Afterward, I inquired as to the cost of this accident. As I remember the figures, it was between $37,000 and $40,000.

I have railroaded more than any man in the United States, ridden more locomotives more miles on different roads of this country and many others. I could tell of a great many near accidents and accidents, resulting in damage to equipment, that I have been involved in from automobile traffic, and so am in a position to speak with authority on this subject. I cannot emphasize the need for caution strongly enough.

Fools will not listen, but every sane and sensible person driving an automobile should apply the same care in driving, particularly at railroad crossings, that he would exercise in negotiating curves on steep mountain grades, expecting every turn to hold unknown dangers.

I feel the railroads have done their share, and more, in bearing the expense of protecting highway crossings. Every safety measure and reasonable precaution have been taken in an effort to reduce crossing accidents. The railroads cannot do it all. They need the co-operation of the Highway Departments of the various states, of you and I and the public in general.

Reasonable care would prevent thousands of accidents. Motorists who will not STOP, LOOK, AND LISTEN in their senseless haste, at least should keep their eyes open. So many fatal crossing accidents happen at points where the automobile driver has an unobstructed view of the track for a long distance in either direction.

You cannot expect the driver who has no apparent regard for his own life to have any thought or care concerning the other fellow, but he should be held responsible for his acts in a financial way. For when he flouts all caution he is certainly flagrantly lawless.

You cannot educate an idiot, and all the crossing warning systems in the world will not stop him from courting destruction, but it remains for the average driver to do his or her share in helping to keep the highways safe for motorists and the railroads safe for trains.

Dedicated to Safety

I have dedicated this chapter to greater safety with the hope that in some small way it may help to further safe driving habits.

One rule I would emphasize strongly, *Never immediately drive onto a crossing behind a train that has just passed.* THERE MAY BE A TRAIN COMING THE OTHER WAY ON THE OTHER TRACK.

Again, *Have your car under absolute control when you approach a railroad crossing—ready to stop, if necessary, or to accelerate safely without fear of stalling.*

I might suggest that the motorist sometime visit a junk yard and look at the remains of a car that has been hit by a railroad train. He will be pretty sure to find one there.

INDEX

131, 132; No. 97, 32; *Royal Blue,* 129, 242; Sentinel Service, 1; *Shenandoah,* 130, 242; Staten Island installation, 291; Staten Island Rapid Transit Lines, 291; Strata-Dome, 129-35, 240-43; traffic Blue Book, 135; White R. Bridge, 355-60
Banister, T. H., 364
Barksdale Field, 123
Barstow, Calif., 9, 221
Baton Rouge, 118, 123, 124, 304
Baylis, Ill., 322
"Bay window" caboose, 129
Beale, Frank D., 140, 143
Bear Creek R.R., 156
Becker, Ind., 230
Beaumont, Tex., 116, 117, 120, 127, 303
Beaumont Hill, 11
Beaver Falls, Pa., 134
Belen, N.M., 80
Belle Telephone Co., 69
Bellevue, Ohio, 59
Bellfield, Pa., 56
Belt Railway of Chicago, 30, 31
Bill Williams Mts., 221
Berger, Tex., 6
Bessemer, Auriel, 109
Bessemer & Lake Erie R.R., 60, 155-76; freight cars, 174-76; freight tonnages, 155-56, 175; incorporation, 156; iron ore transport, 155-56, 159-63; locomotives, 166-73; ore traffic tables, 162-65; rail standards, 157-58; trackage, 157
Bethlehem Steel Co., 133
Bieber, Calif., 38, 51
Bienville, Mont., 124
Big Stoney, Va., 138
Birmingham, Ala., 98, 102, 103, 104, 198, 275, 285
Bitter Root Mts., 146
Black Gold, 106
Blair, T. A., 79
Bledsoe Coal Co., 231
Block signaling, 36, 37, 47
Bloomer, Calif., 39
Blue Bird of the Wabash, 107, 115
Blue Ridge Mts., 309
Blue Ridge, Va., 328
Boca Grande, Fla., 97, 348
Bolokron Unit, 92
Bonnet Carré Spillway, 124
Boston & Maine R.R., 4
Boston, Mass., 80, 270, 275, 370
Braddock, Pa., 133
Branchton, Pa., 166
Brewer, Ill., 227, 229
Brewster, Ohio, 60
Brooke, George D., 140, 143

Brown & King, 160
Brushless train washer, 54
Buchanan, William, 121, 122, 305
Budd Co., 22, 92, 108, 130
Budd Shotweld car-body structures, 114
Buffalo, N.Y., 27, 28, 30, 284
Burbank Junction, 17, 18

C

Cache Creek, Calif., 16
Caddo Parish, La., 119
Caliente, Calif., 11, 14
California, 11, 18, 20, 27, 30, 88, 178, 179, 183, 217, 248
California Zephyrs, 19, 20, 21, 22, 25, 36, 37, 54, 55; make-up, 20, 21; naming of, 21; description of, 22-25; Pullman accommodations, 25
Calumet Steel Co., 231
Campbell Branch, Frisco Lines, 361
Campbell's Creek R.R., 140
Canyon Diablo bridge, 220
Canada, 5
Cape Charles, Va., 275, 372, 373
Capitol, 275
Capitol Limited, 242
Carbofrezer Company, 92, 212
Carbona, Calif., 40
Carbon County R.R., 206, 208, 209
Carloadings, 5
Carrie Furnace, 133
Carrier equipment, 48
Caruthersville Branch, Frisco Lines, 361
Cascade, 82-88
Cascade Line, 83
Cascade Mts., 83, 146, 177, 187
Cascade Summit, 11
Castleman's Rim, 132
Cavalcade, 274
Cayuga, Ind., 227
Centralized traffic control (C.T.C.), 12, 13, 14, 16, 26, 36, 37, 40, 41, 68, 96, 102, 103, 141, 187-95; automatic block change-over, 192-93; carrier equipment, 193; equipment housing, 194; Chicago & Eastern R.R., 224-25; Denver Yard, 267, 297, 307, 324, 326.
Central R.R. of Georgia, 297
Central R.R. of N.J., 291
Central-Southern Illinois line of Chicago & Eastern Illinois R.R., 225
Central States Dispatch, 132, 309
Chaffee, Mo., 229, 298
Charles Pfiger Co., 231
Charleston route of Seaboard Air Line R.R., 187

382

384

F

Fairbanks-Morse Diesels, 58, 146
Fairbanks-Morse track scale, 198
Fairfax, S.C., 96, 188
Falcon Steel Co., 134
Fallston, Pa., 134
Faricy, William T., 340
Farmersville, Tex., 121
Fast freight, 27, 307-11; Virginia R.R.,
  367-68; W. Md. R.R., 307-11;
  "97's," 309
Fast Freight Line, 59
Feather River, 37
Feather River Canyon, 35, 36, 38, 39
Feather River Route, 55
Federal Barge Line, 362
Fendrich & Co., 231
Fernandina, Fla., 96
Finley Junction, Ill., 225, 298
Fitz Henry, Pa., 133
Flagstaff, Ariz., 221
"Flimsies," 36, 37
Flint Kote Co., 231
Florida, 33, 97, 98, 104, 196, 270
Florida-Cuba Special, 100
Florida East Coast R.R., 297
Florida Keys, 97
Flying Crow, 302, 306
Fordyce, Colonel, 305
Fort Erie, 31, 32
Ft. Lauderdale, Fla., 97
Ft. Madison, Ia., 216, 217, 218, 222
Fort Meyers, Fla., 97
Fort Scott, Kan., 102, 103
Ft. Smith, Ark., 198
Ft. Worth, Tex., 102, 104, 105, 286
France, 124
French Acadians, 123, 124
French Quarter of New Orleans, 89
Freight: agents, 4; Bessemer & Lake
  Erie R.R., 159-63, 174-76; coal
  transport, 365-69; cost to haul, 3;
  Frisco Line, 361-64; l.c.l., 362, 363;
  manifest, meaning of, 27; manifest,
  274-75; overnight, 1; perishable, 270-
  83, 285, 286; per diem charges, 2;
  repair, 8; Seaboard R.R., 347-53;
  Chicago & Eastern Ill. R.R., 223-31;
  Virginian R.R., 367
Freight car, 1, 2, 3, 5, 8, 9; advertisement, 6; purchase of, 5; capacity of,
  3; length of, 3
Frigidaire, 26
Frisco Lines, 118, 122, 196-204; Advance, 286; Black Gold, 106; cottonseed oil transport, 361; cotton transport, 361; Eastern Div., 103; fast
  freight, 284-90; Frisco Flash, 286;
  Ford Special, 286; freight, 102, 362,
363; Kansas City–Fla. Special, 105;
  manifest No. 134, 285, 286; manifest No. 136, 285-86; manifest schedules, 287-90; Meteor, 105; modernizing program, 103; Northern Div.,
  103; Packer Special, 285; River Div.,
  105, 286, 361-64; routes, 102, 196,
  198; Southern Div., 103; Southwestern Div., 103; Steam Locomotives,
  103; Springfield Yard, 196; Sunnyland, 105; Texas Special, 105; Traffic Dept., 364; Will Rogers, 105;
  No. 264, 362; No. 265, 362
Frisco Transportation Co., 363
Fulton, Alexander, 123

G

Galesburg, Ill., 216
Gallup, N.M., 220, 222
Galveston, Tex., 286
Gauley-Sewell coal field, 294
Garfield County, Okla., 285
Garnett, S.C., 188
Gary, Ind., 132, 134, 205, 207
General Electric Co., 189, 232, 237
General Mills, 231
General Motors, 19, 129, 302; Diesels,
  89, 99, 100, 103, 114, 247-62; E-8,
  253-54; Electro-Motive Division,
  247, 254, 259; F-7, 249-62; road-
  switching locomotive, 254-59; stand-
  ardization of parts, 258
"General Purpose" (GP), see Loco-
  motives, 103, Diesel
Geneva, U., 205, 208
Geneva Steel Co., 205-11; Keighly
  quarry, 207
Georgetown, S.C., 96
Georgia, 188
Georgian, 298
Gerlach, Nev., 36
Glass-domed cars, 19, see also Vista-
  Dome
Gleed, Ariz., 221
Glen Lyn, Va., 327
Glenwood Canyon, 19
Glorieta Mts., 219
Glorieta Pass, 220
Gold Seal Asphalt Roofing, 231
Goodview, Va., 328
Gould, Jay, 56
Graham, Charles J., 60, 61
Grand Canyon, 221
Grand Trunk R.R., 60
Granite City, Ill., 108
Grass Lake, 11
Gray's Flat, Calif., 39
Great Cacapon, W.Va., 131

385

388

Paxton Grocery Co., 231
Payson, U., 207
Pennsville, N.J., 371, 372
Pennsylvania, 307, 311
Penn. R.R., 27, 28, 30, 60, 275
Pensacola, Fla., 102, 104, 105, 196, 198, 286
Pere Marquette R.R., 140
Perlman, A. E., 269
Petersburg, Va., 95
Peterson, C. E., 88, 317
Petrified Forest, 222
Philadelphia, Pa., 27, 59, 97, 98, 275, 309
Phillips, T. L., 54
Phosphate rock, transport of, 347-53; tidewater loading of, 349-53; sampling of, 352; increase in movement of, 353
Piggot Branch, Frisco Lines, 361
Pinehurst, N.C., 95
Pintsch-Burner lamps, 23
Pioneer, 274
Pit R., 177
Pittsburgh, Bessemer & Lake Erie R.R. Co., 157, 174
Pittsburgh, Butler & Shenango R.R. Co., 156
Pittsburgh & Conneaut Dock Co., 161
Pittsburgh Forge Co., 134
Pittsburgh Junction, O., 56, 57, 59
Pittsburgh & Lake Erie R.R., 60
Pittsburgh, Pa., 57, 133, 155, 205, 309
Pittsburgh Screw & Bolt Co., 134
Pittsburgh, Shenango & Lake Erie R.R., 156, 157-58, 159
Pittsburgh Steel Co., 60
Pittsburgh Tube Co., 134
Pittsburgh West End, 56
Pittsburgh & West Virginia Railway, 56-63; C.T.C. equipment, 56; Clairton branch, 57; coal transport, 58; connection with west side branch, 57; equipment, 57; fast freight, 57; freight, 57, 58; *Michigan Steeler*, 59; Mifflin branch, 57; PSC-1, 59; safety, 61; traffic representative, 61
Pittsburg, Kan., 118, 126
Plainfield, Pa., 307, 308
Plant City, Fla., 97
Pleasure Dome, 213, 216
Pneumatic tube, 72
Pocahontas River coal field, 137
Polk County, Fla., 347
Potomac R., 131
Potomac Valley, 131, 311
Port Arthur, Tex., 116, 117, 120, 126, 127, 128, 301, 302
Port Boca Grande, Fla., 97

Port Covington, Baltimore, Md., 307, 308, 310, 311
Port Covington Terminal, 308, 309
Portland, Ore., 34, 38, 51, 61, 82, 177, 183, 185, 186, 313
Port Neches, Tex., 120
Portola, Calif., 35, 38, 40, 46, 47, 53
Portola, Gaspar de, 35
"Portola Shower," 54, 55
Portsmouth, Va., 95, 98, 275
Potomac Yard, Virginia, 272, 275
Powell, Leigh R., Jr., 276
"Pressurized air conditioning," 90
Princeton, Ind., 227
Princeton, W.Va., 138, 327
Princeton Mining Co., 231
Printing telegraph machine, 50, 51
Promontory, U., 155
Providence, R.I., 309
Provo, U., 207, 210
Pueblo, Colo., 205, 207
Puget Sound, 144, 145
Pullman-Standard, 8, 25
Pullman-Standard Car Manufacturing Company, 85, 177, 178, 181, 240, 246
Pymatuning Swamp, 158

Q

Queen Wilhelmina of Holland, 119
Quick Dispatch, 132

R

Radio, 9
Radio experimentation by K.C.S., 125
Rail Service car, *see* Sperry Rail Service
Railroad Avenue, a book, 158
Railroads at War, a book, 247
Railroads of Today, a book, 46, 135, 247
Railways Ice Company, 76
Raleigh, N.C., 95
Rankin, Pa., 133
Rankin Plant of Bethlehem Steel Co., 133
Raton Pass, 219, 222
Ravenna, Calif., 17
Reading R.R., 59, 291, 307, 309
Red Ball manifest trains, 10, 224-29, 285, 309, 310
Red R., 122, 123
Red River Parish, La., 123
Redding, Calif., 185
Redland, Okla., 126
Reefer Icing, 75
Reefer trains, 1, 4

393

Union Drawn Steel Co., 134
Union Pacific R.R., 1, 105, 113, 206, 207, 208
Union R.R., 60
Union Station, Los Angeles, 221
Union Station, Washington, D.C., 131
Union Switch & Signal Co., 45, 46, 47, 69, 103, 193, 223
Union Track Junction, 224
U.S. Army, 136
U.S. Bureau of Public Roads, 374
U.S. Railroad Administration, 325
U.S. Steel Co., 133, 205
University of Illinois, 299
University of Virginia, 140
Utah, 54, 205, 207
Utley, E. H., 158

V

Vapor Heating Co., 115
Vapor Zone heat, 151
Venice, Fla., 97
VGN 19146, 325, 327, 328, 329, 366-67
Victor Chemical Co., 231
Victoria, Va., 142, 329
Vidalia, La., 122
Villa Grove, Ill., 229
Vincennes, Ind., 227, 229
Vincent, Calif., 17
Vinita, Okla., 105
Virginia, 367
Virginian Railway, 95, 137-43, 325-39, 365-69, 371; board of directors, 143; building of, 138; business handled, 367; C.T.C., 141; CN-2, 3, 67; coal car types, 368; Coal Pier No. 2, 365; coal train movements, 330-39; development, 137-43; electric locomotives, 232-38; fast freight, 367; Guyandot River branch, 329; Kopperston branch, 329; l.c.l., 369; locomotives, 325, 326, 327, 328, 366; mine development, 138-39; modernization, 141; motion weighing of coal, 367; NC-3, 367; New River division, 327; Norfolk division, 328; No. 71, 367; No. 72, 367; second subdivision, 329; tie-up with N.Y. Central, 140; transport of coal, 325-39; VGN 19146, 366-67; Winding Gulf branch, 329
Vista-Dome, 19, 20, 21, 22, 25, 55, 107, 131

W

Wabash R.R., 27-34, 40, 107-15, 230, 277, 318-24; C.T.C., 324; freight

cars purchased, 323; improvements, 321-24; industrial dept., 318-24; manifest trains, 27-34; murals, 107, 108; Passenger and Mechanical Depts., 111; route, 108; Teletype System, 323; Traffic Dept., 318
Wabash Fibre Box Co., 231
Wagon Mound, N.M., 215, 219
Waldo, Fla., 97
Walong, Calif., 15
Wansford Yard, 223, 224, 300
Warren, Calif., 16
Wasatch Mts., 205
Washington, D.C., 27, 97, 98, 130, 273, 370, 372
Washington, 38, 51
Watsonville Junction, Calif., 313
Watts, Okla., 126
Waughmat draft gears, 113
Waukesha, 178
Waukesha mechanical & safety steam jet, 152
Wauwatosa, Wis., 144
Waynor, S.C., 187, 188
Wellington, Kan., 80
West, E. A., 269
West Aliquippa, Pa., 134
West Coast, 17
West Deepwater, W.Va., 141
West Economy, Pa., 134
Western Electric Co., 193
West Lake Wales, Fla., 97
Western Maryland Fast Freight Line, 56
Western Maryland R.R., 3, 59, 60, 307-11, 370; C.T.C., 307; Fast Freight, 307-11; Lurgan Subdiv., 307; Maintenance of Way Dept., 310; manifests, 308, 309-10; Operating Dept., 310; PCS-1, 309; Port Covington Terminal, 308; safety honors, 310-11; No. 1, 309; No. 3, 309; No. 6, 309
Western Pacific R.R., 35-40; communications offices, 50-54; eastern division, 51; Feather River section, 46; freight traffic, 37; western division, 40, 50
West Gilbert, Va., 329
West Homestead, Pa., 133
Westinghouse air-brake equipment, 179
Westinghouse High-Speed Control, 26
Westinghouse HSC Brakes, 115
West Newton, Pa., 133
West Palm Beach, Fla., 97
West Penn & Shenango R.R., 156
West Springfield, Mo., 201
West Tulsa, Okla., 285
West Virginia, 56, 137, 291, 294, 307, 311, 325, 329

394

West Virginia coal fields, 142
Wheat, transport of, 284, 285
Wheeling & Lake Erie Division, Northern Pacific R.R., 60
White, R. B., 136, 360
White River, 230, 355-60
Whiting washers, 55
Whitman, F. B., 55
Wichita, Kan., 102, 198, 284, 285
Wildwood, Fla., 96, 271, 274
Willabit, Va., 329
Willamette R., 177
Williams, Ariz., 221
Williams, Eugene S., 308, 311
Williamsburg, Va., 372
Will Rogers, 105
Wilmington, S.C., 96
Wilson Branch, Frisco Lines, 361
Winding Gulf Branch, Virginian Railway, 329
Winnemucca, Nev., 53
Winnfield, La., 118, 121

Winslow, Ariz., 220, 222
Winter Haven, Fla., 97, 270, 271
Wisconsin, 31, 144
Woodford, Calif., 12, 15

Y

Yale Yard, 285, 286
Yampai, Ariz., 221
Yellowstone National Park, 145
Youghiogheny R., 132
Youngstown, O., 205, 309
Yulee, Fla., 96

Z

Zarfoss, C. N., 311
Zephyrette, 22, 37
Zephyrs, California, *see* California Zephyrs.

Date Due